THE FARMWORKERS' JOURNEY

Dear Emerita,

Please join me in reforming the laws & conditions that impact our farmworkers so that they might look forward to a brighter future.

Sincerely,

Ann Lopez

10/23/11

THE FARMWORKERS' JOURNEY

Ann Aurelia López

UNIVERSITY OF CALIFORNIA PRESS

BERKELEY   LOS ANGELES   LONDON

University of California Press, one of the most distin-
guished university presses in the United States, enriches
lives around the world by advancing scholarship in the
humanities, social sciences, and natural sciences. Its activities are supported by the UC Press Foundation and
by philanthropic contributions from individuals and institutions. For more information, visit
www.ucpress.edu.

University of California Press
Berkeley and Los Angeles, California

University of California Press, Ltd.
London, England

Library of Congress Cataloging-in-Publication Data

López, Ann Aurelia, 1945–.
  The farmworkers' journey / Ann Aurelia López.
    p.   cm.
  Includes bibliographical references and index.
  ISBN: 978-0-520-25072-7 (cloth : alk. paper)
  ISBN: 978-0-520-25073-4 (pbk. : alk. paper)
    1. Migrant agricultural laborers—California.   2.
Migrant agricultural laborers—Mexico.   I. Title.

HD1527.C2L67   2007
331.5'4408968720794—dc22   2006102235

Manufactured in the United States of America

15   14   13   12   11   10   09   08
10   9   8   7   6   5   4   3   2

This book is printed on New Leaf EcoBook 50, a
100% recycled fiber of which 50% is de-inked postcon-
sumer waste, processed chlorine free. EcoBook 50 is
acid free and meets the minimum requirements of
ANSI/ASTM D5634–01 (Permanence of Paper).

*Dedicated to the small producer and subsistence
corn farmers of west-central Mexico and
the farmworkers of California. Proceeds
from the sale of this book will be used to
establish the Farmworker Family Foundation.*

CONTENTS

ILLUSTRATIONS

FIGURES

x / ILLUSTRATIONS

PREFACE

This book grew out of a deep passion I have been experiencing for many years. It began as I read local newspaper articles and editorials about renewed farmworker abuse that often referred to farmworkers in an objectified manner, as if they were inanimate implements of their central valley California corporate agribusiness employers' capital-intensive commercial farming processes.

Although I have no personal history of farmwork in California or elsewhere, this objectification struck a cord of intense dissonance. I viewed the dehumanized references as an affront to any fundamental rational perception of what it means to be a human being. The abuses portrayed were an insult to any standards of tolerable decency and civility. No one in a democracy should be devalued and objectified in this way.

As the articles appeared week after week, my indignation continued to grow. I recall discussing farmworker issues with a class of environmental science students during a lecture about food and agriculture. I questioned students about the appropriateness of the farmworker subjugation and objectification I had read about. Later, I realized that the energy of indignation I experienced must be harnessed and utilized constructively to improve the circumstances of California's farmworkers. My solid commitment to assist farmworkers was born. The newly established Ph.D. program in environmental studies at the University of California, Santa Cruz, provided the avenue by which my all-encompassing task of study and work with farmworkers began.

The binational ethnographic farm-to-farm research summarized in this book derives from almost ten years of collecting data at each end of the migrant circuit between west-central Mexico and Watsonville and Salinas, California. The data collection consisted of extensive interviews with thirty-three farmworkers and their family members in Watsonville and Salinas. I also studied twenty-two subsistence and small producer farms and farm families at the other end of the migrant circuit in west-central Mexico. There, during summer and winter research trips, I learned about the central California farm labor force's farms and families as well as the post-NAFTA effects on the rural Mexican countryside.

The research was time consuming and required great patience and intuitive skill. It is the product of countless hours of participant observation in the form of home visits and social and school involvement—often exhausting and at times even perilous. Farmland in west-central Mexico is subject to unregulated agrochemical spraying in the summer. Avoiding agrochemical exposure and toxic vehicle emissions in some regions is nearly impossible.

The ubiquitous poverty in the region combined with compromised sanitation standards has created a paradigm of familiar hunger and illness in the west-central Mexico countryside. Along with the many viral and bacterial species that plague farm families, serious illnesses also mar the countryside: cholera, dengue fever, malaria, and even several strains of hepatitis. In spite of exercising extreme caution in food and beverage choices and preparation, my research assistants and I found it nearly impossible to complete an entire trip without becoming ill.

I was also not prepared for the heavy emotional load I would have to bear as I listened to often tragic, almost inconceivable stories and witnessed equally tragic life circumstances. Almost from the moment this study began, interactions with farmworkers have often left me awash in an ocean of contrasting emotions, ranging from joy at life successes to deep sadness and anger at the nearly inescapable vicelike grip of poverty most Mexican subsistence farmers and California farmworkers are caught in. The disparity between the comparatively wealthy insulated lives of Californians living in Santa Cruz and the often dangerous, life-threatening, impoverished lives of Mexican farmworkers hidden from public view only 14 miles away in Watsonville motivated me to question local and state government commitment to human rights issues, work safety standards, and democracy in general.

Over time, as an ethnographer I came to enjoy widespread trust (con-fianza) in both the California farmworker community and rural Mexico.

I believe that my ethnicity, maturity, gender, openness, and passion for the work contributed to the high level of trust I experience. Study participants on both sides of the border openly discussed their undocumented status and the mechanisms used to evade the Border Patrol, as well as other sensitive life issues and experiences.

I always made my research purposes clear at the outset of all interviews. I informed each participant that I was undertaking the study ultimately to improve the circumstances they faced in their lives. I also emphasized the value of their input. All individuals with whom I spoke were happy to know that what they told me might be used to improve the binational well-being of their families. I believe that some farmworkers valued my work, and me, and were so willing to divulge rich ethnographic data because participation in the study rekindled long-lost hopes for a better future for themselves and their family members.

I recall asking Florencio Gómez, a farmworker in the Buena Vista migrant camp in Watsonville, why I was so well received in the community. He responded, "That's easy! You're open and down-to-earth." The openness exchanged with farmworkers in California and farmers in Mexico fostered the revelation of deeper personal internal realms that went beyond the confines of structured interview questions. I found that almost every individual interviewed in both California and Mexico retained a reservoir of grief just beneath the surface of a stoic or otherwise pleasant exterior countenance. When the well was tapped, I found myself identifying with the pain of the study participants and emotionally sharing in the harsh realities of their existence.

Some individuals in both California and Mexico were not trusting. On three occasions I arrived for a prearranged interview with a farmworker in Watsonville only to find that he or she was not home when I arrived or that an "emergency" had arisen that required their immediate attention. Attempts to arrange another meeting were dismissed or deemed impossible due to lack of time.

Fortunately, those who distrusted me as an outsider were the exception rather than the rule. With the passage of time, trust and relationships with farmworkers and Mexican farm families have deepened. I feel privileged to continue to be so welcome as a visitor in the homes of farm families on both sides of the border. Farmers, farmworkers, and their families in California and Mexico touched my heart in the deepest way, establishing a life-long connection of friendship and respect. I feel compelled to tell their story. This publication is one step in a continuing lifetime of research, commitment to, and involvement with California farmworkers and their farm families in rural west-central Mexico. I have written all stories and voices exactly as participants in this study expressed them. I use pseudonyms for all farmworker and Mexican farm family members in order to protect their identity.

While engaged in this research, I was able to initiate a variety of community projects to bridge the chasm between the lives of those who live in "mainstream" U.S. society and those who live as farmworkers or farmers in Mexico. In 1999 a Santa Clara, California, Brownie troop prepared small bags of toys and other gifts for each child in all twenty-two families I visited during the 1999 holiday season. My research assistant and I distributed the toys and enjoyed the true meaning of the season through the delight expressed by each child.

In December 1999 I arranged for San José City College students to send 554 pounds of donated clothes and toys to Guadalajara, Jalisco, for distribution to families in villages associated with Cuquio, Jalisco. For Christmas 2001 I organized a "farmworker Christmas" with donations to eighteen of the poorest farmworker families in Watsonville and Salinas; these included a jacket or coat for each family member, clothes, toys, and a visit from a Spanish-speaking Santa Claus.

From May 2000 to November 2001, I developed and taught a preschool science program for the preschool-age children of migrant farmworkers at the Buena Vista migrant camp. I donated science materials from the San José City College biology department to the camp preschool, including rock and mineral collections, astronomy and ecology posters, aquariums, microscopes, and preserved invertebrate samples. In October 2002 I made a presentation to Pajaro Union School District preschool teachers on effective strategies for science instruction to Latino preschool children.

In 2001 I arranged for the donation of forty surplus computers from the San José Community College District to the Buena Vista migrant camp. The Pajaro Valley School District then created a computer lab at the camp staffed with bilingual technicians and instructors for evening farmworker computer instruction.

In 2002 the regional director of the St. Vincent de Paul organization gave me permission to regularly provide bags of free clothing and toys to farmworker families in Salinas and Watsonville. Hundreds of pounds of free clothing, toys, and household items have been provided to families in both areas. In October 2002 I was able to purchase computers and printers with donations for three farmworker families with high-achieving high school students in Watsonville and Salinas.

In 2003 I arranged for a traditional Michoacán meal with a migrant family for a touring church group from Seattle, Washington. Participants in the event were so moved by their experiences with the farmworker family and those who told their stories to the group that they sent a dozen boxes of athletic equipment to the children at the camp after returning to Seattle. In summer 2005 another meal was provided for the San José Human Agenda group, the director of Human Relations in San José, the Mexican consulate, two UC Santa Cruz professors, and apprentices at the UC Santa Cruz Agroecology Center.

In summer 2006, the Human Agenda group returned with guest legislators for a meal. Thirty members of the American Civil Liberties Union visited the camp for a meal later that summer, and UC Santa Cruz farm apprentices visited the camp that September.

Farmworker Christmas has become tradition in my family, with family members donating hundreds of dollars and gifts for California farmworkers each year. In addition, ten children in one of the poorest families I found in Jalisco now have education sponsors in the United States. Several women at a local Felton exercise club, who know of my work, provided the funds for a year of educational expenses for all the children in the family. They are committed to continuing support until the children receive their degrees and are able to find jobs and move out of their impoverished circumstances.

Finally, I am working with a group of equally passionate, interested people to form a non-profit Farm Worker Family Foundation. We have established a website (see Epilogue) and will provide interested individuals with opportunities to participate in projects and make donations designed to improve working and living conditions as well as educational opportunities for binational farm families.

I continue to visit farm families in Mexico every six months and to maintain contact with farmworker family participants in both Watsonville and Salinas. It is my desire and hope that the perspective and information garnered from this project serve to enlighten future immigration and agricultural labor policymakers and to dispel many of the nativist myths and folktales about Mexican immigrants currently in vogue in California and the rest of the nation. In addition, I feel that a "farm to farm" understanding of the human side of migration from west-central Mexico can ultimately serve as a nexus for the development of more enlightened international immigration and trade policy.

This book is organized in such a way that readers can follow and experience the real life circumstances, including human rights abuses, that individuals face all along the binational migrant circuit. I explore the many binational practices, institutions, and laws that promote and maintain the media objectification and subjugation of Mexican farm-workers. Farmworkers are caught up in this binational framework of so-cial, political, and economic institutions and practices, and escape is nearly impossible.

The final two chapters of the book are devoted to a brief review of the most oppressive institutions on both sides of the border. The human rights violations inherent in this framework at each juncture of the mi-grant circuit are itemized and summarized with specific examples from the text.

Chapter 1 presents an overview of the unprecedented displacement of human beings and the high immigration rates currently taking place worldwide.

As an antecedent to addressing the causal factors contributing to this massive human displacement and immigration phenomenon, chapter 2 provides an overview of Mexico's historical sustainable farming prac-tices. All participants in the research on both sides of the border claimed that these sustainable practices provided the foundation for the west-central Mexico campesino farming culture for their own families and for generations of their ancestors. Harvests were consistently abundant, and families were united in their family, farming, and community activities. Furthermore, family members were woven into the ecology of the sur-rounding landscape, ultimately providing an ecologically sustainable lifestyle for millions of Mexico's rural inhabitants.

In chapter 3 I provide a brief overview of Mexico's agricultural polit-ical economy. I present four modern developments that are principal fac-tors contributing to the disintegration and ultimate demise of the west-central Mexico sustainable rural campesino culture: the 1940s introduction of so-called Green Revolution technologies; the overturn-ing of Article 27 of the Mexican Constitution, which privatized the *ejido* lands in preparation for the North American Free Trade Agreement (NAFTA); NAFTA itself; and corporate penetration. Ultimately, as a re-sult of NAFTA's impact on the Mexican economy and particularly on the lives of subsistence and small producer corn farmers, hundreds of thou-sands of Mexican farmers have been forced to flee from their families and land in search of work elsewhere in Mexico and the United States.

In chapters 4 and 5 I discuss the perceived, though unwelcome, alter-native to starvation in the Mexican countryside: migration out of Mex-ico. I address the many factors contributing to subsistence and small producer corn farmers' decision to migrate and the impact this decision has on family members. I also relate several of the more poignant actual immigration experiences of study participants and their family members. Finally, I examine current U.S. immigration policy and its effect on those arriving from Mexico, as well as their family members back home.

Chapter 6 provides a brief history of California's unique corporate agribusiness. Of particular interest is the extent of corporate agribusiness's generation of wealth and prosperity. I chronicle the history and development of California's industrialized farms from the time of California statehood in 1848 and conclude by examining the recent trend toward land and production consolidation. Unlike smaller farms of the U.S. midwest managed by family members and occasional hired help, California's industrial agriculture has always been dependent upon a hired labor force to manage the huge tracts of consolidated land. I review the historical processes of ethnic succession and wage depression that have occurred over the past several decades along with agricultural labor laws that are designed to protect growers while leaving farmworkers with few rights. The chapter concludes with a summary of farm labor attempts to organize, culminating in farm labor's brief episode of victories in the 1960s under Cesar Chavez's United Farm Workers.

Chapter 7 introduces the central California Mexican farm labor force and illustrates the contrasting roles farmers from Mexico experience as they negotiate the transition from farmer with access to land in Mexico to farm laborer in California. Once employment is initially secured, farmworkers engage in a characteristic sequential process of job migration, propelled by job dissatisfaction from one employment situation to another.

The large growers who supply the most benefits and incentives to workers institute an appeasement process that serves to minimize unrest and promote an established loyal labor force that is unlikely to either unionize or strike during the harvest season. The chapter concludes with a discussion of the exploitative working conditions encountered by farmworkers and their abysmally low wages. Most farmworkers work without contracts, legal protections, or a living wage.

The consequences of overwork, low wages, and occupational hazards are the subject of chapter 8. Though they work in a land of prosperity and wealth generation, farmworkers and their children remain impoverished and pay a grave price in compromised mental and physical health. Few have the health insurance necessary to seek medical intervention and remediation.

Chapter 9 addresses the mechanisms by which California farmworkers and their families survive as the poorest of America's working poor. Farmworker housing, extended households, the problems of solitary men, children's education, the impact of overwork on family life, gangs, and family separation resulting from binational life are considered. The chapter concludes with a discussion of the geographic post-NAFTA spread of HIV/AIDS from California to the west-central Mexico countryside, where pre-NAFTA cases of HIV/AIDS were almost unknown.

In chapter 10 we return to the west-central Mexico countryside to observe the impact of mass emigration on rural towns and villages. Many once-vital centers of community activity and commerce have become ghost towns. The majority are home to the elderly and their grandchildren; the working adults are in the United States. Abandoned and depressed women are a norm in the countryside, and everywhere the impact of environmental destruction in its many forms mars the once-pristine countryside.

Fractured families and farming communities no longer function as stewards of Mexico's rich and genetically diverse corn. Without the necessary labor force to carry them out, sustainable intercrop farming practices have been abandoned, resulting in genetic erosion throughout the Mexican countryside. Concomitantly, corporate high-yielding hybrid varieties and genetically modified corn imported from the United States are replacing traditional strains of corn, further exacerbating the loss of genetic diversity.

As cultural and environmental disintegration and death slip through the Mexican countryside, primarily U.S.-originating transnational corporations are enjoying an economic boom and soaring profits by promoting deadly environment-, health-, and culture-destroying drugs, chemicals, and agricultural products. Chapter 11 provides examples of the health-damaging consequences of abandoning the cultivation of traditional strains of corn and replacing them with high-yielding hybrid and genetically modified corn. Additionally, the chapter summarizes the dependence of the Green Revolution's high-yielding corn strains on a variety of agrochemicals and the impact of these chemicals on both human health and the environment of Mexico.

Chapter 12 summarizes the danger Mexican farmers face when they use deadly agrochemicals, often with little information regarding the product's toxicity, with poorly functioning equipment, and without proper clothing and protection. The impact of imported agrochemicals on the lives of adults and children in the countryside is summarized with graphic, specific ethnographic examples. The chapter concludes with a discussion of the traditional Mexican campesino diet and the impacts Coca-Cola Company, PepsiCo, and Marlboro's aggressive campaigns to sell their health-compromising products to the rural poor of Mexico have had on consumption patterns.

Chapter 13 addresses some of the institutional mechanisms that oppress Mexican farmers and their families in Mexico, including the Mexican government and the legacy of the Partido Revolucionario Institucional, the federal military presence in the countryside, the Catholic Church, the inaccessibility of education, *intermediarios* (middle men), caciques, and machismo.

Chapter 14 summarizes the dense, interlocking, co-reinforcing framework of social, political, and economic institutions and practices that extends binationally from the rural west-central Mexico countryside to central California's corporate agribusiness. The human rights violations that are inherent at every juncture of the binational migrant circuit are highlighted with examples summarized from the preceding chapters. The chapter concludes with proactive steps each country and its citizenry can take to ameliorate the deplorable circumstances the binational farmworker community finds itself in.

Finally, the Epilogue relates some of what has been accomplished thus far on behalf of farmworkers, and the work that remains. It includes specific steps that informed consumers can take to promote the well-being of the binational farmworker population, upon which California's entire agricultural economy is dependent.

Berkeley, California
August 2006

ACKNOWLEDGMENTS

So many people have contributed time and energy to this project that it is impossible to recognize all of them in this brief summary. However, I start by acknowledging Professor Patricia Zavella at the University of California, Santa Cruz. She continues to be an incredibly inspiring and enlightened force in all the work I do and have done to benefit farmworkers. I was fortunate to have Professor Zavella's guidance as an advisor for most of my doctoral program. In postdoctoral studies at UC Berkeley, I continued to benefit from her interest in my work, counsel, and inspiration as a most accomplished and published mentor. Professor Zavella is the advisor all graduate students and post-docs dream of working with. She has mastered the art of guidance without criticism. Furthermore, she has always believed in my potential and prompted me to excellence. She has never accepted less from me than my best performance. Without her, this project would not have blossomed into a fruition that includes towns, villages, homes, people, professors, and universities I would never have dreamed of knowing. She continues to be a gift and guiding light in my life.

I wish to acknowledge the University of California Office of the President for providing me with a two-year postdoctoral fellowship so that I could publish my work. Sheila O'Rourke and Kim Adkinson have been most supportive.

I thank J. V. Martinez, my SACNAS mentor, for connecting me with professors at the University of California, Berkeley, and for inspiring my work.

I wish to acknowledge my father, David Amado López, who was born and raised in a San Bernardino Mexican ghetto and, in spite of incredible hardship, became an architect of unique, beautiful homes. He always emphasized the value of education, study, and academic achievement and instilled in me compassion for those who are less fortunate. Throughout my life he staunchly promoted my education.

I wish to acknowledge my daughter, Rosa López, a beautiful, intelligent young woman who has always been a delight and a source of great pride to me. She grabbed onto the reins of educational success through her studies and degree at the University of California, Davis. Her love, warmth, humor, and encouragement have propelled me through many trying moments.

I also acknowledge Margie Maestas-Flores, my dear friend, former colleague, and former farmworker in the Delano grape fields. Though she moved to New Mexico, she was never more than a half-hour away on the Internet. Throughout the development of this work she maintained daily contact with me and scrutinized newspapers across the nation to find and send me relevant current references for my work. Every long day of writing began and ended with an e-mail message of love and encouragement from Margie. She was always there in spirit across the miles.

I am grateful for my friendship with Adrienne Jerman, a teacher at Lincoln Elementary School in Salinas. She was instrumental in connecting me with the Salinas farmworker community and demonstrates to everyone who knows her work how successful culturally relevant bilingual education that includes parent participation can be in promoting Latino children's education.

I wish to acknowledge Michele Lamelin, who provided me with whatever form of assistance I needed to complete this project. She is responsible for typing the entire manuscript and for spending countless, often frustrating hours tracking down the latest, most accurate agrochemical classifications. She has been an invaluable source of encouragement and support.

I thank the farmworker families in Watsonville and Salinas who generously shared often spellbinding information and stories with me, and who were always interested in my work and in ways they could contribute. I treasure the friendships I now have with these families. They have taught me that farmworkers are some of the world's most beautiful, gracious, honest, kind, and loving people. The human virtues of this population have made the knowledge of their inescapable oppressive circumstances nearly impossible to bear.

I express my appreciation for the hospitality offered to me by the families and town and village hotel staffs in west-central Mexico. I am grateful for all the farmers who took the time to share with me the difficult, personal post-NAFTA realities of their lives.

I thank the students at San José City College for their fascination with my work. I recognize that my role as an academically successful Latina provides them with inspiration to pursue their own educational dreams. My students were always in my heart, and my relationship with them often provided the stamina necessary to see this project through to its completion.

Finally, I thank the research assistants who joined me and supported my work on research trips to west-central Mexico, including Shanna Alba, Andres Anaya, Lorenzo Garcia, Maria Izquierdo, Edgar Machuca, Adrian Vargas, and Miguel Zafra. I also thank Meghan Creswell, Sami Monsur, and Alicia Rojas for their assistance with classes and launching the Farm Worker Family Foundation.

ONE

THE FARMWORKERS' JOURNEY

If NAFTA in concept is so good, why are there so many Mexicans coming here looking for work?

**—Louis Escobar, first Hispanic elected to the Toledo,
Ohio, city council**

*Todo sigue igual. ¡Tenemos problemas terribles! Están
tirando café, piña, maíz. No hay ventas.*

Nothing has changed. We have terrible problems here! They
[farmers] are throwing out their coffee, pineapples, and corn.
There are no markets.

**—Alfonso Martinez, municipal government councilman,
Cuquio, Jalisco, August 2001, when asked how the Fox
administration is impacting the farmers of Cuquio**

The small, sleepy village of San Agustín lies in a valley about 25 miles
outside the bustling city of Tepatitlán in the state of Jalisco, Mexico. The
red brick houses and church steeple at the center of town are accentu-
ated by emerald green crops, agave fields, and pastureland surrounding
the village. The provincial, Catholic, pastoral town emanates a demeanor of peace, tranquility, and stability.

The stillness of the pastoral panorama, however, belies the circumstances of families living within San Agustín's small homes. The historically predictable family rhythm of the campesino rural farming life has
been broken by emotional upheaval and uncertainty. Many wives and

mothers who traditionally executed their conventional household responsibilities without interruption are now on high alert, waiting for
word from a husband, son, or daughter that they have safely crossed the
border into the United States.

Faviola de la Cruz hasn't slept well in weeks. She complains of recur-
ring, alternating bouts of grief, depression, and anxiety. Three months
ago her oldest son, 16-year-old Arnuldo Ayala, left his family and the village where he grew up on a solo journey north to the United States. The
last time Faviola spoke with her son was several weeks ago when he
called her after arriving in Ciudad Obregon, a Mexican town north of
San Agustín, about 40 miles from the coast. She hasn't heard from him
since.

With face in hands, she weeps as she recounts her doubts about his
fate: "I don't know whether he has been apprehended by the *migra* [U.S.
Border Patrol agents], thrown in jail, killed attempting to cross the border or what. I am just sick with worry."

Meanwhile, in the village of Chaparaco in the adjoining state of Michoacán, the family members of Maribel Terraza and Joaquin Bejarano
maintain an all-night vigil waiting for the phone call that might reassure
them that 60-year old Maribel has crossed the border safely with the assistance of the family *coyote* (human smuggler). After attempting to secure a visa at the U.S. embassy in Mexico City on three separate occasions over the past year so that Maribel could visit her legally resident
children and grandchildren in Salinas, California, Maribel's husband
Joaquin called the family *coyote* in Tijuana two days ago.

Though Maribel and Joaquin have all the legal requisites entitling
them to a visa for travel to the United States, including land ownership
and a bank account, Joaquin's patience has run out. He angrily recounts
the tale of his three attempts to secure a visa. He complains about the associated costs, including travel to and from Mexico City, hotel, meals, a
long wait in line, and a payment of US$45 on each visit to the U.S. em-
bassy. (In summer 2006, the fee increased to $100.)

Every time he arrived at the front of the long line of people waiting at
the embassy and was able to speak with a U.S. representative, he was
quickly brushed aside after paying his fee, only to be replaced by the next
person in line. His temper flares as he describes the lines in front of the
embassy: "The lines are so long that street vendors earn a living renting
stools to people who stand in line for hours!"

Though the family *coyote* will cost Joaquin and Maribel's family
members living on both sides of the border $2,000 and force them into

further debt, Maribel has been depressed for months. The separation from her loved ones weighs heavily upon her. She cries about the loss every day.

In a phone call, Joaquin advises the family *coyote* that Maribel will meet him at an agreed upon location in Tijuana. The *coyote,* in turn, assures Joaquin that all necessary documents for an "easy" border crossing will be ready upon her arrival.

Maribel flies to Tijuana. Her first attempt at crossing the border fails. Her *coyote* gave her the U.S. passport and visa of a woman named Anastasia. After rehearsing her new name and age several times, she walked *por la linea* (through the line of immigrants entering the United States) in Tijuana, past the Border Patrol guard. When she showed the guard the passport and visa, the agent took the documents from her, insisting that they were false. She was subsequently escorted back to Tijuana, where she waits for another opportunity to cross with further guidance from the family *coyote.*

Unfortunately, the experiences of Faviola de la Cruz and Joaquin and Maribel Bejarano are not uncommon in the world of "free trade." Since NAFTA went into effect in January 1994, millions of Mexican farmers and their family members have reluctantly left their home towns and villages to join the swelling surge of emigrants heading north to the United States. They are taking part in a worldwide migration phenomenon shared by millions of displaced workers and their family members all around the globe.

Today, there are an estimated 185–192 million immigrants worldwide currently living outside their countries of citizenship (United Nations 2005), a population greater that that of the world's fifth-largest country. The number of migrants has more than doubled since the 1970s (United Nations 2002), and it is increasing by approximately 6 million immigrants each year, representing a growth rate more rapid than that of the world's entire population (International Labor Conference 2004).

During the 1980s an estimated 190,000 immigrants settled in the United States each year (García y Griego 1989). This number is increasing by one to four million people of all nationalities each year. From 1996 to 2000, 5.5 million immigrants arrived. In the four-year interval from 2000 to 2004, 6.1 million immigrants were added to the U.S. population (Camarota 2004). These new arrivals are intent upon taking up permanent residence in the United States, either legally or illegally (Martin and Widgren 1996), and now make up almost 12 percent of the U.S. population (Camarota 2004). At 35.7 million, the United States has the largest population of international immigrants in the world and the highest number recorded in U.S. history (Camarota 2004; Passel 2005a, b; United Nations 2002).

Hispanics accounted for nearly half the growth in the U.S. population from 2001 to 2003, and as of July 2003 their population numbered 39.9 million (Armas 2004), with a buying power of over $440 billion (Mangaliman 2001). Two-thirds of new Hispanic residents are of Mexican descent (Armas 2003), and most speak Spanish at home (*Modesto Bee* 2003). From 1980 to 2002 the population of Mexican immigrants living in the United States more than doubled, from 8.7 million in 1980 to 18 million in 2002 (Armas 2002; Durand 2000).

Today, Mexico has the highest emigration rate in the world (Durand 2000). Estimates of the exact numbers of emigrants leaving Mexico for the United States vary considerably. However, it is safe to say that since NAFTA's initiation literally millions of Mexicans have left their families and homes in Mexico to take up residence in the United States. From 300,000 (Consejo Nacional de Población 2004) to 500,000 Mexicans leave Mexico and enter the United States every year (Passel 2005a; Rochin and Castillo 1995). Immigrants from Mexico accounted for 31 percent of all U.S. immigrants in 2004, up from 28 percent in 2000, 22 percent in 1990, and 16 percent in 1980 (Camarota 2004). Currently, one in eleven Mexicans lives in the United States (Passel 2005a).

The overall population of undocumented immigrants in the United States doubled in the 1990s (Armas 2002) and at the end of 2005 was estimated to be 11 million, or 29 percent of all foreign-born residents (Garcia 2004; Grillo 2005; International Labor Conference 2004; Passel 2005a), including 47 percent of the country's 2.5 million farmworkers (Lowell and Suro 2002). Since 1995, the annual arrivals of undocumented immigrants has exceeded documented arrivals (Passel 2005b). Every year from 2000 to 2004, 700,000 undocumented immigrants entered the United States (Passel 2005a). In 2005, 6 million undocumented immigrants were employed in the United States (CBS News 2005).

Fifty-seven percent of all undocumented immigrants in the United States, 5.9 million, are from Mexico. The population of undocumented immigrants from Mexico surged from 1.1 million (18 percent of Mexican-born entrants) between 1980 and 1984 to 2.4 million (85 percent of Mexican-born entrants) between 2002 and 2004 (Passel 2005a). Thus, at current rates, 485,000 undocumented Mexican immigrants are entering the United States every year (Passel 2005b), twice as many undocumented immigrants as entered prior to the heavy border fortification (see chapter 4). During the first eleven months of 1998, the U.S. Border Patrol reported apprehending 1,448,032 illegal entrants, a 2.5 percent increase since 1997 (Annerino 1999). In 2005, 1.1 million arrests were made by Border Patrol agents (CBS News 2005).

One-third of California's 33 million residents are Latinos (Mangaliman 2001), nearly one-fourth of whom (about 2.4 million) are undocumented. California has the largest undocumented immigrant population in the United States (Passel 2005a, b; Wides 2005). One estimate suggests that 1,650 immigrants enter California every 24 hours (Rochin and Castillo 1995). How can these huge shifting flows of humanity be accounted for?

Massive worldwide immigration has occurred simultaneously with the emergence of a global economy wherein countries with formerly restricted borders have opened their economies to the flow of capital, goods, and information (Massey 1998). In the 1960s and 1970s the United States, along with other countries primarily of the developed world, implemented the precepts of the new global economic system. Trade in manufactured goods became increasingly liberalized beginning in the 1960s, though the United States continued to protect and subsidize its farm sector. Once the United States obtained technological superiority in farm production and agroindustrial world dominance, it reversed its earlier position and became the leading advocate of liberalized agricultural trade within the General Agreement on Trade and Tariffs (GATT) and other trading agreements (Barry 1995). Liberalized agricultural trade within GATT was viewed as a means by which the United States could access new markets.

In the 1970s, Mexico's president, López Portillo, managed to resist pressure from advocates of populist and nationalist policies to enter into negotiations that could have resulted in his country joining GATT (Barry 1995). But in 1982, when Mexico could no longer meet the interest payments on its foreign debt, the country became vulnerable to economic restructuring. Additionally, the costs of sustaining its own national food system and the availability of subsidized grains from the United States ultimately resulted in Mexico becoming ever more dependent upon grain imports from the United States. Bowing to international pressure, Mexico eventually joined GATT in 1986 (Cockcroft 1998), which along with pressure from the United States and the multilateral banks paved the way for the NAFTA negotiations in 1990.

A legacy of secrecy about intended dramatic alterations in international economics was initiated in the Western Hemisphere with the

NAFTA negotiations. In both Mexico and the United States, anyone outside of the elite circle of NAFTA originators found it difficult to acquire information about the content and implications of NAFTA beforehand. As late as 1993, labor and government leaders in both countries were unable to obtain copies of NAFTA or information about it. In Mexico, the secretary of commerce and industrial development eventually made a copy of the NAFTA document and its implications available to business leaders, but the document was not available for public scrutiny outside the business community. People in both countries were left to speculate about its contents and relevance to people's lives (Cockcroft 1998; Kingsolver 1996; Markusen and Zahniser 1997).

Juxtaposed against this context of secrecy was a nearly complete lack of democracy in the development process itself (Cockcroft 1998). Socioeconomic groups upon which NAFTA has had a decidedly negative impact were not included in the drafting of the NAFTA accords. Neither students (Kingsolver 1996) nor small corn-growing subsistence farmers in Mexico were included or sought out for their opinions. Indeed, citing inefficiency in corn production, NAFTA originators predicted that millions of farmers would be forced to leave their land and search for employment elsewhere (Nadal 1999).

As a result of NAFTA, which commenced in 1994, and a World Bank structural adjustment loan initiated during the presidency of Salinas de Gortari in 1991 (Barry 1995), all government price supports and subsidies for corn production in Mexico have been withdrawn. The U.S. corn sector is the largest recipient of government farm subsidies. U.S. corn farmers received $10.1 billion in subsidies in 2000 (Fanjul and Fraser 2003). The United States maintains surplus corn stocks and can produce corn at 40 percent of the cost of production in Mexico (Nadal 2000). Grain surpluses in the United States are sent to Mexico while the United States maintains its own food security (Barry 1995). In contrast, Mexico exports labor-intensive agricultural products to the United States (Zavella 2000) while Mexico's once subsidized rural food security has been undermined.

President Salinas de Gortari and his advisors spent over $30 million promoting NAFTA (Kingsolver 1996). Banking industries, agribusiness, manufacturing companies, and multinational corporations presented convincing models, calculations, and rhetoric promising skeptics a rejuvenated Mexican economy with upgraded diets for everyone (Barkema 1992), reduced incentive to emigrate due to a narrowed wage gap between U.S. and Mexican wage rates (Orme 1993), strengthened democracy and improved economic and political stability in Mexico, plus improved health and environmental conditions (Public Citizens Global Trade Watch 1996). The California Farm Bureau Federation proclaimed NAFTA the first "green" trade agreement in history and an ideal way to reduce illegal immigration by creating job opportunity in Mexico (Watte 1992).

The United States played a key military, political, and economic role in the emergence of Mexico's restructured economy and is a primary beneficiary of the trade agreement. Lifted trade barriers have resulted in a boom in U.S. investment in Mexican factories and other businesses, as economic integration between California and Mexico resulted in lucrative profits derived through production in Mexico followed by export to the United States. U.S. direct investment in Mexico increased from $16.9 billion in 1994 to $25.3 billion in 1998 (World Bank figures cited in Anderson 1999). Mexican exports to the United States increased from $49.4 billion in 1994 to $94.7 billion in 1998 (AFL-CIO figures cited in Anderson 1999). Imports from Mexico to California alone more than doubled between 1995 and 2002, from $9.1 billion to $20.3 billion (Shatz and López-Calva 2004). Exports to Mexico of goods originating in California grew an average of 12.8 percent each year from 1988 to 2002, and Mexico has become the largest destination for California exports (Shatz and López-Calva 2004).

One year after NAFTA's initiation, the Mexican agricultural ministry estimated that one million Mexican farmers had already left their land and predicted that one million more would leave the land each year for NAFTA's first fifteen years (Public Citizen's Global Trade Watch 2001; Taylor et al. 1997). In 1995 more than one million Mexicans also reached the age of 15, effectively entering the job market. During this same year the number of jobs in the formal sector of the Mexican economy fell by 200,000 (Taylor et al. 1997). Between the NAFTA years 1993 and 2000, rural Mexico lost between 1.3 million (White et al. 2003) and 1.7 million jobs (National Employment Survey of the Ministry of Labour, as cited in Glipo et al. 2003). Mexico's "comparative advantage" in the restructured "liberalized" international economic arena is its labor force, to be used as a source of workers for factory work, work on large-scale commercial farms in Mexico, and work in U.S. corporate agribusiness.

As a progenitor, promoter, and beneficiary of NAFTA, the United States has been pivotal in creating the conditions that encourage migration, thereby promoting the displacement and immigration of people from Mexico into the United States. The linkages forged between the United States and other countries as a result of the new neoliberal world economy are serving as bridges for international migration (Sassen 1990).

Televised warnings originating in both the United States and Mexico advise campesinos of emigration perils and offer persuasive arguments about the importance of "returning to the land." Widespread publicity touts the Mexican government's responsibility for providing post-NAFTA government aid programs designed to smooth campesino transition into the post-NAFTA economy. Employment "opportunities" in Mexico are also offered as deterrents to immigration.

However, in Mexico, withdrawal of support has left corn-growing rural Mexican farmers completely vulnerable to the vagaries of an economic system in which returns on corn harvests no longer cover costs of production (Barry 1995). Intensifying the rural progression into poverty further has been the failure to honor the NAFTA timetable for tariff elimination on so-called sensitive crops, like corn. In the NAFTA negotiations, a fifteen-year tariff phase-out period was agreed upon in order to allow subsistence and small producer farmers to readjust their lives and locate work elsewhere. In actuality, the tariff phase-out period occurred in a mere thirty months (Fanjul and Fraser 2003; Mexico Solidarity Network 2003).

Rural farmers and their families remaining in Mexico, unable to compete with subsidized U.S. corn production, are paying the price. During NAFTA's first decade, corn-growing rural Mexican farmers were overwhelmed by the flood of U.S. exported corn into Mexico (Tobar et al. 2003) and witnessed farm prices for their own corn plunge by as much as 70 percent (Carlsen 2003; Fanjul and Fraser 2003; Moreno 2003).

The farmers' situation is exacerbated by the fact that Mexico no longer has policies to ensure food self-sufficiency. The cost of food, housing, and essential services in Mexico has risen by 247 percent since the initiation of NAFTA. The cost of corn tortillas has risen by 50 percent. Some products, including milk, chicken, bread, and beans, are more expensive in Mexico than in the United States (Border Action Network 2004). As a result, from January 1995 to June 1996, consumption of basic foods, including corn, beans, and wheat, dropped by 29 percent. Today, one in two Mexicans do not have access to the minimum caloric requirements (2,340 calories) established by the World Health Organization (Suppan and Lehman 1997).

The number of Mexicans living in "severe" poverty grew by four million during the first five years of NAFTA (Inter-American Development Bank, as cited in Anderson 1999). Approximately 81 percent of the rural population in Mexico currently lives in poverty, a 15 percent increase since 1984 (Public Citizen's Global Trade Watch 2001). Over 50 percent of Mexicans in rural areas lives in "extreme" poverty. In the state of Michoacán, one of the most important U.S. immigrant-sending states, 45.6 percent of the population, including 115,000 Mexicans over age 65, live in poverty, some in extreme poverty (Vallejo 2005). In the southern state of Chiapas an estimated 70 percent of the rural population now lives in extreme poverty (Fanjul and Fraser 2003; Public Citizen's Global Trade Watch 2001).

The Mexican Institute of Social Security estimates that 158,000 Mexican children have died and continue to die each year before reaching age 5 from illnesses related to nutrition since NAFTA was initiated. The percentage of malnourished children in Mexico is about the same as in sub-Saharan African countries that have only a tenth of Mexico's per capita GDP (Suppan and Lehman 1997.)

In January 2004, a ten-year accounting of NAFTA's impact clearly demonstrates that most people in all three NAFTA countries (Canada, the United States, and Mexico) are losers under NAFTA, while only a handful of the largest corporations who helped to draft the NAFTA accords secretly are major winners (Mekay 2003). The NAFTA emphasis on a market-based trade economy has disrupted the traditional rural economies of Mexico and exacerbated the economic inequalities within the country (Dalton 2003).

For millions of rural Mexican corn farmers who are attempting to escape rural poverty and starvation, the only viable survival strategy for their families is the abandonment of their land, extended family members, and rural villages and towns followed ultimately by emigration to overcrowded Mexican cities or to the United States. To date at least 1.75 million rural farmers have been forced off their land, migrating to Mexican cities or to the United States as economic refugees (Carlsen 2003). Estimates of the number of people who will ultimately be displaced run as high as 15 million people, or one in six Mexicans (Border Action Network 2004).

The stories of these economic refugee families who attempt to maintain their family unity with family members dispersed between west-central Mexico and central California must be told. They represent one strand of the ever-increasing worldwide migratory flow of humanity and reflect the experiences of migrants all over the world.

The American public has a responsibility to become informed about the human impacts of trade policies that are actively endorsed by their government leaders. U.S. taxpayers must become enlightened and knowledgeable, with answers to the following questions, if they are to mobilize and initiate change on behalf of economically disenfranchised farmworker immigrants: What is the U.S. role in promoting the demise of Mexico's rural subsistence farming culture? What is the experience of Mexican subsistence farmers and their family members as they leave their small farms in Mexico and migrate to the Salinas and Pajaro valleys of central California in hopes of finding work? How are their Mexican villages, towns, and the rural farming culture impacted by their absence? How are U.S.-originating transnational corporations impacting the farming communities of west-central Mexico? Most important, what does the future hold for displaced rural Mexican farm family members living in the United States, and for other family members and farms left behind in Mexico? We can begin to explore the answers to these questions by addressing the history of the Mexican farming culture prior to U.S. trade intervention.

TWO

MEXICO'S HISTORICAL FARMING PRACTICES

Todos comemos de la agricultura. Porque, si no hay agricultura, no hay vida.

Everyone eats as a result of agriculture. Because, if there is no agriculture, then there is no life.

—Consuelo Fernandez, Salinas farmworker

Como no saben hacer otra cosa, tienen que sembrar. Si no siembren, que van a comer?

Since they don't know how to do anything else, they have to plant [corn]. If they don't plant, what are they going to eat?

—Reynaldo Becerra, corn farmer in El Loreto/La Barca, Jalisco

Tecomán is an agricultural hub of the west-central Mexican state of Colima. A modern toll road connects Tecomán with coastal Manzanillo, a world-renowned seaside tourist area. The short stretch of road from Manzanillo to Tecomán passes through verdant coastal tropical vegetation that merges with vast monoculture banana plantations situated between Highway 200 and the coast. As the road approaches Tecomán, banana plantations give way to polyculture agroforestry systems of coconut palms and green lemon trees with intermittent coconut/banana or lemon and mango orchards.

Pueblo Rincón de López is a small pueblo approximately 45 minutes outside Tecomán and is part of a large *ejido* (communal farm; see chapter 3) of 400 farmers *(ejidatarios)*. As the taxi passes through the pueblo of Armería and then begins the steep climb up the road toward Rincón de López, the taxi driver assures me that I won't find Colima campesinos in either Watsonville or Salinas, California. "The port of Manzanillo, local agriculture, and abundant tourism provide plenty of jobs in Mexico for all of Colima's residents."

The main road through Rincón de López is unpaved and lined with concrete houses and small businesses. A confusing jumble of children, chickens, and dogs runs through the dusty road, kicking up clouds of dust. Through the haze and with the counsel of some of the local residents, I find the home of Esmeralda Gómez and Sergio Camacho Machado, the parents of Ana Aguirre, a farmworker in Salinas.

Their house is of concrete construction, barren and stark. The only home furniture is a few plastic chairs and beds in the bedrooms adjoining the home's entrance. Esmeralda keeps a few chickens in the back of the house but claims that they are all sick with a cold. She also keeps two or three pigs for special family feasts.

I observe that one of the most obvious differences between this pueblo and those I have visited in other parts of rural west-central Mexico is the presence of men of all ages in town. Most of the towns in this region are predominantly inhabited by senior citizens, a few young women, and many children whose parents have long since left them for work in the United States. On a walk with Esmeralda's grandchildren by the local river, I see ten young men relaxing and socializing—a very rare site these days.

Sergio Camacho Machado, Esmeralda's husband, is about 70 years old. He and his family moved from nearby Maquilí, Michoacán, to Rincón de López eleven or twelve years ago. When asked about farming, Sergio reminisces about a time fifty years ago when he farmed in Maquilí without using agrochemicals. He relates how he planted a corn, beans, and squash polyculture that never required the chemicals to realize abundant crop yields. Planting and harvesting were all timed with the seasons. The ground was ploughed with oxen and a plow instead of tractors.

Today, Sergio plants his 6 hectares, about 5 miles out of town, in an intercrop of green lemon trees and coconut palms. Some of his land is also devoted to corn production. However, unlike fifty years ago, today he uses a variety of agrochemical fertilizers, herbicides, and pesticides. The local agrochemical distributor is conveniently located right across the street from his home.

Sergio claims that white corn is the only corn he can sell these days, and the corn sells for a very low price. So he stores most of the corn he and his family harvest, and this supply supports their year-round corn consumption. Though his lemons and coconuts garner variable prices, depending on demand and the time of year, the two crops provide enough income for the family to purchase items and services that are not available on his land.

Esmeralda, who listens to our conversation quietly, interjects how she grew crops with her father fifty years ago with no chemical use at all. She recounts how they grew rain-fed crops of tomato, rice, corn, squash, cucumber, beans, and chilies. She talks enthusiastically about her love of the different colors of corn she and her family harvested. Her favorite was the black corn. She bemoans the loss of colorful corn, no longer available because white corn has replaced it for sale on the market.

Esmeralda's voice rises angrily as she describes how harmful agrochemicals are to humans and animals. "The chemicals have poisoned everything! The corn that is grown with chemicals is fed to animals. Meat doesn't taste the same as it did when I was a child because of the chemicals. When I was a child, the animals were only fed corn; now they're fed Purina!"

She continues, talking of the cancers and other diseases she has seen develop in her neighbors because of the agrochemicals. "Even AIDS and tuberculosis incidence have increased because of these chemicals. These diseases were unknown in this pueblo before people began using agrochemicals here thirty years ago. I have a heart condition and problems with my knees. I have not seen Ana [her daughter living in Salinas] for ten years. I can't travel legally to the United States to visit her or my grandchildren. Tell her that I'm going to die, so if she wants to see me, she better come and visit me soon."

THE SUCCESS OF WEST-CENTRAL MEXICAN PRE-HISPANIC AGRICULTURE

Prior to the 1940s introduction of so-called Green Revolution technology into Mexico, subsistence farmers, their families, and neighbors lived close-knit family and village lives by implementing sophisticated, ecologically sustainable irrigation and cultivation practices. These practices predate the Spanish conquest of Mexico and were so successful that they supported Mesoamerican cities of well over 100,000 people. Palenque is but one example.

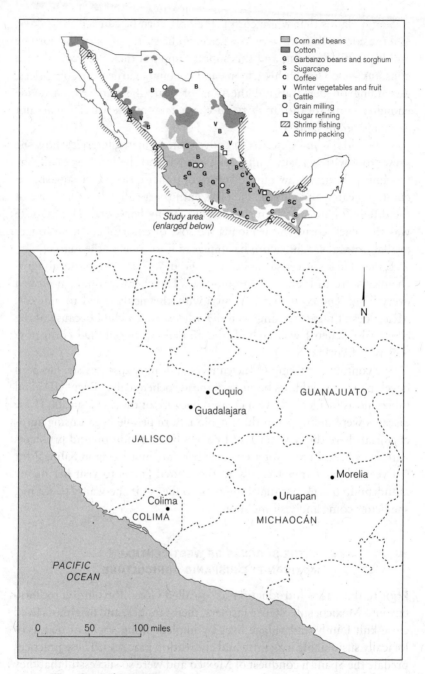

Map 1. West-Central Mexico.

The success of pre-Hispanic agriculture can be attributed primarily to the use of multiple cropping systems, or polycultures. Though temperatures vary throughout the year and region, the primary limiting factor is water for irrigation. Most traditional farming systems are temporal, dependent exclusively upon rainfall for irrigation. Planting and harvesting cycles are thus timed with the May–October rainy season.

In multiple crop systems, more than one crop occupies the same piece of land either simultaneously or in some type of rotational sequence during the season (Gliessman 1992). Prior to the Green Revolution's agrochemicals and mechanization, polycultures were the ubiquitous means of sustenance for farmers and their families. A common traditional multiple cropping system that has been extensively studied is the corn, bean, and squash polyculture. This intercrop is ideally suited for dependency on seasonal rainfall and for insertion into the cleared tropical scrub vegetation characteristic of the region.

The intercrop is typically cultivated in *ecuaros* or *guamiles*, agroecosystems characteristic of west-central Mexico's rocky hillsides. They are cultivated and maintained entirely by hand using pre-Hispanic farming methods. The ubiquitous tropical scrub vegetation is cleared from a cultivation site, and the agroecosystem is subsequently imbedded into the surrounding native vegetation.

This unique cropping system has been studied extensively because of its high corn yields. This form of intercropping corn *(Zea mays),* beans *(Phaseolus vulgaris),* and squash (*Cucurbita* spp.) results in corn yields as much as 50 percent higher than corn planted alone in a monoculture (Fernández 1987; Gliessman 1998). In spite of a reduction in the overall yields for the beans and squash in the polyculture, the total yield for all three crops is much higher per unit of land planted than when the individual crops are each planted in single-crop systems.

Studies have shown that intricate ecological mutualisms among the three crops account for their overall success in a polyculture (Gliessman 1982a, b, 1992, 1998; Letourneau 1986; Risch 1980; Wilken 1987). In the presence of corn, beans have a stronger tendency to form nitrogen nodules as a result of their exposure to *Rhizobium* bacteria in the soil. Fixed nitrogen is then made available to corn through mycorrhizal fungi that connect the root systems of the corn and beans. An analysis of soil nitrogen content after the polyculture has been harvested shows that soil nitrogen concentration actually increases (Gliessman 1998). By contrast, in a corn monoculture, soil nitrogen concentrations decline.

The corn plant stalks also provide support for the bean plants. The

Figure 1. Site of former intercrop embedded in native vegetation, Las Cebollas, Jalisco.

broad leaves of the squash plants shade the ground and thus inhibit weed growth. In addition, potential allelopathic compounds formed on the leaf surfaces are washed into the soil by rainfall. These compounds are suspected of further inhibiting weed growth (Gliessman 1992). Finally, herbivory is reduced in the corn, bean, and squash intercrop because food sources are less concentrated and more difficult to find in the mixture (Risch 1980). The architecture of the intercrop provides microclimatic conditions that attract beneficial insects including predatory insects (Letourneau 1986). Beneficial insects are further attracted to the intercrop by the presence of diverse pollen and nectar sources.

The pre-Hispanic corn, bean, and squash intercrop also included amaranth (*Amaranthus* spp.), which helped reduce herbivory because herbivorous insects prefer the leaves of amaranth to those of the corn plant (S. R. Gliessman, personal communication, 1997). In addition, amaranth appears to be able to withstand the ravages of herbivory more successfully than corn. Amaranth as part of the intercrop thus diverts herbivory away from the more vulnerable corn plants, thereby conserving the corn's photosynthetic surfaces and elevating yields. After the conquest, the Spanish prohibited the growth and consumption of amaranth because of the grain's association with indigenous sacrificial rituals.

In some regions of west-central Mexico in which the rainy season extends beyond October, a second legume crop is planted after the corn, bean, and squash intercrop is harvested. Often a crop of garbanzo beans or other legume that serves as fodder for animals, referred to locally as *janamargo*, is planted as a monoculture, rotationally on the cleared ground. These crops have lower water requirements than corn and are thus successfully dry-farmed after the rains. A small amount of these second crops is typically harvested for family and livestock use, but most farmers sell the majority of the harvest as a source of additional family income.

An example of a west-central Mexican farm family that continues the pre-Hispanic polyculture farming tradition today is the family of Jovita Tejada. Though financial necessity permits family unity for only part of each year, Jovita and her family enthusiastically continue the farming tradition. High in the hills southwest of Tuxcueca, Jalisco, near Lake Chapala is the small, remote village of Las Cebollas. Each year Jovita, her husband, and most of her fifteen children cultivate 3–4 hectares of the labor-intensive corn, bean, and squash intercrop as tenant farmers in an *ecuaro*. Jovita's husband, Jaime Morales, works in corporate agribusiness from May to December each year in Vista, California. His travels to the United States over the past fifteen years have provided income to supplement the family's subsistence efforts.

Jaime attempts to time his travels to California each year so that he is present in Las Cebollas to assist the family in clearing land and planting the intercrop in April, and in harvesting the intercrop in December. In his absence, Jovita and her children maintain the intercrop.

As tenant farmers, the family rents land from a local owner of *pequeñas propiedades* (small properties) in exchange for the crop residues of the harvest. In April, prior to the rainy season, Jovita and her family determine a site for their intercrop. I visited Jovita's farm on several research trips to Mexico. During the summer of 1998, her intercrop was planted on a remarkably high, steep slope of perhaps 30–45 degrees. The view from her *ecuaro* of the breathtaking mountainous farm area surrounding the village was spectacular.

Once the site is determined, weeds are cut down with a machete *(casanga)*, and then allowed to dry for one week. A cool ground fire destroys most of the dried weeds and other native vegetation. Trees and large shrubs are burned, but not permanently damaged by the fire, and

Figure 2. Jovita Tejada and family members in their corn, bean, and squash polyculture, Las Cebollas, Jalisco.

remain as a part of the intercrop. The recovered trees and shrubs provide welcome shade for the workers on the characteristically hot summer days. Ashes from the fire are recognized by subsistence farmers as a source of plant nutrients.

Seeds are planted with a *coa,* a digging stick with an attached metal probe. The probe punctures the ground, and seeds of corn, beans, and squash are deposited into the resultant hole and covered by foot. The variety of squash most commonly planted in the region is referred to by local farmers as *chilacoyote,* a large oval squash with the same mottled skin and size as a watermelon. This form of seed planting occurs throughout west-central Mexico on hillsides on which a slope or an abundance of stones makes the entry of a *tronco de caballos* (horse-drawn plow) impossible.

The intercrop is rain-fed; it depends entirely upon local rainfall. Maintenance of the intercrop primarily involves the constant removal of the rapidly growing pernicious, competitive weeds before they interfere with crop growth. Weeds are removed by hand with a hoe *(azadón)* and *casanga.*

The entire family participates in the harvest. The harvesters wear woven baskets called *chundes* on their backs. The corn enclosed by husks is efficiently and rapidly removed from the stalks. The dried corn on the cob *(mazorca)* is separated from the husks with an iron implement referred to as a *pizcador*. The liberated *mazorca* is then tossed behind the harvester into the *chunde*. Baskets full of *mazorca* are emptied into burlap bags *(costales)* and carried by mule to Jovita's home in the village. The *mazorca* is initially stored in a large 10- by 10-foot concrete bin at the back of the house. Once the corn is removed from the cob *(desgranada)*, it is stored in large drums *(tambos)* for convenient retrieval during meal preparation. The harvest season for December typically yields approximately 400 square feet of corn.

In addition, sacks of beans and *chilacoyote* squash are harvested. The majority of the harvest is stored for family use. A small amount is sold in August when corn is less available and sales result in a higher return. There is thus enough corn for family consumption and for sale. When the intercrop harvest is complete, the landowner's cattle are turned out into the abandoned field to feed on the crop residues. The nitrogen-rich manure excreted by the cattle is incorporated into the soil and improves soil fertility.

Jovita and her family cultivate the same piece of land for two consecutive years, then allow it to remain fallow for four to five years as a means of fertility restoration. When a formerly cultivated piece of land is abandoned for fertility restoration, the family rents another piece of land in the interim. During the period of fertility restoration, the surrounding tropical scrub vegetation reclaims the land. Thus, this minimal-input form of agriculture is completely sustainable and restorative. The agroecosystem supports Jovita's family, and the farming practices do not result in any lasting damage to the adjacent natural ecosystem.

As long as weather conditions are stable with predictable rainfall patterns, the corn, bean, and squash polyculture is a sustainable system with a closed nutrient cycle contributed to by the waste products of animals and the farm family. Corn and beans provide a diet of complementary proteins, which is augmented by beef, chicken, eggs, and milk provided by farm animals. The corn, bean, and squash polyculture has historically provided the foundation for the rural west-central Mexico farming culture.

I asked Jovita why she plants a three-crop polyculture. She responded that the polyculture is an efficient way to harvest three sources of food for her family in December. I asked her if there were any weeds that were conducive to the growth of the three crops and that were not eliminated. She indicated that all weeds are negative because they destroy "the force

Figure 3. Indigenous woman harvesting *maíz criollo*, Las Cebollas, Jalisco.

Figure 4. Harvested *maíz criollo*, Las Cebollas, Jalisco; note genetic diversity.

Figure 5. Native vegetation reclaiming abandoned *parcela*, Las Cebollas, Jalisco.

or energy of the cornfield" *("la fuerza de la milpa")*. During my first visit in the summer of 1998, when I asked Jovita about pests and means of pest control, she responded that she did not have problems with pests in the polyculture and thus was not interested in purchasing the costly agrochemicals sold in nearby Tizapán.

AGRICULTURE AFTER THE CONQUEST

During their conquest of Mexico around A.D. 1520, the Spaniards introduced the concepts of private property and slave labor (Baird and Mc-Caughan 1979). After the conquest, some Indian communities continued to fight for their communal lands, while many fled to the nearby mountains. The Catholic Church seized most of the indigenous arable lands. Indians who could not escape to the nearby mountains were forced into a form of slavery on sugar plantations, in mills, and in mines under Spanish overlords. The 1810 war of independence reorganized the social hierarchy in Mexico to include some Mexican-born Spaniards and *mestizos* but did little to improve the lives of the Indians.

The Spanish introduced horses, mules, and oxen into Mexico along with the plow and other farming implements. Indigenous farming practices were modified with the introduction of this new technology for ground preparation and weeding. The cultivation of relatively flat land in west-central Mexico with a *tronco de caballos* (horse or oxen and plow) continues to be a ubiquitous practice among subsistence farmers who do not have the resources to purchase or rent modern farming machinery. A summary of the typical yearly farming cycle that includes the use of a horse or oxen and plow is as follows:

April–May: Barbecho The rains begin, and land is prepared for planting. A metal plow attached to oxen, horses, or mules by a wooden harness is dragged over the land to turn over the soil *(barbechar)*. As furrows are formed, other family members follow behind depositing seeds into the furrows and covering them with their feet. In recent years some farmers add chemical fertilizers such as urea at this stage.

June: Primer Labor Young corn plants grow to about one foot tall. *Primer labor* (first labor) involves returning to the field with the plow and running it between the rows of corn to eliminate nascent weeds. Plowing at this time also results in the formation of mounds of soil around the corn plant roots and stem. The soil mounds prevent dislodging by the wind. Some farmers claim that the soil next to the roots absorbs sunlight, which heats the soil surrounding the roots and promotes more rapid plant growth.

July: La Segunda At this stage, corn plants have grown to a height of 2–4 feet. Farmers enter the fields a second time *(la segunda)* and remove undesirable weeds *(zacate),* once again using an animal-drawn plow.

August Weeds are dense, pervasive, pernicious, and rapidly growing throughout the growing season in west-central Mexico. They are stalwart corn competitors. Thus a third weeding is often required. In neglected fields in which they have not been removed, weeds quickly overwhelm the corn plants, and corn plant development is stunted; the immature plants never develop sufficiently to produce a harvest. In tended fields, corn plants at a height of 5–6 feet are too tall for weed removal with animals and a plow. Labor-intensive weeding is accom-

Figure 6. Corn planting with a *tronco de caballos*, Los Sauces de Pérez, Jalisco.

plished manually with the use of hoes *(azadones)* and machetes *(casangas* or *os)*.

Late August–September: Jilote Corn plants are mature enough to produce young corncobs *(jilote)* and tassels. Some farmers apply chemical fertilizers at this point to stimulate greater and more robust seed production.

October–November: Elote The rains cease. Soft corn *(elote)* matures. Families typically harvest some of the *elote* to make into tamales. *Elote* is also roasted in west-central Mexico and sold on the street as the popular *elote asado*.

November–December: Harvest Crops are harvested by hand or by tractor. *Mazorca* is harvested by splitting open the cornhusks with a *pizcador;* it is then tossed into *chundes*. Beans *(frijoles)* are harvested initially by disentangling the drying bean plants from the corn plants. Bean plants are piled up on level surfaces on the side or within the cornfield *(milpa)* and beaten with sticks. Beans then detach from their pods and fall to the ground. Young children generally are assigned the task of col-

Figure 7. Harvested squash, Las Cebollas, Jalisco; note genetic diversity.

lecting the fallen bean seeds and placing them in burlap bags *(costales)* for later storage. Either the corn is stored as *mazorca,* with kernels removed periodically prior to cooking, or the kernels are removed prior to storing by hand or by a manually run machine called a *desgranadora* (grain remover). The farmer selects the corn judged to be of highest quality and sets it aside for the following year's planting. Corn and beans are stored in large covered drums or in a concrete bin built into the wall of the home's interior.

In a successful year, farm families in this part of Mexico harvest enough corn to provide for all family members for the entire year, and another third or half of the corn crop can be sold on the market for cash. Prior to NAFTA, the Mexican government subsidized subsistence farm corn production by purchasing the farmers' corn at internationally elevated prices. The cash garnered from the sale of corn could then be used for the purchase of household necessities and services such as clothing, shoes, cooking oil, or a doctor's fee. The remaining corn and all the squash and beans are most often stored for the exclusive use of the family and livestock. All crop residues from the three crops are fed to animals. Families often store crop residues for use during March and April when food supplies are waning; these months are referred to as *los meses críticos* (the critical months).

December–May: Fertility Restoration Livestock are turned out into the fields to consume any remaining crop residues and to keep weed growth in check. While in the fields animals deposit nitrogen-rich manure, which promotes nutrient recovery after the harvest and increases soil fertility during the dry season. Restored fields are then planted again at the beginning of the following year's rainy season.

FARM FAMILY INTEGRATION WITH
AGROECOSYSTEMS AND THE NATURAL WORLD

In west-central Mexico the farming family's relationship to and integration with the corn, bean, and squash polyculture has been an essential component of its success and continuity historically and generationally. The family typically includes a married couple or domestic partners and their children, relatives, extended family members, and even friends. It serves as the focal point for economic allocation. Food, clothing, and shelter are arranged for collectively by all members of the household over the long term (Netting 1993).

In west-central Mexico, men and women more often than not marry a spouse from the same village or from one in the immediate vicinity. When a woman marries a man from a different village or town, she usually moves with him to his location of residence. Esmeralda and Sergio's daughter Ana Aguirre and Fernando Azevedo both grew up in the *ejido* of Maquilí, Michoacán. After they married, Ana moved with Fernando to the United States, where they work as Salinas farmworkers while raising their nine children.

Kinship, family, and household relationships are interwoven with residence, labor, the farm property, and the surrounding natural biotic communities. An efficient division of labor has developed on the basis of gender differentiation. Characteristically, the father and oldest sons are responsible for most of the activities involved with farming fields of crops, such as plowing and driving draft animals. Traditionally, women are responsible for household chores such as cooking, cleaning, washing clothes, and maintaining the *huertas* (gardens) and small animals near the house (Burton and White 1987). Family members forge strong, integrated bonds with one another as they work together day after day.

The labor-intensive agriculture helps to maintain a strong common focus on domestic functions. Time and effort as well as rights and duties of household members are concentrated on crop cultivation. The necessity of this perennial focus on intensive crop cultivation for most of the year fosters awareness among household members of the significance of shared, cooperative activities. Intensive interaction, a division of labor, and a highly socialized level of cooperation among the members facilitate coordination and management of the subsistence household and lands (Netting 1993). The benefits of sustainable agriculture require an emphasis on the most effective combination of production, distribution, transmission, and reproduction among household members. Family solidarity in turn provides the basic framework for mutual aid, control, and socialization.

The household also functions as a repository of ecological knowledge (Netting 1993). West-central Mexico farmers often own title to parcels of land in a variety of environments and ecosystems, and they possess specialized knowledge about the specific microenvironments their *parcelas* (parcels of land) occupy. The agricultural management of each parcel requires a sophisticated level and combination of both agricultural and ecological knowledge in cropping system design for maximum productivity. Conscious experimentation with new crops in specific locations at specific times of the year contributes to the fund of this practical agroecological knowledge.

Members of a household may share an attachment to their farm. Generationally, the family and its farming practices become inextricably interwoven with the natural environment. As "multi-use strategists" (Toledo 1995), family members are dependent upon their immediate environment for food and fiber resources to supplement their subsistence agricultural production. Family members are also contributing parts of nearly closed natural biogeochemical cycles. They extract resources from their immediate environment and return wastes and other biodegradable refuse to the environment.

The fund of ecological information that is so vital to the agricultural endeavor and to the family's relationship to the natural environment is transmitted from one generation to the next through observation, imitation, and the instruction that accompanies the general processes of socialization and cultural education within the family. "Being a campesino is different from having a job. It is a way of relating to land and community. It is a sense of place and identity not easily shaken. The *campo* is the heart and soul of Mexico" (Barry 1995, 5). When asked why many Mexican farmers are unwilling to sell their land, in light of the far-reaching political developments in Mexico over the past ten years, Lorenzo Vasquez, a Salinas farmworker from Zinapecuaro, Michoacán, replied, "*Porque aman a su tierra*" ("Because they love their land").

Economists have noted that the explicit knowledge developed for each plot of land over generations results in the profitability of generations of kin working together and guarding the land holdings within the family. Sales to non-kin are thus less likely than bequests of land to offspring (Rosenzweig and Wolpin 1985). The traditional inheritance pattern in west-central Mexico results in the division of lands among children without regard to gender.

The pre-Columbian polyculture described in this chapter is associated with patriarchal family structures, large families, and social exchange with family and community members. The success and sustainability of the corn, bean, and squash intercrop in its many variations are demonstrated by its continuing popularity among traditional Mexican farmers today (Gardner 1986; Gliessman 1998; Stuart 1985; Stuart and Stuart 1985). Farmworkers in central California and empirical observation in west-central Mexico suggest that the corn, bean, and squash intercrop is still the most common subsistence cropping system among traditional Mexican subsistence farmers in the region. It could also be the continuing, sustainable foundation for small-scale farming in west-central Mexico today if there were adequate support systems for farmers. But the sustainable rural farming culture of Mexico is currently under assault by colossal market and political pressures, making the continuing cultivation of the sustainable foundational intercrop a near impossibility.

Four international developments are responsible for the current demise of Mexico's sustainable rural subsistence farming cultures: the introduction of so-called Green Revolution technology in the 1940s, the overturning of Article 27 of the Mexican Constitution, which privatized *ejido* lands, NAFTA, and corporate penetration. Augmenting the impact of these four factors on the rural farming culture is the Mexican government's continued failure to develop a national agricultural policy that includes subsistence and small-producer farmers. Concurrently, U.S.-led globalization efforts confound rural farming systems by negatively impacting the cohesive family units that once characterized the farming culture of west-central Mexico. In the next chapter we look at the manner in which agriculture in Mexico is impacted by Mexico's political economy.

THREE

ASPECTS OF MEXICO'S AGRICULTURAL POLITICAL ECONOMY

*Nos tiene controlado, el gobierno. Cuando la cosecha es
buena, el precio baja.*

The government controls us [campesinos]. When there is a
good [big] harvest, the price [of corn] goes down.

**—Lorenzo Vasquez, Salinas farmworker and *ejidatario*
with land in Pueblo Viejo, Michoacán**

Los Sauces de Pérez ("Pérez's Willows") is a small *ejido* village near the
town of Cuquio, Jalisco, named after the willows that grow along the
pristine Río Los Sauces. Jesus Acosta's family lives in a handmade adobe
brick dwelling among the many other adobe brick dwellings of the families living in the village. The Acosta family's *ejido parcela* is about an
hour's walk from their home in the village.

The road leading from their home to the 7-hectare *ejido parcela* trav-
erses some of the most magnificent high-country rural terrain in all of
west-central Mexico. Adobe homes share hillsides with beavertail cacti
that grow as tall as trees. In the summer rainy season, verdant green rolling
hills glisten in the sunlight and extend in all directions as far as the eye can
see. Part of the road covers rocky flat terrain. Further along, it leads down
a steep canyon slope and crosses a creek. Pools of water full of tadpoles
fill rock crevices. To reengage the road on the other side of the creek, one
must climb over large volcanic rocks. Between the creek and the *parcela*
the trail is often obstructed by large grass-covered rocks that slow the
walking pace considerably. Jesus's oldest son, Armando, makes this hour-
long journey on foot every day.

Prior to NAFTA, Jesus and his sons planted the traditional corn, bean, and squash intercrop on half of the *parcela* and a monoculture of hybrid corn on the other half. Because of the abrupt decline in the return on corn, Jesus has converted his *parcela* to cattle pasture. On this trip, he shows me several types of grass he has planted, both for grazing and for harvest and storage as cattle fodder.

At the edge of Jesus's *parcela* is a steep cliff that plunges precipitously to the canyon bottom below. A green river runs along the floor of the shaded canyon, the Río Verde. Jesus's farmworker son living in Salinas, California, relayed many stories to me about his camping and fishing trips to the river as a boy. He and his friends and brothers camped out for two or three days at a time, not returning until they had caught and eaten their fill of the river's bounty. Jesus claims that a rich variety of animals live on and around his land and near the river, including wild boars, coyotes, rabbits, armadillos, deer, iguanas, and many kinds of snakes, lizards, and turtles. He points out that they sometimes hunt these animals, bringing variety and nutrition to the campesino family's meals.

Prior to the revolution of 1910, a hacienda owner whose surname was Pérez owned all the land currently farmed by the peasants living in Los Sauces de Pérez. After the revolution, the ancestors of Los Sauces's current residents claimed part of his huge hacienda as their own *ejido* land. The many *parcelas* in the village, originally distributed by lottery, have been passed down to the present day, from one generation of family members to the next.

TOWARD AGRARIAN REFORM

The relevant history behind the *ejido* collective farming villages and the political and economic integration of Mexico and California began with the Mexican War in 1846. This war and the 1848 Treaty of Guadalupe resulted in the transfer of present-day California and much of the Southwest to the United States. Twenty million acres in today's southwestern United States were swindled away from their Mexican owners over the next twenty years (Cockcroft 1998). Northern Mexico to the south became fertile terrain for markets and profit-seeking investors.

After the Mexican War, President Benito Juárez, a full-blooded Zapotec (Barry 1995), attempted to establish free-trade capitalism and the entry of foreign capital into Mexico. His reforms called for separation of church and state (Cockcroft 1998). Indigenous communal lands and clerical lands were expropriated, nationalized, and sold to hacienda owners. Many of the Indians who lived on the former communal land-holdings were forced to work in a system of debt peonage on the haciendas (Baird and McCaughan 1979). The Juárez presidency resulted in the concentration of lands in the hands of a privileged few who justified their land wealth by claiming that Indians were an inferior race whose society and culture obstructed the path to modernization (Barry 1995).

President Porfirio Díaz joined with the United States and Western Europe to alter the Mexican economy permanently (Cockcroft 1998). The Porfirian plan required a massive influx of foreign capital for the construction of railroads, oil fields, mines, and industry, along with agricultural modernization and a rapidly growing export market (Barry 1992). Agricultural development became a primary preoccupation of the government. Agriculture was viewed as the potential source of income from exports with which to develop the infrastructure of an expanded capitalism within the state. Under Díaz's plan, 27 million hectares came under control of primarily U.S. colonizing companies (Baird and McCaughan 1979). The main beneficiaries of these policies were modern capitalist cash crop export enterprises, which were able to combine government assistance with cheap Indian labor to produce crops including cotton, cacao, sugar cane, tobacco, and vanilla for sale to primarily foreign markets.

The Indians who had been forced to relinquish their lands faced exploitation, repression, and a drastic reduction in their standard of living (Cockcroft 1998). By 1910, 38 million hectares had been concentrated into the land monopolies of the hacienda owners and survey companies (Sanderson 1981). Eighty percent of the population depended on agricultural wages and worked for 20,000 landowners (Cockcroft 1998). Having been driven from their ancestral lands, the rural masses were no longer able to farm their sustainable corn crops. Land devoted to corn production dropped from 52 percent to 33 percent (Sanderson 1981). Corn and bean production declined by 20 percent and 25 percent, respectively (Cumberland 1968). As the landless masses scoured the countryside attempting to survive on wild edible foods, they began to organize against the spread of the U.S. monopolies and the underlying political dynamics that resulted in their exploitation and impoverished circumstances.

Díaz's successor, Madero, initially produced a manifesto that included a statute promising the return of stolen lands to the Indians (Baird and McCaughan 1979). However, once elected by popular Indian support, he reneged on his promises and rejected demands for the extensive agrarian reform that would have revolutionized land ownership patterns (Barry 1992; Cockcroft 1998).

Emiliano Zapata organized the hungry, betrayed peasants into a full-scale revolt against the government. Zapata developed a clear set of goals, including recognition of communal land rights and the right of small farmers to control their own villages. He and Pancho Villa fought an ingenious guerrilla war against the Madero government in the Revolution of 1910 until Madero's assassination in 1913 (Barry 1995).

As a result of the Mexican revolution, in which nearly two million Mexicans died (Cockcroft 1998) fighting for *tierra y libertad* (land and freedom), the ruling elite were forced to engage in an agrarian reform program through the enactment of Article 27 of the 1917 Constitution (Grindle 1986). The aim of this land reform was to placate the landless peasants who had brought about the revolution without threatening the future development of capitalist agriculture (Baird and McCaughan 1979).

Article 27 established three forms of land tenure:

The *ejido* (communal farm). As part of agrarian reform, the state could create *ejidos*. Organized groups of landless peasants could stake claim to unproductive farmland by applying to the government for *ejido* status. Plots *(parcelas)* of land on the communal farms not exceeding 10 hectares (DeWalt et al. 1994) were acquired through a lottery system among the *ejidatarios*. The government granted land to members of the peasant communities, but *ejidatarios* could neither sell nor rent their land. In effect, the land continued to be government owned. Typically the *ejido* land relinquished by the government to the peasants was some of the worst in the country. Irrigation, seeds, and technical assistance were not available to the peasants, and some of the land had to be abandoned because of a lack of credit with which to purchase necessary farming supplies.

Ejidos are governed democratically by a general assembly of *ejidatarios* and an elected three-member commission *(comisariado ejidal)* consisting of a president, secretary, and treasurer. All *ejido* towns and villages I visited have a centrally located *comunidad agraria* meeting hall. Meetings are typically held on the first Sunday of each month. The meeting hall is utilized for various community functions at other times. For example, in Tuxcueca, Jalisco, the hall is used for community dances on Friday and Saturday nights. One weekday I met informally with a group of local campesinos at the meeting hall to discuss how NAFTA has affected their lives as farmers. In 2004, an Ensenada-based company selling organic fertilizers and other inputs met in the meeting hall with a group of local campesinos to discuss a farming transition to organic methods.

Propiedad communal (community property). These lands are usually held by indigenous groups and belong to the community at large. The lands of these *comunidades agrarias* could not be sold or leased. Communal land is also located within *ejido* villages. A hill next to the village serves as a communal land resource for the residents of Los Sauces de Pérez. Since converting his *ejido parcela* from corn to pastureland for export cattle production in recent years, Jesus Acosta now cultivates an *ecuaro* (hillside corn, bean, and squash intercrop) near his home. The harvested crops are designated for the exclusive use of his family members.

Pequeñas propiedades. These are small privately owned landholdings subject to free-market forces. It is on these lands that capitalist agribusiness eventually developed a luxury crop and export market by exploiting the lack of legal enforcement of the size and purpose limitations of lands within Article 27. The *pequeñas propiedades* owned by the family of Maria Herrera in San Agustín, Jalisco, are currently utilized almost exclusively for export production. Some of their approximately 45 hectares has been converted to pastureland for export cattle production. Most of the remaining land is planted in agave for lucrative export *tequila* production.

When Lázaro Cárdenas became president of Mexico in 1934, the agricultural census showed that 13,500 people had monopolized 83 percent of all lands in the private sector. The number of landless campesinos at the time had grown to 2.3 million (Cordoba 1974). Strikes raged in both the United States and Mexico. While strikes became commonplace among U.S. agricultural workers protesting low wages and unsatisfactory working conditions in California, more than one hundred farmworker strikes erupted in north-central Mexico. Strikes also erupted in the northwestern states of Mexico, where commercial agriculture and subjugation of peasants had occurred most rapidly (Baird and McCaughan 1979).

Cárdenas and other leaders of the ruling National Revolutionary Party feared another peasant-inspired revolution. They viewed the *ejido* system as a possible means for both pacifying the peasants and advancing the capitalist agricultural goals of the state (Barry 1992). The Cárdenas government thus enacted legislation to collectivize the individual *ejidos*. The intent of the new legislation was to maximize *ejido* productivity and efficiency as larger-scale enterprises. The new legislation gave the *ejidos* preference for water and irrigated land and created the necessary state institutions for their most efficient and productive functioning. The most important state institution financing collectivization was the Ejido Credit Bank (Baird and McCaughan 1979).

The government simultaneously broke up some of the largest landholdings of the rural oligarchy and outlawed debt peonage so that peasants could be made available as a wage labor force on privately owned modernized farms. The intent was to allow for increased production of low-cost food both for the growing urban markets and for export. Thus, between 1936 and 1939, large tracts of land were expropriated and collectivized *ejidos* were established with government financing (Krauze 1999). Some 18–20 million hectares of land was distributed to 800,000 peasants (Baird and McCaughan 1979; Grindle 1986). Hacienda owners impacted by expropriation were allowed to keep 150 hectares of their best land. The largest portion of land distributed to the peasants was not arable but consisted of mountains, forests, or dry grazing lands. Plots of arable land averaged only 5.75 hectares per person.

The willingness of Cárdenas to enact government legislation designed to improve the lives of the campesinos earned him a heroic status that is visible throughout the west-central Mexico countryside today. Towns, parks, fountains, buildings, and streets are named after him, particularly in his home state, Michoacán. In Zinapecuaro, Michoacán, Lorenzo Vasquez spoke reverently of Cárdenas, citing the many unselfish contributions he made to campesinos. He related that the grandfather of a Zinapecuaro resident received a cow from Cárdenas during his presidency. Further evidence of the Cárdenas legacy occurred during the summer 2000 elections in Mexico. Cuatemoc Cárdenas, grandson of Lázaro, ran for the presidency as a liberal, campesino-supported candidate of the PRD (Partido de la Revolución Democrática [Party of the Democratic Revolution]) .

TOWARD AGRICULTURAL INTEGRATION

The agricultural sector experienced an impressive record of growth during the three decades following the Cárdenas administration. From 1952 to 1958, the production of Mexico's twenty-five principal crops grew at an annual rate of 9.7 percent (Contreras 1987). This expansion primarily reflected an increase in cultivated area, from 7.11 million hectares in 1952 to 11.4 million in 1958 (Barry 1995). Farm production outdistanced population growth.

The presidential successors to Cárdenas, however, in essence abandoned the *ejido* model in order to take advantage of the possibility of enormous capital gains internationally. They embraced the opportunity of supplying the United States with cheap raw materials, agricultural products, and cheap labor in the form of easily deportable workers while U.S. industries produced for the Allied war effort. A two-tiered system of agricultural production developed (Barry 1992, 1995; Fernández 1987; Grindle 1986). Small private farmers and *ejidatarios* practiced the subsistence farming of the corn, bean, and squash intercrop on rain-fed parcels and inferior lands. At the same time, the state spent billions of pesos to fortify large-scale privately owned agriculture (Barry 1992; Contreras 1987). By 1982, 85 percent of government-sponsored agricultural credit went to the top 0.5 percent of landowners (Cockcroft 1998). A major part of this investment went to the northwest region.

As another consequence of World War II, U.S. farm laborers began to leave the fields to work in the more profitable war manufacturing industries. The Bracero program was initiated in 1942 as a binational agreement that encouraged campesino migration to the United States. Later, concerns about labor shortages brought on by the Korean War prompted the extension of the program with the establishment of Public Law 78 in 1951 (Heppel and Papademetriou 2001). The Bracero program brought about the irreversible solidification of migration routes between Mexico and the United States.

The damming of large rivers in Sinaloa, Sonora, and Nayarit and the opening of desert lands to agriculture created a land boom that cemented the already strong ties between U.S. and Mexican capitalists in the northwest. Vegetables, sugar, and cotton were grown on these lands with the exploited labor of Mexican campesinos. By the late 1950s, 60 percent of agricultural production was destined for export. The number of landless campesinos employed in agriculture increased between 1950 and 1960 from 2.3 million to over 3 million (Barry 1995).

THE INTRODUCTION OF GREEN REVOLUTION TECHNOLOGY

Green Revolution technology was introduced into Mexico during the 1940s. The impetus for the introduction of hybrid seed technologies into Mexico was based upon the conviction that agricultural techniques were transferable from their sites of development in the United States to the disparate rural environments of Mexico. The focus of the new Green Revolution technologies was on large commercial, irrigated, agricultural enterprises. At the time of Green Revolution technology introduction, subsistence corn farming was responsible for most of the country's corn and bean production (Wade 1974). Surprisingly, the subsistence corn producers were ignored as recipients of the new technology or any other government assistance. Attempts to transfer the technology to subsistence farmers generally occurred at a much later date.

Green Revolution technology depends on commercially produced, hybrid, high-yielding varieties of corn (Gliessman 1998). The new strains require heavy inputs of agrochemical fertilizers, pesticides, and herbicides and were designed to replace the genetically diverse strains of corn *(maíz criollo)*. The hybrid grains were and are currently marketed throughout west-central Mexico as *maíz mejorado* or *maíz superado* (improved corn). Green Revolution agricultural packages consisting of genetically homogenized hybrid seeds and various agrochemical inputs were initially given or sold to commercial and subsistence farmers at below-market prices. Many of the hybrid strains of corn were fabricated so that corn production would not occur unless corn plants were provided with the requisite agrochemical inputs.

Farmers in west-central Mexican towns and villages near large points of distribution such as Guadalajara, La Barca, and Colima claim that Green Revolution technologies were introduced between forty and fifty years ago. The father of Ana Aguirre in Pueblo Rincón de López, Colima, indicated that agrochemicals were introduced forty years ago. Most Mexican farmers in Michoacán and Jalisco claim that agrochemicals and farming mechanization were introduced into the more remote rural areas of west-central Mexico over the past fifteen or twenty years. Residents of very remote villages such as Las Cebollas, Michoacán, by contrast, claim that the introduction spread into their region as recently as ten or fifteen years ago.

The narrow focus of the Green Revolution in support of large commercial agricultural enterprises in Mexico heightened the disparity between commercial and subsistence agriculture (Barry 1995; Grindle 1986). Once farmers adopted the new hybrid varieties, the cost of seeds and the required inputs increased. The carefully hand-selected genetic variability of *maíz criollo* was and continues to be replaced by genetically homogenized corn strains and, more recently, by U.S.-produced genetically modified strains of corn. By 1993 genetic erosion had resulted in only six varieties of commercial corn accounting for 71 percent of worldwide corn production (Gliessman 1998).

Salt residues from excessive agrochemical use are visible on the soil surfaces of many formerly productive fields in west-central Mexico today. The prohibitively high cost of agrochemicals in recent years has rendered their use by subsistence farmers nearly impossible. After being planted in hybrid seed for several years, these lands are often no longer productive without the use of agrochemicals. Sadly, most farmers are uninformed about practices that could restore their fields to former levels of productivity. From 1970 to the present, agricultural productivity has declined, primarily due to the failure of the state to develop agricultural policies that include large commercial farmers *and* small subsistence farmers (Barry 1995).

The presidency of Carlos Salinas de Gortari, beginning in 1988, supported the neoliberal policies promoted by President Reagan in the United States and Prime Minister Thatcher in Great Britain. Neoliberalism—"a set of economic beliefs that subordinates all social and development considerations to the demands of private capital and the world market" (Barry 1995, 54)—is responsible for the current world economic momentum to deregulate, privatize, and liberalize trade and investment.

Salinas de Gortari's most noteworthy contribution to neoliberal economic restructuring included the amendment of Article 27 of the Mexican Constitution in preparation for NAFTA. The 1992 amendment effectively privatized *ejido* lands, ending the agrarian reform resulting from the Mexican Revolution (Cockcroft 1998). *Ejidatarios* were given title to their land and the right to sell, rent, sharecrop, or mortgage their individual *parcelas*. The amendment also allowed them to contract with private investors, including foreign investors. I encountered generalized anger throughout the region regarding Salinas de Gortari's self-serving actions at the conclusion of his presidency. Many campesinos claim that his raid of the government coffers and investment in a Swiss bank account, along with similar government transgressions, are contributing factors to their immobilized, impoverished conditions.

The following example illustrates the dramatic economic and agricultural changes in *ejido* land use that followed the amendment to Article 27 and the initiation of NAFTA. El Guaco, Michoacán, is a large *ejido* southwest of Uruapan, home to three hundred *ejidatarios* and a total population of 1,500. *Parcelas* range in size from 4 to 10 hectares. Two cycles of annual crops are planted and harvested in El Guaco each year. Corn is harvested in October and November. After the corn harvest, cows are turned into the fields to eat the crop residues. In December or January cucumbers are planted under the direction of a representative from Pan American Products. After assessing the U.S. market for cucumbers, this U.S.-based company determines the amount of land to be planted. The company supplies all seeds and agrochemical inputs. In February and March the cucumbers are harvested and shipped to the United States. Because the company has provided the *ejido* with a profitable return on cucumbers, many of the *ejido* farmers contract with the company every year for the use of their land.

NAFTA AND BINATIONAL AGRICULTURAL INTEGRATION

Mexico and the United States are bound together by overlapping economic structures that have integrated the countries for decades. Indeed, Mexican workers and U.S. employers are part of one integrated international agricultural labor market (Acevedo and Espenshade 1992; Bach 1978; Baird and McCaughan 1979; Castro 1986; Herrera 1998; Palerm 1993; Rouse 1991; Sassen 1990). Even before the border was established, labor exchange occurred between present-day Mexico and the U.S. Southwest (Bach 1978). Landless Mexican peasants moved north along railroad lines that carried Mexican-grown commodities into Texas, New Mexico, and elsewhere in the United States (Grebler 1965). In the 1920s, partnerships between Mexican producers and North American distributors were established (Baird and McCaughan 1979). Strawberries have been grown in El Bajío region north of Mexico City since the 1880s. A strawberry freezing industry was started in the 1950s by U.S. entrepreneurs. The tomato processing industry was established in the 1960s for the diversion of fresh market tomatoes grown as an export crop in Sinaloa (Runsten 1987; Runsten and Moulton 1987a, b). Throughout the 1960s and 1970s, profits mushroomed as distributors, U.S. supermarket chains, and banks further expanded Mexican export production.

NAFTA, signed by the United States, Canada, and Mexico on December 17, 1992, formally established the binational system of capital production in the United States and reproduction of the labor force in Mexico. While international entrepreneurs and investors celebrated NAFTA's initiation on January 1, 1994, the poorest of the poor peasants of Mexico sent an alarm around the world with the uprisings in Chiapas (Oppenheimer 1996; Ross 1995).

Today agriculture on both sides of the border is best characterized as a binational system of integrated complementary capitalist enterprises. The linked processes of worker migration from the food processing industrial areas of Irapuato in Mexico's El Bajío region and capital migration from the United States to El Bajío is but one example (Zavella 2000).

The agriculture of northwest Mexico and Baja California is cotermi-
nous with the agriculture of California's Imperial Valley. Producers in
northwest Mexico enjoy a comparative advantage in vegetables and
fresh fruits, especially during the winter. Mexico produces one-quarter
of all fruits and vegetables imported by the United States each year. The
value of its exports of tomatoes, broccoli, and cauliflower to the United
States is greater than that of all other foreign suppliers combined. An estimated 90 percent of the funding for vine-ripened tomato production
from Baja California farming operation originates in the United States
(Rubio and Trejo 1993).

Specialty crop agroexport production is dependent on U.S. markets
and takes precedence over production for the domestic market. Agricultural workers in Mexico and the United States are now susceptible to the
vagaries of a single, integrated international market. Through a network
of organizations, agribusiness has become efficient in the coordination
of production and pricing. The "NAFTA highway" includes three
bridges spanning the border at Laredo, Texas, where 36,000 trucks
laden with produce and processed foods cross into the United States
every day (Zavella 2000).

THE NAFTA VISION BETRAYED

The original NAFTA agreements that have impacted west-central Mexico subsistence and small producer farmers include the following (Cockcroft 1998; CEC 1999; Nadal 1999):

1. All import tariffs on manufactured goods and agricultural products traded among the three countries were to be eliminated.

2. Most tariffs on agricultural products were to be eliminated
   gradually over a ten-year period. Crops such as corn that are
   sensitive to the effects of imports were scheduled for a fifteen-
   year phase-out period.

3. U.S. and Canadian companies operating in Mexico would have
   the same rights as Mexican companies, and vice versa.

4. U.S. and Canadian banks and investment and insurance companies would be allowed to operate in Mexico, and vice versa.

The rationale for including corn, perhaps Mexico's most important
and sensitive crop, was based on the following axioms and assumptions
by NAFTA originators (CEC 1999; Nadal 1999):

1. Campesino corn production is inefficient by international standards.

2. The Mexican government had subsidized corn production and consumers for forty years through CONASUPO and managed subsidies.

3. An end to subsidies would result in a reallocation of resources in the direction of more efficient and productive crop production.

4. Subsistence producers would not be affected because they function economically outside the market economy.

5. The labor force is Mexico's strength (comparative advantage) in the globalized economy. Corn subsidies prevent the labor force from being maximally utilized.

6. Subsistence producers would benefit from new employment opportunities.

The NAFTA assumption that subsistence producers function economically outside the market economy ignores the fact that subsistence households are part of a market economy in which monetary flows are an essential requirement for survival. All corn-growing farmers interviewed in Mexico for this study claimed that one-third to one-half of each corn harvest is sold locally or to the government for income. The remainder is stored for family use. An exception occurs during low-yield years, when corn is stored exclusively for family use and additional income-generating activities are sought elsewhere.

Supplementary income resulting from the sale of corn is used for the purchase of household items that cannot be generated on the farm. Examples include cooking oil, shoes, clothes, farming implements, and agrochemicals. Services are also purchased. For example, many farmers cited the necessity of paying a physician for services when a family member required medical attention.

Moreover, the NAFTA assumption that subsistence producers function outside the market economy and would not be impacted by economic reorganization clearly contradicts the Mexican government's own predictions that millions of farmers would be displaced from their land as a result of NAFTA. Obviously, NAFTA originators were cognizant of the potential of the massive dislocation currently underway in west-central Mexican farming communities when they surreptitiously drafted the document in the secrecy of obscure boardrooms in the finest international hotels.

One of the Mexican government's post-NAFTA goals was to forge a convergence of domestic and international corn prices. As noted above, domestic corn production had been subsidized by the government for forty years prior to NAFTA. Under NAFTA the former corn tariff system was changed to an import quota system that was supposed to be phased in over a fifteen-year period. In 1994, NAFTA's first year, Mexico's tariff-free import quota was set at 2.5 million metric tons of corn. The tariff-free import quota was supposed to expand at a compound rate of 3 percent per year beginning in 1995. By year fourteen of the agreement, in 2008, the tariff-free import quota would have reached 3.6 million tons per year. A similar schedule was established for most basic grains (Nadal 2000).

The quota system under NAFTA was never actualized as planned. All corn imports into Mexico were exempt from tariff payments for thirty months. Public officials claim that reneging on NAFTA's fifteen-year phase-out period for corn, allowing additional tons of imported corn from the United States to enter Mexico freely, is a way to control prices and reduce inflation. However, by failing to honor its NAFTA commitment to the tariff-rate quota system, the Mexican government lost an estimated $2 billion in fiscal revenues from tariffs while simultaneously putting enormous and unanticipated pressure on subsistence and small producer corn farmers (Nadal 2000).

For subsistence and small producer corn farmers, the withdrawal of government price supports has resulted in an unfavorable return on corn production. Frequently, the return on corn production does not even cover the expense of the initial investment. Farmers either break even or lose money on their investment in crop cultivation. Government aid programs are wholly inadequate as buffers designed to compensate for lost income and support for subsistence farmer transition into the NAFTA economy.

Except for brief periods of adjustment, corn prices have fallen steadily since 1982, with an accelerated pre-NAFTA decline in 1993. Implementing NAFTA was a key component of the Mexican government's plan to reform the agricultural sector. However, as a result of abandoning the tariff-rate quota system spelled out by the NAFTA Accords, huge imports of subsidized U.S. corn dumped into Mexico have furthered the steep decline in corn prices by undercutting the corn market in Mexico. The price of Mexican corn has fallen more than 70 percent since NAFTA's initiation in 1994 (Fanjul and Fraser 2003). In NAFTA's first five years, the sizeable gap between the NAFTA vision and the NAFTA reality became glaringly clear. The agricultural sector's first five-year performance resulted in only stagnation, negative growth rates, and mediocre trade balance performance (Nadal 2000).

During the NAFTA negotiations, it was assumed that lower corn prices would result in lower tortilla prices, yielding lower inflation and improved consumer diet. However, tortilla prices actually increased more than 483 percent between January 1994 and January 1999, with an average annual price increase of more than 35 percent.

While the tariff-rate quota system for corn imports was abandoned, tortilla prices were rising, and government subsidies and programs designed to assist corn farmers were either cut or inadequate, the Mexican government *increased* subsidies for the manufacturers of industrial corn flour. The two largest companies (GIMSA and MINSA) enjoyed the greatest influx of these government subsidies.

By 1998, government price supports were removed from tortillas after more than five decades. Increased tortilla prices are, in part, the result of a noncompetitive market for tortillas and the profit-maximizing capabilities of Mexico's largest industrial producers of corn flour and tortillas (Nadal 2000). The abandonment of NAFTA's guaranteed tariff-rate quota system, along with declining corn prices and the skyrocketing cost of Mexico's basic food source (corn tortillas), has resulted in an extraordinary increase in poverty for Mexico's rural farming cultures.

Compounding NAFTA's negative impact on the rural countryside is NAFTA's lack of recognition of a common agricultural labor market between Mexico and the United States despite economists' arguments to the contrary (Acevedo and Espenshade 1992; Delgado 1996; Massey 1998). Nevertheless, Mexico is now generally perceived by California commercial agribusiness interests as the source of a "virtually unlimited supply of temporary and discardable workers" (Chavez 1992, 74), who are needed to maintain high agribusiness production rates in California (García y Griego 1989). Mexican towns and villages have become nurseries that reproduce laborers for U.S. labor markets (Villarejo and Runsten 1993). Additionally, a multiple economic analysis of trade liberalization demonstrates that the U.S. infrastructure creates a situation whereby moving Mexican laborers north to work in the United States is the *only* manner in which wages will begin to equalize as originally predicted by NAFTA (Markusen and Zahniser 1997).

Climatic considerations and cheap labor have accelerated foreign investment into Mexico as an ideal location for the countercyclical production of commercial specialty crops for affluent U.S. markets during winter months (as in the El Guaco, Michoacán, example above). Field research in west-central Mexico confirmed North American agrochemical corporations' view of rural Mexico as a lucrative market for the sale of seeds and agrochemicals to impoverished campesinos. Many of the agrochemicals noted are extremely toxic and have been banned or restricted in the United States for years (see chapters 11 and 12).

Small subsistence farmers in west-central Mexico are disenfranchised as participants in the globalized economy. Their small size and lack of credit, technology, and marketing resources preclude them from participation. Green Revolution technology; NAFTA and the withdrawal of government subsidies; the overturning of Article 27 of the Mexican Constitution and the privatization of *ejido* land; the rise of market intermediaries, commercial agribusiness, and corporate penetration into the countryside— all are contributing to an unprecedented social transformation in the rural west-central Mexico countryside. Post-NAFTA employment opportunities are paltry and often undesirable. With the experience of hunger and malnutrition as an everyday reality and starvation a realistic possibility for themselves and their family members, many corn-growing subsistence farmers feel that they have little choice but to leave their farming lifestyle and head north to the United States in search of employment and a better future for their families.

FOUR

MIGRATION NORTHWARD
TO CENTRAL CALIFORNIA

Imagínase que triste es aquí. Se tiene que separar la familia porque no hay trabajo aquí y hay que emigrar. No hay nada con que mantenerse la familia o no lo suficiente. Si hubiera trabajo aquí, nadie iria.

Just imagine how sad it is for us here [in Mexico]. Family members are separated because there isn't any work here and [members] have to emigrate. There's no way to support a family here. If there was work here, no one would leave.

**—Esperanza Ayala, daughter of Faviola de la Cruz,
San Agustín, Jalisco**

The real losers are the corn producers themselves. This is why many leave their family and farms to travel to the U.S. to find work. It's not that they *want* to work in California or other areas in the U.S. They don't want to leave their families, farms, farming lifestyle, friends, and culture to become slaves in corporate agribusiness. They want to remain in Mexico, but they don't want either themselves or their families to starve.

—José Luis Rubio, municipal president, Cuquio, Jalisco

Four months after Faviola de la Cruz's oldest son, Arnuldo, left home, the phone rings in the San Agustín home. Faviola answers the phone, and suddenly her sullen countenance brightens with a broad smile. "He made it," she shouts to her family members. "Arnuldo is safe! He is in California and has a job in agriculture!" Faviola's ten other children rush to her side. One after another, each child has a private conversation with their oldest brother. After an hour of enthusiastic conversation, the phone call ends. Though completely relieved that her son is safe for the moment, Faviola looks at her other sons and daughters and asks the most important question, "But when will we see him again?"

Over the next few years, Arnuldo becomes established in the United States. His younger brother Beto then immigrates. Beto is greeted by both Arnuldo and a prearranged job as a farm laborer. Gradually, as one son after another emigrates out of Mexico, Faviola's family migration network is established and each successive migrating family member can rely on a larger and larger network of family and friends for assistance. Once all of the men have emigrated, the women follow. In time, the men apply for U.S. citizenship or become legal residents.

Today, only one of her sons and her daughter Esperanza are still living in Mexico. Faviola continues to worry about her children. Though all of her sons are working in the United States either as citizens or with "green cards" indicative of legal resident status, all but one of her daughters are in the United States illegally. Faviola laments, "There has been no real peace in this family since my children's emigrations out of Mexico began years ago."

In Chaparaco, Michoacán, the family of Maribel Terraza continues an all-night vigil waiting by the phone for the call that will confirm Maribel's successful and safe border crossing. After Maribel's first attempt to cross the border using falsified documents failed, her *coyote* next attempted to fit Maribel in a space under a passenger seat in a van owned by another trafficker. However, Maribel is a heavyset woman and could not fit into the allotted space. She eventually crossed the border in the trunk of a *coyote* accomplice's car. On July 23, she and her daughter Elena joyfully called Joaquin and waiting family members from the San Diego airport to report that the ordeal was over. She was in the United States, bound for Elena's home in Salinas where her grandchildren eagerly awaited her arrival.

Faviola expresses her frustration and indignation with experiences similar to those endured by Maribel and Joaquin. She explains how family tradition works to maintain her large family unity and integrity. Those living in the United States visit her in San Agustín every one to three years. Every two years the family remaining in Mexico travels to Salinas, legally or illegally, at Christmas for a reunion. "One way or another," she insists, "all family members are reunited during the Christmas holiday season."

Figure 8. Maribel Terraza making tortillas, Chaparaco, Michoacán.

On more than one occasion Faviola, who also meets the legal qualifications for a travel visa to the United States, has become so frustrated trying to obtain a visa to Salinas that she gave up and hired a *coyote*. She relates that the local U.S. embassy in Guadalajara, Jalisco, gets at least five hundred requests for visas every day. The embassy personnel arbitrarily select one hundred people for visas, at most. All the other people requesting visas are kept waiting for months.

One of her worst memories of an illegal border crossing is of several years past when she had to climb a steep flight of stairs next to a high fence in Tijuana. The *coyote* informed her that there would be a second flight of steps on the other side of the fence to facilitate her crossing. Faviola arrived at the top of the first flight of steps on the Mexican side of the border only to find that the second flight didn't exist. Her *coyote* then yelled to her, "Jump!" She was forced to jump from the top of the first flight of stairs on the Mexican side of the border to the ground on the U.S. side, a distance of some 8–10 feet. Faviola was an overweight woman in her 60s at the time and marvels that she wasn't injured. "I could have broken my leg! Then what would have happened to me?"

The experiences of Faviola and Maribel underscore the often inhumane, degrading, expensive ordeals that older parents of farmworker children are forced to endure, even when they are rightfully entitled to travel visas for brief visits with family members in the United States. The dignity with which Maribel and Faviola conduct their lives, from managing their large families to making tortillas, is impressive. Maribel stuffed into a car trunk and risking asphyxiation, or heavyset Faviola jumping from stairs and risking a broken leg, as their only means of visiting their families in California are images as unacceptable as they are real.

NAFTA'S IMPACT ON SUBSISTENCE
AND SMALL PRODUCER CORN FARMERS

NAFTA has accelerated the process of labor and commodity exchange between Mexico and California. The nearly 2,000-mile Mexican–U.S. border is the busiest border in the world, with trade between the two countries amounting to over $650 million per day. Every year 310 million people, 90 million cars, 4.3 million trucks, and $195 billion worth of goods cross the border (Carral 2003; Consejo Nacional de Población 2004). Mexican farmers are moving north into California to work as farm laborers. Agricultural production in turn is moving south from California into Mexico (Zabin et al. 1993).

Small-scale corn producers are among the most vulnerable economic actors in the Mexican economy. In 1991 alone, 64 percent of all producers operated with losses and yet were responsible for approximately 29.5 percent of total production (CEC 1999). Since NAFTA went into effect, millions of campesino farmers throughout Mexico have lost corn farming as their most significant source of income (Public Citizen's Global Trade Watch 2001).

On December 30, 1999, I met with technical agricultural consultant Ignacio Robles and three other local farmers in the Tuxcueca, Jalisco, *comunidad agraria* meeting hall. The local farmers were Luis Sosa Ortíz, Alfonso Sosa Aceves (president of the *ejido* cattle growers association), and Lic. Adolfo Sosa Cárdenas. All members of the group were actively involved in small-scale commercial corn production at the time. They presented an important summary of a post-NAFTA cost/benefit analysis for 1999 corn production. Their corn harvests are sold to brokers *(intermediarios)* for approximately 1,000 pesos (US$100) per ton. Sorghum nets 950 pesos ($95) per ton, and beans are sold for 5,000 pesos ($500) per ton. The cost of 20 kilograms of commercial hybrid corn seed to sow 1 hectare is approximately 1,000 pesos. The cost of tilling the soil is 500 pesos per hectare. The cost of raking the soil is 300 pesos per hectare. The cost of hiring workers to plant the seed is approximately 300 pesos per hectare. The total cost of production, presumably including agro-chemical inputs, is 4,000–5,000 pesos per hectare. A hectare of land typically yields 3–5 tons of corn. Simple arithmetic demonstrates that income from the sale of their crop barely covers expenses; the farmers do not make a profit. If their yields are low, they lose money (see table 1).

The farmers reflected on a time several years ago when they were able to sell their corn to CONASUPO, a national food staples company that purchased corn and other crops from farmers and then sold the crops to campesinos and urban dwellers at a discount (Barry 1995; Fox 1992) for a "good price." When I inquired about the reasons for the recent changes in corn value, the farmers informed me that "CONASUPO disappeared because of political problems." I probed further by making reference to U.S. corn imported into Mexico. The farmers informed me that this corn is not visibly for sale on the market. It is used almost exclusively in processed food and animal feed because of its poor quality. In the past, Mexican corn was sold for food processing. American corn has thus pushed the Mexican corn farmers out of the market.

On January 4, 2000, I met with the municipal president of Cuquio, Jalisco, José Luis Rubio. Mr. Rubio informed me that the price of corn had fallen precipitously in recent years at the same time that the price of agricultural inputs had increased by 30 percent. "Years ago one kilo of corn could purchase two liters of gasoline. Today the situation is reversed; two kilos of corn are required to purchase one liter of gasoline." Mr. Rubio's assistant informed me that corn was currently selling for 1,280 pesos per ton, approximately one-half of the pre-NAFTA value. I queried Mr. Rubio about the beneficiaries of the recent agricultural changes occurring in the region. He informed me that businesses and corporations, including MASECA, MINSA, Sabritas, and Purina, are the primary beneficiaries. Commercial farmers and *intermediarios* are also benefiting from the changes. The real losers are the small subsistence corn producers.

In Los Sauces de Pérez, Mariano Acosta, Armando Acosta's uncle, informed me that in 1993 a ton of corn sold for 2,000 pesos. He corroborated Mr. Rubio's assistant's claim that the return on harvested corn is roughly one-half of its pre-NAFTA value.

I also discussed corn farming and sales with Joaquin Bejarano, Maribel Terraza's husband in Chaparaco, Michoacán. He pointed out that the

TABLE 1 1999 SMALL-SCALE CORN
PRODUCTION, TUXCUECA, JALISCO
(in pesos)[a]

Income[b]		
Yield	Return per Ton	Profit or Loss
Low: 3 tons	3,000	(−100)
Intermediate: 4 tons	4,000	900
High: 5 tons	5,000	1,900

Procampo Payments[c]		
Yield	Return per Ton	Profit or Loss
Low: 3 tons	3,400	300
Intermediate: 4 tons	4,400	1,300
High: 5 tons	5,400	2,300

Pre-NAFTA Return[d]		
Yield	Return per Ton	Profit or Loss
Low: 3 tons	6,000	2,900
Intermediate: 4 tons	8,000	4,900
High: 5 tons	10,000	6,900

[a] 10 pesos = US$1, 1999. The cost of sowing 1 ha of corn with a project yield of 3–5 tons is 3,100 pesos: corn seed = 1,000; tilling = 500; raking = 300; sowing (hired labor) = 300; misc. hired labor = 500; agrochemical input = 1,000.
[b] 1 ton corn earns 1,000 pesos.
[c] Procampo is a government program to ease corn farmer adjustment to NAFTA economy; assumes average payment of 400 pesos/ha of planted corn.
[d] Assumes average return of 2,000 pesos/ton of corn.

prices for seed, agrochemical inputs, and fertilizers have skyrocketed in recent years:

> After harvesting a crop, prices are so low that people can't even break even. Sometimes they even lose money. Sometimes the prices are so low for the crop that the crop is just destroyed and never makes it to market. Prices have never been secure; one never knows what they will earn for each harvest; so there is never any security. Corn has a government price, but the price is too low. Farmers are paid 1,300 pesos per ton of corn. But fertilizer alone costs 1,500 pesos, so the farmer loses money. Before, the inputs were cheaper and of better quality. Now they are more expensive and aren't working.

EMIGRATION PRESSURES

The husbands of poor families in Mexico are often expected to emigrate as a means of providing for children that would otherwise risk death by starvation. Loreta Medina, the niece of Juan Borrego, has six children and lives in the poorer outskirts of Tuxcueca, Jalisco, on Lake Chapala. She and her husband and children live cramped into two small rooms next to the pigs and other livestock of a local storeowner who rents the rooms to them. The outdoor cooking area where she makes tortillas is literally blanketed with flies in the summer.

In 1998 when I spoke with her, Loreta was distressed about the financial circumstances of her family. A drought resulted in a failed corn harvest in her small corn plot, and she harvested only three sacks of corn. She complained about the high cost of chemical inputs. Her husband is a fisherman in the declining fishing industry of Lake Chapala. As a way of augmenting the family income, Loreta washes and irons clothes for people in town while her oldest daughter, Ana, babysits the younger children in the family. Loreta wants to take birth control pills but can't because of a medical condition. She has considered sterilization, but the cost of the surgery is prohibitive.

In conversations with Lucia Margarita, Juan Borrego's sister, she expressed unbridled contempt for Loreta's husband, who, even with hungry children, refused to leave the family to work in the United States. She found his reluctance to leave his family for work in the United States "unforgivable." She questions how he can stay home and watch his children go hungry when he could be supporting them with income earned in the United States.

The Salinas and Watsonville farmworker participants in this study chose emigration out of Mexico to California as the only viable response to the socioeconomic conditions they confronted in Mexico. The decision to emigrate, especially undocumented, is not made lightly, without serious deliberation among family members (Martin and Widgren 1996). Thirty-two central California farmworkers were asked their work location of preference, Mexico or California, assuming that they could earn a living. Of the 32 respondents, 24 (75%) indicated that they would prefer to live in Mexico, seven expressed a preference for working in California (22%), and one was ambivalent (3%). Those who prefer to live in California have lived in the state for many years and moved their family members from Mexico to California to maintain family unity.

Figure 9. Four of Rosario Morales's sons prior to undocumented emigration to the United States, Los Sauces de Pérez.

Ismena Rocha stated in an interview, "Working here [in California] is a distraction from the sadness I feel for not being with my family in Mexico." Her comment is representative of the reservations expressed by many farmworkers who have left their families and culture behind in Mexico.

Ultimately a combination of complex, powerful structural pressures pushes Mexicans to migrate to the United States. However, I agree with scholars who maintain that the most important factor leading to the decision to emigrate from the west-central Mexico countryside in the post-NAFTA economy, overshadowing all others, is survival (Cornelius and Martin 1993, 6; Girón 1995, 3; Hobbs 2001; Smith and Ellingwood 2001). There is a direct correlation between the price of corn and beans paid to subsistence and small producer farmers in Mexico and undocumented immigration to the United States (White et al. 2003).

The post-NAFTA context of food scarcity and illness is pervasive throughout the rural west-central Mexico countryside, a paradigm in which life is lived and endured at the edge of survival. Hunger is a norm. However, hunger in Mexico isn't caused by the inability of Mexican farmers to produce enough food. On the contrary, in spite of nearly continuous damaging criticism of subsistence and small producer farmers by agribusiness and government in recent years, Mexican subsistence and small producer farmers harvested a record 18 million tons of corn in 1996, according to the Mexican secretary of agriculture (Suppan and Lehman 1997).

The post-NAFTA economy and abrupt government withdrawal of price supports for corn have intensified hunger and malnutrition in the rural countryside. Conversations among campesinos and family members about *aguantando hambre* (enduring hunger) are commonplace. The expression is as common in west-central Mexico as "having a headache" is in the United States. People live in a daily contextual reality of undernutrition. Sunken cheeks and thin bodies or overfed malnourished bodies are the norm. Almost every family can relate a story about a village or town resident who died of starvation, most often a child.

Frequent stomachaches and diarrhea are common. These widespread afflictions are exacerbated by inadequate rural sanitation and a lack of adequate nutrition. Some rural peasants cultivate home gardens full of plants that are deemed herbal remedies for these conditions. For example, in the home garden of Rogelio Durán of Charo, Michoacán, approximately half of all plants are cultivated for the purpose of alleviating stomachaches and diarrhea. West-central Mexican subsistence farmers and their families are desperate and hungry. They emigrate because, if they don't, they may not survive.

Directly related to the issue of survival is the wage differential between the United States and Mexico. Immigration expert Wayne Cornelius maintains that the "U.S./Mexico wage differentials are a more powerful determinant of migration decisions in rural Mexico than outright joblessness" (Cornelius and Martin 1993, 17). A male worker in the food processing industry in Mexico receives about $5 a day for very hard work. This wage rate is about two-thirds what is necessary to support a family (Zavella 2000). Wage differences have continued to differ by factors of eight and fifteen times, and standard-of-living differences are similar (Johnston 2001; Huffman 1995).

In west-central Mexico, wage laborers on farms earn between 16 and 80 pesos per day. This is comparable to approximately $1.60–$8.00 per day. Laborers in California agribusiness can expect to be hired for more than an equivalent rate per hour. This differential is unlikely to change in the near future because of the present huge labor surplus on the Mexican side of the border (Cornelius and Martin 1993). A common expression among would-be emigrants is *"De ser rico en México y pobre en Estados Unidos, mejor pobre"* ("Of the choice between being rich in Mexico or poor in the United States, it's better to be poor in the United States") (Girón 1995, 113).

Other secondary factors contributing to the decision to emigrate include critical opportunities for high-quality education for emigrants' children in the United States, the inability to raise and accumulate capital through any other means, lack of job opportunities in Mexico that pay a living wage, an infrastructure for migration in which migrants learn how to migrate and find jobs and housing in California as a result of concentrating social capital, and the lure of material goods as seen on public television. Over 90 percent of Mexican households now have access to television (Massey et al. 1987, 1998).

Mexico is the largest supplier of immigrants to the United States. Nearly 5.4 million Mexican immigrants entered the United States between 1820 and 1995 (del Pinal and Garcia 1993). By 2003, both men and women from 96 percent of Mexico's 2,350 cities and towns were migrating to the United States (Associated Press 2003), and at least one member of 83 percent of families living in rain-fed subsistence farming areas of Mexico has immigrated to the United States (Girón 1995, 115). The great majority of these immigrants enter the United States illegally (Associated Press 2003).

Undocumented immigration from Mexico to the United States is the largest unlawful migration flow in the world (Rosenblum 2000). Undocumented immigrants attempting to enter the United States in recent years number over a million per year (Annerino 1999; Rosenblum 2000). Near Yuma, Arizona, alone, more than 100,000 immigrants are apprehended trying to cross the border illegally each year (Sterngold 2001).

Mexican immigrants primarily originate in six western Mexican states centered around the city of Guadalajara: Aguascalientes, Guanajuato, Jalisco, Michoacán, Nayarit, and Zacatecas. Twenty percent of Mexico's population live in these states (Runsten and Zabin 1995). International migration from the Mexican sending states of Jalisco and Michoacán has been taking place for at least one hundred years, and the two states were regions of intense bracero recruitment from 1942 to 1964 (Griffith and Kissam 1995).

West-central Mexico has been the locus of some of the highest outmigration rates to the United States in Mexico (Castro 1986; Chavez 1992; García y Griego 1989). Michoacán, Jalisco, and Guanajuato were the most important outmigration states in Mexico from 1990 to 1995 (Mummert 2003). Indeed, almost the entire population of the state of Michoacán is in motion, with most of the forty-one *municipios* classified as regions of high levels of outmigration (XII Censo General de Población y Vivienda 2000, as cited in Mummert 2003). This state accounted for 49.7 percent of migratory flows from Mexico, and 40 percent of the homes in Michoacán had at least one person emigrating to the United States, from 1990 to 1995 (Ramírez 2003). Overall, 40 percent of the more than 100 million people still living in Mexico said they would come to the United States if they had the opportunity (Faux 2006).

Fifty percent of emigrants leaving Mexico for the United States are destined for California, claiming that they prefer to work in California than in any other state. Most of these emigrants were born in west-central Mexico (Consejo Nacional de Población 2004). California in turn absorbs most of the total flow of both legal and illegal immigrants from Mexico (Bustamante 1989). Of the estimated 11 to 12 million undocumented immigrants in the United States (Bybee and Winter 2006; Fox 2002; Garcia 2004; International Labor Conference 2004; Natoli et al. 2001; Ohlemacher 2006; Ruiz 2006), 40–60 percent live in California (Cornelius 1989; del Pinal and Singer 1997; Himelstein and Lascuraín 1993).

Prior to immigration reform in 1965 and 1986, primarily solitary men migrated from west-central Mexico to the United States for seasonal work. They left behind their intact families, villages, and towns and planned to return to them after the harvest season. However, in the past twenty years whole families and even single women are immigrating to and settling in California. About 80 percent of emigrants leaving Mexico for the United States become settlers there; only about 20 percent return to their villages and towns of origin in Mexico. From 1990 to 1995, only 21.5 percent of migrants returned to Mexico; in the six years after NAFTA's initiation and the onset of increased border vigilance, the percentage of migrants returning to Mexico dropped to 17.4 percent (Ramírez 2003).

This recent trend is responsible for the social transformation and restructuring of the rural environment both in Mexico and in California. In California, evidence of settlement including home purchases and U.S. educations has occurred concurrently with the reintensification of California agriculture and the lengthening of the work season (Palerm 2000), NAFTA, increased border enforcement, and increased the cost of *coyotes*, which financially prohibits migrants' return to Mexico.

Although factors such as the productivity crisis in Mexican rain-fed agriculture have contributed to family immigration to California, NAFTA exacerbated the social and economic conditions leading to it. At the same time, expansion of migration networks better facilitated the process. Today, less than 10 percent of farmwork in California is done by those considered to be seasonal workers returning to Mexico after the harvest (Palerm 2000; Villarejo and Runsten 1993).

DOCUMENTED/UNDOCUMENTED IMMIGRATION SUMMARY

Although I never directly asked farmworker interviewees about their immigration status, many Mexican farmers and California farmworkers, in the process of discussing employment and family issues, divulged harrowing tales of border crossings. Farmers, family members, and cab drivers in Mexico were particularly munificent with immigration information. Farmworkers in California, on the other hand, were much more reticent to disclose such information about themselves and family members.

In Mexico, fourteen families and four cab drivers provided vivid accounts of their own and family member experiences. Of the 76 individuals acknowledged as undocumented entrants to the United States, only three immigrated without hiring a *coyote* to assist the crossing. Thirty-three farmers and family members spoke openly about hiring *coyotes*. The mechanism for undocumented entry was not mentioned by 25 individuals. Thus 33–76 individuals associated with the eighteen individuals and families with whom immigration was discussed acknowledged hiring *coyotes*. Only 21 of 100 individuals from Mexico emigrated with documents. Of the 76 individuals in Mexico who acknowledged illegal entry, only 17 ultimately returned to Mexico, resulting in a net flow of 59 individuals from only eighteen random families throughout the region.

These figures support the contention of researchers who have studied the 2000 census. Many assert that the number of undocumented residents is actually much higher than the official estimate of 3 million. As discussed previously, it is now estimated to be over 11 million (Cohn 2001). My total survey, from both Mexico farm family members and interviewees in California who were willing to discuss immigration, records 83 individuals of 113 entering the United States illegally. Only 23 individuals entered with documents. Most of these individuals entered the United States prior to the mid-1980s. In one study of immigration from Gómez Farías, Michoacán, nearly 80 percent of immigrants were destined for Watsonville, California (Castro 1986).

IMMIGRATION REFORM

Migration is possibly the most important international economic phenomenon that is *not* coordinated by an international organization (Rosenblum 2000; Weiner 1993). Immigration policies have remained largely country specific, because NAFTA neglected any provisions for the movement of workers across national borders (Rosenblum 2000). Furthermore, the United States is unwilling to recognize officially that trade-generating mechanisms like NAFTA that ignore a common labor market stimulate undocumented immigration (Muller 1997). Indeed, one of the NAFTA supporters' selling points for the trade agreement was its allegation that, in fact, NAFTA would drastically *reduce* undocumented immigration to the United States by equalizing wages between the two countries and improving the diet in Mexico.

In addition, U.S. residents have always been highly ambivalent about immigration (Chavez 1997; Najar 1999). There is widespread recognition and acceptance of the historical role immigrants from all over the world played in the development of the United States as a First World power. Cultural diversity in this context is viewed positively, as responsible for the country's success as a world leader. But countering this perception is the concept of protectionism and the desire to limit labor market competition and resist the absorption of newcomers. Immigration policy emerging out of this concern is often motivated by nativist politics fueled by xenophobia and racism (Najar 1999). Racism has played a fundamental and continuing role in the development of U.S. immigration policy (Calavita 1989; Healey 1997; Rosenblum 2000). The passage of California's Proposition 187 in 1994, as well as an English-only proposition and the introduction of the California Civil Rights Initiative, introduced a new wave of nativism that ultimately flared into a national "nativist revolt" against undocumented and documented immigrants (Chavez 1997; Golash-Boza and Parker 2006; Ivins 2006; Perea 1997; Santos 2006a, b; Zavella 1997).

In a 2006 *USA Today*/Gallup Poll, nearly 80 percent of those polled indicated that controlling U.S. borders to halt illegal immigrants was extremely or very important; more than 60 percent said that the United States should make illegal immigration a crime (Mangaliman 2006).

Proposition 187 attempted to restrict access of undocumented immigrants to public services including medical services in public hospitals and education in public schools (Perea 1997). In addition, public employees were required to report undocumented immigrants (Feagin 1997). In Proposition 187's wake, conservatives in other states developed comparable legislation (Stefancic 1997). Arizona conservatives sponsored Proposition 200, modeled after California's Proposition 187, in the 2004 election, and ultimately it was voted into law. The Republican Legislative Program for Immigration Reform brought before the U.S. House of Representatives even attempted to deny sixty kinds of federal assistance to millions of *legal* immigrants (Chavez 1997).

In this light, the large influx of new undocumented immigrants from Mexico since the initiation of NAFTA in 1994 prompted the creation of the Illegal Immigration Reform and Immigrant Responsibility Act of 1996. This legislation, dubbed Operation Gatekeeper, enacted by the 104th Congress, substantially expanded funding for border enforcement. By 1999 there were nine thousand agents patrolling 8,000 miles of land and sea borders in the United States and Puerto Rico. Latino agents comprise 41 percent of the Border Patrol's force (Annerino 1999). The number of agents in the Border Patrol's San Diego sector grew from 980 in 1994 to more than 2,200 by November 2000 (Nevins 2000). About 57 percent of the nation's undocumented immigrants are Mexicans, but more than 80 percent of people deported by the federal government in the post-NAFTA period 1996–2002 were Mexicans (J. Gonzalez 2006).

The use of fences, cameras, and motion sensors along urban border areas (Garcia 2004), along with other state-of-the-art surveillance technology and activity, has converted the border into a veritable paramilitarized war zone and transformed the Immigration and Naturalization Service (INS) into the largest civilian gun-carrying force in the world. The total INS budget increased from $214.6 million in 1976 to $4.1 billion as of 1999. INS detention centers are filled beyond capacity, and border residents complain about INS surveillance tactics, which are purported to damage property, and Border Patrol harassment of Hispanic-Americans (Rosenblum 2000).

In the year 2000 alone, four years after the initiation of Operation Gatekeeper, the Border Patrol apprehended 1.6 million immigrants (Smith and Ellingwood 2001). More than 100,000 immigrants were caught trying to cross the border illegally near Yuma, Arizona, each year (Sterngold 2001). Between January and September 2001, more than

7,000 migrants were apprehended at San Ysidro, California (Vause 2001).

Recognizing that the risk of apprehension is much greater at common urban border crossing locations such as Tijuana, many migrants attempt a long trek through the California/Arizona desert region bordered on the north by the Gila River, on the west by the Colorado and Mojave deserts, on the east by the Sonoran Desert, and on the south by Sonora's Gran Desierto (Great Desert). The region is referred to as "America's Killing Ground" because so many people have died of dehydration and overexposure in the attempt (Annerino 1999).

Lacking appropriate clothing or supplies, many try to cross the 20–50-mile stretch of desert wearing jeans and plastic sandals or sneakers, carrying only a gallon of water. Dehydration is an ever-present reality along with scorpions, rattlesnakes, and the threat of capture by the *migra*. When their water supply is exhausted, many resort to drinking their own urine. America's Killing Ground is littered with the skulls, bones, and bloated corpses of would-be Mexican immigrants who never made it (Annerino 1999; Smith and Ellingwood 2001).

Deaths along the U.S.–Mexican border have increased fivefold since Operation Gatekeeper went into effect (Sterngold 2001). In fact, deaths of Mexicans crossing into the United States have become a common, almost routine occurrence in these borderlands (Barry 2003). Within five years of Operation Gatekeeper's initiation, 620 people died attempting to cross into California. If Texas and Arizona are included, the toll is 1,500 (King 2001). In 1998 alone, fifty-three people died of thirst while crossing the Texas borderlands (Annerino 1999).

In 1995 the U.S. government launched a new program, Operation Safeguard, which targeted Nogales, Arizona, specifically. As a point of entry perceived by undocumented immigrants to be more porous than those on the border of California, Nogales was once a favored crossing point for undocumented immigrants. Since Operation Safeguard was initiated, the Bureau of Customs and Border Protection reported thirty-four deaths for every 100,000 apprehensions. Undocumented immigrants crossing the border through Arizona in 2003 were seven times more likely to die than they were in 1998 (Carrol 2003).

In 2002, Arizona reported 145 deaths, and in the nine-month period between October 2002 and July 2003 approximately 105 fatalities were reported along the Arizona–Mexico border alone (Carrol 2003). During just a five-day period in December 2002, fourteen people died in the desert near Tucson, Arizona. The Border Patrol called it one of the dead-

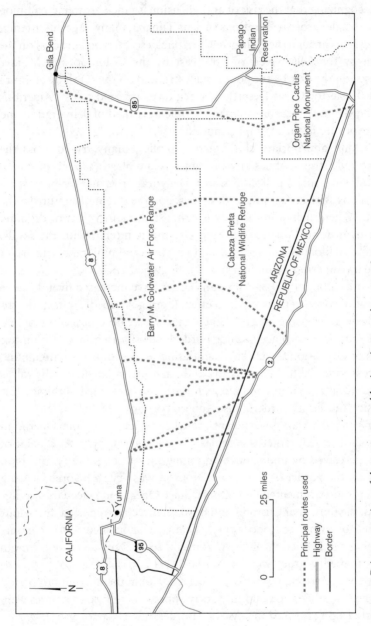

Map 2: Primary section of desert traversed by immigrants since 1996.

liest weekends in recent memory (Klug 2002). In the four-year period from 1999 to 2003, six hundred bodies found along the nation's southern border have yet to be identified (Badger 2003).

Between October 1999 and July 2000, 112 immigrants died in the desert, a 40 percent increase over the year before (Llamas 2000). During the first five months of 2001, deaths occurred at the rate of one per day (Sterngold 2001; Tactaquin 2001). The death toll for the entire year was 1,233, with temperatures on the desert floor of 120–130°F (Reuters 2002). In the six-year period between 1998 and 2004, two thousand migrants lost their lives in the hostile environment of the Southwest desert alone, many of them minors crossing the border in an attempt to find their parents in the United States (Garcia 2004). Since NAFTA was signed into law in 1992, more than four thousand Mexican workers and children, many of them campesinos displaced from their lands, have perished trying to cross the border to find work (Ross 2005).

Tougher border enforcement precludes undocumented parents from returning home to Mexico on vacations to visit their children. As a result, many undocumented workers in the United States send money home to pay for their children's undocumented border crossing. In 2005, the Border Patrol apprehended 93,995 Mexican children ages 17 and under; between October 1, 2005, and April 3, 2006, they apprehended 53,397 Mexican children (Hall 2006).

In May 2001, fourteen immigrants from the state of Veracruz, including an alleged smuggler, died in the Arizona desert after crossing from Mexico (Reuters 2001; Smith and Ellingwood 2001; Sterngold 2001). In May 2003, nineteen immigrants died in an airless tractor-trailer near Victoria, Texas (Tedford 2003). In 2005, 464 would-be immigrants were found dead in the desert. Many other bodies have never been found. Twenty percent of the dead are women and children. The morgue in Tucson, Arizona, had so many corpses to store at the end of 2005 that it was forced to rent a refrigerated truck to hold an extra sixty corpses, at $1,000 per week (CBS News 2005).

In spite of literally billions of taxpayer dollars poured into the endless deterrent strategies each year and the many sophisticated efforts to halt illegal immigration, there is little indication that any of the efforts or expenditures have been effective or have in any way deterred undocumented immigration to the United States (Carral 2003; Garcia 2004; Rosenblum 2000). Rather, desperate, hungry immigrants are willing to take ever more life-threatening risks to arrive in the United States. Many feel that they have nothing to lose and everything to gain. Staying in

Mexico could result in death by starvation for themselves and their families. A job in the United States, on the other hand, offers hope.

> America's immigration policy is a failure. It needs fixing. Everyone can agree on that much. Between 6 million and 10 million people live in the United States illegally. Nobody knows the precise size of this growing subclass. Beefed-up patrols along the border, once hailed as an answer to illegal crossings, have forced Latin Americans to resort to risky and often deadly treks through the desert. People who make it here stay permanently because going back and forth is so dangerous. They come out of desperation for work. U.S. businesses, hungry for cheap labor, are ignoring laws against hiring undocumented workers. So are countless households in need of help that ranges from childcare to gardening. The system is broken. (Natoli et al. 2001, 6P)

In response to the increasing death toll at the border, both the United States and Mexico have taken steps to prevent migrants crossing remote stretches of desert from falling victim to exposure and dehydration. Church groups and activists are setting up water stations and helping migrants with food and water. The Border Patrol added two airplanes and three helicopters to their fleet of seven helicopters to improve patrols. Search-and-rescue patrols in Yuma, Arizona, and in El Centro, California, were expanded in 2001, and the United States also implemented a training program for Mexican agents in search-and-rescue techniques (Fox 2001; Reuters 2001).

Grupo Beta, a humanitarian border unit established by the Mexican government in 1989 to protect migrants making their way north to the United States, also patrols the desert (Carral 2003). The group has posted 125 warning signs around Mexicali and installed 55-gallon drums of water at strategic border points. Agents are armed and arrest smugglers and gangs that attack migrants. More than a hundred Grupo Beta officers patrol the entire 2,000-mile U.S.–Mexican border. Even with the group's comparatively small number of agents, Grupo Beta rescued 14,384 migrants in 2000 and 3,608 migrants in the first four months of 2001 (Smith 2001). In January 2006, the National Human Rights Commission of Mexico began distributing 70,000 maps showing highways, rescue beacons, and water tanks in the Arizona desert in an attempt to curb the death toll (Enriquez 2006; Stevenson 2006a).

A THRIVING MARKET FOR COSTLY INTERNATIONAL SMUGGLERS

Trafficking in people is the fastest-growing organized crime business in the world (Arlacchi 2000). Stepped-up border enforcement efforts indirectly contribute to this brand of organized crime by producing a highly sophisticated class of *coyotes* whose primary and possibly only preoccupation in life is the development of ever more efficient mechanisms for transporting humans en masse across the border illegally. The *coyotes* in turn are matched with a population of desperate west-central Mexican farmers who are willing to risk beatings, robbery, rape, shootings, and even death in their attempt to cross the border (Annerino 1999; Carral 2003; Delgado 1996; Llamas 2000; Stevenson 2006c; Vause 2001).

I did not meet anyone on research trips in Mexico who was documented on their first trip to the United States. All my study's participant post-NAFTA emigrants from west-central Mexican farming communities initially entered the United States illegally. Undocumented immigration is not viewed by these people as criminal activity. They discuss illegal entry into the United States openly and perceive it as a survival necessity. Those who assist and are skilled with the process like the *coyotes* are viewed as heroes, not villains (Castro 1986) and ultimately as essential providers of a service necessary for family well-being not unlike a family doctor or dentist.

Family study participants in San José Ixtapa, Guerrero, and Confradia de Duendes, Jalisco, have a family member *coyote* at the border who is willing to offer reduced rates or free passage to immediate family members and their relatives. The family of Maribel Terraza and Elena Martinez in Chaparaco, Michoacán, maintains contact with a *coyote* in Tijuana. All that is necessary is a phone call and transportation to the border. Preparations and falsified documents are ready upon arrival.

The positive image *coyotes* enjoy plus the lucrative returns for minimal though dangerous efforts invested in illegal human transport across the border fuel an apparently ever more sophisticated and growing class of *coyotes*. As of summer 2004, a *coyote* fee ranged from $300 for an infant to $2,500 for an adult. By January 2005, family members in Mexico informed me, the cost of a border crossing had increased to $3,000. However, in a March 2005 discussion with Elsa González, who has worked in Watsonville's berry fields for the past four years, I learned that she paid $3,500 to a coyote in 2001 for a comparatively "easy" half-hour trek through a desert region of the border followed by van and taxi transportation to Watsonville.

As border vigilance becomes more specialized, *coyote* fees increase accordingly. Many *coyotes* do not deal in the transport of single individuals. Groups of *coyotes* and their accomplices lead, guide, hide, and fly twenty to thirty undocumented immigrants across the border at a time.

Elsa crossed the border with nineteen other undocumented immigrants. Her *coyote* and his accomplices managed to earn a whopping $66,500 for about a day's work.

THE IMMIGRANT STRUGGLE CONTINUES: THE ETERNAL QUEST FOR AMNESTY

At the end of December 2000, the U.S. Congress reauthorized Section 245(i) of the Immigration and Nationality Act (Silverman and Nagiecki 2001). Undocumented immigrants living in the United States who wish to apply for legal residency are no longer required to return to Mexico for the application process. Instead, provided that they have a close family member who is a U.S. citizen or legal resident, they can apply for legal residency in the United States.

Rogelio Alvarez is undocumented. Two years ago he moved to Texas with his undocumented wife and four children. He is currently a homeowner employed in Texas agriculture. His sister, Adela Lozano, came to the United States illegally from Uruapan, Michoacán, approximately fifteen years ago with her young twin daughters and son. Her husband was killed in Mexico, and she had no other means of providing for her young children. She has worked in the fields and in vegetable and fruit packing houses in and near Watsonville for the past fourteen years. In 2001 her daughters were fifteen years old and star pupils at the local high school. Both aspired to continue their education after high school at a university. However, after recognizing that their undocumented status would preclude them from receiving most scholarships for their educational advancement, they gave up their dreams of pursuing academic degrees. Today, one is a farmworker and married with a young son. The other lives with her boyfriend and two small children in her mother's cramped Watsonville apartment. She is also a farmworker.

On January 8, 2001, I attended a meeting with Adela at the Santa Cruz County Immigration Project in Watsonville. Droves of Mexican immigrants with fatigued, saddened faces filled the building on Main Street. The employee who conducted the meeting made it very clear to all attendees that the new law is useful only to those with close relatives who are legal residents or citizens. Those without legal resident or citizen relatives cannot benefit from the law.

It soon became obvious that most of the immigrants crammed into the small meeting room, including Adela, could not benefit from the new law. They attended because they anticipated an *amnistía* (amnesty). In

1986, Congress passed the Immigration Reform and Control Act (IRCA), and over a million undocumented workers became documented as a result (Wells 1996). The IRCA is now referred to as an amnesty within the farmworker community.

As the employee droned on about apparently arbitrary immigration rules and regulations, including exorbitant "penalties," filing fees, extended required absences away from family members after filing, and so forth, the mood among the attendees changed from one of hope and anticipation to palpable distress and sadness.

The Immigration Project employee's only parting words of reassurance included an admonition to save all documents that could be used as evidence of extended residence in the United States. He advised attendees to hope and pray for another immigration amnesty. As I left the building, I looked into one distraught face after another. Some people were allowing their deep sadness and sense of hopelessness to express itself in overflowing tears—the legacy of NAFTA's repudiation of a common binational labor market.

FIVE

IMMIGRATION EXPERIENCES

Si no nos ayudan allá, entonces no nos comemos ni aún frijoles.

If they [her undocumented sons in California] don't help us in
the U.S., then we won't even have beans to eat.

—Rosario Morales, Los Sauces de Pérez, Jalisco

Three men from Jalisco squat behind a ramshackle, abandoned storage
shed within yards of a crossing point on the Arizona–Mexico border. For
days now they have traveled, mostly on foot, from Jalisco's high mountains to this remote location in the northern Mexican desert. All three
consider themselves lucky to have avoided apprehension thus far. Their
rations for the trip have run out, and they are weak, exhausted, hungry,
and thirsty from the demanding journey.

Nonetheless, at this moment they are anxious, with adrenalin pumping
through their veins. "What time is it?" asks Juan while elbowing his friend
Lorenzo. Lorenzo, staring into the evening shadows through a dusty, broken shed window, his eyes fixated on their border crossing point, looks
away just long enough to glance at his watch. "It's 8:52," he whispers.

The next eight minutes seem like an eternity. The men are ready. At
exactly 9:02, the men quickly jump to their feet and make a run for it.
At 9:12 they cross the border, just before the start of the next INS shift,
which begins at 9:15. The newly arrived Border Patrol officer noncha-
lantly takes up his vigilant stance, oblivious to the undocumented immigrants who have just entered the United States under the cover of darkness in the fifteen-minute gap between shifts.

IMMIGRATION IN THE AFTERMATH OF SEPTEMBER 11, 2001

Prior to the tragic events of September 11, 2001, in New York and Washington, D.C., there was widespread discussion and public controversy over the Bush administration's consideration of another mass amnesty program that would legalize millions of undocumented workers in the United States (Schmitt 2001; Shorey 2001). The government of Mexican president Vicente Fox grew increasingly assertive in its demands on behalf of the millions of Mexican citizens residing illegally in the United States—demands that included taxpayer-funded welfare assistance, education benefits, free health care, and driver's licenses (Milanese 2001; Schmitt 2001).

In the San Francisco Bay area, proponents like Richard Hobbs, an immigration attorney and Santa Clara County's director of the Office of Human Relations, argued that "immigration is not a matter of choice but of survival" (Hobbs 2001). Mexico's government and American unions united to urge President Bush to grant legal status to undocumented Mexican immigrants (Greenhouse 2001). The National Council of La Raza stated, "By legalizing immigrants who live, work, and contribute to life in the United States, this debate could deal fairly with hardworking people who have responded to an economic reality that has been ignored by our laws" (Navarrete and Muñoz 2001).

On the other hand, anti-immigration advocates argued that legalizing immigrants currently in the United States illegally would reward people for breaking the law and increase unemployment, traffic, and crime as well as strain energy resources (James 2001; Shorey 2001; Sutton 2001). Some suggested granting temporary work permits. Others expressed anger at ineffective Border Patrol policies and immigration legislation.

President Fox was scheduled to visit President Bush in September 2001, at which time Bush was expected to announce his immigration proposal. And then the unthinkable occurred on September 11, 2001. As 2001 came to a close, U.S. government priorities shifted to a focus on preventing future "terrorist attacks" (Gedda 2001). U.S. government leaders postponed discussions of immigration reform, though they continued to express an interest and intent in the development of some kind of legal residency policy for Mexican migrants already living in the United States (*San Jose Mercury News* 2001c).

The terrorist attacks precipitated renewed discussion about security enhancement along the border (Gedda 2001). Approximately 30,000–35,000 pedestrians cross the border daily into the United States. "Stricter reviews" of the people who cross the border into the United States went into effect, with corresponding long delays at border crossing points. All pedestrian border crossers were required to convert their border-crossing cards into new high-tech "laser visas" by October 1, 2001, for instant background checks. Yet an estimated two million Mexicans, many uninformed, failed to convert their border-crossing cards by the October deadline. U.S. citizens were required to present photo identification before entering the United States (Ellington 2001).

Since September 11, Mexico and the United States have entered into negotiations and formulated bilateral border security agreements devised to encourage cooperation between the two countries. In 2003, the Integral System of Migratory Operation and the Migratory Predocumentation System were developed in Mexico with the goal of accessing information on the migratory status of all foreigners visiting and living in Mexico. The United States and Mexico have signed the U.S.–Mexico Border Partnership Action Plan and implemented the twenty-two points of the agreement with the goal of increasing border security without disturbing the flow of goods and people. Furthermore, the two countries have joined forces and increased binational cooperation and shared intelligence in confronting organized smuggling operations functioning at the border (Carral 2003).

While the United States and Mexico discuss increased national security measures, the lives of millions of hard-working undocumented farm laborers and other low-wage workers who are not a threat to U.S. security and, in fact, contribute to U.S. prosperity, continue to hang in the balance. Several undocumented laborers informed me that the tightened security at the border has had little impact on their plans to travel back and forth between Mexico and the United States. The *coyotes* are as active and as effective at facilitating border crossings as ever.

The structure of the illegal immigration trade discriminates against the poorest of the Mexican poor and favors those individuals who are financially stable enough to save some money, or those who have several family members working in the United States. The funds from these resources on both sides of the border can be pooled and used to purchase a comparatively safe, uneventful border crossing that proceeds without incident most of the time. Those individuals who lack funds and do not have relatives working in the United States who can pay the high *coyote* fees are the ones most likely to die in their attempts to reach the United States. Many are not knowledgeable about the best, safest routes for an undocumented border crossing through scorching desert and frigid mountains. They often set out without any information about the hazardous journey they will face.

Thus, not only does Operation Gatekeeper support a thriving market of ever more costly illegal smugglers at the border, but the illegal, organized crime market it fosters is structured in such a way that it discriminates against the poorest of Mexico's poor. These poor, in turn, are the ones most negatively impacted by NAFTA policies, and for whom there are the fewest survival options. The Southwest desert border region of the United States and Mexico is littered with the bones of some of the most economically disenfranchised people in the world.

IMMIGRATION STORIES

"But how do they get across the border?" This question represents an expression of some of the greatest curiosity and mystery for those attempting to understand the complexity of border dynamics. In this section I present several undocumented immigrant/*coyote* stories related to me by farmworkers and their family members in Mexico. Of particular interest are the relationships the traffickers sometimes develop with Border Patrol officers, and the dynamics of these interactions during the trafficking process.

I describe the immigration experiences of several study participants who were generous enough to extend *confianza* and describe their experiences and travails in detail, even at considerable risk. I elucidate several different examples with the intention of demonstrating the great diversity, creativity, and inexhaustible forms the undocumented immigration experience can take. Some stories reveal a unified, coordinated binational family effort in which immigration impacts family members on both sides of the border.

Alberto Carranza

Alberto Carranza of Uruapan, Michoacán, left Mexico for the United States in 1999 as an undocumented farmworker. From 1999 to mid-2000 he worked in the fields of Visalia, California, pruning peach and plum trees. He then left California for northern Sonora near Nogales to work in a small grocery store. He claims that the *migra* isn't nearly as vigilant in the area of this border town as it is in California. He related that at one time it was so easy to cross the border in the Nogales area that all he had to do was cut a single wire that defined the border in the region and walk across.

Alberto stated unequivocally that people who die in the desert perish because they don't know what they're doing when they cross and don't know the best geographic area for a border crossing. According to him, they shouldn't cross through the desert but should travel directly to Nogales, Mexico. A desert crossing is dangerous and takes at least eight days. However, if they hire him as their *coyote,* a border crossing through Nogales is comparatively inexpensive and takes only three days.

Alberto charges $1,000 for each undocumented person (termed *pollo*) he assists in a border crossing. He related three different strategies he has used to traffic clients across the border in the region of Nogales. He uses the grocery store where he is employed as a point of contact for prospective clients.

In one strategy, Alberto uses bicycles to traffic ten *pollos* at a time across the border. He directs each client to obtain a bike. Then all ten clients and Alberto ride their bikes to a point on the border where he, the *coyote,* cuts the wire fence defining the border. After crossing the border, the *coyote* leads his *pollos* as they ride their bikes on *migra*-monitored roads. They ride as swiftly as possible until the *migra* appears in a car. When stopped by an officer, they get off of their bikes and run off the road on foot, carrying their bikes on their shoulders. When an officer gets out of the car and starts chasing them on foot, they run back to the road, get back on the bikes, and again begin frantically peddling away. If a *pollo* gets caught, the whole group benefits, since the officer becomes preoccupied with processing papers for the one individual who is caught while the remaining nine *pollos* and Alberto escape.

In a second strategy Alberto uses his truck, which is designed to carry a maximum of eight people. He piles sixteen people on top of one another and covers them with a tarp. On one occasion while he was driving the truck on the usual roads patrolled by the *migra*, a Border Patrol officer walking on foot pointed a gun at the truck driver and ordered him to stop. Alberto was asked about the number of people he was carrying in the back of the truck. Alberto replied that there were "about sixteen." The officer then asked him if he knew his truck was designed to carry no more than eight people and demanded that Alberto get rid of eight people, since he was exceeding the *coyote* capacity of *pollos* in the truck.

Alberto acted confused, not knowing how to choose which eight people to leave behind. At this point all sixteen *pollos* began to beg the *migra* to let them through. The *migra* asked them if they didn't mind being squashed together in a space designed for half as many people. They all responded that they didn't mind. The officer then waved them on, and all sixteen got through, while Alberto earned $16,000 for a few hours' work.

In a third strategy, Alberto leads a group of *pollos* across the border at night, under cover of darkness. On one occasion a Border Patrol officer observed Alberto and his group through heat-sensitive goggles. He and his group were subsequently stopped, and the officer accused Alberto of being a *coyote*, insisting that he had observed Alberto leading the group the entire time. Alberto queried the officer about how he was able to observe him leading the group at night, under cover of darkness. The officer proceeded to show Alberto how the heat-sensitive goggles work, then escorted Alberto and his group back to Mexico. However, Alberto was never arrested.

Alberto claims that he is not at all concerned about being arrested as a human smuggler. The first offense carries only a three-day jail sentence. The second offense results in a ten-day jail sentence. Even a third arrest carries a jail term of just three weeks. With the lucrative monetary gains *coyotes* are able to garner in a very short period, and his penchant for helping his fellow campesinos, Alberto claims that it only makes sense for him to continue his work and help people as a smuggler.

José Moreno

José Moreno emigrated to the United States illegally from near Tlalpujahua, Michoacán, with the assistance of his legal resident uncle in Marina, California, who loaned him the money for a *coyote*. Initially he lived in Marina with his aunt and uncle. Currently he maintains a small two-room home in a substandard Salinas apartment complex. He lives with his undocumented wife, two undocumented children, and a citizen baby recently born in the United States His home serves as a "switchboard" house for emigrating members from his small rancho in Michoacán.

My frequent visits with the family reveal an ever-changing panorama of human beings newly arrived from José's community in Mexico. Most initially take up residence in the apartment. On one occasion there were ten visitors living in the apartment with José and his family. José's wife Elena functions as the hub and organizer of the group by maintaining the apartment, cooking meals, and tending to her children and the continual stream of undocumented guests arriving from Mexico.

Jorge Rosales

Jorge Rosales from Catalina, a rancho near Apatzingán, Michoacán, im-migrated to California in 1985. Family members paid for his *coyote*. He initially lived with his aunt, who owns her own home. In time he went to live with a brother in Redwood City. Eventually he established him-self in a steady job in Salinas, acquired California permanent resident sta-tus, and then arranged for his wife's immigration. Jorge's wife is undoc-umented, and his son, born after Jorge and his wife came to California, is a U.S. citizen.

Consuelo Fernandez

Consuelo Fernandez is originally from Nueva Italia, Michoacán. More than twenty-two years ago, in 1983, Consuelo was the first in her fam-ily to immigrate to the United States. She immigrated illegally with some friends after she lost her husband in Nueva Italia. Her brothers in Mex-ico encouraged her to immigrate in order to locate work to provide sup-port for her three young children. Initially, she left her children with her family in Nueva Italia. According to Consuelo, she then "struggled and suffered" for two or three years until she found a job and housing and managed to complete her own documentation. Then she traveled home and returned to the United States with her children.

Joaquin Bejarano

Joaquin Bejarano and Maribel Terraza have four adult children, Pedro, Marisol, Mariana, and Elena. Elena, her husband Salazar, and their three children are all legal residents living in Salinas. Until Elena sustained a serious work-related spinal injury, she was employed as a mustard picker in Salinas corporate agribusiness. Her husband has picked celery in Salinas for many years.

Joaquin and Maribel's son Pedro is documented, and his wife is un-documented. The family has a *coyote* on call in Tijuana to assist mem-bers with border crossings when necessary. The family paid the *coyote* $1,500 in 1998 to assist Pedro with his wife's border crossing. Pedro's two children were born in the United States and are U.S. citizens. Once the entire family was reunited in the United States, they initially took up residence with relatives. They have since moved to Livermore, California.

In Mexico, Pedro and his family, like many families with strong ties to their communities in Mexico (Castro 1986; Zavella 2000), are in the process of constructing a spacious, fully furnished home behind Joaquin and Maribel's home in Chaparaco, Michoacán. The family typically lives nine months to a year in a single rented room in Livermore while Pedro works in construction and his wife is employed as a house cleaner. They return to Chaparaco for three months each year at Christmas to enjoy their new home and holiday festivities with other family members in Mexico.

Maribel and Joaquin's son-in-law Lorenzo also immigrated to Livermore in early 1998. Once he became established as an undocumented construction worker, he sent for Marisol, Maribel and Joaquin's daughter. Marisol crossed the border in July 1998 using the services of the family *coyote*, for $1,500. Her two-year-old son crossed the border with a woman *coyote (coyota)* for $300. The documented *coyota* held the child's hand as she led him *por la linea* (through the line), across the border. The child was then reunited with his mother waiting on the U.S. side of the border.

Maribel and Joaquin's third daughter, Mariana, lives with her three sons and daughter in an apartment in the nearby agricultural city of Zamora, Michoacán. Her husband Geronimo is a bus driver with routes extending throughout west-central Mexico.

Joaquin and Maribel hoped to visit their children, grandchildren, and other relatives and friends in California for the 1998 holiday season. Joaquin and Maribel both have Mexican passports and all the requisites for obtaining a travel visa: marriage license, property title, home ownership, and a bank account. Joaquin's unsuccessful efforts to obtain a visa for travel are related in chapter 1. On one occasion, in desperation, he made copies of his documents and gave them to me to take to the U.S. embassy in San José, California, on his behalf. When I attempted to discuss his case with an INS agent, I was told that "he must have done something in Mexico that is keeping him from obtaining a visa." It is difficult to imagine a man with Joaquin's level of integrity and concern for others "doing anything" that could have prevented him from obtaining a visa.

When Joaquin Bejarano wanted to visit his children and grandchildren living in Salinas in May 1999, he telephoned the family *coyote* prior to leaving Chaparaco. He traveled to Tijuana from Guadalajara. The *coyote* was waiting with a bogus passport. A picture of Joaquin was taken and embossed onto the passport. He practiced his "new name" on the passport several times and then crossed the border *caminando por la linea* (walking through the line) in Tijuana, where identification papers are checked by INS agents.

He was met on the U.S. side of the border by an accomplice and driven to the San Diego airport. He took a plane from San Diego to San José, where his daughter Elena and her family were waiting for him. Walking effortlessly through the line in Tijuana is considered a relative luxury among undocumented migrants. The *coyote* that arranges such a crossing also exacts a correspondingly high price. Joaquin paid $2,000 for the service.

In July 1999, a visit to the family in Chaparaco confirmed that Joaquin had successfully crossed the border and was enjoying a visit with Elena's family in Salinas. While Joaquin and Maribel visited their children and grandchildren in Salinas, Mariana, Geronimo, and their children rented their apartment in Zamora and moved into Joaquin and Maribel's home in Chaparaco in the couple's absence. Pedro was due to return from Livermore in August to plant Joaquin's *parcelas* in potatoes and tomatoes. Pedro planned to assume all of Joaquin's farming responsibilities in his absence.

Maria Herrera

This is an example of a family migration network gone awry. Maria Herrera was the victim of an unscrupulous *coyote* and a U.S. attorney of Mexican descent. These individuals, in combination with the peculiar system of U.S. immigrant "justice" that denies due process and is reserved exclusively for immigrants, seriously compromised Maria and her family financially, legally, and emotionally.

Maria, the daughter of Faviola de la Cruz, currently lives in Salinas, California, with her husband and four children. She works year-round packing radicchio for Premio. Her husband picks broccoli in the fields of Salinas corporate agribusiness. The entire family has had legal resident status since 1994. Six months after Maria and her family immigrated to Salinas, Maria's son-in-law immigrated illegally, to Hamilton, California.

During the subsequent three years, the son-in-law was able to return to his home in San Agustín only one time to visit his wife and two sons. After three years in Hamilton, separated from his family, he and his other family members in California made arrangements for the undocumented U.S. entry of Maria's oldest daughter and grandsons. Maria's daughter and two grandsons subsequently crossed the border with a *coyote* near Yuma, Arizona.

Upon their arrival in Yuma, the daughter called Maria to inform her of their safe U.S. entrance. Maria then traveled to Yuma to meet her daughter and the children. The *coyota*, oldest daughter, two grandsons, and Maria drove toward Los Angeles in the early hours of the following morning. The *coyota* was to be paid upon arrival in Los Angeles.

A suspicious Yuma policeman tipped off immigration officials in Indio, where the group was stopped. After extensive interrogation, unknown to Maria, the *coyota* informed the INS officials in English that *Maria* was the *coyota*. Maria and her family are monolingual Spanish speakers and were unable to decipher the English conversation between the *coyota* and the official. Maria was subsequently detained and charged with instigating the illegal immigration of her daughter and grandsons. Her daughter and grandsons were deported and returned to Tijuana.

Maria was eventually released, and she returned home to Salinas. Next, the same *coyota*, who suffered no consequences from the Indio encounter with the INS, drove to Tijuana to assist her deported daughter and grandchildren cross the border and enter California again. The undocumented daughter and grandsons are currently living in Hamilton.

Eight days after Maria returned to Salinas, she received a letter from the INS. The letter was printed in English, which Maria cannot read. Fortunately, her children read English and were able to translate the letter for Maria. The letter designated a court date and admonished Maria to hire an attorney for the appearance.

A neighbor recommended an attorney who then accompanied Maria to court on September 14, 1997. The attorney's fee was $1,100. All proceedings were in English. The judge asked her three questions: her name, residence location, and telephone number.

One week later Maria received another letter. She was again required to appear in court with her attorney. The attorney's fee for this second visit was $550. The same questions were repeated.

Maria then received a third letter. Another court date was scheduled for May 1, 1998. Her attorney's fee was again $550. At this court hearing she was not asked any questions. Again, all proceedings were in English.

Seven days later, Maria received a letter from the INS revealing the court's verdict. She would be deported for ten years, and she must leave the United States by June 1, 1998. Again the letter was in English and translated for her by her children. Neither the judge in court nor her attorney ever informed her that she was in danger of deportation.

Maria was shocked and terrified at the thought of leaving her children, home, and job in California. She then approached a second attorney, who informed her that he could do nothing to assist her. Maria and one of her brothers began a search for a third attorney. A third attorney reviewed her paperwork and charged a hefty fee. Ultimately, the attorney was able to delay the deportation for two years.

Two years later, Maria received a letter informing her that she was required to leave the country by June 6, 2000, or risk forceful deportation. When she again visited the third attorney, he informed her that the matter would have to be handled in San Francisco with his "representative." She was informed that she must appear in San Francisco on June 6 with the attorney's representative. For this "service," she paid the attorney $7,000.

On June 6, one of Maria's brothers transported her to San Francisco to meet the representative. She met him at the immigration office, and he promptly turned her over to immigration authorities.

When Maria entered the immigration office, officials searched her purse. She was forced to remove her watch, necklace, hair ornaments, and all money and turn them over to INS officials. She was then ordered to sign papers. She was never informed about the papers' content; she was only ordered to sign. In her state of terror, she complied. Maria was then directed to a room with other women. She was menstruating at the time and was not allowed to use a restroom to change her sanitary product. She was eventually ushered out of the office, hands and feet shackled, and onto a "private *migra* plane" bound for San Diego with 150 other undocumented immigrants.

In San Diego, all 150 immigrants were taken to an office in which the shackles were removed and their personal effects returned. The immigrants were then escorted to a waiting car and driven to Tijuana. Upon her arrival in Tijuana, Maria found a hotel and called her Salinas family members to inform them of her disastrous fate. One of her brothers in California and a daughter traveled to Tijuana with some of her clothes and money. Her brother bought a plane ticket to Guadalajara and notified their mother, Faviola de la Cruz, in San Agustín of her pending arrival. Gabino Ayala, Maria's brother, picked her up at the airport in Guadalajara and drove her to San Agustín.

Maria has since returned to Salinas to be with her family. She continues to work in the radicchio fields under an assumed name. She has consulted with other attorneys regarding her plight. Most inform her that she must allow enough time to pass (ten years) so that her case can be reopened with the possibility of a positive outcome. She lives in constant fear regarding her now illegal status in the United States and potential risk of incarceration.

In March 2005, after living and working in the United States for five years since her deportation, she again met with a qualified San José immigration attorney. He informed her that she must hide out for another five years. After a total of ten years from the time of the judge's verdict, he can reopen her case and resubmit her application for legal residency. When asked why she doesn't return to Mexico, she tearfully responds, "I can't leave my family."

Elena Esparza

Elena Esparza's husband, Emanuel, began undocumented treks to the United States to work as a farm laborer in 1985. From 1985 to 1988 he traveled back and forth between Huacao, Michoacán, and Watsonville, working in the strawberry and bush berry fields from March to November. On each trip to the United States he hired a *coyote* to lead him and as many as twenty other undocumented immigrants over the mountains near Tecate. If the *migra* interfered, the *coyotes* led the *pollos* over the mountains at a different location on the border to California or Arizona.

In 1990, Emanuel and Elena married and their two oldest sons were born over the next two years. In Huacao they lived with Emanuel's family in a two-room adobe dwelling. Each family lived in one of the rooms. Elena related that the room she and her family occupied was so small that the only furniture that fit into it was a single bed. The two parents and two sons slept in the same bed. The only means of acquiring food was by growing a corn, bean, and squash intercrop as sharecroppers on less than a single hectare.

When asked why she and her entire family immigrated to the United States, Elena informed me that they came in search of work. In 1994, Emanuel traveled back to Watsonville to work during the agricultural growing season. Elena and her two sons took a bus to Nogales, Mexico, during the season of Lent. For eight weeks they harvested and sold *nopales* (beavertail cactus stems) and earned 2,000 pesos. Emanuel received a $1,600 income tax refund and had also saved other money for his family's undocumented border crossing. By pooling their financial resources, Elena was able to pay a *coyote* $2,250 to traffic her and her two boys across the border in a bus. Emanuel was waiting on the U.S. side to meet them and transport them to Watsonville.

Initially the family lived with Emanuel's brother in a garage while they searched for an apartment. Eventually they were able to rent an apartment with two bedrooms to share with Emanuel's brother's family. Each family and their children stayed in one of the two bedrooms. From there, Elena and Emanuel moved to a one-bedroom bungalow they share with two other families during the harvest season.

Elena bemoans the economic necessity of her absence from her birthplace in Huacao. She especially misses her mother. Her voice drops as she relates that, in 2005, it's just too dangerous and costly to risk an undocumented border crossing. If she went back to Mexico, she could not afford to pay a *coyote* for a safe return to the United States, and her family is now settled in Watsonville.

Since their immigration to the United States in 1994, Elena and Emanuel have had two daughters and another son. In 2005, Emanuel acquired legal residency and continues to work at his new year-round place of employment in the mushroom industry. Elena is undocumented and works for a company that grows organic bush berries. Their family is representative of many farmworker families in which immediate family members have differing documentation. Emanuel is a legal resident, Elena is undocumented, their two oldest sons are undocumented; and the two daughters and youngest son are U.S. citizens.

Aurelio Toledo

Many farmworkers and their family members spoke of arriving undocumented in the United States *por el cerro* or *brincando por el cerro*. "Leaping over the hill" refers to the necessity of leaping over crevices and dry streambeds in the border desert hills near Tecate, Baja California.

Aurelio Toledo, a former farmer from Poncitlán near Guadalajara, explained how he has managed to work as a tree trimmer in Pasadena, California, for many years and then return for periodic visits with his wife and family members. Aurelio boards a plane for a $120 flight from Guadalajara to Tijuana. He then travels to Tecate. Early Sunday morning he enjoys a full meal of tacos in Tecate, where he meets the two *coyotes* who will facilitate his crossing over the desert hills. He carries a satchel full of *pan Bimbo* (a familiar sliced white bread) spread with mayonnaise and one gallon of water. He will sip the water judiciously throughout the two-day journey.

The two *coyotes* begin the trek with a column of as many as twenty undocumented immigrants at 10:00 on Sunday morning. One *coyote* leads the column, the other follows the last person in line. Both *coyotes* scout continuously during the journey for *migra*. The immigrants walk day and night without sleep until they arrive in the United States on Tuesday morning.

If *migra* are spotted during the journey, the migrants fall to the ground and seek out any ground depression to conceal themselves. They then quietly crawl on their stomachs until they find a tree, rock, or bush to hide behind or under. Mounted *migra* have difficulty navigating on horses through the hills. There are no roads for cars. Therefore the migrants cross the hills during daylight hours and cross open spaces at night.

The press has cited many incidents of Border Patrol abuse. The Border Patrol is known to be responsible for incidents of racial profiling at the border in which drivers are stopped based only on their race or ethnic appearance (Reinhardt 2000). Furthermore, agents side with ranchers who own property along the border of southwestern states and sometimes deal harshly with immigrants who trespass (Booth 2000). Such incidents, however, belie Aurelio's encounters with officers working along the California border.

Aurelio spoke of the kindness he has experienced from the Anglo officers on his many journeys over the years. He cited instances in which guards offered him and other migrants orange juice and then told them to go and hide for an hour until they (the Border Patrol) were gone. Other times, when he and his companion migrants were caught, they explained to the Border Patrol their intention to work in California to support their families and their lack of involvement with the drug trade. With these reassurances, the immigrants were often allowed to continue their journey to California. Aurelio claims to have been treated courteously and returned to Tecate on the many occasions when he was caught and detained.

Aurelio acknowledged seeing evidence of only one death on his many binational journeys. He observed a corpse in the mountains that he described as a young man who appeared to have fallen off a cliff and struck his head on a rock. The young man's head was covered with dried blood. Aurelio believes the victim must have died instantly from a fall.

Other immigrants who made the journey *por el cerro* spoke of routinely observing dead bodies. When I interviewed Eduardo Sousa, a Watsonville farmworker, he spoke with agitation about seeing two dead bodies in the desert mountains when he first came to the United States with a *coyote* in 1984. He was able to establish legal residency in 1986 under the Immigration Reform and Control Act and is thankful that he no longer has to subject himself to such sightings on his return trips from visits to Mexico.

Aurelio also spoke of the manner in which some Border Patrol officers are bought off by the *coyotes*. In April 2001 an undocumented immigrant paid a *coyote* a fee of $1,800 for a comparatively painless border crossing. For this then-elevated price the prospective immigrant could cross the border by simply waiting in Tecate for the *coyote*'s "all clear" signal and then walking across between Tijuana and Tecate without incident, thereby avoiding the arduous two-day crossing over the desert hills. Conspiring Border Patrol officers regularly update *coyotes* regarding a time of day or night for safe border crossing without detection. Aurelio mentioned that this effortless border crossing procedure is usually reserved for women and children. Men more typically traverse the mountains.

After the two-day trek over the mountains, a van meets the migrants on a dirt road parallel to the border and escorts them to a "safe house" in San Diego. At the safe house, four migrants are loaded into the trunk of each of five waiting sedans. The sedans proceed up the California coast to the San Clemente INS checkpoint. Once the checkpoint has been successfully passed, the migrants exit the trunk, enter the passenger portion of the car, and complete a journey to a Los Angeles safe house. Upon his arrival at the safe house, Aurelio calls his sons who live in Southern California. The sons travel to the Los Angeles safe house, pay the *coyotes* $1,400 for their services, and whisk their father off to one of their homes.

Aurelio related one attempt to cross the border in which he was returned to Tecate by the Border Patrol on six different occasions. While he waited for each attempted trip over the hills, he stayed as an all-expenses-paid guest in a house or hotel provided by the *coyotes*. Until a successful trip is made, the *coyotes* provide for all food and lodging at the border in Mexico. On this particular occasion he remained in Tecate for two months at *coyote* expense, until his seventh attempt over the mountains was successful.

According to Aurelio, it is no longer possible for undocumented migrants to arrive at the San Diego airport with the intention of booking a flight elsewhere in the country. The airport currently checks all passenger identifications thoroughly before booking flights. Aurelio acknowledged, however, that if a migrant can secure passage to the Los Angeles airport there are no problems. Flights to any part of the United States can be arranged without detection.

Finally, Aurelio discussed another manner in which undocumented immigrants make border crossings. The back of a van is filled with immigrants lying in layers on top of one another. The immigrants are then covered with cardboard. A black man drives the van. His wife and child accompany him as they drive across the border. Aurelio surmises that this method of illegal transport is successful because the *migra* do not suspect that a black man and his family would be involved with the illegal transport of Mexicans.

Roberto Fonseca

Roberto Fonseca is originally from Gómez Farías, Michoacán. When he first immigrated to California, his brothers in California provided funds for the *coyote* fee. They also arranged for employment with the company they were working for. His brothers taught him how to work in the strawberry fields. They also shared their home and meals with him. After living three years with them, Roberto moved from his brothers' home to his own apartment. By the time he married, he was established with a car, an apartment, and a job. He acknowledged that if he had not established himself first, before marrying, and traveled to California with his wife, he would have felt "lost and blind," not knowing where to go for housing, jobs, or any other necessities.

In the early 1980s, as a single man and before obtaining documentation, Roberto followed a route over the mountains similar to Aurelio Toledo's. After he married, he expressed his concern about taking his wife *por el cerro*. The route of travel over the Tecate hills is often considered a viable option only for men. In 1985 he accompanied his wife on an attempt to enter the United States. Twenty to thirty undocumented immigrants boarded a van at night. He recalled that the van traveled without lights of any kind. The van entered some sort of field and bounced over the field's furrows and waterholes. One *coyote* drove while another charted the van's direction.

Eventually the van entered a U.S. freeway and headed north. The passengers were taken to a hotel in San Diego. They spent the night, bathed, and recuperated from the journey. The next day they boarded a plane for San José, California. Roberto indicated that the journey was comparatively painless because he had prior experience traveling to the United

States as an undocumented laborer. He knew what to expect and how to function in California.

Paulo Miranda Espinoza

Paulo Miranda Espinoza is a cab driver who lives in Morelia, Michoacán, with his wife and three children. He considers immigration to be a requirement for survival in Mexico. Without immigration he cannot afford to feed and clothe his family and provide education for his children. As of summer 1998, he had emigrated illegally to California six or seven different times. Each time he hired a *coyote*, which he claims is essential with the continued progressive militarization of the border. *Coyotes* can be hired in Michoacán to facilitate the journey from there to the border. Paulo says that federal and state police stop all Mexicans suspected of emigrating and force them to return to their states of origin. However, Paulo indicated that they can be bribed for about 20 pesos.

Coyotes charge separate fees for the trip from Michoacán to the border and for the trip across the border into the United States. The farther north into California the *coyote* must secure passage for the emigrant, the higher the fee. *Coyotes* aren't paid unless the immigrant is delivered successfully without apprehension by the *migra* to the agreed-upon destination.

A *coyote* travels between Michoacán and Tijuana or Tecate with as many as fifty emigrants at a time. According to Paulo, groups of ten people at a time actually cross the border in Tijuana. Paulo crosses the border with a *coyote* in a trailer. Emigrants lie under crates of fruit, which are placed on a shelf above them. When the trailer reaches the border and a border guard inspects it, the top of the trailer is opened, exposing only fruit.

Crossing the border in Tecate does not expose the would-be emigrant to as great a risk of apprehension as crossing the border in Tijuana. But one of the risks of crossing in Tecate is the long trek through the California desert mountains. Contrary to Aurelio's assessment, according to Paulo the mountains are full of mounted *migra* by day. Most emigrants hide under trees and scrub during the day and travel only at night. Some migrants are not prepared for the physical rigor of the crossing and die of exposure and dehydration.

Paulo has relatives living in Los Angeles and Indio, California. Once he gets into the United States, he stays with relatives for a few days before beginning to look for work in Indio. In Indio he lives in a "switchboard" house with other men, most of whom are also undocumented. A flourishing market in the production and sale of falsified documents exists in both Mexico and the United States (Castro 1986). In summer 1998, he paid approximately $200 for a fraudulent green card, or *mica*. He claims that he has never been hired by an employer who checks the authenticity of his card. As long as he can show them a card, he gets hired.

Arturo López Navarro

In the summer of 1998, Tomasina López Santos lived with her two grandsons, Arturo López Navarro (age 13) and Jorge Esteban Navarro (age 14), in Confradia de Duendes, Jalisco, near the town of Tecolotlán. The parents of the two teenage boys and their two sisters had emigrated illegally to the United States in 1995. Since then, neither boy had seen either parent or their sisters. The parents in the United States agreed to pay for a *coyote* to assist the boys with emigration once they completed high school in Mexico.

One year later, in the summer of 1999, Arturo and twenty-two other undocumented Mexicans boarded a small plane and flew across the border at Nogales, Arizona. From Nogales a *coyote* transported him to his waiting family in Salinas. He is currently living with his mother in Salinas and working in a flower shop.

Sofia Ornelas

Sofia Ornelas told me of a harrowing adventure crossing the border at Nogales in 1996. She, her husband, and their young daughter were directed in Nogales, Mexico, by two young girls, fifteen or sixteen years of age, to an underground bridge leading to the entrance of a sewage outfall pipe that extends into Nogales, Arizona. She recalled the unpleasant experience of trudging through the wastewater with her young daughter crying, "Mommy, we're going to drown!"

Eventually they arrived at the end of the pipe in the United States. Another underground bridge led them out of the pipe to the surface. Ultimately they located a nearby, prearranged pizza house. A waiting car at the pizza house transported the family to her brother's home in Mesa, Arizona.

THE FUTURE OF UNDOCUMENTED
IMMIGRATION TO THE UNITED STATES?

Increased flows of Latinos into the United States in NAFTA's wake have given U.S. hate groups a new target, and hate crimes against Latino immigrants are on the rise throughout the country (Poovey 2005). By October 2005, three undocumented immigrants were killed in apparent vigilante violence, and seven others were confirmed wounded (Southern Poverty Law Center 2005a).

Unfortunately, those who are uninformed about the plight of undocumented immigrants and the role the United States has played in displacing them from their land in Mexico are fomenting anti-immigrant sentiment. In March 2005, when the agricultural season begins, hundreds of civilian "Minutemen" volunteers, some armed, converged on a 20-mile stretch of Arizona's border with Mexico in an attempt to stop the yearly predictable increased flow of undocumented immigrants entering the United States to work (Hall and O'Driscoll 2005).

The Minutemen enjoyed neutral to positive press throughout 2005 in spite of the fact that one of the group's leaders made public bigoted statements, that some Minutemen demonstrators are affiliated with neo-Nazi groups, and that the group includes other known white supremacists. In fact, the Minutemen group received positive reviews from both California governor Arnold Schwarzenegger and Colorado congressman Tom Tancredo. Governor Schwarzenegger lauded the project as a great thing that should be emulated and claimed that the Minutemen had done a "terrific job" and were welcome to come to California (Berkowitz 2005a).

Additionally, in 2005 the federal Department of Homeland Security increased the number of Border Patrol agents by 25 percent. Human rights advocates, in turn, responded by sending groups to the border to document the inevitable human rights abuses by vigilante violence (Shields 2005). In late July 2005, Texas Republican representative John Culberson and forty-seven other legislators introduced the Border Protection Patrol Act (H.R. 3622). If passed, the bill would create a Border Protection Corps that would be allowed to "use any means and any force authorized by state law to prevent individuals from unlawfully entering the United States" (Berkowitz 2005b).

In September 2005, a group of one hundred Californians calling themselves the Friends of the Border Patrol Border Watch received classroom and field training from those with military or law enforcement experience to watch for illegal border crossings in California. Volunteers monitor "undisclosed" stretches between San Diego's Border Field Park and the city of Calexico in Imperial County. The group operates its patrols on private property, and only former and current law enforcement agents are armed (Gazzar 2005).

As the year 2005 came to a close, President Bush continued to push for a temporary-worker program akin to the Bracero program (see chapter 3) in an uninformed attempt to curtail the flow of undocumented immigrants into the United States. His program calls for 300,000 people to be given temporary visas for three years. The visas would be renewable for three years (Bacon 2005a). His other enforcement strategies, along with those of most of the other congressional representatives and senators, are punitive at best and racist at worst.

His proposal advocates "interior repatriations" that will send Mexican immigrants back to the interior of Mexico rather than leave them on the Mexican side of the border where they can engage in repeated attempts to cross. He emphasizes "catching" undocumented immigrants by further expanding surveillance monitors, infrared cameras, and pilotless surveillance aircraft. Furthermore, he proposes tougher enforcement of laws against employers who hire undocumented workers (Bacon 2005a).

The consequences of this approach were tested on April 19, 2006, when federal agents arrested seven current and former managers of IFCO Systems, a manufacturer of crates and pallets, on criminal charges. More than 1,100 people were arrested on administrative immigration charges at more than forty IFCO sites in the United States. Most of the 1,187 undocumented immigrants arrested were subsequently processed for deportation (Gaouette 2006; Miga 2006).

As a result of the nationwide raids, rumors of immigration roundups prompted thousands of undocumented immigrants to stay home for indefinite periods of time; construction and agriculture were industries most impacted by the absence of workers (Wides-Muñoz 2006). Agribusiness warned that food prices would increase with unnecessary labor shortages (Stebbins 2006). From Watsonville to Washington State, organic growers complained that INS raids and harsh border policies were causing a serious labor shortage in the care and harvesting of their labor-intensive crops (Barbassa 2006). The executive vice president of Associated General Contractors of South Florida claimed that 50 percent of workers on construction jobs in the region had not shown up for work following the IFCO raids, costing contractors millions of dollars a day (Wides-Muñoz 2006).

In concert with the president's punitive biases, House Armed Services chair Duncan Hunter and Representative Tom Tancredo even called for the construction of a high-tech fence along the nation's entire border from the Pacific coast to the Gulf of Mexico as a proposed solution to undocumented immigration, at any cost (Alonso-Zaldivar 2005; CBS News 2005).

In mid-December 2005, a federal judge lifted the final legal barrier to completing a 14-mile stretch of fencing in San Diego designed to thwart undocumented immigrants. The fence would cross steep, rugged canyons, including "Smuggler's Gulch," a common area where undocumented immigrants travel before entering the United States (Spagat 2005). Within a few days of the approval for San Diego's fence extension, the House of Representatives approved building 700 miles of fence in the area of Laredo, Texas, much to the chagrin of the Mexican government (Grillo 2005).

Arizona's two Republican senators, John Kyl and John Cronyn, introduced a bill that would create temporary visas lasting six years, for farmwork and other unpopular types of work. Undocumented workers in the United States would first have to move back to Mexico to obtain the visa, and they would have to return to Mexico permanently once the visas expired (San Jose Mercury News 2005b).

In addition, the bill calls for machine-readable, tamper-proof Social Security cards to be issued to every American in the workforce. These cards would purportedly prevent undocumented workers from getting jobs. The bill would fund the hiring of ten thousand new Department of Homeland Security personnel for seeking and eliminating undocumented workers from the workforce, and an additional thousand for detecting immigration fraud. Ten thousand new Border Patrol agents would be recruited over five years, all at a total cost of approximately $12 billion (Elser 2005).

By the end of 2005, the U.S. government had spent $20 billion since NAFTA went into effect attempting to stem the tide of undocumented immigrants entering the United States. Eleven thousand Border Patrol agents, three times the pre-NAFTA number, have been hired to "secure" the border. Neither of these extreme, expensive measures has done anything to stop or even deter undocumented immigration. One-half million undocumented immigrants entered the United States in 2005 (CBS News 2005).

The flow of undocumented immigrants from Mexico and the attendant national hysteria, as demonstrated by the plethora of recent congressional bills demanding punitive solutions to their "invasion," could readily and rapidly be curtailed by relatively simple rural development interventions sponsored by the United States (see chapter 14). These rural development interventions would cost only a fraction of the bill U.S. taxpayers are currently saddled with and would simultaneously give Mexican NAFTA economic refugees an escape from the unwelcome prospect of emigrating to survive, leaving their families, homes, and land behind.

As 2005 drew to a close, the U.S. Congress continued to promote some of the most punitive, repressive immigration policy in U.S. history. In spite of the fact that not a single "terrorist" has ever been identified entering the United States through Mexico (CBS News 2005), the House of Representatives approved HR 4437, the Border Protection, Antiterrorism, and Illegal Immigration Control Act of 2005, sponsored by Representatives James Sensenbrenner (R-Wisconsin) and Peter King (R-New York). If passed by the Senate in 2006, the bill will further divide families, criminalize undocumented status, and drive undocumented workers deeper underground. Representative Tancredo's bill would institute mass deportations (Bacon 2005b).

The cost and logistics of ridding the country of 12 million people are prohibitive. The Center for American Progress has put the cost at approximately $215 billion over a five-year period (Mendoza 2006). The punitive legislation and potential felony status for undocumented immigrants sent a shockwave throughout the entire U.S. Latino community. While mainstream America watched Sensenbrenner's bill pass the House with little controversy or divisiveness, on its way to the Senate for approval, Spanish-language radio and television stations across the country sounded the alarm with lively, impassioned discussions about the implications for the future of undocumented immigrants in the country if the bill passed the Senate.

Enormous protests were organized across the country. To the utter surprise and amazement of mainstream America, literally millions of immigrants and their supporters poured into the streets of 140 major cities at the end of March and beginning of April 2006 to protest the punitive legislation (A.N.S.W.E.R. 2006; Bada et al. 2006; Cooper 2006; Gailbraith 2006; Gumbel and Buncombe 2006; May et al. 2006; Mintz 2006; Molloy 2006; Ostrom 2006; Prengaman 2006; Villagran 2006). Students walked out of classes (Bogado 2006; R. J. González 2006;

Lohse and McPherson 2006; Rubin and Cho 2006; Sagara 2006), and church groups issued statements in support of immigrants (del Toro and Vives 2006).

On May 1, 2006, International Worker's Day, immigrant organizers planned "A Day Without Immigrants" and encouraged all Mexican workers and students to leave their jobs and schools for the day to march. In Mexico City, thousands of Mexicans took to the streets to support migrants in the United States by celebrating what they called "A Day Without Gringos." They encouraged Mexicans not to purchase items from U.S.-owned supermarkets, fast-food restaurants, and other American stores (Stevenson 2006c; Thompson 2006). Immigrant supporters are likening the outpouring of protest fueled by punitive anti-immigrant legislation to a second civil rights movement (Gumbel and Buncombe 2006).

Finally, a massive boycott of all Kimberly-Clark products including Kotex, Depend, Poise, Kleenex, Scott, Little Swimmers, Pull-Ups, Huggies, and Viva was initiated during the first week of May 2006 throughout Latin America. These brands are best sellers in more than eighty countries, and Rep. Sensenbrenner is heir to the Kimberly-Clark family fortune. As one of the initiators of the Kimberly-Clark boycott stressed, "All Hispanics who purchase some of the world's most recognized brands . . . are putting money in Sensenbrenner's bank account (www.AxKC.net).

To date, no U.S. or Mexican legislation calling for comprehensive immigration reform and accounting for the United States and Mexico's mutual responsibility in fomenting the mass exodus of farmers from rural Mexico in the first place has been proposed. The United Nations Convention on the Status of Migrants and Their Families has, however, established a new set of rights for migrants who have been displaced by the trend toward the globalized economy. The Convention holds both sending and receiving countries responsible for the welfare of immigrants and proposes the goal of equal status for both migrant and non-migrant people. The United States has not ratified this guarantee of migrant human rights (Bacon 2005a). On the contrary, in June 2006, President Bush ordered the National Guard to further "protect and secure" the southern border. Operation Jump Start assigned 2,500 Guardsmen from across the nation to the Mexican border by the end of June, and a total of 6,000 over a two-year period, time enough to recruit and train 9,000 new Border Patrol officers (Billeaud 2006a; Clancy 2006).

In the meantime, as illustrated by innumerable undocumented immigration stories from countless immigrants who have made the journey to the United States from Mexico successfully, border crossings continue in record numbers, albeit at ever increasing cost to the migrant. *Coyotes* and undocumented border crossings are the institutions that serve to maintain the unprecedented flow of immigrants to the United States. Creative and inexhaustible illegal border crossing mechanisms plus an ever more sophisticated cadre of illegal human smugglers keep pace with sophisticated state-of-the-art border surveillance technologies, allowing passage of more than one million undocumented immigrants every year.

Once in the United States, migrants must contend with arbitrary, ever-changing, and ever more punitive immigration laws at both the state and federal level, along with potentially unscrupulous attorneys who prey on the farmworker community. While the number of undocumented immigrants in California continues to swell as they fill up rural farming communities in the central valley and elsewhere, most find employment in California's corporate agribusiness.

SIX

CALIFORNIA'S CORPORATE AGRIBUSINESS

En California la gente vive para trabajar; aquí en México, tra-bajamos para vivir.

In California people live to work; here in Mexico we work to live.

—José Martínez Espino, mango farmer and Director of Rural Development, Municipal Government, Coa-coyul/Zihuatanejo, Guerrero

Porque aquí está un poquito más esclavizado que en México . . . tiene uno que apegarse a sus leyes . . . leyes . . . reglas de . . . de la compañia.

Because here [in California, workers] are a bit more enslaved than they are in Mexico; one is obliged to adhere to the company rules.

—Lorenzo Vasquez, cauliflower picker, Salinas, California

Farmers and their family members who arrive from Mexico to work in the California central coast's corporate agribusiness as farm laborers become part of a farming system that is historically, politically, economically, and ethnically unique. The federal and state legislation governing the lives of farmworkers is often dualistic and arbitrary in both content and enforcement. One example is the manner in which border policy is enacted and enforced. When the need for undocumented labor in the fields of California's corporate agribusiness is high, border enforcement declines, regardless of the legislative mandates in effect at the time. Similarly, when the need for undocumented labor is low, border enforcement is increased (Hanson and Splimbergo 1999). Although the INS is responsible for enforcing immigration laws, in practice the Border Patrol has never had the budget, staffing, or apparent inclination to enforce the law at the California–Mexico border, largely because of pressures from agriculture (Wells 1996, 66).

GENERATION OF WEALTH AND PROSPERITY

California's corporate agribusiness is unique as the leader and pinnacle of modern capitalist agricultural development in the world today (Palerm 2000; Wells 1996). Wealth and prosperity abound (Taylor et al. 1997; Palerm 2000). California is the nation's most important food producer, generating more than half the nation's fruits, nuts, and vegetables and $27–$30 billion per year (Fernandes 2005; Martin 1989; Villarejo and Schenker 2005). The remarkable productivity of the land in combination with a mild climate results in greater output per acre in crop value than elsewhere in the nation.

From 1998 to 2000, the total value of principal commercial vegetable crops, both fresh market and for processing, increased by nearly $1 billion from about $4.7 billion in 1998 to more than $5.6 billion in 2000 (USDA 2001). By 2003, the total value had increased to almost $5.9 billion (USDA 2004). In contrast, yearly production value in Arizona and Texas is only a fraction of California's yearly production value, and vegetable crop values there actually declined in the 1998–2000 period and the 2001–3 period.

As the nation's leading agricultural producer in 2002 (*California Statistical Abstract* 2003), a growth industry, and a world leader of capital-intensive agricultural enterprises, California agribusiness is envied and emulated worldwide (Martin et al. 1995a; Palerm 2000). As a growth industry, California's agriculture was one of the few healthy sectors of the state's economy during a recent recession (Palerm 2000; Wells 1996). In the U.S. farm crisis year of 1986, California's fruit and vegetable crops increased in value by 12.3 percent (Wells 1996). A comparison of the three-year average crop production for 1970–72 with the three-year average crop production for 1990–92 shows a 98 percent increase (Villarejo and Runsten 1993).

Today California producers are enjoying the benefits of the globalized economy by marketing their products overseas. U.S. agricultural exports topped $53 billion in 2002, up from $11 billion ten years earlier. U.S. agricultural imports in the same year totaled $41 billion, for a trade surplus of 12 percent (USDA 2003). California agricultural exports in 1995 totaled $11.7 billion (Carter 1997). Almonds are California's largest agricultural export commodity, recording $662.4 million in export sales in 2000 and accounting for 71 percent of all California almond sales (Scripps-McClatchy Western Service 2001). A year later export almond sales reached $685.5 million (*California Statistical Abstract* 2003). Cotton ranked second, with exports worth $616.2 million, a gain in export value of 39 percent over 1999. Seventy-eight percent of California's cotton crop is exported (Scripps-McClatchy Western Service 2001).

In 1994, Fresno, Tulare, Kern, and Monterey counties combined led all other U.S. counties in the value of their crops, accounting for more that $6 billion, or approximately one-third of the year's California total (USDA 1995). Eight years later the crop values for these same four top agricultural counties had doubled to over $12 billion (*California Statistical Abstract* 2003). The central coast of California alone supports a nearly $8 billion agricultural industry that includes more than two hundred crops and employs more than 60,000 people (AWQA 2005; Diringer and Gilman 2006).

Monterey County

Salinas is located in the Salinas Valley of Monterey County. It is one of the richest farming regions in the world (FitzSimmons 1986) and is referred to as the nation's "salad bowl." Monterey County's 2003 agricultural commissioner's report boasts a page of "million dollar crops" (Lauritzen 2003, 19), including leaf lettuce valued at $552 million; head lettuce valued at $489 million; broccoli valued at $280 million; and strawberries valued at $253 million.

In 2000, the gross production value for head and leaf lettuce in Monterey County alone was $775 million, an increase of nearly $200 million over the preceding year (Lauritzen 2000). By 2003, the gross production value for head and leaf lettuce had increased to over $1 billion (Lauritzen 2003), an increase of more than $250 million from 2000. The county's gross value of agricultural production in general steadily increased from $1.93 billion in 1994 (Palerm 2000) to $2.37 billion in 1999 to $2.92 billion in 2000 (California Agricultural Statistics Service 2001, 1). By 2003, the gross value of agricultural production had increased to $3.29 billion, an increase of 10 percent over 2000.

Monterey County producers are becoming even more affluent by exporting produce. In 2003, 520 million pounds of produce was exported. The top produce export commodities were lettuce, broccoli, celery, strawberries, cauliflower, carrots, green onions, asparagus, and tomatoes. In addition, county producers exported almost 17 million pounds of nursery stock, 3 million pounds of seeds, and over 200,000 pounds of cut flowers (Lauritzen 2003, 17).

Santa Cruz County

Watsonville is located in Santa Cruz County, and strawberries are the county's most lucrative crop, with per-acre net returns surpassing those of almost every other crop in the state (Wells 1996). In 1999 the gross farm income from strawberries for Santa Cruz County alone was more than $109 million, while strawberry acreage increased from 2,716 in 1998 to 3,458. By 2003 the value of Santa Cruz County's strawberry crop had increased to more than $121 million. Even though total acreage planted in strawberries declined slightly, from 3,586 acres countywide in 2002 to 3,201 acres in 2003, production in tons per acre actually increased, from 25.6 in 2002 to 26.81 in 2003 (Moeller 1999, 2003).

Total berry production in Santa Cruz County, including strawberries, red raspberries, and bush berries, yielded a gross farm income of over $133 million in 1999 and increased by over $100 million to almost $239 million within the next four years (Moeller 1999, 2003). Santa Cruz County agricultural commodities sold for $289 million in 1997, representing a 13.2 percent increase over 1996 (California Agricultural Statistics Service 1997). By 2003 the total gross production value of Santa Cruz County agricultural commodities had grown to more than $371 million (Moeller 2003).

Strawberries

California is the U.S. leader in strawberry production, accounting for 82 percent of the nation's strawberry crop. With growers investing $30,000 in each acre (Hamilton 2004), strawberries are farmed so efficiently and intensively that each acre produces an average of 21 tons annually. The central coast is one of two regions in California where most of the strawberry crop, both conventional and organic, is harvested (Ohmart 2003).

Statewide, the 1995 gross farm income from strawberries was $552 million (Johnston 1997). By 2003 the total value of California's strawberry crop had increased to almost $778 million (California Agricultural Statistics Service 2003), with 32,636 acres planted in strawberries in the state (California Strawberry Commission 2005). In 2003, over 16 million trays of fresh strawberries and 22.9 million pounds of frozen strawberries were exported. Fresh strawberry exports surpassed those of 2002 by 26.9 percent (California Strawberry Commission 2004).

Together, Santa Cruz and Monterey Counties constitute the largest single strawberry-producing region in California (Wells 1996). With 10,759 acres devoted to strawberry production in 2001 (California Strawberry Commission 2001) and 12,250 planted in strawberries in 2005, the region boasts 37.5 percent of the state's strawberry acreage (California Strawberry Commission 2005). Four-fifths of the U.S. strawberry crop originates from agribusinesses in the Watsonville area, and 20,000 workers are employed there in the strawberry industry alone (Maestas-Flores 1997).

U.S. fresh produce buyers prefer lucrative California strawberries because they have the highest quality and longest shelf life (Wells 1996). Strawberries and cherry tomatoes are California's most capital- and labor-intensive crops (Palerm 1991). Approximately 50 percent of the $25,000–$30,000 invested by a grower in each acre for strawberry production is expended on the labor necessary to grow and harvest this valuable specialty crop (Wells 1996).

Particularly in the Pajaro Valley, growers have the highest nonlabor investments in their crops per acre (Wells 1996). Eduardo Sousa claims that in 2000, Coastal Berry's 800-acre company invested $1,100 per acre to fumigate with methyl bromide, and approximately $25,000 was spent per acre for labor and other expenses. He indicated that to become a strawberry grower on a small farm of 3–5 acres would require an initial investment of at least $25,000. Because of their high investment, growers are keenly interested in developing labor crews with a strong commitment to quality labor. They are especially interested in worker satisfaction and invest in the stability, care, and commitment of labor (Wells 1996).

LAND PRODUCTION AND CONSOLIDATION

California agriculture is different from agriculture elsewhere in the nation in several ways: land consolidation has resulted in land tenure dominated by large holdings which, overall, are larger than farms elsewhere in the nation; the productivity of the land in combination with climate results in greater output per acre in crop value than in other regions; and California farms are completely dependent upon hired labor, rather than on family labor, for most of the work in the fields.

In combination, these three characteristics result in an agricultural system that can best be described as "industrial," with "farms" that have the characteristics of factories: "factories in the field" (McWilliams 1939). Agricultural industrialization includes "increased labor productivity, purchased farm inputs and machines, crop specialization, land reorganization, huge irrigation works, international markets, complex output processing, and the appearance of large corporations" (FitzSimmons 1986). This agribusiness system, which can be traced historically to the original Spanish land grant system that preceded California statehood, is unique in all the world (Runsten 1981).

California's agriculture has been characterized historically by a trend toward land and production consolidation. Over time, huge tracts of land became concentrated into the hands of a few wealthy landowners (FitzSimmons 1986). This trend can be seen in three separate stages in the history of California land acquisition and distribution (McWilliams 1939).

Centralization of land ownership can be traced to Mexican land grants originally issued to Mexicans under Spanish rule, prior to 1844 when California was a province of Mexico. The Mexican War of 1846–48 and ensuing Treaty of Guadalupe Hidalgo brought U.S. statehood to California. At this time, the Spanish land grants were transferred directly to individuals through various unscrupulous political and legal machinations. In addition, the federal government gave huge tracts of land to railroad companies for the development of a transportation system. Southern Pacific Railroad was a key beneficiary.

Inaccurate land speculation also contributed to California agricultural land centralization. The federal government gave large areas of "wastelands" to the state government. Speculators were subsequently allowed to place a monetary value on the land. In so doing they purposely devalued the land. The "wasteland" was then sold for ridiculously low prices, sometimes as little as $0.25 per acre. Greedy speculators could then buy up large tracts of land easily (McWilliams 1939).

By the 1930s, fourteen men and a few railroads owned most of the land in California. These land monopolies were the most important contributing factors to the industrialization and development of capitalist agribusiness in California (McWilliams 1939). Initially, the cattle ranching activities of the Mexican period were replaced by extensive wheat

Figure 10. Industrialized agricultural "factories in the field": broccoli harvest with mechanized processing and packing, off Boronda Road, Salinas, California.

farming throughout the state. Wheat grown in California was exported to a lucrative European market. Sugar beets succeeded wheat in the late 1800s. In the early 1900s, with the completion of the railroads connecting California and the East Coast, farmers began to diversify their crops. Field crops such as sugar beets and barley were gradually replaced by a growing fresh vegetable industry (Palerm 2000).

The shift to labor-intensive specialty crops, including strawberries, fresh vegetables, wine grapes, and nursery crops, occurred after World War II as a result of the development of transportation, storage methods, and new markets (Wells 1996). By 1978, for example, specialty crops occupied 85 percent of the harvested land in the Salinas Valley (FitzSimmons 1986). From 1960 to 1989, fruit and vegetable crop acreage increased by nearly 200 percent throughout the state, while field crop acreage decreased by more than 60 percent (Palerm 1991). Between 1980 and 1994, the share of the state's farm value attributable to field crops decreased dramatically while fruit and vegetable production increased dramatically (Palerm 2000).

In Santa Barbara and San Luis Obispo counties, labor-intensive, high-value crops such as snow peas, baby vegetables, vine tomatoes, tomatillos, and grapes replaced grain and livestock (Palerm 1994). Specialty crops have now completely displaced grains and dry beans in the central coast area (Wells 1996).

The amount of land farmed in California has remained relatively stable, at about 37 percent, or 36,600,000 acres, since 1945. However, the trend has been toward a dramatic decrease in the overall number of farms with the consolidation of farmland into fewer, ever-larger farms. In 1945 there were 138,917 California farms. By 1972 the number had fallen to 57,000, with 12.2 percent of all farms in ownership of almost 32 million acres (Thomas and Friedland 1982).

Prior to 1960, nearly four thousand farms produced tomatoes for processing. By 1972, with the introduction of the tomato harvester, the number had declined to less than seven hundred (Friedland et al. 1975). In 1940 the three largest lettuce growers accounted for less than 20 percent of all lettuce production in California and Arizona. By 1978, four of the largest grower-shippers were responsible for shipping about 40 percent of California/Arizona lettuce (Friedland and Thomas 1978).

In the 1990s, increased crop yields and values occurred at a time when total farm acreage and cost of farm wages declined (Villarejo and Runsten 1993). In the late 1990s and the new millennium, production has become more intensive, creating more value, more jobs, and more income for the state (Palerm 2000). Currently the largest 2.5 percent of California farms operate 60 percent of the state's cropland, and net farm incomes are 2.5 times the national average (Wells 1996, 22).

In 1996 in Santa Cruz County alone, of 58 vegetable farms, seven farms of more than 500 acres accounted for 78 percent of vegetable acreage. Of 149 tree and vine farms, ten farms of 100 acres or more accounted for 42 percent of all tree and vine crops. Of 127 berry farms, twenty-two farms greater than 100 acres accounted for 58 percent of berry farm acreage (Runsten 1998).

The "reintensification" (Palerm 2000; Wells 1996; Zavella 2000) of agriculture that began in the late 1970s and 1980s has been accompanied by an expanded growing season. The high employment season, which formerly extended from May to September, is gradually becoming protracted. The protracted growing season, in turn, requires an ever-greater labor force to grow and harvest the specialty crops effectively. California agriculture has thus become more dependent on migrant labor over the past few decades. Farm labor requirements for crops such as almonds, lettuce, strawberries, broccoli, and cauliflower doubled from 1970 to 1989 (Palerm 1991).

ETHNIC SUCCESSION AND DEPENDENCE UPON A HIRED LABOR FORCE

In California's corporate agribusiness, control over labor costs is often the single most important determinant of profitability (Wells 1996). In order for growers to accumulate capital as a result of crop sales, they need to control the price and performance of manual labor. Labor costs in fruit and vegetable agriculture are typically 20–40 percent of the total cost of crop production (Martin 1989). As indicated earlier, the cost of manual labor in strawberries is even higher, at approximately 50 percent of the total per acre expenditure. Indeed, harvest labor costs in this crop have increased steadily over the years (Wells 1996, 49). Growers have limited control over the market value of their crops, and they cannot reduce the costs of inputs. Thus, the costs of labor as well as labor quality are critical as more flexible components of the production process over which the grower has some control.

Wealth generation in California's corporate agribusiness is, in turn, uniquely dependent upon the labor of a tractable, low-paid labor force, characteristically "invisible" and detached from mainstream California society. The invisibility and disconnection can be accounted for by ethnic and linguistic dissimilarities as well as by the often-isolated geographic location of farm labor housing.

Historically, whenever an ethnic group associated with farm labor became too militant for growers to control, threatened growers typically organized and employed a variety of tactics, including violence and murder, to suppress potential strikers. With local, state, and federal law enforcement acquiescing to or supporting them, growers have been instrumental in reinstating the tractable labor force status quo by either forcing compliance by the existing ethnic group or ousting the perceived militant ethnic group and recruiting an entirely new foreign immigrant labor force. Two illustrations of the development of worker militancy and the resultant grower-instigated repercussions are the sugar beet strike of 1903 (Almaguer 1994) and the cotton workers' strike of 1939 (Ruiz 1987).

In addition to grower-initiated suppression of militant farmworkers and unionization, strict statewide legislation is often enacted which compounds the growers' and mainstream society's attempts to restore the group to the former, more familiar status of compliance and invisibility.

In a familiar cycle sometimes referred to as "ethnic succession" (Zabin et al. 1993), ethnic recruitment is followed by eventual ethnic militancy and visibility, punitive grower-instigated retaliation, enactment of discriminatory legislation, the return of that group to invisibility, and recruitment of a new ethnic minority to work in the fields. Such a sequence has occurred repeatedly in California (Friedland and Barton 1975).

In the late 1800s, beginning with the Chinese who worked in the fields after the completion of the transcontinental railroad, a succession of ethnically diverse farm laborers have been recruited to cultivate and harvest crops. In 1882, as a result of the increasing visibility of Chinese workers and their success in purchasing farmlands, the first Chinese Exclusion Act was passed in 1882, effectively excluding Chinese from land ownership in California. The Geary Act of 1892 continued the provisions of the 1882 Exclusion Act and provided for the deportation of all illegal Chinese (McWilliams 1939).

While Chinese were being legislatively discriminated against by the state, growers began to quietly recruit Japanese as the next ethnic group destined for the difficult hand labor required for beet cultivation. Japanese were purported to have the characteristics deemed valuable by the growers—docile, uncomplaining and obviously foreign in a land of predominantly Anglo men and women (Kushner 1975).

Largely in response to Japanese ingenuity, competition, and success at leasing and purchasing California agricultural land, the grower-supported Alien Lands Acts were passed in California in 1913 and 1920. This legislation prohibited foreign-born Japanese from leasing or owning land in the United States. After the enactment of this legislation, most Japanese workers became sharecroppers in California's central coastal farmlands (Wells 1996). The federal Immigration Law of 1924 further restricted Japanese immigration to the United States, and Japanese internment in concentration camps in 1942 effectively removed them as laborers and competitors from all sectors of California society.

Hindu workers appeared in California's agricultural fields for a few years between 1907 and 1910. Hindus in the Imperial Valley harvested the first cotton harvest of any commercial value. Subsequently, Hindus quickly moved into farm ownership. After their success in farm acquisition, the Immigration Act of 1917 was enacted to exclude further Hindu immigration.

Growers recruited Mexican workers as many fled Mexico in the wake of the revolution of 1910. By the time the Dust Bowl "Okies" and "Arkies" succeeded Japanese and Hindu workers in the 1930s, approximately 75,000 Mexicans were working as farm laborers (McWilliams 1939).

John Steinbeck's *Grapes of Wrath* poignantly elucidates the plight of the Dust Bowlers and California's agricultural fields as sites of illness, impoverishment, servitude, and other forms of oppression. During the Depression years, with the migration of the Okies and Arkies in the 1930s, over 50,000 Mexican workers, many of whom had acquired U.S. citizenship, were deported (Kushner 1975). Older Mexican Americans in the United States today continue to harbor the scars and sense of betrayal elicited by their own deportation experiences (Olivo 2001).

Growers, however, continued to look to Mexico for a supply of cheap labor that was efficient and docile. Mexican laborers in the early 1900s were believed to be the perfect solution since they either would return to Mexico after the harvest or could easily be deported (Kushner 1975). For the past sixty years, California growers have depended primarily on Mexican nationals and Mexican Americans to work in the fields (Palerm 2000).

Along with Mexicans, a large number of Filipinos have historically been hired as farm laborers. Many Americans viewed the influx of Filipinos into the fields with alarm, as the third successive "invasion" of Asians into the domestic labor force. Growers, by contrast, often viewed Filipinos as more desirable than Mexicans, since they were perceived to be even more docile, low-paid, and hard working (Kushner 1975). Filipinos have, however, been some of the most active organizers in the field (see below).

There is a hierarchy of farmworkers and their experiences. The conditions of corporate agribusiness employment in California are largely dependent upon the stratum on which new recruits find themselves on the farmworker hierarchy. New migrants often replace settled farmworkers who work directly for unions, growers, or growers associations (Lloyd et al. 1988; Mines and Anzaldua 1982).

Currently, the California farm labor market is undergoing a new cycle of ethnic replacement. California growers and farm labor contractors now have access to Mixtec workers from Oaxaca, who are at the bottom of the ethnically stratified farm labor force. The sharply rising flow of indigenous migrants from southern Mexico is the most significant development within the California farm labor market in recent years (Villarejo and Schenker 2005). Their vulnerable situation forces the migrants to accept lower wages and poorer working conditions than *mestizo* (of Spanish and American Indian descent) Mexicans who are at higher levels on the hierarchy and still make up the majority of the California farm labor force (Zabin et al. 1993). To date, Mixtec workers are beginning to appear in significant numbers in central coast agriculture. The number of farmworkers of indigenous origin is growing rapidly and is often considered the fastest-growing segment of California's farmworker population (Aguirre International 2005).

Historically, employer recruitment of successive, ethnically differentiated, foreign-born workforces has been the most important factor in wage depression and the maintenance of agricultural wages at a level that is substantially below that of manufacturing jobs (Zabin et al. 1993). Each successive wave of migrants unintentionally fosters wage depression by their willingness to work for lower wages than their predecessors (Palerm 1991, 1993).

Though California's agriculture has undergone major changes in recent years with its reintensification, transition to fewer and larger farms, mechanization, and greater production of fruit and vegetables resulting from greater consumer demand, hired farmworker employment has not changed (Martin 1989; Palerm 2000). Communities of stable, settled farmworkers who were able to break through recurrent cycles of poverty have never developed in the state (Zabin et al. 1993).

AGRICULTURAL EXCEPTIONALISM

Just as U.S. immigration law and court proceedings operate with a separate and unique interpretation of "due process," California farmworkers are subject to employment laws that are unique to the farming system and different from those affecting workers in the manufacturing sector (Martin and Taylor 1995c). The differential treatment of agriculture and agricultural workers and their exclusion from most protective labor legislation originated primarily from government's attempts to deal with the agricultural crisis of the 1920s. Agriculture has consistently been presented as a special case that should be governed by separate laws in order to protect the nation's food supply. Other arguments include the seasonality of the work, the unpredictability of weather patterns, and the perishability of agricultural products (Heppel and Papademetriou 2001).

Another contributing factor to the paucity of protective legislation for farmworkers has been the decades-old, generally romanticized perception of American family farms. A distinction between farming as a way of life on Midwestern farms and the profit-seeking motivation of California's corporate agribusiness has never been made legislatively (Martin 1989; Martin and Taylor 1995a). The confusion has resulted in government legislative intervention in agriculture that has favored large, commercial farms, still perceived as "family farms," over actual small and medium-size family farms with less political representation (de Janvry et al. 1988). The resulting principle of "agricultural exceptionalism" continues to guide national policy (Heppel and Papademetriou 2001).

An example that occurred in November 1999 illustrates this point. The federal Occupational Safety and Health Administration proposed an ergonomics standard that would regulate workplace hazards that cause musculoskeletal (back and neck) injuries, the most common source of injuries and physical complaints among the farmworkers in my study. The proposed standard would cover workers in general industry but would exclude agricultural workers (Davis 2000).

Another example: As part of New Deal legislation, the Fair Labor Standards Act of 1938 was designed to curtail poverty among workers by establishing a minimum wage, discouraging excessively long hours of work, and eliminating child labor. Farm laborers were completely excluded from these legislated protections (de Janvry et al. 1988). California set the standard work week for farm and agricultural processing workers at sixty hours.

Agricultural workers are also not entitled to overtime pay for work performed beyond the federally mandated forty-hour work week. Furthermore, though the minimum age in nonagricultural jobs is 16 years, children of 12 or 13 can be employed in agriculture as long as their employment is outside school hours and takes place in a nonhazardous environment (Heppel and Papademetriou 2001). Currently teenagers 14–17 years old, very young teens, and preteens make up an estimated 6–10 percent of the U.S. harvest labor force (Aguirre International 2000).

Documented immigrant farm laborers lack privileges and supports that are extended to citizens. Their presence in the United States and access to benefits is directly contingent upon active labor force participation. They must have an offer of employment before entering the country. They can be deported if they are unemployed for a long period. They are eligible for unemployment insurance and workers' compensation insurance, but they may not receive state or federal welfare assistance until they have lived in the country for five continuous years (Wells 1996).

The National Labor Relations Act of 1935 provides employees with the right to organize and bargain collectively. However, farmworkers continue to be completely excluded from this law. The California Agricultural Labor Relations Act, signed into law on June 5, 1975, has provided some legal concessions to farmworkers, giving them the right to organize, the right to hold harvest-time elections, and the right to bargain collectively without employer interference. This law also provides an avenue for the determination of and prevention of unfair labor practices. An appointed counsel and five-member board, the Agricultural Labor Relations Board, was created to address farmworker complaints and unfair labor practices (Wells 1996). The effectiveness of the Board in supporting farmworkers with grievances is, however, entirely dependent upon the prevailing political climate in Sacramento and the political ideologies of the governor-appointed board members (see below).

Even with some semblance of protective legislation in California, farmworkers remain unhealthy (Villarejo 2001; Villarejo et al. 2000) and impoverished and continue to work long hours without appropriate compensation. At the height of the strawberry season in June and July in Watsonville, California, many spend up to 13 hours per day, six or seven days per week, bent over at the waist, picking strawberries in 90-plus degree heat.

Several farmworkers in this study are United Farm Workers or Teamster union members. Others are in regular contact with Western Service Workers in Santa Cruz, an organization that represents and supports low-income workers. Yet, in spite of their difficult employment circumstances, none of the farmworkers interviewed for this study appear to be knowledgeable of the very few rights and protections they do have under federal or California state law.

FARM LABOR ATTEMPTS TO ORGANIZE

Overall, one of the biggest fears haunting growers in their relationship with farmworkers has always been that of union organization among exploited workers. Along with the persistent fostering of prejudice against anyone "foreign," growers have always sought to maintain the status quo through four principal strategies: overrecruitment of workers for harvesting crops; pitting of ethnic groups against each other; repatriation programs; and manipulation of agrarian mythology to gain community support for undermining worker organizations and breaking strikes (Guerin-Gonzales 1985)

Historically, employers often provided separate encampments for laborers of different ethnic groups in order to promote distance and distrust among them. Myths were central in maintaining the caste labor sys-

Figure 11. *Los agachados* ("the bent over ones"), strawberry pickers, Watsonville, California.

tem in California agriculture by promoting Mexicans as transient workers who return to Mexico and minimizing the reality of their contribution to corporate agribusiness development in the state.

The remarkable success of Cesar Chavez and other core organizers of the United Farm Workers (UFW) in the creation of an enduring farm labor organization can largely be attributed to a unique and brilliant style of labor organizing. Chavez brought techniques used in community organizing from his work with the Community Service Organization to the task of organizing farmworkers. He named his initial organization the National Farm Workers Association (NFWA). His strategy involved building solidarity by offering services to farmworkers. By serving genuine needs and developing organizations within which farmworkers could develop trust, Chavez and the NFWA founders created a climate for forging bonds of solidarity among workers (Thomas and Friedland 1982).

Chavez and his group of organizers traveled extensively throughout the state, making personal contact with farmworkers and establishing information networks. Ethnic, cultural, and religious symbols were also used to promote unification. Most meetings were conducted in Spanish.

The community organizing phase of the movement was a time when an extensive organizational infrastructure of farmworkers was developed and solidarity among farmworkers congealed (del Castillo and Garcia 1995).

Chavez was successful in union organizing because he so brilliantly organized and forged alliances with multiple constituents, including consumers, church and political leaders, and students. Many alliances were formed with powerful community figures such as Father Donald McDonnell, a Roman Catholic priest in San José, and Father Thomas McCullough of the Archdiocese of San Francisco. Concurrently, he politicized farmworkers so that they engaged in huge public protests. The protests encouraged farmworker visibility and renewed public support for the plight of farmworkers (Kushner 1975).

By the summer of 1965, several social, political, and economic factors were in place to provide a fertile context for the development of the UFW and new protective farm labor legislation. As a result of the work of the Industrial Workers of the World and the Cannery and Agricultural Workers Industrial Union, a precedent had been set for solidarity among farmworkers of all creeds, nationalities, and cultures. The exploitation of farmworkers by employers advertising jobs in excess of those available was exposed by the Wheatland riots. An ABC television documentary, *Harvest of Shame,* aired in 1960 and exposed the deplorable work and living conditions of U.S. farmworkers (Majka and Majka 1982). The Bracero Program had ended, and the civil rights movement was in full swing with prominent supporters such as Dr. Martin Luther King and Robert Kennedy. Everywhere among the country's youth, capitalist individualism was under sharp attack. In addition, an unpopular war in Vietnam was philosophically tearing the country apart. With their involvement in the Delano grape strike, Cesar Chavez and his farmworkers would become a lightning rod for a much greater movement of the time—a movement that included all those individuals who shared a commitment to end the injustices of racism, the war in Vietnam, the suffering of the poor, and the degradation of farmworkers.

The Delano grape strike developed out of a protest by Filipino workers who were members of the Agricultural Workers Organizing Committee (AWOC) over wage inequities. Early in 1965, California growers in the Coachella Valley received a temporary dispensation from the labor department to allow the importation of braceros to harvest the grape crop. Braceros were to be paid $1.40 per hour. For the same work, Filipino workers received $1.25 per hour and Mexican Americans received $1.10 per hour (Kushner 1975).

In May, AWOC went on strike and won a raise for both Mexican American and Filipino workers. With continuing strikes, the Filipinos eventually recruited NFWA for support. The Delano grape strike covered a 400 square mile area and involved thousands of workers. The organizational efforts of the UFW that resulted in the strikes and national consumer boycotts were unsurpassed in the history of U.S. farm labor organizing. Initially three crops were targeted: table grapes, wine grapes, and lettuce (Kushner 1975; Wells 1996). Ultimately, on July 29, 1970, twenty-six Delano employers of more than 7,000 workers signed the historic table grape agreement. By 1977 the union had won 180 separate contracts to administer in the grape, lettuce, tomato, strawberry, and nursery industries (Thomas and Friedland 1982).

The UFW found a willing and militant concentration of farmworkers in the Salinas Valley. Many in leadership positions in the lettuce industry were ex-braceros. Having survived the injustices of the bracero era in the United States, they were highly class conscious, hostile to growers, and receptive to union activity (Wells 1996). Strikes involving Salinas Valley lettuce workers were also particularly militant and effective because lettuce workers tend to work in unified crews, putting organization and solidarity among workers in place before the strikes. The UFW initiated a paralyzing general strike in August–September 1970, which spread to and decimated the strawberry harvests that year (Wells 1996). Meanwhile, central coast turmoil was further enhanced by heated and often violent confrontations between the UFW and Teamsters regarding union representation.

Ultimately, the UFW was a major force behind the extension of the minimum wage, unemployment insurance, and workers' compensation insurance to farmworkers. It was also instrumental in the passage of California's Agricultural Labor Relations Act and the establishment of the Agricultural Labor Relations Board (ALRB) in 1975. The chaos of this period of California's farm labor history is detailed in the Board's records; its Salinas office is at the top of the list for number of union election petitions and unfair labor practices charges filed from 1975 through 1981 (Wells 1996). The reverberations of UFW striking farmworkers in central coast agricultural industries continue to influence growers' relationships with farmworkers today.

The unanticipated death of Cesar Chavez on April 23, 1993, as well as dissension within the UFW curtailed union momentum and effectiveness in the following decades. By 1984 only fifteen of seventy grape growers in the Delano area were under union contract (del Castillo and Garcia 1995). The union won fewer and fewer elections, membership dropped considerably, fewer and fewer strikes occurred, and the UFW reduced the number of organizers in the fields.

By 1980, with the defeat of Proposition 14 and the election of Ronald Reagan as president, the country began to take on a more conservative mood. In California this resulted in the appointment of pro-grower representatives to the Farm Labor Board (del Castillo and Garcia 1995). The new representatives consistently ruled against the union in many of the grievances brought before it. Newly elected Republican governor George Deukmejian slashed the ALRB's budget and appointed board members hostile to the UFW. The number of unfair labor practice charges that were moved forward fell sharply. The UFW charged that fewer workers were willing to challenge their employers' conduct because they did not expect fair treatment by the ALRB. Ultimately, the UFW withdrew its participation from the ALRB completely (Wells 1996).

Though the current UFW staff and membership are but a small vestige of their size and strength during the 1970s, the union persists, in spite of the many political and economic obstacles it continues to encounter. Its longevity of over thirty years has earned it the distinction of being farm labor's longest-lived and most durable union (Thomas and Friedland 1982; Wells 1996).

Although Chávez and the UFW provided brilliant and effective organizational strategies that resulted in temporary victories for farmworkers throughout the state, interview data acquired in this study suggest that the UFW has lost its pervasive appeal among farmworkers. Indeed, many farmworkers expressed outright indignation about the organization and justified their indignation by citing a variety of complaints ranging from nonresponsiveness to union members' complaints to suspected graft within the organization. The *Los Angeles Times* corroborated these views in a detailed four-part series on the UFW in January 2006 entitled "UFW: A Broken Contract" (*Los Angeles Times* 2006). The articles allege that the UFW is no longer focused on organizing farmworkers to confront their oppressive circumstances but rather on garnering memberships and donations, while financing projects that frequently have little to do with the improvement of farmworker working conditions and well-being.

In the meantime, most farmworkers today continue to suffer the same inhumane conditions and indignities of the past. Cesar Chavez is dead, and with the exception of some minor concessions and contrived grower appeasement mechanisms the plight of farmworkers remains as difficult as in earlier periods of the state's history. Farmworkers continue their lives as the poorest of the state's and nation's working poor and, in many instances, have once again become publicly invisible (Griffith and Kissam 1995; Jourdane 2004).

SEVEN

FARMWORKERS IN CENTRAL CALIFORNIA'S CORPORATE AGRIBUSINESS

People in California are slaves to their work.

—Consuelo Fernandez, mushroom picker, Watsonville, California

Estaría bueno andar como perro, digo, los perros andan con cuatro patas. Digo, a lo mejor no va doler ya uno allí.

It would be good [to walk like] a dog. Dogs walk on four feet. At least as a dog, one wouldn't be in pain.

—Roberto Fonseca, disabled strawberry picker Watsonville, California

It's 5:00 A.M. at Elena Esparza's Watsonville apartment in a low-income housing unit sandwiched between agricultural fields, far removed from the actual city of Watsonville. The alarm sounds, and Elena's hand emerges from under the warm covers. She gropes for the button on the alarm clock that will switch off the offending noise. While the rest of the family continues their slumber, she takes a few moments to sleepily re-view the events and expectations of the day. She checks the clock face again: 5:05, time to get up.

Elena nudges her husband Emanuel in an attempt to wake him. He worked twelve hours picking mushrooms yesterday and didn't arrive home till late. Neither Elena nor Emanuel have ever figured out what the odd odor that permeates his clothing at the *honguera* (mushroom farm) is. All they know is that, when he returns home from work, the first thing he has to do is take off all his clothes and quickly bathe in order to prevent the odor from spreading throughout the house.

Emanuel and Elena emerge from their bed. While Emanuel gets dressed, Elena throws on a robe and shuffles to the two adjoining bedrooms to wake the couple's five children. As the oldest four children sleepily get dressed and wash up, Elena wakes and dresses two-year old Jaime. In a flurry of activity, she makes lunches for all five children, her husband, and herself while passing out granola bars to her four older children for breakfast on the schoolbus en route to school. She dresses quickly and takes Jaime to the babysitter, who lives in an apartment nearby. By 6:00, Elena and Emanuel's apartment is empty, as each family member enters the outside world to start their day.

Elena drives an old Chevy pickup to her job at Rancho Santa Maria near the Santa Cruz County fairgrounds. It's a half-hour drive from the family's apartment. On the way she experiences the familiar pangs of anxiety. "What if the police stop me? They'll confiscate my car and send me back to Mexico. What will happen to my children?" Fortunately, she's always made it to work without being apprehended. Because she is undocumented, she can't get a license or automobile insurance. She recounts with agitation in her voice, "If I'm ever stopped for a traffic violation, my whole world will fall apart."

As she drives along, with fields of strawberries and blackberries whisking by her on either side of the road, she is further plagued by thoughts of her husband's precarious work environment. Though he has a valid green card, he works in an agroindustry that is notorious for worker accidents. Four of their neighbors fell off the walkways surrounding some of the highest mushroom beds onto the concrete floor below and were severely injured. None have been able to return to work, and their disability payments are minimal compared to the money they earned in year-round work. Teenage sons of relatives in Mexico were forced to immigrate to Watsonville for work in order to continue the flow of remittance money to Mexico that supports other family members and disabled workers and their families, both in Mexico and in the United States. The disabled workers' spouses continue to work in the field.

Elena recalls the frightening images Emanuel created in her mind as he described his first days cutting mushrooms from the highest serial "mushroom beds" positioned from floor to ceiling. "My legs were trembling so much as I stood on the foot-wide walkways that I could hardly work. I was afraid that I'd trip, fall off the ramp, and end up paralyzed like our neighbor, Gonzalo. I think I am gradually getting used to working in the high beds, though, and I feel much steadier on the walkway now."

By 6:30, Elena arrives at her seasonal job at Rancho Santa Maria. Her anxiety is allayed as she leisurely converses with other workers until 7:00, when the workers enter the blackberry and raspberry rows to begin the day's harvest. She will earn $3.10 per hour, plus $2.15 for each case of twelve baskets picked. When the berry harvest is plentiful—mid-May to mid-June and mid-August to October, Elena can pick three to four cases per hour, for an hourly salary of $9.55–$11.70.

On the other hand, when the berry bushes aren't producing abundantly, at the very beginning and end of the harvest season, she harvests only a single case in an hour, for an hourly salary of only $5.25, which is $1.50 below California's minimum wage of $6.75 per hour. To make matters worse, she loses her seniority with the company every two years at the end of the season. That's when her boss checks her green card and discovers once again that her Social Security number is bogus. She is then required to return to work the following season with a new fake green card, at the bottom of the seniority list. She and her boss have done this dance for several years now. They both know the routine well.

The benefits of seniority include the opportunity to work the longest and most productive stretches during the harvest season. Elena's documented co-workers are able to quit early at the end of the season because they can draw unemployment and financially survive the intervening winter months until the next year's harvest season begins. Their unemployment checks are just about equivalent to what their income would be if they picked berries during a light harvest for $5.25 per hour. So why work at all during this time?

Of course, Elena is ineligible for such benefits. She wishes that she had an unemployed female relative with a valid green card like her undocumented sister-in-law, Elsa Gonzalez. Elsa also immigrated from Huacao, Michoacán, and has used her mother's name and green card with a valid Social Security number for the past two years she has worked for the company. Since her mother doesn't work, Elsa works right alongside Elena in the blackberry fields and enjoys all the benefits of progressively higher seniority status over time. At the end of the season when the Social Security numbers are checked, Elsa passes the test with flying colors and is able to move to a higher seniority rank the following season.

However, Elena reflects on Elsa's *coyote* debt when she first arrived in the United States. Whereas Elena and her family arrived in Watsonville debt free because they earned money to pay for their *coyote* before crossing, Elsa's first order of business when she arrived here was to work to pay back her family members who put up the money for her $3,500 border crossing (see chapter 4). As a new lowest-wage employee at the bottom of the seniority hierarchy, and with the inclement weather that plagued the region in 2001 and 2002, Elsa had to labor nearly an entire year as an indentured worker to support herself while paying off the debt. She was unable to save any money at all that year, but she was relieved at the end of the year when the balance due was finally cleared.

Elena works hard throughout the day, with 15-minute breaks at 10:00 and 3:00. She enjoys her half-hour lunch break at noon, when she can exchange information about family members with other relatives and friends. She reflects on the fact that, even though she loses seniority every two years, she is fortunate to be working in organic bush berry fields where she doesn't have to worry about her cotton clothes, sweater, hat, and *pañuelo* (bandana) absorbing the terrible odor from chemicals that Emanuel returns home with from the mushroom farm. She also is grateful that she doesn't pick strawberries and have to work all day bent at the waist. Furthermore, she is thankful for the plastic chairs offered by the company at lunchtime. Before this "benefit" was instituted as company policy, she and her co-workers ate their lunch seated on the ground at the side of the road.

It's late April, and today Elena will leave the fields early, at 3:30, after only seven or eight hours of work. She's gearing up for the big harvest that begins May 15. At that time she can expect to work 10 1/2 hours per day without overtime pay. She's pleased to have the opportunity to work and earn more money for her family at this time of the year, but she complains about the terrible fatigue she experiences at the end of each workday and on her one day off per week.

THE MEXICAN AGRICULTURAL LABOR FORCE

Nationwide, more than two million year-round and seasonal migrant farmworkers, including 100,000 children, work in U.S. agriculture (Oxfam 2004). Thirty-six percent, an estimated 684,000 individuals (Aguirre International 2005), are employed in California's corporate agribusiness each year by 35,000 employers (Campos and Kotkin-Jaszi 1987; Furillo 2001; Martin 1989, 2001; Martin and Mason 2003; Olvera 2001; Palerm 2000; *Sacramento Bee* 2001; Villarejo 2001). Forty-four percent of the nation's fruit, vegetable, and horticultural farm laborers are hired in California (Aguirre International 2005). About 95 percent of California's agricultural labor force is immigrant, and almost all workers are Latino from Mexico (Oxfam 2004).

Though there are no definitive accurate data regarding the number of undocumented workers currently holding down jobs in the United States, it is estimated that about half of farmworkers here, 25 percent of household workers, and 10 percent of restaurant employees are undocumented (Malone 2002; Perrin and Williams 1999). In California, undocumented farmworker estimates run as high as 85 percent (M. Jourdane, personal communication, 2005). One in ten farmworkers is a U.S. citizen (Aguirre International 2005).

In Monterey and Santa Cruz counties, 93 percent of farmworkers are Mexican or Mexican American and 97 percent are Spanish speaking (Parsons 2001). In contrast, 90 percent of California growers are of European descent (Zabin et al. 1993). Depending on the crop, 20 percent (Martin and Mason 2003; Aguirre International 2005) to 50 percent (Palerm 1991, 2000) of California's farmworkers are women. Women are broadly represented in the strawberry and bush berry industries of central California.

Monterey County was home to the third-largest California county farmworker population in 2000, with an estimated 86,941 farmworkers, including 46,687 seasonal workers. Santa Cruz County was home to the fourteenth-largest county farmworker population, with nearly 20,000 farmworkers. Though no official estimates are available primarily because of the large number of undocumented immigrants entering California, based upon housing demand alone officials in both counties agree that the migrant farmworker population increased significantly from 2000 to 2005.

FARM LABOR ROLES IN MEXICO AND CALIFORNIA

Most farmworkers view California farmwork as a form of drudgery akin to slavery, in which their labor is used to generate wealth for a frequently unknown, distant grower who ultimately profits from the harvest. When farmworkers whose families own land in Mexico were asked to compare their role as farmers in Mexico with their role as farmworkers in California's corporate agribusiness, the following comment made by Lorenzo Vasquez was typical: "In Mexico I farmed for me and my family, and we owned the land. In California, I'm an employee farming for someone else." Florencio Gomez expressed similar sentiments: "In Mexico, a farmer does all the work and the entire harvest is his. In California, one works for a company that owns the harvest."

Figure 12. Women lettuce harvesters on a break, Salinas, California.

The landless farmworkers from Gómez Farías who worked as wage laborers for growers in the Zamora, Michoacán, strawberry fields are generally much happier with the labor conditions and regulations in California. They related stories about having to purchase their own tools and baskets for the harvest in Mexico, slogging through freezing mud with bare feet as they planted the strawberry plants, and being sprayed indiscriminately with agrochemicals in Mexico. Most were paid very low wages and complained about not having an opportunity to work for enough hours each day to support themselves or their families.

By comparison, in California many claimed that they are not allowed to enter fields if the terrain is muddy and slippery. They can wear shoes to work on the dry ground, the grower provides work implements and materials, and there are regulations governing the use of agrochemicals. In addition, they can earn as much money in one hour picking strawberries in California as they could earn in an entire day picking strawberries in Mexico.

JOB MIGRATION

Upon their arrival in California from Mexico, and with a family member or friend's recommendation, farmworkers frequently initially begin working seasonally for farm labor contractors or smaller growers. The increased employment of farm labor contractors by growers to hire and supervise farmworkers is the most significant labor development in California agriculture in recent years (Furillo 2001; Martin 1989; Martin and Taylor 1995c; Villarejo and Runsten 1993). They serve as intermediaries between the farmworker and the grower. California farmworkers are more than twice as likely to be employed by farm labor contractors as are farmworkers elsewhere in the United States. Fully 37 percent of California's farmworkers were hired by farm labor contractors between 2003 and 2004 (Aguirre International 2005).

Thirteen of the thirty-three farmworkers interviewed for this study indicated that they were initially hired by a Latino farm labor contractor or worked on farms owned by Salinas Valley or Pajaro Valley Mexican farmers. Most central coast farms owned by Mexican growers are small, less than 15 acres, and occupy marginal land with highly erodible steep slopes. Additionally, low-resource Mexican growers are minimally integrated into local farming networks (Mountjoy 1996; Wells 1996).

The farmworker's social network is critical at this stage. None of the study participants was recruited directly by a farm labor contractor. Rather, a family member or friend knew of or worked for a labor contractor and made the connection between the labor contractor or grower and the farmworker seeking employment. Seventy-four percent of Watsonville farmworkers and 52 percent of Salinas farmworkers found jobs through family and friends. Some farmworkers acquired employment through their own initiative by going directly to the farm and soliciting employment or by filling out an application.

Network hiring among Latino immigrants is impacting all aspects of labor relations in California. Latino social networks of family and friends are so important to the composition of workers in enterprises that hire unskilled labor "from urban Los Angeles to the fields of Monterey" that labor union organizers don't even consider mounting a campaign leading to a possible strike without first mapping the workplace family relationships, including the leaders, outcasts, and old rivals. In addition, social networks have impacted the dynamics of contract negotiations and grievance procedures (Cleeland 1999).

Elena Martinez is one example of a farmworker with an extensive social network. Every time I have visited her family in Salinas, her home is full of family and friends from Mexico and locally, from Salinas. Conversations often center on work-related topics. Before sustaining a spinal injury, she was able to secure a comparatively high-paying, stable, long-term job as a mustard picker/packer with D'Arrigo Brothers through her contacts with friends, in only a single job change.

On the other hand, Antonio Moreno functions as a comparative loner, openly acknowledging that he has little contact with even immediate family members such as his two brothers who live and work in Salinas. He has changed jobs six times since he and his wife left Pine Canyon Ranch after twelve years when the ranch owner died and the farm was turned over to a *contratista* who paid them substandard wages. Since then, the longest Antonio has worked for any one employer is six years. He usually works for an employer for only a year or a season at any given location. For the past two years, he has worked as a foreman for Gavilan View, a strawberry enterprise near Salinas. However, now he is dissatisfied with this employment arrangement because a labor contractor manages all labor, and workers do not receive benefits of any kind. He continues to work for characteristically short periods before moving from one job to the next and never "lands" in an acceptable, stable employment situation.

Family relationships are also important on the job. The majority of farmworkers are employed with at least one immediate family member or relative at the same job site. Among the Watsonville farmworkers, in 27 percent of the current and past jobs held by farmworkers, spouses were working for the same employer. In 41 percent, siblings were working for the same employer. Many worked with both their spouse and siblings or other relatives.

Job turnover is not as great in Salinas because a higher percentage of the interviewees have settled in California and are no longer migrating. In 13 percent of the current and past jobs held by Salinas farmworkers, spouses were working for the same employer. In 19 percent, siblings were working for the same employer. The data on farmworker job acquisition and family members at the same job site clearly underscore the vital importance of family members and friendships to Watsonville and Salinas farmworker employment.

Small growers typically provide a low wage and few, if any, benefits (Wells 1996). Faced with seasonal employment, the necessity of supporting dependents and sending remittances to Mexico, and intolerable wages and working conditions, farmworkers eventually become motivated to seek employment elsewhere. My research suggests that the high farm labor turnover rate (Alarcón and Mines 2001) in central California's agriculture is a manifestation of a characteristic sequential process, propelled by job dissatisfaction that farmworkers engage in as they move from farm to farm in an attempt to improve their employment status. Though two of the farmworkers in this study maintained that they were "let go" due to flood conditions that destroyed a crop (Antonio Moreno) or a general company strike (Rosa Maria Guzman, in 1985), none of the farmworkers in this study claimed that they were ever terminated in their employment. The initiative to move on was generated by the farmworkers themselves.

Although farming enterprises owned by Japanese Americans are common, especially in the Pajaro Valley, and make up 46 percent of the grower population (Wells 1996), most farmworkers in this study worked primarily for Mexican-owned (initially) or Anglo-owned (after gaining experience) agribusinesses. However, three farmworkers in this study moved sequentially from small Mexican grower farms to Japanese grower farms. Japanese strawberry growers typically own medium-sized farms of 15–49 acres on farmland characterized by gentle and moderate slopes with slightly to moderately erodible soil. They often belong to co-ops that assist members with purchases, technical assistance, and fruit marketing (Mountjoy 1996; Wells 1996).

After moving from one untenable job situation to another, many farmworkers eventually find work with a large grower such as Coastal Berry Company or Driscoll Strawberry Associates in Watsonville or Bud-Antle, Tanimura & Antle, or D'Arrigo Brothers in Salinas. The Anglo grower-owned strawberry companies typically possess large farms with a mean size of 249.5 acres. Their farmland is characterized by flat to gentle slopes with only slightly to moderately erodible soil. Anglo growers are the most educated ethnic group involved in strawberry production. They are also well connected with agricultural suppliers, marketing agents, and university researchers (Mountjoy 1996).

The larger companies purportedly provide higher wages plus benefits and working conditions that are sometimes nominal but still a step ahead of the smaller growers (Wells 1996). Most important, many large growers provide some workers with year-round, stable employment. Workers who have moved from job to job and been burdened with a familiar history of employee dissatisfaction are frequently relieved to find stable, often year-round employment with the benefits most large companies provide; thus, they tend to remain loyal to the company and employed there indefinitely. Worker attrition is then reduced, and the labor force is stabilized. This pattern is particularly noticeable among Watsonville workers on large farms.

In addition, the number of job changes prior to long-term employment with a large grower or corporation appears to be directly related to the extent of the worker's accrued social capital. The farmworkers who maintain extensive social networks learn about the most desirable, highest-paying jobs from friends, family, and their contacts employed by the industry. Individuals in their social networks serve to secure employment with a large company through recommendations and the favorable status they may hold among farmworker ranks within the company.

Simultaneously, the large growers, who supply the most benefits and incentives to workers, have instituted a system of employee appeasement in their employment relations with farmworkers. This process includes both behavioral dynamics on the part of company personnel and material bonuses in various forms. Appeasement serves to minimize unrest and promote an established, loyal, labor force that is unlikely to either unionize or strike during the harvest season.

Rosario Ramirez has picked strawberries in Watsonville for over twenty years. Before acquiring employment with Reiter Berry in 1984, she worked for a year or two at a time at six other agribusiness enterprises. When I asked her about the conditions of her present employment, she smiled and glowed with approval about the way company personnel treat workers, exclaiming enthusiastically that the company owner and supervisory staff are *"muy buena gente"* ("really good people"). She spoke at length about the appreciation she feels for the way the company respects its workers and expressed gratitude that the company owner is "on the side of the workers" and supports them.

She claimed that the owner himself walks through the fields asking each worker, *"Como te sientes?"* ("How are you feeling?"), *"Como estás?"* ("How are you?"), *"Como te tratan?"* ("How are they treating you?"), *"Si tienes una queja, dímela."* ("If you have a complaint, tell me [about] it."), *"Si tienen un problema que no puedan resolverlo con el mayordomo, yo estoy para ustedes a la hora que ustedes me llamen."* ("If you [speaking to all of the workers] have a problem that you can't resolve with the foreman, I'm here for you at the hour that you call me."). The owner always uses informal personal pronouns when addressing farmworkers as a means of engendering familiarity and promoting the notion that he and his employees are on the "same team."

Teresa Costa, also an employee of Reiter Berry Farm, confirmed Rosario's view by indicating that the supervisors are "understanding people." She even expressed her conviction that they must take classes to learn how to treat workers with respect.

This company hosts four parties for the workers between May and

November during the harvest season. Workers look forward to a party in May, at the beginning of the harvest season. The company hosts a Fourth of July celebration for all of the workers and their families that includes a barbeque, band, and dancing. Another party is given in October, and a fourth on the last day of the season in November. I spoke with Rosario in 2003 on the last day of the season. She informed me that the season had officially ended at 11:45 A.M. that day, and that she and the other workers had danced and partied until 4:00 to celebrate.

The company has instituted the practice of providing lunchtime tables and chairs for workers, who are no longer allowed to sit on the ground. Rosario complained that many workers prefer to sit on the ground while eating their lunch in order to rest their backs. The tables and chairs have provided a means for workers to celebrate farmworker birthdays, however. Each worker in a crew with a member celebrating a birthday brings a food dish or drinks to work with them. At lunchtime the food is arranged on the tables as a buffet. Workers contribute money to purchase a cake, and the company allows the workers an extended time for lunch, beyond the usual half hour. Rosario adamantly insisted that the company's provision of tables and chairs plus additional time at lunch for birthday parties "does not occur anywhere else."

At the end of the season, workers who have been employed for at least a thousand hours during the season receive a bonus. The bonus rewards longevity with the company by paying farmworkers who have worked for at least four years 4 percent of earned wages for the season. Workers with one to three years of experience earn 2 percent of earned wages for the season. Rosario credits the many "benefits" the company provides the workers, as well as the respectful manner in which farmworkers are treated, for her longevity with the company. She informed me that some workers have worked for the company twenty-five years.

Most of Florencio and Rosario Gomez's Watsonville farmwork while living at the Buena Vista migrant camp was also with Reiter Berry. Like Elena Esparza, they are both grateful that they picked bush berries and could work *parejo* (upright). While living at the camp, they often commented about their good fortune in not having to work *agachados* (bent over) all day like their *fresero* (strawberry picking) friends. Both Florencio and Rosario expressed how much they enjoyed and appreciated the frequent parties given by the company for the farmworkers and their families. The parties include a barbeque, band, dancing, and even gifts of flowers.

Nearly twenty years ago and upon the recommendation of his

brother, Antonio Juárez was able to avert the sequential employment pursuit altogether by acquiring initial employment as a lettuce cutter with Bud-Antle in Salinas. He is so satisfied with his employment and has accrued so much seniority with the company over the years that he has no desire to seek employment elsewhere. He receives comprehensive health insurance, end-of-the-year bonuses, and retirement savings.

The company also provides strong incentives for workers *not* to report accidents, by providing monthly gifts to crews of workers with no reported accidents. For each month his crew of thirty-three workers does not report an accident, the company rewards them with gifts. He proudly showed me the watch he was wearing, which he received from the company the month before. In addition, he pointed out a cooler and pencil holder and mentioned that he has also received several sweatshirts. Other prizes include hats and radios.

If the crew does not report accidents for six months, each worker becomes eligible for a raffle at the end of the season. Farmworkers have an opportunity to win impressive prizes at the raffle, including microwave ovens, televisions, stereos, and video cassette players. The grand prize is a small truck or van. Crews that work in each crop have their own raffle with comparable prizes.

When Antonio's father was ill several years earlier, the company owner permitted him to return to Mexico to be with him. The owner assured him that his job was secure and would be waiting upon his return from Mexico.

Eduardo Sousa acquired employment with Coastal Berry Company in 1988 after working for a Mexican grower during the preceding four years. He has moved up in the company and now enjoys year-round employment working on the company's irrigation systems. In addition to medical insurance for his entire family, paid holidays, gifts as incentives for unreported accidents, and parties, Eduardo claims that one of the greatest company benefits is a chance to play football. Coastal Berry Company has set aside an area for football. Each of the twenty-two company crews is a team and plays regularly. The games both unify crew (team) members and provide diversion.

Most farmworkers view the benefits and working conditions provided by the large companies as a great improvement over their previous experiences with other growers. The majority are content to remain docile, primarily because they know that their circumstances could be much worse. Thus, the large companies essentially use the intolerable previous work histories of farmworkers to their advantage. The combination of behavioral and material benefits provided by large growers results in a stabilized caste of large company workers ready and "willing" to be exploited for capital generation. Like Eduardo Sousa, in some cases a farmworker who has worked seasonally for a large company for many years may be able to improve his or her employment situation within the same company, by moving into higher-paying year-round work in other, more stable jobs such as machine operator, irrigator, mechanic, cooling plant and warehouse worker, labor foreman, crew boss, and the like (Palerm 1991). Small growers and farm labor contractors, on the other hand, are not able or inclined to provide the opportunities or level of benefits the larger growers provide and still realize acceptable profit levels. Thus, smaller growers are inevitably subject to high rates of employee turnover, as employees leave to find more favorable employment opportunities.

Some farmworkers, like Antonio Moreno, never complete the sequential continuum, remaining in the tedious limbo between their first labor experience and the possibility of year-round employment in a large company. Their perpetual dissatisfaction, sense of social injustice, indignation, and often inability to accept substandard, oppressive employment demands prompts them to remain on the employment move, never arriving at a permanent employment destination.

Roberto Fonseca, a seasonal migrant resident at the Buena Vista migrant camp, was on the employment move for many years after his first employment experience with a farm labor contractor in 1975 at the age of 15. He worked for and became dissatisfied with four other employers, never finding a satisfactory, life-long employment location. His wife Esperanza worked with him from 1985 to 2002, when he sustained a permanent disabling back injury picking strawberries and was unable to return to work.

Roberto, a member of Western Service Workers, claims that he moved from job to job because the working conditions were intolerable or he never got along with his supervisor. He indignantly described the conditions he was subjected to while working for a farm labor contractor. His wage was low, there wasn't a clean place to eat lunch, bathrooms were dirty, and he never met the farm owner.

He and his wife worked almost ten years with his two brothers for a Japanese grower. Still, he complained, his wages were too low, there wasn't a clean place to eat lunch, and the bathroom consisted of a hole in the ground, "the same as in Mexico." Roberto angrily noted that sometimes the hole was completely "full."

WORKING CONDITIONS

Growers exploit farmworkers regardless of the company size or benefits provided. By the thousands, agribusiness employers break state and federal labor laws by underpaying, or not paying what they promise, tens of thousands of farmworkers in California. Violations of labor laws are so prevalent that farmworkers often expect to be cheated (Furillo 2001).

In 2001, one study estimated that at least 2,800 employers cheated 42,000 workers out of minimum wages in any given pruning season—a loss to employees of more than $4.2 million. Though few farmworkers in this study complained that their employer never paid wages for services rendered, a review of court and state records cited eighteen instances between 1999 and 2001 in which agricultural employers statewide completely failed to pay an estimated 1,600 farmworkers $820,0000 in wages (Furillo 2001).

Most farmworkers are required to work long hours in excess of the federally mandated forty-hour work week, without overtime pay. Wages are substandard for the work performed and health risks involved. Farmworkers typically work up to eleven or even thirteen hours per day during the height of the season. Not a single farmworker in this study claimed to have received overtime pay for overtime work. As illustrated in Elena Esparza's story at the beginning of the chapter, the workday typically begins between 6:00 and 7:00 in the morning. Farmworkers are allowed 15-minute breaks at 9:00 and 3:00, and at noon they have a 30-minute lunch break. Most workers eat lunch seated by the side of a field; some eat lunch in their vehicles.

In a study of farmworker health by the California Institute for Rural Studies, 82 percent of farmworker subjects and 96 percent of farmworker subjects in a National Agricultural Workers Survey (Aguirre International 2005) reported that their employer provided toilets, wash water, and clean drinking water (Villarejo et al. 2000). My study corroborates these findings. Most farmworkers claim that clean drinking water and wash water are provided on the job, as well as clean bathrooms. The majority also claim to have a good relationship with their foreman or supervisor; few, as indicated earlier, have contact with the farm owner.

FARMWORKER WAGES

Labor surpluses in recent years and the use of *contratistas* have resulted in an overall decline in farm wage rates statewide (Martin and Taylor

Figure 13. Grower-provided wash water on the side of portable restrooms, Watsonville, California.

1995c; Sherman 1998). In the 1980s, farmworkers' wages declined by 15 percent (Villarejo and Runsten 1993). This decline in agricultural wages occurred 50 percent faster than the decline in manufacturing wages. In addition, many employers have eliminated employer-paid benefits such as health insurance (Villarejo and Runsten 1993).

In the 1990s, even with increasingly widespread prosperity, farmworker wages lost ground. By 2000, wages adjusted for inflation had dropped from the 1990s average of $6.89 to $6.18 per hour. As a consequence, farmworkers lost 11 percent of their purchasing power (Aguirre International 2000).

Farm wages in general have remained at approximately half the levels of manufacturing wages since before 1950 (Heppel 1995). California wages for farmworkers reached their highest level in 1978 as a result of farmworker strikes and grape boycotts resulting from unionization efforts by the UFW. Farm labor wages declined until 1983, then recovered slightly from 1983 to 1989 before declining sharply after the Immigration Reform and Control Act of 1986. Overall, between 1974 and 1996, wages dropped about 15 percent and, though they have risen slightly since 1996, they still remain below the 1978 peak (Alarcón and Mines 2001; Huffman 1995).

In 1998, California farmworkers earned on average $6.26 per hour (Employment Development Department 2000). In 2002, the median hourly wage for farmworkers in a number of crops was $7.24 (USDL 2002). However, with 61 percent of California farmworkers reporting seasonal employment (Aguirre International 2005), at an end-of-the-season hourly rate of $5.25 undocumented workers like Elena Esparza often didn't even earn a minimum wage for seasonal work in 2005.

Typically, farmworkers are paid in one of two ways: by the hour and the number of cases (one case equals twelve baskets) of fruit picked, like Elena Esparza, referred to as *horas y cajas;* or by the number of cases picked, referred to as *por contrato.* If a farmworker elects to be paid *por contrato,* the wage per case is higher than if he/she is working *horas y cajas.* Most farmworkers agree that, if the harvest is good and the crop is abundant, it is best to elect to be paid *por contrato.* They make more with piece rates because, as efficient harvesters, they can exceed the normal pace and earn a higher wage. In contrast, if the crop is light, most farmworkers feel that it is best to elect to be paid by the hour and the number of cases of fruit or vegetables picked. Then they can at least count on a minimum hourly wage. These two systems of payment are particularly prevalent in the strawberry and bush berry industries.

Farm wages for strawberry pickers during the bracero era averaged only $0.95 per hour. By 1969 they had increased to $1.80 per hour. In 1976 the hourly wage was $3.60, and by 1985, after the grape strikes, they reached $7.20 (Wells 1996). In 2000, Rosario Ramirez earned $4.65 per hour and $0.70 per case of picked strawberries. In 2001 she earned $4.75 per hour and $0.75 per case of picked strawberries. As an *horas y cajas* worker, she estimates that she earns approximately $7.20 per hour at the height of the harvest when berries are plentiful. In the early and latter weeks of the season, when ripe strawberries are less plentiful, she earns much less. Thus, wages for strawberry pickers have remained stagnant or declined over the past twenty years. Adjusted for inflation, most farmworker's salaries are about the same as they were before the UFW grape strikes in the 1960s (M. Jourdane, personal communication, 2005).

An undocumented relative of Florencio Gomez revealed that, in 2001, Garroutte Farms paid her $3.50 per hour and $2.00 per case to pick bush berries. She indicated that at the season's height, when berries were plentiful, she could pick two to three cases per hour. Her seasonal salary maximum was thus $7.50–$9.50 per hour. She related that in many weeks, and especially with inclement weather, harvestable berries are scarce and she was lucky to pick a case in an hour. Elena Esparza agrees. In 2005, when the harvest was light, she picked only a case an hour, for a salary of only $5.25 per hour ($3.10/hour and $2.15/case).

Like Roberto Fonseca, Josefa Rodriguez's husband sustained a disabling back injury as a result of work in the strawberry fields in 2000. Thus, when Josefa and her family return to the Buena Vista migrant camp, she must shoulder the entire financial responsibility for her family of three children. Esperanza, Roberto Fonseca's wife, is caught in the same predicament. Josefa informed me that she often earns only $100 or $120 per week at her job picking strawberries with a sharecropper. Her low income barely enables her to pay the rent and buy groceries for the family. She is unable to save money or purchase any clothes at all for her growing children.

Maria Herrera is paid approximately $14 per hour to pack radicchio year-round for Premio in the Salinas Valley. Her income, in combination with the lower hourly wage of her husband who picks broccoli, is sufficient for her family to own a condominium in one of Salinas's lower-income neighborhoods.

UNIONIZATION

Only seven of the thirty-three farmworkers interviewed for this study had a union-negotiated employment contract with the company they were employed by. The seven union members reported varying degrees of satisfaction with their union membership and representation. Four of them work at Monterey Mushrooms, a company with a UFW contract.

To discourage UFW membership, many growers offer workers the same benefits the union offers. Farmworkers are then able to save the 2 percent of their meager salaries that are required each month for union membership. The incentive to join the UFW is thus obstructed (M. Jourdane, personal communication, 2005).

Three interviewees worked for companies with Teamsters Union contracts. The Teamsters have a questionable history of worker advocacy. In addition, during the UFW-sponsored grape boycotts of the 1960s, the Teamsters were instrumental in undermining UFW success by arranging "sweetheart contracts" with growers. Because of the lower wages that could be paid to Teamsters-affiliated farmworkers, growers signed contracts with their union instead of with the UFW. Throughout the state, grower-Teamsters alliances developed as a weapon against the UFW (Thomas and Friedland 1982).

Nevertheless, two workers in particular appeared to be remarkably satisfied with their Teamsters-supported work environment and company benefits. For his $19 monthly Teamsters dues, Antonio Juárez, the Salinas lettuce cutter who works for Bud-Antle, claims that he receives a decent wage, full health insurance coverage for himself and all immediate family members, retirement, bonuses, and four hours of guaranteed salary if he shows up for work, even if it rains and he can't work that day. Antonio has worked for Bud-Antle for over eighteen years.

Ismena Rocha has worked for River Ranch Packing House for over seven years. A Teamsters contract was signed with the company three years after she began working for the packing house. She claims that conditions at the company were never really bad. However, Ismena spoke with pride about the manner in which the Teamsters "empower workers" and inform them of their rights as workers. The union has negotiated an excellent benefit package including medical, dental, and vision health insurance as well as disability insurance. Ismena knows the company owner, and the company provides employees with a dining room for meals, including a microwave oven and icemaker. Ismena also reports that the restrooms are always clean.

The remaining farmworkers in my study are working without contracts or a living wage. As a disempowered caste, they are faced with only negative choices in their employment location preferences. Farm labor and immigration laws as well as the system of employee appeasement discussed above serve to institutionalize many of the difficult and unjust conditions farmworkers struggle with as employees in California's industrial agricultural enterprises. They work for short periods of time in one employment situation after another in an attempt to locate a situation that will pay the most and cost them the least in terms of energy and health risks. Each job becomes a part of the continuum in the sequential process, ultimately, in many cases, leading to long-term employment with the largest, wealthiest growers.

EIGHT

AN IMPOVERISHED, ENDANGERED, AND OVERWORKED PEOPLE IN THE LAND OF PLENTY

*Hay cuando duerme uno . . . está soñando que está traba-
jando uno, por el mismo cansancio, la presión que tiene uno
en aquel trabajo. No descansa uno ni de noche.*

Oh, even while sleeping one dreams that they are working.
It's because of the exhaustion and the pressure one experiences in that [strawberry picking] work. One doesn't rest,
even at night.

**—Mirna Ramirez, strawberry picker, Watsonville,
California**

At 3:30, Elena Esparza carries the cases of blackberries she's picked for the day to the edge of the field where the *ponchadora* (case counter) waits while tired workers begin to line up. Since it's late April and still the beginning of the season, the harvest is light. Elena has picked only ten cases all day. At $2.15 per case, she can count on $21.50 for the cases plus $24.80 for eight hours of work at $3.10 per hour *(horas y cajas)*—that's $46.30 grossed for a day's work. She's hoping to earn at least $8,000 during the seven-month season. About half of this sum must be saved for the winter months when there is no employment available for her on the berry farms. She knows that her yearly income is low, but at least it helps pay some of the bills.

At 4:15 she throws off her hat and bandana and steps into her truck for the ride home. On the way back to her apartment she stops at a local Mexican market and buys some pinto beans, rice, masa, onions, and Kool-Aid for the children. They ask her for fruit, but fruits and vegetables are so expensive that she can only really afford to purchase the chilies needed to spice up her *pozole* and *frijoles,* along with some cabbage.

When Elena finally arrives home at 5:20, she picks up Jaime at her neighbor's apartment and then checks to see that her other four children are either in the apartment watching television or playing on the playground. Satisfied that her children are all accounted for, Elena walks home to make dinner for the family at 6:00. She feels fortunate that she has the time now for a brief stop at the store, and time to check up on her children. At the height of the harvest season in another two weeks, there will be no time.

At 6:45 her husband Emanuel returns home, tired from a long day at the *honguera*. After greeting him, Elena finishes making dinner while he showers and dresses in clean clothes. By 7:15 the family is all seated around the large table enjoying a dinner of beans with salsa, rice, and homemade tortillas. Elena attempts to eat her meal with young Jaime seated on her lap. Between bites, she tries to engage him in the process of eating. Tonight he is much more interested in playing with the spoons on the table than in eating.

At about 8:00, with everyone fed, Elena admonishes the children to take turns bathing and to start their homework. While some children bathe, others begin their assignments, and Elena washes the dishes and begins cleaning house. Her youngest third-grade daughter asks her a question in Spanish about her English assignment, then recalls that she'll have to guess at the answer. Her mother doesn't know English. Elena worries, "How can my children progress in school if I can't help them with their homework like the Anglo parents do? How will they get a decent job later on if they can't get an education? I don't even have time to visit their schools or meet their teachers. No one tells me anything about what they are learning."

For the next hour, Emanuel relaxes with a beer on the couch and watches his favorite TV program. The children work on their homework assignments and bathe, and Elena continues to clean house, scrubbing floors and the downstairs bathroom. On some nights, if she can finish the housework early enough, she has time to make the next-day's family lunches in the evening. She prefers this routine, because then the next morning isn't quite so hectic.

By 9:00 the children are bathed and ready for bed. Elena climbs the stairs to the bedroom, carrying Jaime on her hip. The other children follow. Once all the children are in bed, Elena at last has time for the bright spot in her day, a bath. By 10:30, Elena and Emanuel are in bed, attempting to relax enough from their hectic day to get much-needed rest before the 5:00 alarm rings the next morning.

FARMWORKER HEALTH AND OCCUPATIONAL SAFETY

While offering only substandard wages, and thus relegating workers to a life of impoverishment, farmwork is one of America's most dangerous industries (International Labour Office 2003). In California alone, from 1985 to 1994 there were 385,411 paid claims to farmworkers for job-related injuries, illnesses, and deaths—133,802 cases involving disabling injuries or illnesses and 501 for occupational fatalities (Williams 1998).

Immigrants are at greater risk than the U.S.-born of dying in a job-related accident (Pritchard 2004). Immigrants made up 14 percent of the U.S. workforce in 2000, and the number killed at work rose to 849 in the same year, a 17 percent increase over 1996 (*San Jose Mercury News* 2001a). The Bureau of Labor Statistics claims that, of the 6,023 occupational deaths reported in 1999, 725 were Latino workers. These deaths included several incidents in which migrant farmworkers died when overcrowded vans crashed while their foremen drove them to the fields (Greenhouse 2001).

An Associated Press investigation found that the jobs Mexican immigrants encounter in the United States are killing them at the rate of one victim per day (Pritchard 2004); the average death rate for farmworkers is five times greater than that of workers in other industries (Ahn et al. 2004). Evidence suggests that some employers who hire Mexican workers for the most perilous work regard Mexican workers as disposable human beings (Pritchard 2004).

The National Safety Council (2002) reported farmwork as the most hazardous U.S. industry of 2001, with 700 deaths and 130,000 disabling injuries reported. In 2002, the death rate for agriculture was almost six times greater than that for all other industries, with a death rate of 21 per 100,000 workers; the general occupational injury death rate for all industries in 2002 was only 3.6 deaths per 100,000 workers. There were 730 agricultural deaths in 2002, while another 150,000 people suffered disabling injuries (National Safety Council 2003).

No state is deadlier than California, with 725 Mexican worker deaths on the job between 1996 and 2002 (Pritchard 2004). Farmwork is California's second most dangerous industry after construction. In 1999, 76 California agricultural employees were killed on the job, according to the California Division of Occupational Safety and Health. The figure represents a 33 percent increase over agriculture's 1995 fatality figure of 57. During the same time period, industrial deaths dropped by 8 percent, from 646 to 591 (Furillo 2001).

In addition, California accounts for 26 percent of all reported disabling occupational injuries among hired farmworkers (Rural California Report 1998). Occupation-related injuries and illness and workplace safety violations occur at astonishing rates (Williams 1998). Approximately 30 percent of California farmworkers are paid on a piece-rate basis *(por contrato),* which may be the source of increased injury because attention is focused on maximizing production, potentially at the cost of worker safety (McCurdy 1997).

The findings of a binational farmworker health survey of 140 California farmworkers confirmed that 27 percent of farmworkers reported having at least one injury while working on U.S. farms. A total of 140 injuries were reported, with eleven respondents reporting two injuries. The most commonly reported injuries occurred as a result of falls. Forty-three farmworkers, 30.7 percent of those surveyed, reported falls as the cause of their injuries. In addition, four workers lost fingers, one lost a hand, and two suffered a loss of sight during accidents (Mines et al. 2001).

Nearly one-quarter of California farmworkers surveyed in a recent National Agricultural Workers Survey (Aguirre International 2005) reported suffering from at least one musculoskeletal problem. Twelve percent experienced skin problems, and about 15 percent experienced watery or itchy eyes and runny or stuffy noses. All of these percentages show increases over data collected since 1999.

The California Institute for Rural Studies claims that 18.5 percent of farmworker subjects reported having a workplace injury at some point in their farmwork career that was compensated by a payment to them under the California Workers Compensation Insurance System. However, only one-third thought that their employer had such coverage, despite the fact that California law requires it (Villarejo et al. 2000). The state-mandated legal requirement explains grower motivation to encourage their workers not to report injury while at work. When injuries are not reported and claims against the insurance are not made, presumably premiums are kept at a minimum.

Back injuries among farmworkers are commonplace and discussed within the farmworker community in much the same way that people outside of the community discuss headaches. Among the thirty-three primary farmworker interviewees for this study, six (18 percent) sustained disabling back injuries either at the time the research for this study was in progress or at some time during the course of their careers as farm laborers. Fernando Azevedo's two brothers both sustained disabling back injuries from falls while working for Monterey Mushrooms.

AGROCHEMICAL EXPOSURE

One of the greatest occupational hazards farmworkers face is the day-to-day exposure to toxic pesticides. California farmworkers are more affected by environmental exposure to pesticides than any other human population (Moses 1993). Though California pesticide safety laws are among the strictest in the nation, the state Department of Pesticide Regulation and the County Agricultural Commissioners are not enforcing the laws (Barnett 1989; Liebman 1997). In fact, enforcement is weakest in the counties with highest pesticide use (Reeves et al. 1999).

The Department of Pesticide Regulation has proposed cutting its budget and scaling back the pesticide use reporting system (Liebman 1997). County agricultural commissioners are said by some to be so closely identified with the interests of the growers that they have been reluctant to enforce the laws (Barnett 1989). Agricultural interests, with the encouragement and support of the U.S. Department of Agriculture, continue to block any changes in pesticide policy that would protect farmworkers (Moses 1993).

Even the company doctors who service the few farmworkers with health insurance are reluctant to report or acknowledge the possibility of pesticide-related illness. In February 2000, Rosario Gomez underwent surgery for thyroid cancer after working twelve years as a bush berry picker for Driscoll Associates. When she questioned the company doctor about a connection between pesticides used at her worksite and her cancer, the physician denied any connection. When she requested a disability leave, the doctor informed her that she was cured and should return to work immediately. Rosario knows of one other young woman, in her crew of sixty, who has developed thyroid cancer, and two others who have developed uterine cancer.

The EPA estimates that as many as 300,000 farmworkers suffer from pesticide poisoning each year nationwide (Human Rights Watch 2000). In 2001 the California Department of Pesticide Regulation reported that farmworker injuries and illnesses caused by pesticides ran about 150 per year, statewide, down from about 280 in the early 1980s (Furillo 2001). My research suggests that the incidence of illness or symptoms associated with agrochemical exposure is much higher. Nine farmworkers (28 percent) experienced chronic skin irritation and skin eruptions. Seven (22 percent) complained of irritated eyes and nasal membranes. The complaints are probably from exposure to pesticides or other agrochemical products producing symptoms of acute toxicity (see appendix A: U.S. EPA Acute Toxicity Ratings; Moses 1993).

Whereas the EPA estimates that 10,000–20,000 agricultural workers experience acute pesticide-related illnesses each year (Reeves et al. 2002), with 475 reported in California in 2000 (Reeves et al. 2002), my research suggests that the poisonings are not acute, one-time events. A significant number of farmworkers I interviewed display symptoms indicating that they are exposed to acutely toxic substances for the entire duration of their employment with a company. In other words, they continuously have irritated skin, skin with welts or other eruptions, irritated eyes and nasal membranes, often with accompanying nausea.

Thomas Gamsky of the University of California, Davis, and his associates studied the prevalence of dermatitis and risk factors for skin disease in 759 California farmworkers who worked in the grape, citrus, and tomato fields. Of those who participated, 2 percent displayed contact dermatitis and 13 percent displayed lichenified hand dermatitis (a particularly severe form of dermatitis). Grape workers were the most likely to report rashes and were more likely to have contact dermatitis and lichenified hand dermatitis than citrus and tomato workers. Increased hours in the fields, male gender, and not wearing gloves were all associated with more lichenified hand dermatitis (Gamsky et al. 1992). Grapes are grown with some of the highest levels of agrochemicals used on any crop.

Farmworkers reported a range of other complaints suggestive of pesticide exposure. Florencio Gomez spoke of the intense nausea he experiences while working during the winter months for Sierra Citrus in Lindsay, California. He developed serious diabetes during spring 2001. Consuelo Fernandez also spoke of the intense nausea she feels in her work at Monterey Mushrooms. Ana Aguirre discussed the flu-like symptoms experienced in her work at Smuckers. Juan Borrego stated that, when he worked near farm areas subjected to spraying, he developed terrible headaches. Lorenzo Vasquez spoke of workers in his crew having to be hospitalized for severe headaches.

The California Institute for Rural Studies claims that only 57 percent of farmworker subjects said they had received pesticide safety training (Villarejo et al. 2000). However, a 2005 National Agricultural Workers Survey report claims that 86 percent of farmworker participants reported receiving training or instruction regarding the safe use of pesticides (Aguirre International 2005). All farmworkers employed by Driscoll Associates acknowledged that workers are consistently informed about the name, chemical composition, and possible physical side effects of agrochemical use and exposure at employment locations. Fields are blocked off and entry is not permitted after spraying. Monterey Mushrooms holds an annual meeting in Spanish that all workers are required to attend, in which agrochemical usage information is divulged.

However, during interviews, when I queried farmworkers with physical symptoms for the names of the agrochemicals that had been utilized at their employment sites, none could give me either the brand name or the chemical composition of a single agrochemical compound. I asked them to inquire at the company regarding the names of the compounds. Later they informed me that their foremen, supervisors, and others were unwilling to discuss or identify the names of the agrochemicals used. Indeed, all affected farmworkers agreed universally that employers and their hired intermediaries continually reassured farmworkers about agrochemical product safety. Some company personnel told the workers that the offending compound was innocuous sulfur or "Cal," a harmless calcium carbonate product used on tree trunks in Mexico.

Pesticide-related illness is an important cause of acute morbidity among migrant farmworkers in California. Organophosphates, carbamates, inorganic compounds, and pyrethroids account for over half of the cases of acute illness. Exposures occur in various ways, indicating that the use of pesticides creates a hazardous work environment for all farmworkers (Das et al. 2005).

In a November 2001 Cancer Registry of California study, the agency found that Hispanic farmworkers have a higher incidence of brain, leukemia, skin, and stomach cancers than other Hispanics in California. In addition, female Hispanic farmworkers have more cases of uterine cancer than other Hispanic women. The registry also compared cancer incidence data from 146,581 farmworker union members with the data on California's general Hispanic population. During the period, 1,001 farmworkers were diagnosed with cancer. There were 59 percent more reports of leukemia and 69 percent more reports of stomach cancers among farmworkers than in the general Hispanic population (Baca 2002; *San Jose Mercury News* 2002a).

Other studies that have evaluated cancer risk in farmworkers suggest that they are experiencing excesses of multiple myelomas and cancers of the stomach, prostate, testes, buccal cavity, pharynx, lung, and liver and cervical cancer (Zahm and Blair 2005).

Though these studies did not conclude a direct link between pesticide exposure and increased cancer incidence, the UFW blames the elevated cancer frequency in farmworkers on pesticide exposure. A future study will examine the agrochemical identity and length of exposure time in afflicted farmworkers. Nevertheless, in 2005 a conclusive relationship between agrochemical exposure and cancer was identified at the University of Massachusetts, Lowell, which reported scientific evidence linking involuntary environmental and occupational exposures to industrial and synthetic chemicals used in agriculture to nearly thirty types of cancer. Many of these chemicals are dispersed throughout the environment. Included in the report's conclusions are the associations between herbicide exposure and non-Hodgkin's lymphoma and between childhood leukemia and pesticide exposure (Clapp et al. 2005).

The Pesticide Action Network has grouped the most toxic pesticides into two primary categories: "Dirty Dozen" pesticides and "Bad Actor" pesticides (see appendix A). Some of the agrochemicals classified in each of these two groups were banned from use in the United States many years ago but continue to be used in Mexico. Collectively, the Dirty Dozen pesticides cause many deaths and widespread environmental damage every year. Most have been banned or restricted in the industrialized countries because of their known hazards. Bad Actor pesticides are *at least* one of the following: known or probable carcinogens; reproductive or developmental toxicants; neurotoxic cholinesterase inhibitors; known groundwater contaminants; and pesticides with high acute toxicity.

Glyphosate, the active ingredient in Monsanto's Roundup, is the most commonly used pesticide in U.S. agriculture (Richard et al. 2005). Between 85 and 90 million pounds of this weed killer are used in U.S. agriculture each year. Several genetically modified crops have been developed as "Roundup Ready" crops (see chapter 11); the grower sprays Roundup on Roundup Ready crops, and weeds are eliminated with no adverse effect to the crop plants. Glyphosate is also the second most commonly used nonagricultural pesticide, with 8–11 million pounds used in the United States each year. Roundup is readily available for sale in a variety of stores and retail enterprises across the country and has been linked to the onset of non-Hodgkin's lymphoma in adults (Beyond Pesticides 2005; Organic Consumers Association 2006d).

A peer-reviewed 2005 study conducted in France determined that glyphosate causes fetal endocrine disruption at concentrations ten times lower than recommended concentrations for agricultural use. The Roundup formulation of glyphosate enhances bioavailability and bioaccumulation, impacting fetal cells at concentrations one hundred times lower than recommended for agricultural use. The study found that a mammalian enzyme critical to sex steroid hormone synthesis and sex differentiation is disrupted in the presence of Roundup. The effects are noticeable on human placental cells after only eighteen hours (Richard et al. 2005).

In a European study, researchers concluded that there is a direct link between pesticide exposure and the onset of Parkinson's disease. A study of almost three thousand people in five European countries led investigators to conclude that, the more pesticide exposure an individual experiences in his/her lifetime, the higher the risk of developing the disease. High-exposure people such as farmers and farmworkers were 43 percent more likely to develop Parkinson's (Coghlan 2005). Though the European study did not indicate a particular pesticide as the causative factor in Parkinson's development, other studies have suggested a link between the onset of Parkinson's and exposure to either paraquat, a Dirty Dozen herbicide, or Maneb, a Bad Actor fungicide and suspected endocrine disruptor (Beyond Pesticides 2001b).

About one-third of the pesticides used in California are classified as Bad Actors (Reeves and Schafer 2003). The use of pesticides linked to cancer grew by 7.5 million pounds from 1994 to 1998, a 32 percent increase (Arax 2000). Organophosphate agents that interfere with nerve function by inhibiting cholinesterase activities are heavily used in agriculture. Over 9 million pounds are used annually in California alone (McCurdy 1997). Strawberries are the most intensively treated crop in the state, receiving an average of more than 300 pounds of pesticide active ingredient per acre per year (Liebman 1997).

Jaime Valenzuela, an Aptos Berry Farm labor contractor in this study, is a consistent purchaser and user of agrochemicals. In his interview he recited a list of fourteen agrochemicals used regularly in his strawberry production enterprise. Four chemicals from his list are Bad Actors:

Captan, a powerful fungicide, is acutely toxic and a proven carcinogen. Some formulations were banned in the United States in November 1992. Jaime, however, was using it in 1998.

Chloropicrin is classified as an acutely toxic carcinogenic insecticide. In addition, the compound is a human reproductive and developmental toxin and a neurotoxin. It is also toxic to aquatic organisms. Some formulations of the compound have been banned in the United States.

Malathion, an insecticide, is moderately toxic, a possible carcinogen, a cholinesterase inhibitor, and a suspected endocrine disruptor.

Methyl bromide is a broad-spectrum soil fumigant widely used to control insects, pathogens, nematodes, weeds, and rodent pests (Prentice and Broome 2004). It is acutely toxic, mutagenic, a developmental and reproductive toxin, and listed as an EPA Category I fumigant (see appendix A). The fumigant is often mixed with the insecticide chloropicrin and injected into the soil, where the combination temporarily kills anything alive (Hamilton 2004).

California is one of the largest users of methyl bromide in the world. In 1998 more than 4 million pounds of methyl bromide, about 30 percent of the state's total of 14 million pounds, were applied to California strawberry fields alone. In 2000, 10.9 million pounds were used throughout the state. Nineteen people in California died from methyl bromide exposure between 1982 and 1997. In January 2000, the California Department of Pesticide Regulation issued draft regulations on methyl bromide that do not protect school children, farmworkers, or residents living near strawberry fields (Hamilton 2004; Levey 2002; PANNA 2001a).

Air monitoring at Pajaro Middle School outside Watsonville and three other schools in Monterey and Santa Cruz counties from 2000 to 2002 confirmed methyl bromide levels above the state guidelines of 1 part per billion. At Pajaro Middle School concentrations were almost eight times greater than the mandated state guideline. Yet state regulators refused to take steps to curtail levels of the fumigant, even though benign alternatives to methyl bromide use have existed for some time (Prentice and Broome 2004).

San Luis Obispo County residents of Halcyon complained in 2002 about methyl bromide drift from adjacent strawberry fields, claiming that the fumigant made them ill. They also complained of illness following malathion application. Residents demanded more monitoring and health studies to determine if they are being exposed to harmful chemicals. However, county agricultural officials insist that they carefully monitor pesticide application and have found no evidence of pesticide drift into the neighborhood (*Santa Cruz Sentinel* 2002).

Because the bromine in methyl bromide is fifty times more destructive to the ozone layer than the chlorine in chlorofluorocarbons (PANNA 1995), in a 1999 amendment to the Clean Air Act the U.S. Congress required the EPA to phase out the use of methyl bromide. The phase-out schedule was established as follows: 25 percent reduction in 1999, 50 percent reduction in 2001, 70 percent reduction in 2003, and 100 percent reduction by 2005 (Environmental Protection Agency 2001). The

United States signed the Montreal Protocol, committing to phase out methyl bromide completely by 2005 in an effort to protect the planet's ozone layer (Beamish 2005). However, bowing to pressure from fruit and vegetable farmers in California and other major agricultural states, the Bush administration petitioned to postpone the global phase-out of methyl bromide in March 2004 (Nesmith 2004). On December 15, 2004, the EPA extended methyl bromide use into 2005 by creating a "critical use exemption" framework that granted "critical use allowances" to producers and importers of methyl bromide.

As 2005 came to a close, the Bush administration was making plans to ensure that methyl bromide remains available at least through 2008 in order to protect agricultural and manufacturing interests (Beamish 2005). In the meantime, the EPA and the State of California are both considering the registration of methyl iodide as a new replacement agrochemical for methyl bromide. Methyl iodide is highly carcinogenic and is even used by cancer researchers to induce cancer in mammalian cells for study (PANNA 2005c). While synthetic chemical methyl bromide replacements are aggressively sought by agricultural and manufacturing interests, methyl bromide continues to be the strawberry grower's soil sterilization fumigant of choice.

Jaime's recital of agrochemicals is but a microcosm of the expansive use of these products in agriculture statewide. California is literally drenched with hundreds of millions of pounds of agrochemicals applied to crops each year (Liebman 1997). In 2002 alone, pesticide use accounted for the release of almost six times more toxic materials into the environment than manufacturing, mining, or refining facilities. Of the 174 million pounds of pesticides reported to be used in California in 2002, 90 percent were capable of drifting from the site of application to become airborne toxins (PANNA 2005a).

The destructive impact of many specific agrochemicals in many species is well documented. For example, amphibians all over the world are in trouble, with declining numbers. Atrazine is the most commonly used herbicide in the United States and possibly the world. Tyrone Hayes and his associates found that when leopard frogs, *Rana pipiens,* are exposed to atrazine levels at concentrations as low as 1 part per 10 billion, their larvae developed into hermaphroditic frogs incapable of reproduction (Hayes 2003). Similar experimental results were found in another frog species, *Xenopus laevis.*

A comprehensive medical monitoring study in nearby Washington State found that, when blood samples were regularly taken from both field workers and pesticide sprayers, dangerous levels of blood pesticide levels were found in both groups (Farm Worker Pesticide Project et al. 2005). Tests primarily involved measuring cholinesterase inhibition by organophosphate and carbamate pesticides. Cholinesterase is an essential enzyme for proper nervous system function. Organophosphates and carbamates tend to depress cholinesterase levels in affected individuals, resulting in nausea, neurological problems, seizures, respiratory distress, and even death. Over the course of the first year, one in five of the pesticide handlers had blood pesticide levels capable of significantly impacting the nervous system. Of this group, 4 percent had levels so high that they had to be removed from the job. Other tests revealed that the urine of nine out of ten field workers, as well as every pesticide handler, contained organophosphate residues.

Farmworker family members are also affected by pesticide drift (Farm Worker Pesticide Project et al. 2005; Kegley et al. 2003; PANNA 2005a; Reeves and Schafer 2003). Pesticides that drift through the fields are brought home on workers' skin, hair, and clothing, even when they don't work directly with pesticide application. Thus, the family members and children of farmworkers become inadvertently exposed.

The Washington State study revealed that four pesticides were responsible for the greater number of serious cholinesterase depressions: chlorpyrifos (Lorsban), azinphos methyl (Guthion), carbaryl (Sevin), and formetanate (Carzol). All four of these agrochemicals are classified as Bad Actors, and use of most formulations has been prohibited in the United States.

Of interest is the fact that, in a large percentage of the cholinesterase depression cases, there was no evidence of noncompliance with worker protection standards. State and federal laws allow open cabs on air-blast pesticide sprayers towed by tractors, even though enclosed cabs reduce pesticide exposure (Farm Worker Pesticide Project et al. 2005).

There are few comprehensive studies of the short- and long-term effects of chronic exposure to pesticides in central California. However, the Center for Health Assessment of Mothers and Children of Salinas study (CHAMACOS) may provide valuable information with which to assess pesticide exposure in the future (Rodebaugh 2000). This study, funded by the EPA and National Institute of Environmental Health Sciences, is currently in progress to ascertain the effect of pesticide exposure on pregnant farmworkers and their babies. The comprehensive Salinas Valley project includes research on the possibility of intervention strategies to reduce pesticide exposure among farmworkers as well as on the impact of pesticide exposure (CHAMACOS website, 2005).

In March 2006, CHAMACOS researchers published a paper indicating that some newborns may be 26–50 times more susceptible to exposure to the organophosphate pesticides diazinon and chlorpyrifos than other newborns, and 65–130 times more sensitive than some adults. Susceptibility is dependent upon the inheritance of an enzyme that breaks down the toxic metabolites of organophosphate pesticides. Infants are at particular risk because the level of the detoxifying enzyme in newborns averages one-third or less than that of adults. It may take six months to two years for an infant to develop mature levels of the enzyme.

The CHAMACOS researchers intend to pursue the implications of infant susceptibility in future research, particularly the impact of exposure and increased organophosphate susceptibility on neurodevelopment in young children (Furlong et al. 2006; Yang 2006). University of Sydney scientists have already determined that regular exposure to organophosphate pesticides plays a role in the causation of some cases of deadly motor neuron disease (Beyond Pesticides 2006).

CHAMACOS researchers also studied the impact of DDT on children's development. DDT, an organochlorine, persists in the environment long after use, accumulating in the food chain and in the fatty tissues of animals and humans. Thirty-three years after its use was banned in the United States, DDT is still detectable in 5–10 percent of people, and its breakdown product, DDE, is detectable in nearly everyone.

Pregnant agricultural workers were tested for blood levels of DDT. Then the researchers tested the mental and physical skills of the women's babies at six, twelve, and twenty-four months using established tests to measure the children's development. For each tenfold increase in DDT level measured in the mother, the team found a corresponding two- to three-point decrease in the children's mental development scores. Children with the highest DDT exposures in the womb were associated with a seven- to ten-point decrease in test scores. Physical skill tests on the children showed a comparable pattern (BBC News 2006).

In May 2006, another published study indicated that mothers and their daughters share an inherited body burden of industrial chemicals. The study shows an unexpected body burden link between mothers and daughters and suggests the long-lasting influence of both pollution passed from mother to daughter and the common exposure to chemicals shared throughout the daughter's childhood (Environmental Working Group 2006a).

Pesticides and industrial chemicals are so pervasive in California and elsewhere in the United States that scientists have even detected pesticides in cigarette smoke. Researchers tested three pure-tobacco-type cigarettes, an experimental reference cigarette, and eleven commercial cigarettes. All showed the presence of three pesticides in tobacco smoke (Dane et al. 2006).

While scientists and researchers, many working abroad, continue to confirm how ubiquitous and damaging to health toxic pesticides and industrial chemicals are in the environment, the Bush administration proposed in April 2006 to roll back Americans' right to know about chemical hazards in their neighborhoods. The proposal would allow California industries to handle almost 1.5 million pounds of toxic chemicals per year without telling the public. In Los Angeles County alone, nearly 630,000 pounds of chemicals a year from 160 facilities would no longer be subject to reporting. Chemicals for which reporting would be slashed or curtailed include some of the most hazardous to human health (Environmental Working Group 2006b). In an unprecedented move, a union of more than 9,000 EPA scientists lashed out against this policy, saying the profits of the pesticide industry are taking priority over public health considerations (Organic Consumers Association 2006b).

THE WORST OF THE THIRD WORLD FOLLOWED BY THE WORST OF THE FIRST WORLD

In the 2005 National Agricultural Workers Survey, 9 percent of California farmworkers reported being told by a doctor or nurse that they suffered from a serious health condition such as diabetes, high blood pressure, tuberculosis, heart disease, a urinary tract infection, or asthma. California Institute for Rural Studies research corroborates the poor health of California's farm laborers. Its study included one thousand farmworkers throughout the state. Eighteen percent of male subjects had at least two of three risk factors for chronic disease, including high serum cholesterol, high blood pressure, or obesity. Both male and female subjects showed a substantially greater incidence of high blood pressure as compared to all U.S. adults. Eighty-one percent of male subjects and 76 percent of female subjects had unhealthful weight. Both male and female subjects were more likely to suffer from iron deficiency anemia than other U.S. adults. More than one-third of male subjects had at least one decayed tooth. Nearly four of ten female subjects had at least one broken or missing tooth (Villarejo et al 2000).

In late 2001, the University of California published a study indicating that immigrant farmworkers from Mexico would be healthier over the long term if they stayed south of the border. Undocumented farmworkers from Mexico tested significantly healthier than their counterparts of the same age living legally in the United States. The only difference between the two groups is the length of time spent here. The longer immigrant farmworkers remain in the United States, the sicker they become. "As we see it, the lifestyle of farmworkers, which is driven by work and poverty, translates into a deterioration of their health status due to poor access to care, a failure of preventive education, and their own diets. When they get here, they have the worst of the Third World, and then they get the worst of the First World" (Villarejo 2001).

Other studies indicate that the health and academic achievement of child immigrants deteriorate the longer they are in the United States, exposed to the mainstream North American culture (Shields and Behrmann 2004). When they arrive here, the children of immigrants from Third World countries have lower rates of asthma and obesity than U.S.-born children. In Mexico the diet is more nutritious than that of many Americans because of its emphasis on legumes and corn products (McLaughlin 2004).

By the time immigrant children become teenagers in America, many have gone years without health insurance, adopted sedentary lifestyles and bad eating habits, or become sexually promiscuous, thereby potentially compromising their health (Shields and Behrmann 2004). Another study of Latinas confirms this by relating level of acculturation to mainstream U.S. values with a lifetime history of smoking, risky sexual behavior, low fruit consumption, and high fast-food consumption—all factors that compromise health status. Latinas who are most acculturated and presumably have been in the United States the longest are the most likely to engage in these health-compromising behaviors (Kasirye et al. 2005).

MENTAL HEALTH

A broad binational health study completed in 2001 found chronic illness to be the most prevalent illness category among more than one thousand participants (Mines et al. 2001). One in four participants reported having a diagnosed chronic ailment. High-blood pressure, gastrointestinal problems, and diabetes were the most common. Of interest is the overwhelming majority (80 percent) of respondents who acknowledged the need for relief from stress or anxiety. Many are purchasing strong medications in Mexico and elsewhere to deal with psychological disorders. Some are taking antidepressants and sedatives, but without clinical follow-up or counseling of any kind.

Twenty-two percent of the participants reported a loss of motivation or feelings of depression so severe that it affected their ability to work. The majority of these individuals claimed that their condition was the result of separation from family members. Many participants reported that pain and bodily injury are tolerated because it "comes with the job."

Numerous health providers report an increase in drug use among farmworkers, especially men, to help them withstand the hardship of farmwork. A recent study in the South documents the provision of crack cocaine along with food, alcohol, and cigarettes by some labor bosses to the farmworkers they supervise, in order to control them through a system of debt peonage (Bletzer 2004).

The American Psychological Association reported in 2001 that minorities in general tend to be disproportionately represented in groups with high rates of mental illness. Mexican American youths are more likely to report depression, anxiety, and suicidal thoughts than are white youths (Feder 2001). "The Latinos we work with are cut off from their old community and familiar smells, sounds, colors, language. There's a shock to the system. We see a high incidence of symptoms of anxiety, depression, post-traumatic stress disorder" (Zimmerman De La Torre, as cited in Feder 2001).

A 2006 federal study found that Hispanic teenage girls are an endangered group in the United States. They attempt suicide more often than any other group. A shocking one in six young Hispanic women attempts suicide, a rate one and a half times as high as that among non-Hispanic black and white teenage girls. They also become mothers at younger ages, tend not to complete their education, and are involved in increasing rates of drug use and other social problems (*New York Times* 2006).

In a study of Mexican women age 35–50 who migrated, researchers discovered that satisfactory adjustment to life in the United States is heavily dependent upon the resolution of interpersonal stressors associated with breaking up social networks in the sending nation (Mexico) and replacing those ties in the receiving nation (United States). However, study participants who prefer to learn the culture of the United States over Mexican culture have the highest levels of depression (Vega et al. 1987). In addition, as one facet of adjustment to the North American lifestyle, Hispanic women smoke cigarettes more often in the United

States than they do in their native countries. Similar smoking increases are not seen in Hispanic men (Bethel and Schenker 2005).

Epidemiologist Bridget F. Grant of the National Institute on Alcohol Abuse and Alcoholism in Bethesda, Maryland, and her coworkers found that 48 percent of Mexican Americans born in the United States developed at least one psychiatric disorder, including alcohol and drug disorders, major depression, mania, panic disorder, social phobia, and general anxiety disorder. Among those born in Mexico but living in the United States, psychiatric disorders afflicted only 29 percent. Of particular interest is the finding that illicit drug disorders occurred in 12 percent of U.S.-born Mexican Americans, compared with only 1.7 percent of their foreign-born counterparts living in the U.S. (Bower 2004).

Latino children face higher health risks than other minorities and whites. They are more likely to consider suicide (20 percent), be exposed to higher levels of air pollution (34 percent), lack health insurance (27 percent), have a higher proportion of teeth with cavities (65 percent), and have less dental work such as filling cavities (Tanner 2002). In addition, nearly 25 percent of Latino children are overweight, and only about 40 percent at age 3–5 are enrolled in early childhood care and education programs, compared to over 60 percent of blacks and whites (Federal Interagency Forum on Child and Family Statistics 2005).

In spite of the prevalence of mental illness within U.S. Latino communities, few Latinos seek mental health services. Latinos as a group use mental health services at noticeably lower rates than other groups. Mental health taboos within the culture, poorly funded community mental health programs, and treating mental illness as a nonissue within the family all contribute to the underutilization of mental health resources (Hernandez 2005).

INSUFFICIENT REST, PROSTITUTION, AND MOLESTATION

Additional risks to farmworker health became apparent during the interviews for this study. Beyond the obvious ubiquitous pesticide exposure, strawberry pickers complained about unremitting exhaustion caused by overwork. Mirna Ramirez spoke of dreaming about strawberry picking while she sleeps. Many injuries in agriculture may be the result of excessive working hours and inadequate daily or weekly rest (International Labour Conference 2004).

Antonia Carranza is the single parent of five children from five different fathers. She lives in the well-known prostitution district of Salinas.

She took up prostitution as a means of supplementing her meager farm wages so that she could support her five children. She, her children, and her niece and fatherless baby all live in a small, run-down three-room apartment. Though prostitution and repeated pregnancies are a less common health risk among central coast farmworkers, Antonia's case underscores the desperation many farmworkers experience in their attempts to survive in California with substandard wages.

Women are sometimes the inadvertent prey of doctors with ulterior motives. A local 60-year-old white male gynecologist allegedly sexually abused farmworkers near Half-Moon Bay, California. Mexican farmworkers with little English speaking ability enlisted the doctor's services because he offered them free of charge. The doctor even provided transportation to his clinic and bought the women lunch. After allegedly molesting farmworkers for years, his case was finally brought to trial (De Sá 2001). In 2001 he was acquitted of molestation charges by a San Mateo County jury. However, the Medical Board of California revoked his license, concluding that he performed inappropriate, unethical, and nonprofessional sexual acts on is patients (Webby 2003).

MEDICAL INSURANCE

Latinos are the group of North Americans most likely to lack medical insurance (Navarrete and Perez 2001). According to a University of California, Los Angeles, study, in 2003 half of California's 4.5 million uninsured residents were Latinos (*San Jose Mercury News* 2003b). In 2003, only 58.1 percent of Latinos in Santa Cruz County were covered by health insurance (Dominican Hospital 2004).

Seventy percent of all persons in a study by the California Institute for Rural Studies and in the National Agricultural Workers Survey (Aguirre International 2005) lacked any form of health insurance. Undocumented workers were the most likely to be uninsured, with 83 percent reporting that they had no health insurance. Only 7 percent were covered by the various government-funded programs for low-income people. A mere 16.5 percent of farmworkers worked for employers that offered health insurance. Nearly one-third of the same workers did not participate in the offered insurance plan because they could not afford the required premiums or copayments.

Thirty-two percent of male farmworkers indicated that they had never been to a doctor or clinic in their lives. Half of all male farmworkers and two-fifths of female farmworkers had never been to a dentist. More than two-thirds claimed that they had never had an eye-care visit (Villarejo et al. 2000). In the binational follow-up study, 58 percent of farmworkers had no medical insurance and 50 percent reported that no member of their family had insurance (Mines et al. 2001). When asked who paid for the majority of the cost of the last health care visit, 41 percent of workers claimed that they paid most of the bill from their personal income (Aguirre International 2005).

· Even if farmworkers are fortunate enough to have some form of health insurance, there is no guarantee that they will receive good-quality health care. Both the federal Institute of Medicine in 2002 and the National Agricultural Workers Survey in 2005 concluded that there are pervasive racial and ethnic disparities in health care quality, even when members of different racial groups have the same symptoms, insurance, and income (Aguirre International 2005; Lyons and Bazely 2002). Minority groups in general receive lower-quality health care than Anglo Americans. For example, in one study of 13,000 heart patients, for every 100 Anglo American patients who went through a procedure to clear their heart arteries, only 74 African Americans were prescribed the same treatment (Lyons and Bazely 2002).

An already poor family without health insurance can be left in ruinous financial circumstances when serious illness or a medical mishap affects a family member. A case in October 2001 illustrates this point. Teresa Martinez, a Watsonville strawberry farmworker, was pregnant with twins and continued to work throughout her pregnancy. She delivered the twins at Stanford Hospital by caesarean section and then died two days later from complications of the surgery. The family had no medical insurance. Her husband was thus left with the daunting task of caring for the newborns and an older daughter while attempting to pay off medical and burial expenses (*San Jose Mercury News* 2001b).

In spite of a serious medical insurance deficit among Latinos in general and nativist claims to the contrary, immigrants are not swamping the U.S. health care system; they use it far less frequently than native-born Americans. Health care spending by the government, insurers, and patients themselves averaged approximately $1,139 per immigrant compared to $2,564 for non-immigrants. Immigrant children spent or cost $270 per year, compared to $1,059 for native-born children. Thirty percent of immigrants use no health care at all during the course of a year (Reuters 2005a).

THE FARMWORKERS' DIET

The California Institute for Rural Studies examined young farmworker subjects who would normally be expected to be in prime physical condition and concluded that the risks for chronic disease such as heart disease, stroke, asthma, and diabetes are "startlingly" high. The report further concluded that poor diet is the most likely contributor to these conditions.

For the impoverished, fruits and vegetables may be a luxury. Those with very limited food budgets tend to concentrate their diets around energy-dense foods composed of refined grains with added sugars and fats as lowest-cost food options. A family's poor, unbalanced diet may quell hunger pangs while leading to obesity among family members, even as they suffer from malnutrition due to the lack of vitamins, minerals, and fiber provided by fresh plant products (Drewnowski and Specter 2004).

Corn is the staple of many Latino households in California. With the advent of prevalent corn "pharma" crops and other genetically modified forms of corn that have contaminated conventional U.S. corn food crops in recent years (Andow et al. 2004; Mellon and Rissler 2004), California farmworkers and other low-income Latinos face a future of possible further health deterioration (see chapter 11).

Potentially exacerbating farmworker health problems still further are fruits and vegetables that are deficient in important nutrients. Data released from a 2006 study by the U.S. Department of Agriculture show that the amounts of such key nutrients as protein, calcium, phosphorus, iron, riboflavin, and vitamin C in vegetables and fruits have declined noticeably over the past fifty years (Gay 2006). Thus, the few vegetables and fruits that farmworkers can afford to purchase may be significantly lacking in the nutrient quality necessary to maintain health.

In a state renowned for its agricultural abundance, 6.4 million people live in households that experience hunger or food insecurity. This figure includes about 2.5 million low-income children for whom hunger results in poor health and poor academic performance. Roughly 30 percent of California's Latino children live in households that cannot provide adequate food for a healthy life (Arnold 2002). "It is a tragedy and more than a little ironic that the labor force that is responsible for producing such a great abundance of healthy food in California should themselves be suffering from the effects of inadequate diet" (Villarejo et al. 2000, 31).

NINE

FARMWORKER HOUSEHOLD
SURVIVAL IN CENTRAL CALIFORNIA

*Ellos tienen que estudiar, tienen que aprender para que sea
diferente su forma de vida a la que nosotros viviendo.*

They [her children] *have* to study, they *have* to become educated
so that their lifestyle is different from the one we are living.

—**Rosa Maria Guzmán, strawberry picker, Watsonville,
California**

*Pues aquí tenemos muy poquito tiempo para estar con los
niños.*

Well here [in California], we have very little time to be with
the children.

—**Leticia Romero, strawberry picker, Watsonville,
California**

Farmworkers originating in the west-central Mexico campesino culture
immigrate to the United States with a strong work ethic and the intention
to work hard (Castro 1986). Indeed, in interviews in both central California and Mexico men spoke of hard work and supporting a family as
if they were perceived as dimensions of fulfilling male and female gender
responsibilities (Alonso 1992; Salgado de Snyder 1993). To be deprived
of an opportunity to work hard is intolerable. Many insist that one of
their primary motivations for immigrating to the United States is to take
advantage of the many opportunities available to work (Segura 1994).

Seventy-five percent of all individual farmworkers nationwide and 52
percent of all California farmworker families earn less than $15,000 per

year. Nearly one-quarter of farmworker families have incomes below the federal poverty level (Aguirre International 2005). Despite wages that are too low to meet basic needs without public or private assistance according to the California Self-Sufficiency Standard and nativist accusations of allegedly draining public services such as welfare, food stamps, and Social Security (Chavez 1997), California farmworkers rarely use welfare services or other forms of state and federal public assistance (Agricultural Worker Charitable Trust 2005; Aguirre International 2005; Chavez 1992, 151; Palerm 1991, iii; 1997, 25; 2000, 335; Taylor 1997, 46). Even with declining wages in the periods 1994–1995 and 1997–1998, only 20 percent of all farmworkers reported receiving unemployment insurance, and just 10 percent reported receiving benefits from the Women, Infants, and Children program. The use of Medicaid and food stamps has actually decreased over time (USDL 2000).

Indeed, undocumented farmworkers as a group contribute not only their labor to California's agricultural economy but also significant capital to federal and state funds by paying an estimated $337–$410 million every year in taxes (Perrin and Williams 1999). This sum represents a contribution of roughly 7 percent of California's gross state product (Cockcroft 1998).

The extent of the contributions of undocumented immigrants to Social Security alone is striking. The funds amounted to 10 percent of the surplus in 2004, that is, the difference between what the system currently receives in payroll taxes and what is distributed in pension benefits. In 2002 alone, 3.8 million households headed by undocumented immigrants generated $6.4 billion in Social Security taxes, benefits that they will never be able to collect (Porter 2005). The National Academy of Sciences found that the average immigrant contributes $1,800 more in taxes annually than they receive in benefits. Over their lifetimes, immigrants and their children each pay an average of $80,000 more in taxes than they receive in local, state, and federal benefits combined (Southern Poverty Law Center 2005b).

California's central coast has one of the lowest levels of welfare receipt in the state, even with poverty rates twice as prevalent there as the entire San Francisco Bay area (Hill 2004, 66). In a 2001 Farm Worker Housing and Health Needs Assessment Study of the Salinas and Pajaro valleys, less than half of the poorest respondents in the study accessed social services such as unemployment insurance, food stamps, or Temporary Aid for Needy Families, for which they may have been eligible (Giuriato et al. 2001).

CENTRAL COAST FARMWORKER HOUSING

Data released by the U.S. Census Bureau on November 20, 2001, indicated that San Francisco Bay area counties were among the wealthiest in the nation, with a unique mix of educated and highly paid immigrants (Bazeley and Kang 2001). A 2001 Community Assessment Project report released by the United Way confirmed that, for the general population, income increased less than 10 percent while home prices increased 30 percent and rents increased 20 percent over the year 2000. In November 2001, average rents in Santa Cruz County ranged from $792 per month for a studio apartment to $2,497 per month for a four-bedroom apartment (Boerner 2001). In 2005, a two-bedroom apartment cost the renter $825–$1,600 per month in Monterey County and $1,000–$1,775 per month in Santa Cruz County.

According to the U.S. Department of Housing and Urban Development, affordable housing should cost 30 percent or less of gross income. In the San Francisco Bay area, including Santa Cruz and Watsonville, one household in three in the general population pays more than this recommended percentage (Giuriato et al. 2001; Rubenstein 2001).

From 1996 to 2002 in Santa Cruz County, the cost of a median-priced home shot from $209,000 to $420,000, an increase of 101 percent in just eight years. During the same period, median family income increased from $53,100 to $69,000, an increase of only 30 percent (Dominican Hospital 2004). Latinos living in Santa Cruz County spent over twice the recommended affordable housing percentage, or 76.7 percent of their household *take-home pay,* on housing costs in both 2003 and in 2004 (Dominican Hospital 2003, 2004). By 2006 the median value of a single-family home had risen to $594,000 (www.trulia.com/CA).

Home ownership represents a profound dividing line between the "haves" and "have nots" in California today. The majority of whites (71 percent) and Asians (59 percent) are home owners, while the majority of Latinos (55 percent) and blacks (51 percent) are renters (Baldassare 2004). Whereas all but the wealthiest find the prospect of home purchase or apartment rental in Santa Cruz and Monterey Counties to be a daunting financial prospect, farmworkers are by and large completely economically disenfranchised from the housing market.

Latinos are the worst hit by the disparity between income and cost of living (Boerner 2001). The median housing cost paid by farmworker families in the Central California Housing and Health Needs Assessment Study of 2001 was $400 per month. This sum is approximately 40 per-

TABLE 2 INCOME AND HOUSING COSTS
(2004, 2005)

	Annual Median Family Income[a] (all families)	Annual Gross Average Income[b] (farmworker families)	Monthly Renter Costs (2-bedroom apartment)	Median Value of Single-Family Home[a]
California	$58,327	$9,500–$15,000	$914 (median)	$391,102
Monterey County	$56,489	$9,500–$15,000	$825–$1,600	$500,161
Santa Cruz County	$75,759	$9,500–$15,000	$1,000–$1,775	$577,139

SOURCES: [a]U.S. Census Bureau, http://factfinder.census.gov, accessed December 17, 2005. [b]National Agricultural Workers Survey 2005, *The California Farm Labor Force: Overview and Trends from the National Agricultural Workers Survey*, Aguirre International, http://www.epa.gov/region9/ag/docs/final-naws-so92805-pdf. *Monterey Herald*, www.montereyherald.com, accessed December 17, 2005; *Santa Cruz Sentinel*, www.santacruzsentinel.com, accessed December 17, 2005.

cent of their income, an amount that exceeds the affordability threshold by 10 percent. Thirty-five percent of farmworker respondents paid more than 50 percent for housing, and 17 percent paid more than 80 percent of their income for housing (Giuriato et al. 2001).

The only farmworker participants in this study who acknowledged payment of rents less than $400 per month were those living in the state-supported Buena Vista migrant camp. In October 2001, farmworkers in the city of Watsonville were paying $600–$675 for one-bedroom bungalows and "apartments." In some cases three families with a total of twelve people shared a single unit.

In recent years, the topic of inadequate farmworker housing in the midst of skyrocketing central coast real estate values has become a topic of public concern. The middle class of Watsonville is shriveling up, while growing income disparities foster a two-tiered community made up of the wealthy and the poor, including farmworkers. In 1997, Santa Cruz County became the second least affordable place to live in the nation. The unemployment rate in Watsonville increased to 15.2 percent in the same year (Jacobi and Lee 1999).

A 1980 study by the Farmers Home Administration calculated an unmet demand of 756,196 housing units for farmworkers nationwide. This estimate occurred prior to California's reintensification of agriculture. In 1995, a study by the UC Center for Cooperatives calculated a shortage of 250,000 housing units for farmworkers in California alone. The study further estimated that 300,000–400,000, or 40–60 percent, of California farmworkers are either homeless or lack adequate housing for some significant period of the year. At the same time, the number of employer-provided housing camps dropped from 1,424 in 1982 to about 900 in 1994. Some estimates reveal that in the 1950s and 1960s there were as many as 5,000 employer-provided housing camps (Perrin and Williams 1998).

Housing Shortage in Watsonville

Former Watsonville mayor Oscar Ríos acknowledged that nothing has really changed in his beleaguered city. Affordable housing scarcity continues to be a serious problem. He mentioned six hundred units of affordable housing that have been built since 1999, which, according to the mayor, is a mere token gesture and barely addresses the need. In addition, 3,000 jobs are needed to reduce the unemployment rate in Wat-

Figure 14. Farmworker housing, Watsonville, California.

sonville; 1,500 have been created, but most are low-paid jobs in the retail business (interview, Oct. 18, 2001).

The problem of overcrowding was clearly evident when I visited study participant Rogelio Alvarez's residence. In 1998, Rogelio and his family lived with his brother Juan's family and his sister Adela Lozano's family in an apartment carved out of a rambling Victorian house in central Watsonville. Several other farmworker families lived in pieces of the same huge Victorian house. I counted nineteen adults and children in the three families, all living in approximately 1,000 square feet with a single bathroom.

In order to afford high rents, several families often live in a housing unit designed for a single family. The approximately 250-square-foot farmworker housing units in figure 14 are each home to ten to twelve people from two or three different families. The rent for each unit in October 2001 was $600–$675.

Housing Shortage in Salinas

Salinas is also plagued with a housing shortage for low-income farm laborers, many of whom reside there throughout the year to work the three or four annual harvests produced in the valley. As nearby Silicon Valley housing prices skyrocketed at the end of the 1990s, many Silicon Valley employees bought houses in Salinas for half the cost of a Silicon Valley home (Kaplan 2000). Much of the land in the 19-square-mile city is already built up with expensive single-family homes designed to house top wage earners and potential buyers destined for employment at Cisco Systems' 20,000-worker site in nearby Coyote Valley.

In the city's poorest neighborhoods, the shortage is forcing families to triple or even quadruple up in apartments with nowhere for children to play but a parking lot. In 2000 one estimate indicated that some Salinas neighborhoods housed as many as 22,000 people per single square mile (Kaplan 2000). Anna Caballero, 2001 mayor of Salinas, claimed that in fact 31,000–34,000 people per square mile lived in Census Tract 7 in the area of Del Monte Avenue, with 30 percent of households housing seven or more people (interview, Oct. 19, 2001).

Most of the Salinas farmworkers interviewed for this study live in substandard housing in Salinas's poorest neighborhoods. José Moreno's family often houses as many as ten people in a deteriorating unit of less than 400 square feet. Fernando Azevedo and his wife Ana Aguirre live in a four-bedroom apartment with eight of their children, three of them married. The married children and their families, in turn, each occupy one of the four bedrooms. The apartment is equipped with two large refrigerators, one of them in the living room. There is a freezer on the front patio. At any given time, there may be twenty to twenty-six adults and children living here.

In 1999, Juan Borrego lived in a two and one-half room deteriorating unit in the same poor neighborhood of Salinas. He had approximately 300 square feet, with a living area, a small kitchen, and a tiny sleeping area off to the side of the kitchen. Juan and his wife slept in the sleeping area. All three of their daughters shared a hide-a-bed in the living area.

In 1998, Antonia Carranza lived in a ramshackle apartment building in the purported prostitution zone of central Salinas. Her unit consisted of approximately 300 square feet, with three rooms arranged in a slightly different configuration than those in Juan Borrego's apartment. Antonia lived in the apartment with her three children and conducted her prostitution business from a bedroom that faced the street. Her niece occupied the front living area with her infant son.

Both mayor Anna Caballero and former mayor Oscar Ríos feel strongly that their respective counties, Monterey and Santa Cruz, have ignored and not taken responsibility for the tremendous low-income, affordable "essential" housing deficit and demand. Besides the huge agribusiness demand for cheap labor in both counties, these two counties include coastal cities that are common tourist attractions. Santa Cruz, Monterey, Pacific Grove, and Carmel are preferred Pacific coast marine enthusiasts' locations. The adjoining coastal mountain ranges offer many opportunities for a variety of recreational activities. In addition, the cities and towns are recognized art and cultural centers.

Comparable to the cheap labor force in agribusiness, the backbone of the thriving tourist industries is a workforce of predominantly low-salaried Latino workers in restaurants, hotels, and numerous tourist attractions. Their low wages prevent them from living in the central coast towns and cities where they work. Oscar Ríos commented that the overloaded buses that transport low-salaried Latino workers between Watsonville and Santa Cruz every morning and evening are a clear indicator that Santa Cruz is not doing its share to house its own "essential" workers.

At the end of 2004, with rents and housing costs beyond the reach of most farmworker families, I visited several families, in housing units designed for single families, with three or four families totaling twelve to twenty-six people living in them. These housing arrangements are not atypical. Impoverished Mexican farmworkers often survive by living in household clusters or networks of households centered around a key relative in which skills and services are traded and shared (Chavez 1992; Healey 1997; Vélez-Ibañez and Greenberg 1992). Other kin and their households form peripheral households. Collectively, the residents of household clusters share funds of knowledge that include skills with application to a wide range of life necessities, including car repair, botanical medicinal treatments for illness, how to navigate through the social services bureaucracy, babysitting, and cooking.

As a survival strategy, young farmworking families without multiple wage earners often pool their resources with other families in order to diminish housing and living expenses, as well as to share child care responsibilities (Chavez 1992; Palerm 1991; Vasquez et al. 1994; Zlolniski 1996). A domestic group of friends and other single relatives, such as siblings or cousins, provides another convenient way for single people to share the cost of housing (Chavez 1992).

In Monterey County and Santa Cruz County, another parent, family member, or friend typically cares for farmworkers' young children. Only 16 percent use licensed day-care facilities, and only 6 percent have children in Head Start programs (Parsons 2001). The funds of knowledge shared among immediate and extended family members enable Mexican families to share the burden and demands of everyday living and to cope with their impoverished circumstances (Chavez 1992; Moll et al. 1992; Vasquez et al. 1994; Vélez-Ibañez and Greenberg 1992, as cited in Zavella 1996).

MEXICAN FARMWORKERS IN CALIFORNIA: PROBLEMS AND CHALLENGES

Housing shortages and isolation, along with unhealthy living conditions, have become institutionalized as a result of the low wages received for difficult, often perilous work and inadequate housing opportunities. In addition, farmworkers face other challenges at home and in their California communities.

Extended Households

Although extended households with pooled resources among members offer farmworkers a means of economic and social survival, there are often inherent problems. Overcrowding with the consequent lack of privacy can generate psychological stress and family tensions, possibly accounting in part for the exaggerated levels of mental illness in U.S.-born Mexican Americans (see chapter 8 and Zlolniski 1996).

In addition, economic stratification within the household sometimes results from unequal access to employment opportunities, material, and public resources available to members of the same household. As discussed earlier, household residents frequently hold differing documentation status. A farmworker's legal status determines access to government social benefits and welfare. Economic stratification and whether a household member is eligible for government benefits often create a situation in which living standards among members of the same household differ markedly (Zlolniski 1996).

In these situations, only limited income pooling occurs in order to cover basic living expenses such as rent and utilities. Budgets for items such as food, clothing, and medical care are kept separately. The complex interplay of factors such as overcrowding, employment opportunity availability, and economic stratification often results in conflicts that ultimately lead to the dissolution of extended households, followed by their reconfiguration with a new group of workers, thereby potentially resulting in considerable household instability (Zlolniski 1996).

Solitary Men

Since the Bracero program, many unaccompanied male newcomers have entered California willing to work in agribusiness for wages that are not economically sustainable (Alarcón and Mines 2001). There are social costs associated with having large numbers of solitary males separated by 2,000 miles from their wives and girlfriends in Mexico. Their living and working conditions foster and intensify socially undesirable behaviors such as prostitution, alcoholism, and other forms of drug addiction.

Prostitutes follow the migrant seasons, showing up at labor camps and bars on farmworkers' paydays. A 1997 study found that about 45 percent of Mexican migrant workers questioned reported having sex with prostitutes in the United States, and condom use was reported to be rare (Garcia 2001). According to Artemiza Avalos, the farmworker outreach coordinator for the Monterey County AIDS Project, many farmworkers have never used a condom, though there are programs that attempt to provide education regarding condom use (Garcia 2001). The legacy of socially undesirable behaviors engaged in by solitary, lonely males in California can be passed on to unsuspecting family members in Mexico when they return to their hometowns and villages (see below).

Education

The highest level of schooling attained by most farmworkers is the sixth grade in Mexico (Aguirre International 2005). Many associate their difficult work and low pay with a lack of education. The last formal question I asked farmworkers in Salinas and Watsonville interviews was, "What are your hopes for your children's future?" Universally, without exception, all farmworker parents in this study want their children to become educated so that they don't have to work as farm laborers when they reach adulthood. This finding corroborates the work of researchers who have found that Mexican immigrants hope their children will be better educated and find better, less menial jobs (Chavez 1992). Other researchers have found that U.S.-born children of foreign-born hired farmworkers were not interested in pursuing their parents' line of work (Villarejo 2001).

Indeed, the commitment to encouraging education and dissuading their children from considering farmwork as a viable employment option is so strong that many parents take their children to the fields to observe the hardship firsthand. After taking his children to the fields to watch people working like "burros," Rogelio Alvarez gave them an ultimatum: either take an interest in school and study hard, or go to work with him in the fields. He reported with satisfaction that his children have since maintained an interest in schoolwork.

Elena Fonseca, a migrant farmworker who lives in the Buena Vista migrant camp, expressed her hopes for a better life for her children as follows: *"Pues, están aprendiendo que no sirve."* ("They're [her children] learning that [farmwork] isn't a good employment choice.") Xóchitl Flores of Salinas commented, *"Les digo a ellos, 'Estudien, para que no andan como yo.'"* ("I say to them [her children], 'Study so that you won't have to walk through life like I am'").

Still, Latinos in general have the lowest rates of high school and college graduation of any major population group in the United States (del Pinal and Singer 1997). For every one hundred Latinos who enter the U.S. educational system, only forty-seven graduate from high school and only eight receive a B.A. degree (Solorzano and Ornelas 2007). In 1996, the President's Advisory Commission on Educational Excellence for Hispanic Americans called upon the nation

> to improve education for Hispanic Americans. The Call to Action goes out to Hispanics and non-Hispanics alike—rich, middle-class, and poor—to work in partnership with the leadership and resources of government and the private sector.
>
> The nature of the problem with the education of Hispanic Americans is rooted in a refusal to accept, to recognize, and to value the central role of Hispanics in the past, present, and future of this nation. The education of Hispanic Americans is characterized by a history of neglect, oppression, and periods of wanton denial of opportunity. (1998, 13)

The obstacles encountered by farmworker families whose most passionate objective in life is for their children to become educated and escape the onus of farm labor are formidable. Ninety-eight percent of the children of immigrants come to the United States with the hope and desire to learn (de la Torre 2002). Yet migrant children's academic lives are often adversely affected by the failure of schools to address their needs (López 1999). Schools exhibit both structural barriers and cultural and linguistic discontinuities that contribute to the exaggerated numbers of educational casualties among Latino students. Structural factors include racism and discrimination and their resultant manifestations in the schools. They also include practices and policies in schools that are contrary to the goal of equal and high-quality education for all students (Nieto 1996).

In addition, cultural and linguistic discontinuities make life particularly difficult for students from economically oppressed and non-mainstream groups (Nieto 1996). There is a pervasive disconnect, both culturally and linguistically, between the monolingual Spanish-speaking homes farmworker children are raised in and the California educational system, which is predominantly represented by Anglo Americans who speak the English language and ascribe to a very different, frequently conflicting set of Anglo American cultural and educational values. Often mainstream, middle-class values predominate to the degree that teachers and administrators are culturally blind and incapable of appropriately contextualizing what they perceive as either individual or cultural deficiency in their students (López 1999).

Even though Latino parents value education highly, and high levels of parental involvement in schools at an early age have been shown to affect student performance through high school (Henderson 1987), many feel intimidated by the school environment and lack an understanding of the culture of California schools. Schools seldom have programs or mechanisms designed to involve monolingual Spanish-speaking parents meaningfully in classroom activities or in planning and policy decisions (Vasquez et al. 1994). The result is that few Latino parents initiate contact with the school, and few know how to respond to contacts initiated by the school (Delgado-Gaitan 1990).

Like Elena Esparza, many farmworkers express helplessness because of their inability to assist their children with school assignments. Most farmworkers are uneducated beyond elementary school and speak little, if any, English. Their children's requests for assistance with English and math assignments at home often go unanswered. Problems associated with their inability to assist their children are exacerbated by teachers who have little confidence in their students' educational potential and little interest in their cultural reality.

In school conferences and workshops early in my research, I heard teachers publicly make inappropriate, denigrating remarks about their Latino students and family members. Several expressed indignation at the mere suggestion that contact with students' families in the communities might further the students' academic progress. Most appeared to have little or no interest in learning about the culture or in interacting with family or community members. This schism is disconcerting when one considers the importance of education and the significant level of respect and esteem afforded teachers in general by farmworkers and their children. It may also be viewed as a contributing factor to the inflated dropout rate of students from this ethnic population.

Carolina Evans-Román has a long history of elementary school teaching in the Watsonville Pajaro Union School District, where many schools have majority populations of farmworker children. She claims that most elementary school teachers are Anglo, with a poor grasp of the Spanish language and the farmworker culture. Many express fear at the prospect of home visits where they could extend classroom invitations to parents, thereby reducing the intimidation many parents feel (personal communication, 2005).

Numerous young people living on the central coast are not even enrolled in school. This immigrant youth population, ages 16–24, has California's lowest enrollment rates among immigrant youth. In addition, the central coast ranks lowest in the state in English language proficiency, with more than 20 percent of young people reporting that they are not fluent in English. Nearly one in five central coast students enrolled in high school is limited English proficient, the highest number for any region in California (Hill 2004).

No Time for Family

Sixty-four percent of California farmworkers are married, and about 54 percent have children. The median number of children per farmworker family household is two (Aguirre International 2005). Several farmworkers and their spouses complained bitterly about *el exceso del trabajo* (too much work). They view the many hours spent at work away from their families as a source of disharmony and family disruption, both within their immediate families and among extended family members living in the area. Eduardo Sousa expressed his frustration about how much easier it was to maintain family unity in Mexico. According to Eduardo, U.S. farmworker family members live in different cities, and it has become next to impossible for them all to spend time together. Veronica Madrigál has not seen or visited her sisters in Florida for six years because the harvest season in Florida does not coincide with that in California. Family reunions in Huitzó, Michoacán, thus occur at different times of the year. She has never met her nieces.

Juan Borrego of Salinas works a day shift. His brother who lives only a few miles away from him works a night shift. Juan complained that he rarely sees his brother. When he arrives at his brother's home in the daytime, his brother is sleeping. His brother only has time to visit him when he gets off work in the middle of the night—when Juan and his family are asleep.

Some farmworkers express concern about not having the time to be with their children. Armando Acosta rarely sees his own children, who live with him in Salinas. He claims that he has no time for family because he is always working. He works 52 weeks per year, twelve to fifteen hours a day. He has time for family interaction only on rare occasions when work slacks off and he can leave early. His children are still in bed when he leaves in the morning and are in bed again when he arrives home from work.

Armando reminisced about his family life in Los Sauces de Pérez before immigrating to the United States. In Mexico, family members spend 60–70 percent of their days and nights with each other. In California he says he feels lucky to be with family members 10 percent of the time. When I asked him about his young daughters, he could not recall the age of one of them and had no knowledge about what any of them were studying in school.

Gangs

Rosa Maria Guzmán concurs with other study participant families who claim that the incidence of gangs and gang-related violence in Watsonville is a direct result of farmworker family disruption *within* California. Rosa Maria argues that in Mexico the mother was always home working and was always available when her children needed her. Her own father worked only eight hours a day, so there was plenty of time for family unity, even though the family lived in extreme poverty.

Low wages provided by farm labor in California result in women who must work along with their spouses to support their families. Women's employment, in turn, sometimes results in children being neglected. Parents working in California's corporate agribusiness and local packing houses often are required to work twelve- or thirteen-hour days. According to Rosa Maria, many parents have no idea where their children are, what they are doing, or if they need their parents.

Rosa Maria's husband Manny chimed in with his assessment of the contrasting values of young people in Mexico and California. In rural

Mexico young people are interested in growing crops and raising and caring for animals. In California their priorities shift to an interest in cars, electronic devices, fashion, and music. According to Rosa Maria and Manny, the combination of job-related parental neglect and "distorted modern values" leaves no time for family interactions that promote family unity. "Corrupt" values and lack of family unity encourage young people to take to the streets to join a gang as a social replacement for family.

Binational Families

The defining characteristics of farmworkers and "intact" nuclear families as well as the definition of the traditional family on both sides of the border are in a state of flux. "Intact" nuclear migrant families are often fluid, changing, and resilient (Palerm 1991; Zavella 1996). In Mexico, as a result of emigration as well as other economic constraints, the traditional Mexican family structure is undergoing disruption and reorganization. The traditional family structure in Mexico, which included a breadwinner father as head of the household and a wife at home with children, is regularly being replaced by a family structure in which both spouses work and must rely on multiple sources of income for survival (Zavella 2000). Family commitment to binational life is exemplified by the fact that about 13 percent of Mexican farmworkers maintain homes on both sides of the border (Rochín and Castillo 1995).

In this study, the dispersion of family members binationally followed a relatively predictable pattern. In general, older parents remain in the villages and towns of the Mexican rural countryside, while their younger children emigrate to the United States. Twenty-seven of thirty-one primary farmworker interviewees who provided information regarding the binational nature of their families indicated that at least one of their parents lived in Mexico. For most families in which both of the farmworker's parents were still living, both parents continued to reside in their home towns and villages. Five of the thirty-one interviewees indicated that "their entire family" had immigrated to the United States. Fourteen other families indicated that more than five of their immediate family members had immigrated to and settled in the United States.

HOMES AND FAMILIES LEFT BEHIND IN MEXICO

Central California farmworkers maintain contact with their binational family members in Mexico by means of telephone calls, letters, and visits to their home towns and villages. However, as corroborated by the studies of other researchers, contact with migrant family members in Mexico is often infrequent and results in characteristically painful separation and serious family disruption (Hondagneu-Sotelo and Avila 1997; Salgado de Snyder 1993, 1996).

The social costs of emigration to California for the families, villages, and towns left behind in Mexico are often extreme. Family separation means that a generation of Mexican children is being raised without fathers (Alarcón and Mines 2001; Salgado de Snyder 1993). In some cases absent fathers in the United States either abandon their families in Mexico entirely or marry another woman in California and start a second family in the United States (Gledhill 1995).

Stories of spousal family abandonment and marriages to second wives are lively topics of discussion throughout the west-central Mexico countryside. Abandoned wives with children in Mexico are frequently left with no means of support and no way to contact their spouse in the United States. Some families in Mexico break down entirely as a result of the migratory process (Gledhill 1995, 136). I encountered many abandoned and seriously depressed women quietly mourning the separation from and loss of loved ones, in both central California and west-central Mexico.

Jorge Becerra of El Loreto Occidental, Jalisco, left his wife and young children in Mexico over twenty years ago to work in Salinas's corporate agribusiness. He subsequently married a second wife in the United States and has two children with her. As a tractor driver, his wages are substantially higher than those of less skilled farmworkers. He appeared to be economically better off than all other farmworkers I interviewed in Salinas. His salary is high enough for his California family to afford a new two-story home in Salinas. He also supports his oldest son's education at the University of California, Santa Cruz.

While Jorge lives a comparatively affluent lifestyle with his wife and two children in Salinas, his first wife, seven children, and mother all live together in squalor in Mexico. They have a very small home with beds crowded into each room. Jorge's Mexican wife claims that the only forms of support her husband provides for his family in Mexico are annual one-month visits and payment for the children's education beyond elementary school in Mexico.

The small household of Tomasina López Santos in Confradia de Duendes, Jalisco, represents the multiple levels of painful separation and abandonment potentially experienced by family members in a single family with members living on both sides of the border. Tomasina's husband spends most of the year living with his grown children in Salinas, while Tomasina takes care of their livestock and *parcelas* in Confradia. Though well into his 60s, the husband continues to work seasonally in California's corporate agribusiness.

Tomasina's youngest daughter, Maricela, and her baby son were also living with her when I visited the family initially in 1998. Maricela's un-documented husband was working in Santa Ana, California, at the time. Maricela was planning to be reunited with her husband that summer by making an undocumented border crossing with her son. When I visited the family one year later in summer 1999, Maricela and her son had not yet emigrated. She finally emigrated in summer 2000. By then her baby was over 2 years old and had never met his father.

Another of Tomasina's daughters emigrated to the United States with her husband and daughters, leaving her two sons, Arturo López Navarro and Jorge Esteban, to live with Tomasina just as they were entering their teen years. When I visited Tomasina in summer 1998 and summer 1999, both boys were thin and obviously depressed. Fortunately, the boys were reunited with their family in central California at the conclusion of their teen years.

It is not uncommon for family members in California to have never met or had contact with immediate family members living in Mexico. As of summer 2000, the family of Jesus Acosta and Rosario Morales of Los Sauces de Pérez, Jalisco, had not seen their eldest undocumented Salinas farmworker son, Armando, for over eleven years. Armando, in turn, had never met his two younger sisters still living in his home rancho. His parents had never met his wife or their grandchildren born in the United States. Family members infrequently conversed by phone from El Ter-rero, a larger pueblo with a phone many miles away.

Sometimes immediate family members are lost altogether. While shar-ing a meal with the family of Joaquin Bejarano of Chaparaco, Mi-choacán, at a local, popular, outdoor seafood restaurant, his wife Mari-bel Terraza reflected on the distribution of her family members between Mexico and the United States. She attempted to recall the last time she had contact by phone or otherwise with one of her brothers, who had

Figure 15. Members of the family of Jesus Acosta and Rosario Morales, Los Sauces de Pérez, Jalisco.

emigrated to Arizona thirty or forty years ago. She finally concluded sadly that she had not had contact with him for over thirty years. *"Es como si fuera muerte."* ("It's as if he were dead.")

Central California farmworkers leave behind families and a familiar rural campesino farming culture when they emigrate to the United States. In order to buy the survival opportunities offered by corporate agribusiness, they and their loved ones in Mexico pay high social and health costs. None of the farmworkers in this study appreciated the poverty they and their family members endured in the rural countryside. However, most recall with nostalgia the freedom experienced back on the farm and the day-to-day unity experienced by family members. After years of work in California's corporate agribusiness, many return to the post-NAFTA rural Mexico countryside only to find a markedly changed world.

SOME HEALTH CONSEQUENCES OF BINATIONAL FAMILY LIFE

In addition and related to the often tragic social costs inherent in binational family life, the incidence of the transfer and spread of the deadly

AIDS virus among farmworkers in California (Castañeda and Zavella 2005; Zavella 2005), and from California to the towns and villages of the west-central Mexico's rural countryside, appears to be increasing (Magis-Rodriguez et al. 2004). The states of Jalisco and Michoacán, which supply many farmworkers to California's corporate agribusiness, are among the hardest hit by the epidemic (Garcia 2001; Magis-Rodriguez et al. 2004). Husbands and boyfriends in California engage in illicit sexual activities and contract the disease. They then return to Mexico and inadvertently and unknowingly pass the virus on to their unsuspecting wives and girlfriends. Pregnant wives, in turn, pass the disease on to their unborn children.

The impact of this tragedy is aggravated by the fact that AIDS *(La Sida)* is viewed as a horrible stigma in the west-central Mexico countryside. Infected individuals quickly become outcasts. Families are forced from their neighborhoods. Parents are fired from jobs, and children are expelled from schools (Garcia 2001). Thus, even if California farmworkers returning to Mexico are aware of their HIV-positive health status, they are unlikely to report their condition to others.

Prior to NAFTA, AIDS was rare in the Mexican countryside. In 1995, rural areas of Mexico accounted for only 4 percent of Mexico's reported AIDS cases. In the post-NAFTA years from 1994 to 2000, the number of AIDS cases in the rural countryside grew by 80 percent. By 2001, the percentage of AIDS cases in the rural countryside of Mexico climbed to 10 percent and included more women and children than ever before (Garcia 2001; Mena 2000). As of 2001, 48,000 AIDS cases were documented in Mexico, but health officials believe that the HIV-infected population involved at least 177,000 people. They estimate that 30 percent of AIDS cases in Michoacán, the source of tens of thousands of workers in California's Bay Area, including corporate agribusiness, originated in the United States (Garcia 2001). Their estimate is corroborated by more recent studies indicating that Michoacán has the highest percentage of AIDS cases among rural persons with background residence in the United States (Magis-Rodriguez et al. 2004).

HIV/AIDS researchers recognize that migrant labor plays a major role in the geographic spread of HIV (Mena 2000, A13; National Center for Farmworker Health 2004; Organista et al. 2004). Migrant farmworkers in the United States are among the most vulnerable to contract sexually and drug-use-transmitted diseases including hepatitis C. California has the highest incidence of HIV/AIDS in the United States (National Center for Farmworker Health 2004), and because the population of HIV-infected individuals is so large in the United States compared to that in Mexico, the risk of acquiring HIV/AIDS is 5.5 times greater in the United States (Magis-Rodriguez et al. 2004).

According to the National Commission to Prevent Infant Mortality, migrant farmworkers as a group are ten times as likely as the general U.S. population to acquire HIV (Garcia 2001). The California Department of Health Services reports that the percentage of Mexican or Mexican American AIDS cases increased from 36.5 percent in 1995 to 47.7 percent in 2000 (Sanchez and Lemp 2003). Their family members in rural Mexico are at high risk for sex-related transmission of HIV (Salgado de Snyder et al. 2000). The burden of the disease contracted in California is thus borne by Mexico, which lacks sufficient funding and medical infrastructure to treat the burgeoning number of people contracting the disease in the rural countryside (Mena 2000).

TEN

MEANWHILE, BACK ON THE FARM

Todo el rancho se va; hay casas vacías sin nadie. Toda la familia está allá.

The whole village is leaving; there are empty houses [in the village] with no one living in them. The whole family is there [in the United States].

—Tomasina López Santos, Confradia de Duendes, Jalisco

Fox has been a disaster! It is difficult to describe his record as it is full of irrational behavior. Yes, you can say that he has worked to benefit large corporations, but even that's inaccurate because he and his crew of incompetent cabinet members have made so many mistakes that if I were a big business guy, I would be furious with them!

—Alejandro Nadal, economist and coordinator of the Science, Technology and Development Program, El Colegio de México

Cocula, Jalisco, is the mariachi capital of the world. Mariachi bands from all over the globe converge on the small rural town during the summer months to play their lively songs and compete for the title of best mariachi band in the world. The town is surrounded by sugar cane fields, an important crop in this region, and visitors can purchase a wide and colorful variety of tasty Mexican candy manufactured locally from the cane.

The road leading from Cocula passes through La Sauceda, an average-size village. Along the side of the road near the village, the traveler observes several dormitories where sugar cane harvesters who migrate from Guerrero live while the cane harvest is in progress from November 20 to May 1. At last, the remote village of San Nicolás appears on the horizon. Entering San Nicolás reminds one of how Mexico must have been one hundred years ago. Adobe houses and buildings line narrow cobblestone streets. Farmers on horses and mules packed with forage for their animals ride down the streets. Chickens run about helter skelter, while the lowing of cattle, hee-hawing of donkeys, grunting of pigs, and songs of birds fill the air. Within the immense tranquility of the rancho, the smells and sounds of nature mingle with the smells and sounds of the domestic animals and cooked meals emanating from the houses. The only indicators of a modern era are the empty modern houses built with remittances from the United States, a new elementary school, and a recently built Baptist church.

The yard in front of Consuelo Segura Camacho and Salvador Alfaro's house is fenced with rustic stacked rocks. A tree at the yard's entrance acts as a support for an enormous prostrate, scalloped-leaved cactus plant growing on the branches. Consuelo tells me that the name of the unusual cactus is *pitajalla*. Several huge white cactus flowers hang from its stems, sending their floral perfume into the surrounding air. Consuelo informs me that the beauty and fragrance of the flowers earned them the name *reina de la noche* (night queen).

Pots and cans full of plants line one side of the yard. A huge mesquite tree fills the yard in front of the house and provides perches for the family's pet bird, Paco. The yard is swept immaculately clean. The small home at one corner of the large yard has an adjoining brick outhouse. The other side of the yard looks out onto an approximately 25-square-meter lot planted in corn and squash.

Consuelo, Salvador, a research assistant, Juana Alfaro Ramirez, and I all sit together around a table in the shade of an overhanging tree to discuss the family's binational life and the farming practices in the region. Juana is the cousin of Consuelo and Salvador's oldest daughter, Ismena Rocha, who works in Salinas's corporate agribusiness. Seated on Juana's lap is her three-year old granddaughter, Margarita. Margarita sobbed inconsolably the entire afternoon of our visit, never stopping. When I queried Juana about the source of the child's grief, she responded, "Margarita is sad because her mother has left her. Margarita's mother and father successfully completed an undocumented border crossing fifteen days ago. When they establish themselves with steady employment, they will send for their daughter."

Juana's husband and six of Juana's nine children, two daughters and four sons, have emigrated without documents to the United States. Juana says that one of her sons crossed the border a total of fifteen times in a three-week period before crossing without being caught and returned to Tijuana. All of her sons are working in construction.

She speaks of the importance of family members in the United States regularly getting together with other family members still living in Mexico. Because they are in a foreign country, the importance of family contact and unity is even more important than if the entire family lived in Mexico. She maintains that when family members return to Mexico they are starved for family contact and want to interact with family members in Mexico almost continuously.

Salvador worked as a bracero in California and Arizona agriculture in 1955, picking carrots, beans, artichokes, and lettuce in Salinas and cotton in Arizona. He used to grow the corn, bean, and squash intercrop in Mexico on his 3-hectare *pequeña propriedad*. He planted two crops per year on the rain-fed land. His intercrop developed from May to November. Then, after the November harvest, while the ground was still damp from the rains, he grew a crop of garbanzo beans from November to January. Cattle and horses grazed on the land after the bean harvest, depositing manure and restoring the land for the next year's intercrop.

Salvador claims that, at 82, he is too old to work the land, and his land is too far from the village for him to walk there anymore. He now rents his land to a farmer who plants a monoculture of hybrid corn imported from the United States. According to Salvador, the renter relies heavily on the use of agrochemicals, including chemical fertilizers and herbicides, for maximum crop production. The rent for land use is fifteen truckloads of *mazorca* (harvested dried corn) each year.

Salvador maintains that agrochemicals were introduced into San Nicolás twenty to twenty-five years ago. In the small corn plot in front of his yard, he uses only the chemical fertilizer urea. He argues that he doesn't like to use herbicides or insecticides because the herbicides kill his squash plants and insecticides are unnecessary since he has never had any problem with pests. Besides, he knows of several people who died of pesticide poisoning. Juana's son ate sugar cane after it had been sprayed with herbicides and became so ill that he had to be taken to the hospital in Cocula for treatment. Fortunately, the son recovered from the ordeal.

A walk through the village after our conversation further confirms the vision of this village as an example of the rural Mexico of antiquity. Adobe houses painted in a variety of colors line the extensive cobblestone streets. I marvel at the labor involved in making adobe bricks, building the homes, and placing cobblestones for roads in the village.

At one point we pass by a huge house with two cars parked in the driveway and a large locked fence in front. Beautiful blooming rose bushes line the driveway. Juana informs us that the house belongs to her cousin. She unlocks the gate, and we proceed into the yard. I peer through the windows of the house and discover a beautiful home interior with tiled floors, wooden kitchen cabinets, and many pieces of furniture, all wrapped carefully in blankets. The house was built seven years ago, and Juana's cousin has returned to the house only one time since then. While her cousin works in the United States, Juana cares for the home and garden. I am taken aback by the infrequency of visits by this cousin, who has built the most modern house in the village. I ask Juana why her cousin doesn't visit more often. Juana giggles and responds, *"Pues, por ser mojada."* ("Well, because she's undocumented.")

CAMPESINO FARMLAND TRANSFORMATION

For thousands of years, the campesinos of west-central Mexico have been the guardians of Mexico's genetic corn diversity. By methodically selecting the most productive corn from their yearly harvests, they have artificially selected thousands of unique strains over generations of family farming activity to match the unique environmental conditions of untold numbers of unique microclimates and ecology.

With market forces compelling key family breadwinners to flee their farming communities, the social fabric of the communities and the family and community institutions that have historically been instrumental in protecting the land, seed stocks, and the environment are unraveling. The dearth of a community farm labor force to continue the labor-intensive practice of intercrop farming has, in turn, truncated the campesino farmer's valuable role as guardian of Mexico's corn genetic diversity, leading to widespread genetic erosion in corn (Nadal 2000).

In response to the pressures wrought by NAFTA, corporate penetration, and Green Revolution technology, the farmlands of the west-central Mexico countryside are undergoing rapid transformation away from the sustainable polyculture foundation. In a desperate attempt to generate income for family support, some campesinos who eschew emigration are attempting to convert their lands to industrial monoculture corn production, hoping for elevated yields by relinquishing their traditional hand-selected corn seeds and adopting the heavily U.S.-promoted hybrid seeds and their requisite agrochemicals. Others are converting their intercrop land to pasture for export beef production. Some replace their corn, bean, and squash intercrop with export crops of strawberries, broccoli, tomatoes, and cauliflower. Still others leave their land fallow in the care of a relative when they migrate. Some even sell their land under great duress.

While the potential for campesino land sales resulting from the overturn of Article 27 has opened the door to land consolidation with fewer and fewer farmers owning more of the land, the social costs of foundational intercrop disruption on the campesino culture have been extreme. As described in chapter 4, whole families are fleeing the countryside and emigrating to the United States in an all-out struggle to survive and stave off potential starvation. Mexican and California newspapers carry stories about emigrating individuals who are willing to risk their lives daily in dangerous undocumented border crossings.

GHOST TOWN PUEBLOS AND RANCHOS

Mass emigration out of west-central Mexico's countryside, particularly in the states of Michoacán and Jalisco, has transformed the once bustling pueblos and ranchos into virtual depopulated ghost towns (Zendejas and De Vries 1995). Men typically emigrate first, leaving behind their wives and children (Castro 1986; Delgado 1996; Katel and Lloyd 2001). For most of the year, many towns and villages are occupied exclusively by the elderly, primarily elderly women; women with husbands and boyfriends who have emigrated; and young children whose parents have emigrated. Most of the houses in many towns and villages are unoccupied *casas tristes* (sad houses) (Zavella 2000).

Of the 2,200 people who lived in Florencio Gomez's Michoacán village of Huacao in 1990, only 400 post-NAFTA residents remain (Thompson 2001). Once again, most of those left behind are women, children, and the elderly.

In the winter California off-season, some California immigrants return home to their towns and villages of origin, temporarily repopulating them to former near normal levels. However, summer visits to pueblos and ranchos present a different landscape. In Tecolotlán, Jalisco, as the sun sets townspeople make their way to the central plaza to socialize. Clusters of elderly men socialize on the plaza benches and reminisce about their families, farms, and migration experiences. Young women with babies in their arms stroll with their mothers around the plaza, occasionally stopping to chat with a neighbor. Groups of children run about the plaza laughing and playing. With the exception of a few students who attend a local university, young single people and men under age 60 are visibly absent from the social milieu.

In Gómez Farías, Michoacán, children, elderly women, and single people are generally the exclusive occupants of the village from January to October (Castro 1986). When I visited the village in summer 1999, there was literally no one in sight. The empty dusty streets were lined with homes. The front doors of some houses were boarded up, and as I walked through the empty streets an occasional curious elderly resident peaked through a window.

In Chaparaco, Michoacán, Elena Martinez owns a home near her parents' home (Joaquin Bejarano and Maribel Terraza) on Lázaro Cárdenas Street. Her home is rented out indefinitely while she resides in Salinas, California. Three other family members also own homes in Chaparaco. All are vacant since they emigrated to the United States.

The currency emigrants send to Mexico from the United States as remittances each year is substantial and growing as the U.S. Mexican immigrant population continues to increase. In 1998 remittances totaled $5 billion (Osuna 1998). By the end of 2001, remittances had increased to $9.6 billion, an increase of 40 percent over 2000. Since the September 11, 2001, terrorist attacks in the United States, remittances, rather than falling, actually increased (Associated Press 2001; *Financial Times Information* 2001). In 2005, Mexican migrant workers in the United States sent $17–$20 billion back to Mexico, about 3 percent of Mexico's national income. In fact, individual money transfers are now Mexico's greatest source of foreign exchange, with revenues even larger than those garnered nationally from oil exports and tourism. Remittances now total more than ten times the amount of U.S. aid sent to Mexico (Havice 2005; Morris 2006).

In the Colonia 22 de Octubre, Michoacán, near Uruapan, the neighborhoods are filled with small, impoverished homes covered with corrugated tarpaper roofs. The foundations and walls are constructed of rocks, concrete blocks, branches, and pieces of wood assembled somewhat haphazardly to enclose the inhabitants who dwell within. Across the road from Marisol Carranza's home, however, are three strikingly modern two-story concrete homes painted blue and white, peach pink, and lime green, respectively. The parents of Marisol's former neighbor, the owner of the peach pink home, inhabit the blue and white home. According to Marisol, her former neighbor who owns the peach pink home is working in the United States and almost never returns to the *colonia*. In the meantime, she sends remittances to her parents for their support, while her parents take care of her home just two doors away. Marisol informed me that the lime green home is also consistently vacant. The owner of this *casa triste* also resides in the United States.

Of the twenty-two farm towns and villages I visited in west-central Mexico between summer 1998 and summer 2006, the only ones populated by a significant number of men for most of the year were Pueblo Rincón de López, Colima; San Agustín, Jalisco; and El Guaco, Michoacán. In Pueblo Rincón de López, the lemon harvests brought a high enough return that male farmers were able to remain in the village and support their families. In addition, the international port at Manzanillo and a thriving coastal tourist industry provide local supplementary employment opportunities in the geographically small state.

The El Guaco *ejido* was also noticeably populated with both men and women. The joint binational agricultural ventures that have been established between U.S.-based export companies and the *ejido* provide a high enough financial return to obviate the necessity for emigration.

When I visited San Agustín, Jalisco, in summer 2000, the tequila industry had surged suddenly in response to a growing international demand for tequila from the region. A nearly continuous parade of trucks full of harvested agave stems moved through San Agustín's streets en route to Zapotlanejo near Guadalajara. On my preceding two visits to this village, the streets were, by comparison, nearly empty.

Gabino Ayala informed me that the agave grown in the narrow valley here is manufactured into the best tequila in the world. The agave stem appears to concentrate sugars more efficiently, resulting in its preferred status among tequila distilleries. Gabino spoke excitedly of a new tequila refinery, which he referred to as La Laja, in Zapotlanejo. According to him, as of summer 2000, the refinery supported the local economy with a good return on the sale of harvested agave. The refinery manufactures José Cuervo tequila and was purchasing 60–70 percent of San Agustín's agave. Whereas the local refinery at Ojo de Agua de Latilla paid growers only 5 pesos per kilogram of agave stem in 2000, La Laja paid 12 pesos per kilogram. The return translates into $60–$120 per large agave plant.

Laborers who work in the fields as stem harvesters earn as much in Jalisco as they would earn in the United States, about $500 per week. By contrast, other farm laborers earn only 500–600 pesos per week. Gabino informed me that, because of the high wages in San Agustín, emigration to the United States out of the region was at a standstill. Workers were no longer forced to migrate because they could support themselves and their families in Jalisco.

The San Agustín economic boom was short lived, however. A local newspaper interview with Félix Bañuelos Jiménez, president of the Administrative Council of Tequila Producers, revealed that the tequila industry was in crisis due to the increasing demand for tequila and the growing scarcity of agave stems. Agave was scarce in the region because unseasonal snowfall over a three-year period had destroyed much of the crop.

In response to the crisis, at least eighty tequila manufacturers planned to stop purchasing agave stems altogether for fifteen days in July 2000 in order to halt tequila production entirely. The manufacturers hoped to put pressure on agave growers to lower their asking price for agave to half the current market value. Jiménez reported that the manufacturers were forced to take such drastic action in order to keep tequila prices from "rising as high as the clouds" (Flores 2000).

By summer 2004, the hillsides throughout the states of Jalisco and Michoacán were replete with blue-green agave plots of varying sizes. Gabino reported that the agave bonanza had ended. Return on agave stems was extremely low in 2004–5, as *todo el mundo* (the whole world) was planting agave, and supply exceeded the demand of the refineries.

ABANDONED AND DEPRESSED WOMEN

Another obvious and tragic testimony to the social transformation I encountered in west-central Mexico is the remarkable number of women who openly express their feelings about being depressed or abandoned by their spouses and family members. Many of these women are part of an increasingly elderly population whose families have already emigrated. They continue to live in the west-central Mexico ghost town pueblos and raise their grandchildren while their undocumented children struggle to earn a living and the necessary fee for their children's *coyote*. Their grandchildren eventually join their parents in the United States, leaving their grandparents behind and alone in the pueblo.

Male emigrants are at least granted considerable publicity when Border Patrol officers foil their crossings, or when injury or death occurs en route to the United States (see chapters 4 and 5). It is the women unseen and left behind in Mexico who silently bear the emotional burden as part of the social costs of NAFTA's legacy. The intense gender subjugation characteristic of the Mexican farm culture frequently results in the abandonment of women emotionally or physically. But the already harsh reality of women's abandonment experiences has been further exacerbated in NAFTA's wake.

Even though this enormous, ubiquitous population of abandoned and depressed women is apparent and widespread, and many abandoned women regularly express overt manifestations of chronic depression, V. Nelly Salgado de Snyder of the Mexican Institute of Psychiatry claims that there are few comprehensive studies that address the psychosocial aspects of wives and children who remain in Mexico. Salgado de Snyder studied women in rural and semirural communities in Jalisco and Michoacán who had never been out of Mexico and were married to immigrant workers living in the United States. She found that the family's psychological and social structure suffers important changes when one of its members emigrates (Salgado de Snyder 1993, 1996).

Though most women in Salgado de Snyder's studies acknowledged that migration had provided material advantages, they also consistently disclosed that migration had dismembered families and destroyed domestic life. Many study participants expressed fears of family disintegration, an increase in family violence, fear of being abandoned, and fear of being infected with the AIDS virus. Loneliness and lack of support from the absent husband were identified as sources of stress. Twenty-three percent reported that their spouses had never returned to Mexico after departing to the United States, though they maintained contact with the family. Five percent claimed that they did not even know where their spouses were in the United States.

Studies of immigrants living in the United States indicate that they are equally troubled by family disintegration. Concern for the welfare of family members left behind and guilt for having left the family were found to be important sources of stress related to psychological distress and depression (Salgado de Snyder 1993).

Salgado de Snyder and her associates also found that Hispanic immigrant women are more at risk than their male immigrant counterparts for experiencing psychological difficulties resulting from breaking life-long ties with family members, friends, and community. Additionally, women must cope with the stressors associated with their multiple roles as mothers, wives, and employees.

In the California Institute for Rural Studies report on the health status of 971 farmworkers cited in chapter 8, 9 percent reported depression, 16 percent reported that they suffered from other nervous conditions, and 13 percent indicated that they were angry much of the time (Villarejo et al. 2000). Rick Mines's follow-up study in 2001 further confirmed the prevalence of psychiatric disorders in the binational population (Mines et al. 2001).

The following examples of women's depression or abandonment resulting from family circumstances beyond their control represent but a microcosm of a veritable epidemic of tragic loss, loneliness, and abandonment suffered by the women of the west-central Mexico countryside.

The Family of Arturo Acosta

Arturo Acosta is the oldest son of Jesus Acosta and Rosario Morales. His wife and three children live in Los Sauces de Pérez. Arturo is documented and spends most of the year working in Salinas, California. The remittances sent to his family in Los Sauces de Pérez support them. He visits his wife and children only one time per year during the Christmas holidays. He has applied for family reunification documents from the U.S. embassy that would allow his family to join him in California. However, the family is aware that it may be years before the necessary permits are forthcoming.

The Family of Marisol Carranza

Marisol Carranza was abandoned when her husband was shot and killed in El Guaco, Michoacán. When I visited her family in Uruapan for the fourth time in January 2000, Victoria, one of her daughters, was seated in the living room area of their home with a new baby. I was shocked, since I had visited the family only six months earlier during the summer months and there was no mention of a pregnancy. Victoria informed me that the baby was 43 days old. The father was living with and committed to another woman in Uruapan with whom he already had two children. He was not interested in assuming responsibility for any of the support for Victoria's new daughter.

I asked Marisol how she felt about her new granddaughter. She replied that she was still very angry about the baby and thought it unfair to have a baby with no father and no commitment from the father. Victoria related how she was able to hide her pregnancy from her mother for the first six months. When her pregnancy became obvious at about six months, she ran away to the home of a cousin. She related that she feared that her mother would beat her if she discovered her condition. The cousin called Marisol and informed her of the pregnancy. Somehow Marisol and Victoria managed to reconcile, and Victoria returned home. She gave birth to the baby in a government hospital, and her mother and aunt purchased clothes and other necessities for the baby.

In the meantime, Marisol's second son, Alberto, impregnated his girlfriend before emigrating to the United States as an undocumented worker at the end of 1999. In January 2000 he was working in Visalia, California, pruning peach and plum trees. Much to Marisol's chagrin, her son had no intention of marrying his former girlfriend or supporting their child. Alberto's girlfriend gave birth prior to the birth of Victoria's daughter. The girlfriend's family lives in the same *colonia* as Marisol's family and has since cut off all communication with Carranza family members.

In 2004, Alberto moved to Nogales, Mexico, and supports his new family in Nogales, Arizona, with his earnings as a *coyote* (see chapter 5). In 2004 he proudly showed me pictures of his 2-year old son with the son's mother in Arizona. When I asked about his daughter in Uruapan, he denied that he had fathered the child but acknowledged sending his former girlfriend funds from the United States to cover prenatal care.

The Family of Maribel Terraza

I visited Maribel Terraza (see chapter 4) and her remaining family members in Chaparaco, Michoacán, on several trips to west-central Mexico. She consistently complained about depression. She lamented on several occasions that she just couldn't accept the fact that her family was fractured, with members living on both sides of the border. Tears streamed down her face as she described how much she missed her children and grandchildren living in the United States.

Women in Maquilí and San Juan de Lima, Michoacán

Fernando Azevedo's sister Rosa lives in Maquilí, Michoacán, with her husband, Rogelio. Rosa and her brother are the only two siblings still living in the rancho. The remaining five siblings and their families, including Fernando, have all emigrated to Watsonville or Salinas. When I visited Rosa and her sister-in-law in summer 1998 on a Sunday, the streets of Maquilí were nearly empty. Rosa's sister-in-law informed me that the streets were deserted and that most of the village's houses were empty because the majority of the village's population had already emigrated to the United States.

When I attempted to broach the subject of family with Rosa in order to garner information about her children, she quickly changed the subject. Later, when she appeared to be more relaxed, Rosa informed me that all ten of her children had emigrated to California and Washington. Although her children visit her in Maquilí on occasion, she views their visits as a mixed blessing. After a brief visit the children return to the United States, leaving her with bitter sadness *(gran tristeza)* and a tremendous sense of emptiness inside *(vacío)*. As we sat together and conversed, the sadness and emptiness evident in her voice as she spoke mirrored the emptiness of the village's homes and streets.

When I returned to the United States and informed Fernando Azevedo that I had visited his sister Rosa in Maquilí, I asked him why she did not come to California so that she could be in closer contact with her siblings and children. He informed me that her husband had been apprehended in the United States on drug charges. Rogelio returned to Mexico and could never again visit the United States without risking arrest and a jail sentence. Rosa was forced to choose between a life with her husband or close proximity to her siblings and children in the United States. She chose to remain with her husband in Mexico.

While visiting Maquilí, my research assistant and I stayed at a somewhat run-down Mexican resort in San Juan de Lima. I discussed my interest in family immigration with the proprietors of the concrete-block motel rooms, Teresa and Manuel Valenzuela. Teresa informed me that she attended elementary school with Fernando Azevedo in Maquilí and knew his family well. She acknowledged that the populations of all of the coastal villages near San Juan de Lima were declining as people emigrated to the United States. She then spontaneously, very unexpectedly, began sobbing despondently as she described the departure of her youngest son a month before my visit. As she cried, she said that she would never be able to accept the emigration and loss of her children to the United States. Her husband later informed me that she cries and is depressed most of the time since her son's emigration. Before I left, Teresa made me promise to call her son and tell him how much she missed him.

The Family of Pedro Delgado

One of Tomasina López Santos's daughters, Catalina, lives year-round in Confradia de Duendes, Jalisco, with her two children. Her husband,

Pedro Delgado, works in the broccoli, cauliflower, and artichoke fields of Watsonville, Salinas, and Castroville for nine months each year. Catalina's home is one of the nicest in the village, built with Pedro's remittances earned in the United States. The home is about a half mile from her mother's home on the main road near the entrance of the village.

In 1995, Catalina and Pedro applied to the U.S. Immigration Service for documents that would allow her and the children to travel with Pedro to the United States. As of summer 1998 they had not received any response from the Immigration Service. Pedro acknowledged that sometimes as many as six years elapse before legal papers allowing emigration to the United States are granted. In the meantime, Catalina and her children, like her mother, remain in Confradia de Duendes alone for most of the year.

ENVIRONMENTAL DESTRUCTION

The demise of the rural countryside is at the root of Mexico's environmental crisis. The government knew decades ago that, if farmers continued their intensive use of agrochemicals to boost production (see chapters 11 and 12), the soil would eventually collapse. However, officials at the time refused to consider more practical, restrained farming methods. Erosion, deforestation, and desertification threaten the land, resulting in declining agricultural productivity and more intensive uses of land, from logging to overfarming. More than 60 percent of Mexico's farmland is severely degraded, and another 30 percent is in varying stages of ecological decay (Morales 1994; Simon 1997; Watson 2000).

There is a strong correlation between environmental destruction and migration. In Michoacán and Jalisco, more than a quarter of the land is eroded and degraded (Watson 2000). Economic pressure forces many campesinos to extend their farming activities into marginal lands that are easily damaged by intensive farming practices. Community farming practices designed to mitigate soil loss and conserve soil are weakened by the progressive loss of social cohesiveness, ultimately leading to aggravated soil erosion. When I asked campesinos why soil fertility levels in Mexico were declining, they almost universally responded that the land is worked too intensively with no opportunity "to rest." Many lamented the fact that their land "is tired."

In summer 2006, campesinos complained about climate change in their region. The rains did not begin until July. Some informed me that they had planted their corn fields as many as four times that year. The rains were three to four months late, and rats, birds, and insects dug up and consumed the seeds before they even had a chance to sprout. For the first time in my studies, I observed corn fields with plants growing at differing stages of development. And, then, when the rains finally did come in July, they were so cold and intense, often including hail storms, that many corn plants were destroyed.

While migrants vacate the pueblos and ranchos of the rural countryside, and women, the elderly, and children are left behind to fend for themselves, there are ecological warning signs everywhere that environmental integrity is crumbling. Forests are disappearing, steep hillsides are being converted to fields and orchards, and the once pristine rivers run brown with eroded soil. The government of Mexico has neglected the formulation and enforcement of effective environmental legislation designed to protect Mexico's varied natural resource base and biodiversity. In 1982 it created SEDUE (Secretaría de Desarrollo Urbano y Ecología [Ministry of Ecology and Urban Development]), the equivalent of the U.S. Environmental Protection Agency. Mexico's first major environmental protection code was legislated in 1988. Both of these legislative attempts at environmental protection were grossly underfunded and ineffective (Cockcroft 1998).

President Salinas replaced SEDUE with SEDESOL (Secretaría de Desarrollo Social [Ministry of Social Development]), which included environmental concerns but was equally ineffective. Both presidents Salinas and Zedillo prioritized economic growth over environmental concerns and initiated legal reforms to attract foreign investment by relaxing environmental codes (Cockcroft 1998).

Not surprisingly, environmental degradation in Mexico has worsened as a result of NAFTA. Although Mexico entered NAFTA in 1994 as a nation recognized for its great biodiversity, 98 percent of its tropical forests had already been destroyed and one-third of its total land mass had been converted to desert as a result of the indiscriminate extraction of natural resources and the implementation of Green Revolution technology (Cockcroft 1998).

Article 106 of the NAFTA treaty prohibits any environmental regulations that might be a "disguised restriction on trade" (Simon 1997). NAFTA critics from around the world view NAFTA as a treaty that grants the United States easy access to Mexico's oil, natural gas, uranium, and other natural resources. Even the gene pools of tropical flora and fauna, of use to the pharmaceutical companies, are now available to the international business community (Cockcroft 1998).

As a result of NAFTA, Mexico has experienced greater environmental destruction than either the United States or Canada. Not only is Mexico viewed as a source of natural resources by the United States, the country is also becoming a kind of North American dumping ground and hazardous waste disposal area. The combined costs of soil erosion, water and air pollution, and the depletion of nonrenewable resources from 1980 to 1997 came to 8.5–15 percent of Mexico's GDP. Workers and poor people are suffering the worst effects of pollution and environmental devastation (Cockcroft 1998; Moyers 1990).

In 2000, Vicente Fox campaigned for the presidency of Mexico and promised to resolve environmental problems plaguing Mexico. When he came to office, he promised that his administration's policy would require environmental indicators to be included in calculations determining GDP. Environmental services would be considered in the cost of doing business. Six years after taking office in 2000, none of Fox's environmental promises had been kept (Greenpeace 2004e, 2006a; Nauman 2002).

On the contrary, the election of the PAN (Partido Acción Nacional [National Action Party]) candidate and the end of the PRI's seventy-year dominance have in fact exacerbated Mexico's environmental crisis. New development proposals threaten the 800-mile Baja California peninsula. Fox has proposed an initial $20 million government investment in a "nautical ladder" of new marinas and infrastructure to entice U.S. boat owners into Baja's Sea of Cortez (Russel 2002). In 2001, Fox announced his comprehensive plan for a major transportation and industrial corridor that would extend from Puebla, Mexico, to Panama. The plan, dubbed Plan Puebla Panama, or PPP, calls for the displacement of native communities, rampant and uncontrolled ecological destruction, and colossal industrial development (Call et al. 2002; Revolutionary Worker 2001). Because Mexican energy policy is subordinate to the needs of the United States, without taking into account environmental or social concerns the Fox government is filling the border with thermoelectric plants, refineries, and gas pipelines to supply Arizona and California energy needs (Rivera 2001).

In September 2003, Fox removed the federal government's top environmental officials, including the minister of environment and natural resources (SEMARNAT) and the head of the Mexican environmental attorney general's office (PROPEPA) responsible for enforcing environmental laws. One source claims that the PROPEPA disclosure of the extent of illegal deforestation in the monarch butterfly overwintering forests of Michoacán may have been the primary cause for the dismissals (Rosés 2003).

In 2004, El Programa de las Naciones Unidas para el Medio Ambiente (PNUMA) claimed that Mexico's environment continues to deteriorate. The organization predicts that in three decades most of the country's natural resources will be lost to posterity unless urgent measures are taken to manage the country's forests and water resources better (Greenpeace 2004a).

Deforestation

After Lorenzo Vasquez introduced me to his village and *parcelas* in his home village of Pueblo Viejo, Michoacán, he took me on a drive through the mountainous region nearby. At one point clouds began to concentrate, leading to heavy rainfall. We stopped to wait out the storm by the side of the main highway near a logging road. During the 15–20 minutes we waited as the storm passed overhead, we watched five logging trucks emerge from the logging road. Each large truck was loaded to capacity with tree trunks.

Although there are protective forest management laws on the books, they are not enforced. Lorenzo claimed that the deforestation is the result of widespread poverty. Anyone with a truck can enter the forest and harvest wood for sale. Gerardo Bocco, an ecologist at the Universidad Nacional Autónoma de México, estimates that as much as 80 percent of current logging in Mexico is illegal.

I observed piles of garbage randomly strewn by the side of the road while Lorenzo reminisced about his childhood years when he and his friends camped in the mountains and enjoyed walking among the trees. Not only were the forests healthier, all the trees were tall with wide trunks, he claims. The forests were also much cleaner, and there were no piles of garbage in the forest at that time.

Pedro Alvarez-Icaza and his associates of PAIR (Programa de Aprovechamiento Integral de Recursos Naturales y Desarrollo Social en Areas Rurales de Subsistencia [Program for the Integrated Utilization of Natural Resources and Social Development in Areas of Rural Subsistence]) conducted an interdisciplinary study of the progressive environmental deterioration taking place in six *municipios* located in the forested, predominantly Purépecha Sierra region between Pátzcuaro and Uruapan, Michoacán. His group attributes the growing problems of deforestation to the impoverished conditions, with no opportunities for livelihood improvement, that most of the Purépecha rural farmers are trapped in. The farmers living in the region studied are socially and economically marginalized. Most lack basic infrastructure such as running water, electricity, and sanitary sewage disposal mechanisms (Alvarez-Icaza et al. 1993).

Their plight is further aggravated by the fact that the mountainous regions are subject to unforeseen crop losses to snow or hail at the high altitudes. The growing population and its food insecurity in combination with forest industries' financial interests have unleashed an economic and environmental crisis among the campesino forest dwellers that places ever greater and growing pressure on the forest resources.

In addition, there is constant tension between the campesino communities and the government. The government organizations purportedly responsible for protecting the forests, including Las Unidades de Conservación y Desarrollo Forestal (UCODEFO), are so burdened with bureaucracy and a reluctance to meddle in the affairs of powerful timber contractors and industries that they are extremely inefficient at controlling deforestation.

The forests are home to diverse populations of pine, oak, fir, grassland, and tropical dry forest species. Alvarez-Icaza and his associates determined that 45 percent of the soil and vegetation resources in the area studied are damaged. The damage was caused by deforestation, the development of pastureland for cattle, and the introduction of Green Revolution Technology hybrid crop species.

Interestingly, there are no official figures regarding the extent of illegal deforestation. However, technical experts who work in the region estimate that for every 3 cubic meters of timber processed in local sawmills and wood factories, 2 cubic meters are illegal (Alvarez-Icaza et al. 1993, 167). Growing social and economic pressures have resulted in a drastic reduction of forested land in the region. Of the 127,000 forested hectares in the region in the 1960s, only 74,000 remained in 1992—representing more than a 47 percent loss of forested land in slightly more than thirty years (Alvarez-Icaza 1993, 237).

In 1995, one year after NAFTA's initiation, then-governor Ruben Figueroa Alcocer of Guerrero signed a five-year agreement with the U.S.-based transnational timber company Boise Cascade. The agreement granted Idaho-based Boise Cascade exclusive rights to purchase timber from members of twenty-four mountainous Guerrero *ejidos*. The controversial pact reinvigorated the timber industry in the region and forced local sawmills to increase their production as much as tenfold over a three-year period (Amnesty International 2001). According to satellite images taken of eighteen areas in the Petatlán and Coyuca de Catalán mountains from 1992 to 2000, 86,000 hectares (38 percent) of forest were lost from the 226,203 hectares that existed in 1992. Furthermore, the excessive logging and destruction of the region's native vegetation led to a 446 percent increase in clearcut area. In 1992, 37,636 hectares had been clearcut. By 2000 the figure had reached 130,595 hectares (Worldwide Forest/Biodiversity Campaign News 2000).

Alarmed local residents staged a well-orchestrated protest of the wanton destruction of their *ejido* lands by constructing roadblocks to prevent lumber from leaving the region. Because of their concern about the impact of increased logging and its impact on agricultural production, two courageous *ejido* activists, Rodolfo Montiel Flores and Teodoro Cabrera Garcia, formed the Organization of Campesino Ecologists of the Sierra de Petatlán and Coyuca de Catalán (OCESP). On May 2, 1999, both men were arrested by soldiers of the 40th Infantry Battalion of the Mexican Army for alleged ties to a guerrilla movement and trumped up charges of "eco-guerilla organization," illegal possession of weapons, and drug trafficking.

Both men were imprisoned for over two years and subjected to bodily torture by members of the Mexican army. The torture was inflicted as a means of extracting confessions for the trumped-up charges and resulted in injuries to the eyes, genitals, and thighs as well as glandular inflammation (Agence France Presse 2001). While in prison, members of Montiel and Cabrera's organization were murdered by local caciques (see chapter 13, and Worldwide Forest/Biodiversity Campaign News 2000). Specialists from a Danish medical organization presented evidence of the torture at the Unitary Tribunal of Chilpancingo, Guerrero. The tribunal denied Montiel and Cabrera's appeals, despite the evidence, reconfirming an extended sentence for both men (Environment News Service 2001).

An international outcry by environmental and human rights organizations focused attention on the abuses the two forest activists were subjected to, as well as to the serious problem of deforestation in the region, and demanded that the activists be released. While in prison, Montiel received a $175,000 award from the Goldman Foundation in April 2000. In February 2001, the Sierra Club presented its prestigious "Chico Mendes" award to Montiel (Agence France Presse 2001).

The Mexico City–based Human Rights Center Agustín Pro Juarez A.C. (PRODH) defended Montiel and Cabrera. In August 1999, their attorney, Digna Ochoa y Placido, was kidnapped for several hours and beaten while being driven in the back of a car. The situation escalated until Digna Ochoa was found shot to death in her Mexico City office. A note was left near her body threatening other attorneys at PRODH (Amnesty International 2001).

Finally, on November 8, 2001, under mounting international pressure, President Fox ordered Montiel and Cabrera's release on "humanitarian grounds," after they had spent two years in prison. Montiel and Cabrera called for democracy in Mexico and an end to the practice of torture. Montiel claims that he cannot return to his village for fear of reprisal by local *caciques* (*OnEarth* 2002). His experiences underscore the danger farmers encounter when they attempt to protect their lands by confronting corporate economic interests in Mexico.

And More Deforestation

In February 2004, Greenpeace Mexico demanded that Mexico's federal administration make forest and rainforest preservation one of its most important priorities. According to the UN Food and Agriculture Organization, 785,000 hectares of forests and rainforests are cut down each year. Mexico is now fifth in the world in forest destruction after Brazil, Indonesia, Sudan, and Zambia (Greenpeace 2004b).

President Fox and his administration have long assured the Mexican public that forest protection is a matter of national security. However, his budget priorities and allocations don't fit his rhetoric. In fact, Fox's 2005 federal budget for forest protection actually promotes deforestation (Greenpeace 2004c). To remind President Fox of the importance of forest conservation and responsible forest management under Forest Stewardship Council principles, Greenpeace Mexico presented him with a chair made from FSC certified wood from the forests of San Juan Parangaricutiro, Michoacán (Forest Stewardship Council 2004).

In May 2005, Centro Mexicano de Derecho Ambiental (CEMDA), Greenpeace, and Centro de Derechos Humanos de la Montaña "Tlachinollan" demanded that the governor of Guerrero release Felipe Arreaga from prison. Arreaga was arrested on trumped-up charges while he worked to impede deforestation, promote massive reforestation campaigns in the region, and support community organization to improve the lives of the forest-dwelling campesinos (Greenpeace 2005a).

Later in May 2005, two of Alberto Peñalosa Domínguez's children were killed as they returned home in the evening. Domínguez and his family live in the same mountainous region of Guerrero as Arreaga. Like Arreaga, Dominguez is a strong leader in the Organización de Campesinos Ecologistas de la Sierra de Petatlán y Coyuca de Catalán (OCESP) (Greenpeace 2005a). He and two of his other children were severely injured in the gunman's attack. These events underscore the intense conflict currently in progress in the Mexican countryside, where campesinos are forced to fight against big financial interests who want to exploit, and ultimately destroy, their forest resources for profit.

Monarch Forests of Michoacán

The Michoacán forests of the unique *oyamel* pine, which makes up only 2 percent of Mexico's total forest cover and provides shelter for millions of migratory monarch butterflies from November to March every year, are the locus of some of the most violent conflicts between conservationist campesinos and illegal loggers. Though Mexico's national park service and conservation organizations are taking steps to stop the illegal logging in the Mariposa Monarca Biosphere Reserve, illegal loggers carry weapons and are intolerant of anyone who interferes with their deforestation activities. Many park service personnel are afraid to even enter the forests (Appleby 2004).

Altered Ecosystems Fueled by Campesino Desperation

In a desperate attempt to feed their families, rural subsistence farmers remaining in west-central Mexico are encroaching upon undisturbed communal land within *ejidos* and planting as much corn as possible. In some areas the only land I observed that still supported original native vegetation was in inaccessible areas, or in the most remote parts of the countryside. En route to Maquilí, Michoacán, there are entire hills that appear to have been "shaved" of their original pristine native plant cover for crop production.

Uruapan is the avocado capital of the world. Literally tons of avocados are shipped to the United States from Uruapan weekly. Nearly all of the oak and pine forests that historically surrounded the city of Uruapan for miles have been removed and replaced with avocado orchards.

Off the main highway from Yahualica to Tepatitlán, Jalisco, the only remaining forested areas are those that are inaccessible. The vertical cliffs of some of the higher mountainous areas still boast remnant examples of the tall dramatic native organ pipe cactus. Two or three species of *Op-*

untia intermingle with flowering legume trees. Vines with rich foliage grow abundantly over the trees and cacti in these uncommon pristine patches. The remaining terrain has been denuded for firewood or corn cultivation.

A hill next to the Los Sauces de Pérez *ejido* in Jalisco contains some of the most undisturbed habitat I observed in west-central Mexico. The stream flowing next to the hill is still full of pools of tadpoles in summer. *Selaginella* and a great variety of ferns, mosses, and wildflowers dot the streambanks and emerald green grassy hillsides.

In response to the changed economy wrought by NAFTA, Jesus Acosta has converted his *ejido parcelas* to pastureland and is now growing corn, beans, and squash in a *guamil* on the hillside using small amounts of agrochemicals. It is only a matter of time before other farmers join him, remove the native vegetation, and permanently alter the pristine habitat of the hillside's biotic communities.

Deterioration of Water Resources

The consequence of the ubiquitous denuded terrain with exposed soil is pervasive, serious soil erosion. A third of Mexico's 50 million acres of farmland has been severely eroded. A full 86 percent of the land is suffering from some degree of erosion (Morales 1994; Simon 1997). As the summer rainy season revisits the countryside, soil is washed off the land into the abundant, once pristine rivers and streams that course through the countryside. Bearing their atypical load of soil, west-central Mexico's rivers and streams run brown. With the exception of Río Cupatízio, which runs through Uruapan, Michoacán, all of the rivers observed in my explorations were brown, carrying a load of silt.

The most serious form of soil erosion, gully erosion, is common in the farmed areas. The loose soil texture in much of the region prevents soil particles from readily adhering to each other. When the soil becomes too moist, it crumbles. Thus, with the removal of the natural vegetation and with uninformed farming practices, the soil in many areas of west-central Mexico is washed into rivers adjoining the land, leaving behind nonarable eroded terrain. The gushing water of Río Grande de Santiago Lerma, the huge river entering Guadalajara, carries tons and tons of sediment from soils that were eroded in the surrounding countryside.

Lake Chapala, Mexico's largest freshwater lake, is drying up (Burton 1997, 2000, 2001). About three-quarters of Lake Chapala's shore are in the state of Jalisco; the other fourth is in Michoacán (Sociedad Amigos del Lago de Chapala 2005a). In summer 2000, the new president of the College of Jalisco's Urban Architects issued a warning that the lake was in danger of disappearing altogether (Orozco 2000).

The lake is the source of 60 percent of the water flowing into Guadalajara (Orozco 2000). Dam construction on the rivers and streams feeding the lake have reduced the flow of water, causing the lake's volume to decrease over time. In addition, the governments of four of the states near the lake—México, Querétaro, Guanajuato, and Michoacán—support nearby industrial and agrarian interests that demand and expect cheap water from the lake to maintain their endeavors. The Mexican National Water Commission is responsible for managing Mexico's water resources. Commission members have discussed various tactics for saving the lake, but they have accomplished nothing to protect it to date (Sociedad Amigos del Lago de Chapala 2005a).

Lake Chapala is home to hundreds of plant and animal species and hosts a variety of migrating birds every winter. Several of the fish species living in the lake are endemic (Burton 1997). However, pollution levels are extreme, and fish species are disappearing. Fifty-one percent of the lake's water is highly contaminated, 41 percent is moderately polluted, and a paltry 8 percent is considered "clean and acceptable." The lake is polluted with industrial waste, domestic sewage, and agricultural chemicals (de Anda et al. 2004). Sewage treatment plants are either not functioning at all or are not efficient. Even Guadalajara, a major city of over 6 million people, has no waste water treatment plant (Sociedad Amigos del Lago de Chapala 2005b).

More than 2,000 people living in the immediate area of the lake basin attempt to make a living by fishing. The lake was once full of native fish, including three species of white fish, which have brought culinary acclaim to the region. Today these species are almost extinct. Another native species, once sold in huge quantities, *popocha,* is also virtually extinct. Finally, five species of *charal* are endemic to central Mexico. All five fish species are in serious decline. State fisheries' departments claim that total catches declined 69 percent in a period of just eight years (Burton 1997).

The Lerma-Chapala Basin is the depository for more municipal discharge than any other hydrological system in Mexico. Levels of DDT from industrial farming and hexachlorocyclohexano (HCH), classified as a high-level carcinogen and suspected endrocrine disruptor, are remarkably high, causing fish deformities and widespread death among livestock and birds. The waters are also contaminated with agricultural chemicals, copper, lead, chromium, zinc, cyanide, and phosphorus, and untreated water is used for the irrigation of agricultural crops exported to Canada and the United States. Doctors in the region advise local residents not to eat the fish because of heavy metal contamination (Sociedad Amigos del Lago de Chapala 2005b).

Juan Borrego, who grew up in Tuxcueca, Jalisco, bordering Lake Chapala, recalls his childhood when the lake was unpolluted and full of fish. He, his brother, and friends took their nets to the lake to fish for gilthead, carp, bass, white fish, *vagre,* and *charal.* He excitedly explained how on one occasion he and his brother caught a string of fish that stretched 12 feet end to end. He recalls buying vegetables in town, borrowing a large pot from his mother's kitchen, building a fire by the side of the lake, and cooking fish stew with his friends. He and his brother also dried the fish in the sunshine and stored it in the shade of their home for meals and snacks. Juan claims that the dried, stored fish was edible for up to two years.

He related that fishermen used to make a living by catching fish for the people of the villages and towns bordering the lake. The fish provided an important source of protein for local residents. Gradually, however, the fish populations declined. When fishermen caught small fish, rather than return them to the lake they threw them on the ground to die. During the breeding season *(la veda),* all fishing in the lake was prohibited in order to allow the fish to reproduce. Many people ignored the prohibition, however, and fished anyway. Overfishing and water contamination have resulted in fish populations so scarce that it is now nearly impossible to make a living as a fisherman on Lake Chapala.

The west-central Mexican farming culture is rapidly disintegrating. The agricultural and social crisis in the Mexican countryside could result in a rural exodus of as many as 15 million people (Bejarano 1993). Unable to survive on their farms in the countryside, they are forced to abandon their lands. Amid the ever-increasing hunger, starvation, and environmental degradation, it is principally the women in both Mexico and the United States who mourn the economically and politically forced fracturing of their families. They live with the reality of a crumbling culture and environment all around them in west-central Mexico.

ELEVEN

TRANSNATIONAL CORPORATIONS AND THE U.S. LEGACY IN WEST-CENTRAL MEXICO

Los Estados Unidos siempre nos evia todo lo peor.

The United States always sends us the worst of everything.

—Adrián Cornelio Gonzalez, 2005 municipal president and owner of Fertilizante Gonzalez, Cuquio, Jalisco

The cultural farming system of Jalisco and Michoacán that has been in place since pre-Hispanic times has been broken by two processes that have occurred over the past 20 years: the introduction of "Green Revolution" seeds and agrochemicals resulting in the commercialization of agriculture, and the globalized economy. The breakdown of the long-standing cultural farming system has forced people to emigrate to the U.S. in order to survive.

—Dr. L. I. Gallardo, veterinarian, Cuquio, Jalisco

As cultural disintegration and death slip through the Mexican country-side, disrupting one farm and family after another, transnational corporations are enjoying an economic boom (Wright 1990,185; and see websites of, e.g., Dow, Monsanto, and Syngenta). Spurred by NAFTA, their profits are soaring. While the United States spends billions of taxpayer dollars unsuccessfully attempting to stem the tidal flow of illegal drugs from Mexico (Johnson 2001; Wagner and Flannery 2000), predominantly U.S-originating transnational corporations are exporting and aggressively promoting deadly environmental, health, and culture-destroying drugs, chemicals, and agricultural products to Mexico with impunity. As purveyors of addiction and even genetic and human death, their hybrid and bioengineered seeds, agrochemicals, caffeine, and nicotine products exacerbate the already compromised health of an impoverished, undernourished, and malnourished rural population in Mexico.

Primed by the authoritarian institutional mechanisms in place in the rural countryside (see chapter 13), largely uneducated rural campesinos are easy corporate prey. The price of succumbing to the lure of corporate wares is high. Campesinos ultimately risk their health, lives, and even the traditional corn foundation of their culture. This damaging and deadly transnational corporate contribution constitutes the United States' shameful legacy in the west-central Mexico countryside.

AGRIBUSINESS IN MEXICO:
GENETIC EROSION AND GENETIC ENGINEERING

Development of Traditional *Maíz Criollo*

Scientists speculate that somewhere between 7,000 and 12,000 years ago Mesoamerican farmers created traditional corn by crossbreeding wild grasses. As corn diffused to the south and north, hand-selected seeds from corn plants that thrived locally led to new strains adapted to different soils, pests, moisture levels, and growing seasons. Thousands of traditional corn varieties, each adapted to a unique microclimate, developed through this process. For thousands of years, these genetically diverse corn varieties were the staple food source for small farmers and their families dispersed from South America to the Arizona desert (Warwick 2000; Wolkomir 1995; Wright 1990, 154–155).

Introduction of Commercialized
High-Yielding Hybrid Corn Varieties

As a result of extensive plant breeding leading to highly productive strains of commercial hybrid corn and subsidies of billions of dollars to huge U.S. agribusiness operations, the United States is the largest commercial corn producer and exporter in the world. The U.S. corn sector is the largest recipient of U.S. government subsidies, totaling $10.1 billion in 2000 alone. This enormous sum of taxpayer-generated money is ten times greater than the total Mexican agricultural budget (Cunningham and Saigo 1999; Fanjul and Fraser 2003; Weiner 2002).

With NAFTA's "free-trade" policies, huge U.S. commercial corn surpluses are being shipped into Mexico; the U.S. Department of Agriculture estimates that imports of U.S. corn to Mexico have increased
eighteen-fold since NAFTA went into effect in 1994. As a result, 24 percent of total corn consumption in Mexico is now commercial corn imported from the United States (Carpentier and Herrmann 2004; Weiner
2002).

Since the 1940s introduction of Green Revolution technology, the
Mexican government has promoted agriculture as an instrument of industrialization rather than a legitimate way of life (Wright 1990). In contrast, Mexican campesinos continue to experience their farming practices
as much more than just a job. In fact, corn farming is a lifestyle in which
farming practices, community relationships, and family members are integrated into the farming process and the natural environment (see
chapter 2).

Many farmers in west-central Mexico who can afford to purchase the
costly *maíz mejorado* (improved corn) seeds are replacing their traditional *maíz criollo* corn seed, hand-selected for generations and a unique
genetic fit to their land, with genetically homogenized commercial strains
from the United States. Others who cannot afford the costly hybrid seeds
have been exhorted by their government to exchange their traditional,
genetically diverse seeds for hybrid seeds in the government-sponsored
kilo por kilo program (a kilogram of traditional seed exchanged for a
kilogram of hybrid homogenized seed).

As agents of industrialization, U.S. corporations are well represented in
Mexico by a few agribusiness giants. About 75 percent of global cereals, including corn, is controlled by only two multinational companies, Cargill
and Archer Daniels Midland (Smaller 2005). These two mega-corporations
are the largest corn exporters to Mexico and the primary beneficiaries of
corn exports (Fanjul and Fraser 2003). In addition, agribusinesses in the
west-central Mexico rural countryside include Monsanto's Asgrow and
Cargill, DeKalb and Hartz (Spitzer 2003), as well as Dupont's Pioneer.
Company signs are posted along roadsides next to commercial hybrid corn
fields throughout the countryside, advertising the replacement of traditional corn varieties by the commercial homogenized imported strains.

As of March 2002, 70–80 percent of the corn grown by farmers in
rural Cuquio was hybrid corn (Hector Figueroa, personal communication, 2002). Agribusiness and feed stores throughout west-central Mexico advertise and sell their inventory of primarily U.S.-originating commercial seed stocks and the required agrochemical inputs as "packages."

Figure 16. Commercial hybrid seeds in the countryside, Cuquio/Los Sauces de Pérez, Jalisco.

In El Loreto/La Barca, Reynaldo Becerra reported that the most common Monsanto Asgrow corn strains grown in the region are *pantera, bufalo,* and 4575. The most common Pioneer strains are 3046, 3028, and 3076. He also informed me that Cargill sells its own set of corn strains.

The loss of genetic diversity has progressively narrowed corn's worldwide genetic reservoir to such an extent that, in 1993, 71 percent of the world's commercial corn crop was derived from only six genetic varieties (Gliessman 1998). The U.S. southern corn leaf blight is an example of the devastation that can occur in monoculture fields of commercialized corn. The blight destroyed 15 percent of the U.S. corn crop, over 700 million bushels, in 1970 (Wolkomir 1995).

The narrowing and genetic distortion of corn stocks ultimately places corn, one of the three grains that support all of humanity, at risk. In west-central Mexico, the foundation of the entire campesino culture is at risk. Angus Wright eloquently asserts that "the effect [of the introduction of commercialized hybrid strains] was to eliminate the system of security and stability built into agriculture by thousands of years of peasant technology practiced under widely varying circumstances and

adapted to those differing conditions" (Wright 1990, 180). Genetic diversity is the raw material for plant breeding. Loss of diversity may restrict opportunities for future breeding efforts. Genetic diversity is an essential component of environmental resistance and protects crops from extensive loss due to disease, herbivory, or unpredicted variations in environmental conditions. Genetic diversity also promotes crop flexibility, enabling plants to adapt to changes in seasonal conditions over time (Gliessman 1998).

Genetic erosion creates genetic vulnerability whereby genetically uniform plant varieties become susceptible to pest and disease epidemics or to losses caused by extremes in the weather. Genetically uniform crops provide the ideal conditions for the rapid outbreak of pests and plant diseases. Pests and diseases, in turn, have the capacity to undergo rapid genetic change, potentially quickly adapting to changes in their hosts' defenses (Gliessman 1998). In Mexico, 7.9 million hectares were planted in corn in 2001. About 1.5 million hectares of this maize consisted of hybrid varieties, developed mainly by transnational companies (Carpentier and Herrmann 2004).

Health-Damaging Effects of High-Yielding Green Revolution Crops

Whereas Green Revolution high-yielding crop varieties were once thought to be the answer to global famine because they produce several times as much grain per unit area as the traditional varieties they are replacing, their legacy is worldwide intellectual deficits in the developing brains of children. So-called miracle crops are contributing to widespread brain impairment in the developing world because they do not absorb essential micronutrients including iron, necessary for successful brain and intellectual development (Lean 2000).

Christopher Williams, a research fellow with the Global Environmental Change Programme, claims that approximately 1.5 billion people, roughly one-quarter of the earth's population, are affected by "Green Revolution iron deficiency." The condition has impaired the learning ability of more than half of India's schoolchildren. Figures from the United Nations show that half of the world's pregnant women are anemic because they have too little iron, thereby putting both themselves and their babies at risk. Iron deficiency may be responsible for as many as 200,000 deaths per year (Lean 2000).

Introduction of Transgenic Corn Varieties

As huge commercial corn shipments from the United States continue to invade the Mexican countryside, biotechnology companies are manufacturing newer, ever more biologically bizarre transgenic (genetically modified) corn varieties. In 1999, 98.6 million acres worldwide of transgenic crops were planted, and in 2000 global acreage of such crops rose to 109.2 million, a land area equivalent to more than twice the total landmass of Britain (Evans 2002; Wheelwright 2001). In 2003, one million acres of genetically engineered crops were planted in the United States alone (Koons-Garcia 2000).

Without fully comprehending or testing the health and ecological effects of the new strains, the firms are manufacturing, among others, "Terminator" corn strains and corn strains with gene transfers of biological endotoxins functioning as pesticides, such as "Bt corn." These new endotoxin-bearing seeds were initially advertised as the solution to excessive pesticide use in the United States, since the plants are designed to eliminate pests by carrying transgenes that destroy herbivorous plant predators. However, a report by the Northwest Science and Environmental Policy Center in 2003 confirmed that the planting of 550 million acres of genetically engineered corn, soybeans, and cotton in the United States since 1996 actually increased pesticide use by about 50 million pounds (Benbrook 2003).

Genetically altered Terminator plants produce sterile seeds and cannot be used to plant the following year's crops (Warwick 2000). The sterile seeds are genetically manufactured by the addition of three genes to the corn plant. The seeds from the modified plants are then treated with an antibiotic. The plants that grow from the treated seeds then produce a toxin that renders their seeds sterile (Kaiser 2000). Farmers who plant Terminator plants are forced into a cycle requiring the yearly purchase of Monsanto agribusiness transgenic corn seeds (Allen 1998; *Consumer Reports* 1999; Kluger 1999; Perian 1999).

Considered the most controversial and immoral agricultural application of emergent genetic engineering to date, Terminator technology has created worldwide outrage among thousands of people in sixty-two countries. They cite the technology as a global threat to the livelihood of 1.4 billion people, including the subsistence farmers of west-central Mexico, who rely on hand-selected seed for the following year's crop (Barnett 2000; *Global Pesticide Campaigner* 2005; Kluger 1999; Warwick 2000).

Since maize pollen can travel as far as 60 feet from the plant that produced it (UC Mexus 2004), ecologists and other members of the scientific community claim that corn pollen from neighboring fields can easily be transferred by the wind to the cornfields of subsistence farmers and thus render their crops sterile (Kaiser 2000). Some scientists further claim that pollen from Terminator plants could be transported by the wind, crossing with ordinary crops *and* wild plants, spreading from species to species until flora all around the world become irreversibly sterilized (Kluger 1999; Milius 2003).

The new technology is viewed as a serious threat to food security that could exacerbate the problems of widespread hunger in developing countries (Allen 1998; Perian 1999). The Rural Advancement Foundation International estimates that by 2010 the majority of the world's non-subsistence farmland will be planted in bioengineered Terminator crops unless the technology is banned. Thus, in less than a few years of a single lifetime, thousands of years of farmer-saved artificially selected seed and community plant breeding could be irreversibly lost (Warwick 2000).

In 2000, Monsanto Corporation was poised to purchase Delta and Pine Land Company, which, in partnership with the USDA, holds the patent to Terminator technology. After an initial halt to the biotechnological development of Terminator plants resulting from the international uproar, USDA officials announced in August 2000 that they would continue to develop the technology because of its "scientific promise" (Kaiser 2000; Koons-Garcia 2000).

Monsanto genetic engineers argue that there is no real risk of pollen from Terminator plants causing widespread sterilization in other plants and suggest that border fields planted around crops that are wind- or insect-pollinated could serve as a safeguard against interspecies contamination (Kluger 1999). However, the social and economic structure of subsistence farming cultures around the world could be dramatically undermined if, instead of saving the best seeds from their crops and replanting them the following year (see chapter 2), farmers were forced to purchase Terminator seeds every year from transnational corporations because pollen from Terminator varieties had landed on their traditional crops, rendering their traditional seeds sterile.

In the west-central Mexico countryside, subsistence farmers' fields do not have the necessary borders around them to protect their crops from cross-contamination. Rather, their crops are often planted directly adjacent to the fields of farmers who plant commercial hybrid varieties, with little more than a row of rocks or a wire and wooden fence separating the fields. Lacking knowledge of the risks they face, and with the lax environmental laws and enforcement in Mexico, subsistence farmers could be left to discover that their altered *maíz criollo* no longer germinates. Perhaps rather than relying on "borders" around fields to ward off Terminator contamination, a better solution to cross-contamination is one suggested by scientific advisors to the USDA who propose that Monsanto and Delta and Pine Land Company should be held legally liable for Terminator plant damage to a neighbor's field (Kaiser 2000).

The controversy rages on, and Terminator technology nearly surfaced again at the Convention on Biological Diversity in 2005, with the support of the Canadian government. Then, in January 2006 at the fourth meeting of the Ad Hoc Open-ended intersessional Working Group on provisions of the Convention on Biological Diversity in Granada, Spain, parties clashed once again over the moratorium on Terminator technology. Ultimately, the moratorium was reconfirmed, but Australia insisted on modifying the field test moratorium to allow further research and studies on potential impacts and other aspects of Terminator technologies on a case-by-case risk assessment basis, thereby weakening the "de facto" UN Biosafety Protocol agreed on in January 2000 (Ching 2006).

The UN Biosafety Protocol provides basic international rules that allow mainly developing countries to regulate the safety of transgenic foods, crops, and seeds. It has been ratified by 132 countries, but the three main countries that grow these crops, the United States, Argentina, and Canada, refuse to support it. On the final day of the meeting, the Working Group finalized its recommendation, which was subsequently forwarded to the eighth meeting of the Conference of the Parties to the Convention on Biological Diversity, held March 2006 in Curitiba, Brazil (Friends of the Earth International 2006).

For two weeks prior to and during the convention, the call for a ban on Terminator technology took center stage. Thousands of peasant farmers, including those from Brazil's Landless Workers Movement (Movimento Sem Terra), protested daily outside the meeting to demand a ban, and women of the international Via Campesina movement of peasant farmers staged a powerful silent protest inside the meeting on March 23. Protests also took place in India, Peru, Spain, New Zealand, and Canada. Ultimately, the governments of the world upheld the de facto moratorium unanimously (etcgroup 2006; Organic Consumers Association 2006a; Osava 2006b).

Of interest at the convention proceedings were the roles of the United States (not a convention member) and industry in their attempts to undermine labeling practices for transgenic (GMO, genetically modified organism) products. Initially Mexico, Paraguay, Peru, Brazil, and New Zealand supported GMO-containing products labeled as "may contain GMOs," instead of the stronger, more truthful "contains GMOs." Ultimately, largely because of the influence of protesters and those opposed to GMO technology, all countries agreed to go with the stronger label, thereby undermining the influence of industry and the United States in the negotiations (Organic Consumers Association 2006a).

Nonetheless, environmental and indigenous activists left the conference disappointed with the proceedings, primarily because they were not conducted democratically, providing opportunities for environmental and indigenous groups to participate in the negotiations; nor did the convention result in any concrete, practical decisions. Greenpeace International called it a "failure." "The Convention on Biological Diversity is like a ship drifting without a captain to steer it," said Martin Kaiser, Greenpeace political adviser. According to Kaiser, the convention failed to determine the means for financing the fulfillment of the goal of significantly reducing loss of biodiversity by 2010 (Osava 2006a).

In the meantime, a farmer who lives near Cuquio, Jalisco, claimed in summer 2004 that his corn seeds saved from the preceding year never germinated. Has the Terminator already arrived in west-central Mexico?

In 1998, 25 percent of corn grown in the United States was genetically modified with a bacterial gene (endotoxin) that renders the plants poisonous to caterpillars (Wheelwright 2001). Bt corn contains a gene from the bacteria *Bacillus thuringiensis* that directs the corn plant to produce a toxin to destroy the corn worm commonly visible at the end of the mature corn cob, once the corn sheaths have been removed.

In 2000, environmental organizations began to blow the environmental whistle on genetically altered Bt corn because of the potential harmful effects the altered corn pollen could have on caterpillars (butterfly larvae) in the environment. Agribusiness interests supported by the EPA insisted that Bt corn poses little risk to butterflies (Howie 2001; Meredith Corporation 2001). The scientific community, however, viewed the altered corn with greater skepticism (*Consumer Reports* 1999; Zangerl et al. 2001). Cornell University researchers raised monarch butterfly larvae on common milkweed plant leaves spread with Bt pollen. Monarch butterfly larvae's specific food source is the common milkweed plant. After only four days, 44 percent of the larvae exposed to the Bt pollen died, and the surviving Bt-exposed larvae were reduced in weight by more than 60 percent. The control groups of larvae consuming either plain milkweed leaves or leaves spread with pollen from non-genetically altered corn had a 100 percent survival rate (Tokar 1999).

In 2001, the National Academy of Sciences reported significant reduction in growth rates of black swallowtail butterfly larvae that was "likely" to be caused by transgenic corn pollen exposure. The Academy report called for thorough testing of transgenic corn strains to reduce their potential negative environmental impact (Zangerl et al. 2001).

In another study, German researchers discovered a gene transfer from genetically engineered rapeseed to bacteria and fungi in the gut of bees. The rapeseed strain was genetically engineered to resist the herbicide glufosinate. Pollen from the transgenic plants was fed to young bees in the laboratory. The researchers found that, when the bees ate the pollen, the gene for resistance to the herbicide was transferred to bacteria and yeast living in the gut of the young bees, resulting in an interkingdom transfer of genetic material (Reiche et al. 1998).

Gene flow from one species to another has been substantiated in several studies. For example, in a study of wild sunflower patches that had grown near farmed commercial sunflowers for up to forty years, 115 wild plants that researchers tested carried at least one genetic marker characteristic of the commercial sunflower plants. A rare genetic marker found in conventional alfalfa crops has been documented in stray plants up to 230 meters away from the alfalfa crop (Milius 2003).

Monsanto's own study of genetically modified corn fed to rats showed that, over time, the animals developed kidney and blood abnormalities. The secret study was leaked to reporters of the U.K. *Independent* newspaper and traversed the world on the Internet almost overnight (Beyond Pesticides 2005). As a result, environmentalists and food security activists in India insisted on a moratorium on all genetically modified foods and crops (Devraj 2005).

In 2000, 135,000 acres of a genetically altered hybrid corn referred to as StarLink were planted in Iowa. The EPA restricted the corn as a potential food allergen to humans. Growers were warned that the corn could be sold for animal feed only, not for human consumption. When corn-containing foods were sampled from a Maryland Safeway store, however, at least one was found to contain the genetically modified StarLink corn. The corn was subsequently quickly and quietly removed from the market (Wheelwright 2001).

Millions of bushels of genetically engineered corn approved only for animal consumption are currently in the U.S. food supply (Kaufman 2000). An estimated 70 percent of processed food on U.S. supermarket shelves contains some genetically engineered ingredients that have not been adequately tested for impacts on human health or the environment (Cain 2002; see also www.thecampaign.org). These foods include such common, innocuous items as baby formulas, tortilla chips, drink mixes, taco shells, "veggie" burgers, muffin mixes, and even McDonald's McVeggie Burgers (*Consumer Reports* 1999).

By 2006, substantial U.S. acreage had been planted in yet other new forms of genetically engineered corn plants designed to produce drugs and vaccines ("pharma crops") and industrial chemicals. Since 1991, the USDA has approved between 100 and 200 or more applications for pharma crop field tests in almost every state in the union. Each permit often allows biotechnology companies to grow pharma crops in several states. For example, between 2000 and 2004, the USDA granted seven permits to Monsanto, Dow, and Pioneer, a Dupont subsidiary, to grow pharma corn crops in California and other states. A permit issued to Pioneer in 2004 allows the company to grow 7,475 acres of pharma corn crops in California and twenty-one other states. Some applications include more than one pharma crop site per state. This information and the exact locations within a state planted in pharma crops are withheld from the public as confidential business information (Union of Concerned Scientists 2006).

Agronomists and crop scientists maintain that using food crops like corn to produce pharmaceuticals and industrial chemicals virtually guarantees the genetic contamination of traditional corn seed crops destined for corn products in the U.S. food supply (Andow et al. 2004). Crops not associated with food crops such as guayule could be used instead of corn as pharma crops without the risk of harming the food supply (Daniell and Gepts 2004).

The authors of one study of corn contamination by pharma transgenes estimate that a minimum of 0.1 percent of 1.6 trillion corn seeds planted yearly in the United States—that is, 1.6 billion corn seeds—carry pharma transgenic sequences. This number is so huge that it would take about 25,000 50-pound bags to hold the 1.6 billion contaminating seeds. When Union of Concerned Scientists members traveled through the United States to purchase traditional food seeds supposedly free of genetic modification, 50–100 percent of the samples they obtained were contaminated (Jacobs 2004; Mellon and Rissler 2004).

Bioengineered Corn in Rural Mexico

Prior to NAFTA's initiation, the International Service for the Acquisition of Agri-biotech Applications (ISAAA) expressed its intent to bring "innovative agricultural biotechnological techniques to the developing world's farmers." The stated Third World goal of the organization is for farmers to use the new biotechnological methods as a means of achieving greater productivity while cutting the necessity of chemical pesticide use. In 1992, ISAAA targeted Mexico, Taiwan, and Costa Rica as the countries where the new methods were likeliest to succeed (Gershon 1992).

In 1998, Mexico banned the planting of any genetically modified corn in order to protect its traditional strains of *maíz criollo* (Elias 2002; UC Mexus 2004). However, since NAFTA began in 1994, the United States exports 5.5 million tons of corn to Mexico every year (Carpentier and Herrmann 2004; *International Herald Tribune* 2005)—30–50 percent of it genetically modified (A. Nadal, personal communication, 2005; Dyer-Leal and Yúnez-Naude 2003; UC Mexus 2004; Weissart 2004). Because this corn is subsidized with U.S. taxpayer money, it can be sold in Mexico for less than the cost of growing corn in Mexico (Koons-Garcia 2000).

Additionally, it is impossible to separate commercial corn stocks targeted for animals or humans in the United States. Genetically modified corn sent to Mexico does *not* have to be labeled as genetically modified corn. In rural Mexico, with less distributor and farmer sophistication and regulation, no agency is monitoring the corn varieties farmers choose to plant in their fields. Many farmers plant whatever corn is available. Thus, inevitably traditional corn varieties have and will continue to become contaminated with bioengineered strains.

Since the initial introduction of hybrid commercial seed varieties, critics have been vocal about the risks associated with the disappearance of traditional corn varieties (Wright 1990). Reports of genetic contamination began surfacing in 2001 when Ignacio Chapela and his graduate assistant, David Quist, created a firestorm of controversy with their discovery of transgenic DNA in ancient Oaxacan strains of corn (Quist and Chapela 2001). With further testing, other labs in Mexico found transgenes in corn varieties elsewhere in Mexico (Milius 2003). By 2005, transgenic corn varieties had been registered in *most* of Mexico's states, including Jalisco and Colima (Greenpeace 2005b). The probable source of transgenic corn genes in Mexico is U.S.-exported genetically modified corn (Dyer-Leal and Yúnez-Naude 2003).

Biologically, the replacement of traditional corn varieties with commercially produced, hybrid, high-yielding varieties or genetically bioengineered varieties is tantamount to the potential mass extinction of corn's genetic reservoir produced over at least 7,000 years. Carelessness, ignorance, and greed could wipe out what nature and Mexican farmers spent thousands of years developing—a food crop inseparable from the history, environment, culture, and cooking of Mexico (UC Mexus 2004).

Transgenic Corn and Global Trade

Although there is mounting controversy regarding genetically modified grains in the United States, at least there is discussion and some attempt to regulate bioengineered varieties and control their dissemination. In 2001, 80 percent of farmers complied with all planting restrictions for corn that is genetically engineered to produce its own pesticide, a significant increase from 71 percent the year before (Brasher 2002). There are, however, no functional, enforceable state or federal controls for imported transgenic strains of corn sold or brought into the west-central Mexico countryside.

Until recently, and under pressure from the WTO, the European Union prohibited the importation of genetically modified corn from the United States, at an approximate annual loss to U.S. transgenic corn farmers of $200–$300 million (Brand 2003; *Consumer Reports* 1999; Koons-Garcia 2000). In January 2003, the United States, backed by Canada and Australia, filed suit with the WTO, arguing that the ban violated global trading rules (Brand 2003).

The six-year biotech moratorium ended in 2004 when the EU head office finally approved a type of genetically modified corn for human consumption. Unlike corn product labeling in the United States and Mexico, all genetically modified corn products sent to Europe must be labeled as such (Geitner 2004). With the influence of "free trade" and the lax health and environmental regulations already in place in Mexico, the pressure to export U.S. stocks of bioengineered corn to Mexico will only increase.

If tragedies comparable to the southern corn leaf blight in the United States afflict Mexico's corn producers, resulting in huge crop failures, unless the United States can make up for crop losses with added imports, widespread famine in Mexico could easily result. And if corn considered a biotechnological failure in the United States, such as StarLink, is imported and dumped into the Mexican countryside, the ecological and human health ramifications in the region's already compromised, degraded, fragile ecosystems remain a matter of disquieting speculation.

Transgenic Crops and Agrochemicals

Some crops are genetically designed for and require agrochemicals for productive yields. For example, Monsanto's Roundup Ready corn, soybeans, and cotton strains are genetically designed to withstand Roundup (glyphosate, an herbicide). The transgenic corn plants are unharmed by the herbicide, while competing weeds are destroyed. To grow Monsanto's Roundup Ready crops, the farmer must have the funds to purchase both the seeds and the herbicide to rid the fields of weeds. In California, glyphosate exposure is the third most commonly reported cause of pesticide illness among agricultural workers (Cox 1995). The herbicide can drift away from the site of its application as far as 800 meters. Monsanto's Roundup Ready soybeans and cotton are already planted in Mexico. How soon Monsanto's Roundup Ready corn invades the countryside remains to be seen.

Aggressive strategies by biotech companies, particularly Monsanto, have promoted the supposed advantages transgenic crops provide to the environment, consumers, and farmers. They have misrepresented the performance of these crops, exaggerated the benefits, and ignored entirely the negative impacts, both actual and potential, they may have on the environment and future generations (Friends of the Earth International 2006b).

Critics claim that the conversion of world agriculture by a small, elite group of biotech companies has little to do with corporate greed. Rather, they view it as a geopolitical issue, consistent with what Pentagon planners refer to as "full spectrum dominance." This includes global military dominance, dominance of the world's oil supplies, control of the world's reserve currency, and future and growing control of agriculture through control of transgenic patents and crops. They argue that, if present trends continue, global dominance by the United States will be based on control of the planet's food supply (Engdahl 2005).

The dangers and difficulties associated with controlling the spread of genetically modified crops into the food supply became abundantly clear in August 2006 with the disclosure that the rice supply on the market in England is contaminated by genetically modified rice, code-named LL-RICE601, produced by Bayer CropScience. This rice appeared in several storage locations owned by Arkansas-based Riceland, the world's largest miller and marketer of rice. The European Commission and Japan prohibited any shipments from the United States unless they could be proved free of the banned rice (Lean 2006). In addition, Bayer's transgenic Liberty Link 602 rice was found on the market in the United States. Neither the transgenic rice strain imported into England nor the one for sale in the United States has been authorized for sale or for human consumption. Mexico is the principal importer of rice from the United States (Greenpeace 2006b).

AGRIBUSINESS IN MEXICO: AGROCHEMICALS

Farmer Perceptions about Commercial Agriculture

The Green Revolution and bioengineered strains of commercialized corn *(maíz mejorado)* that continue to pour into Mexico are part of agribusiness packages that require farmers to use chemical fertilizers, herbicides, and pesticides to realize elevated crop yields (Wright 1990). The new plant varieties, in turn, result in increased numbers and species of pest infestations, requiring more pesticides (Watson 2000). Throughout west-central Mexico I asked farmers when their problems with pests began initially. Almost all reported that pests were never really a problem until the introduction of agrochemicals and farm machinery.

Corroborating the farmers' perceptions is an inter-institutional collaboration of scientists and an agricultural economist who found that organic farming produces the same yields of corn and soybeans as does conventional farming but uses 30 percent less energy, less water, and no pesticides. The study is a review of the Rodale Institute Farming Systems Trial, the longest running comparison of organic and conventional farming in the United States. The research compared soil fungi activity, crop yields, energy efficiency, costs, organic matter changes over time, and nitrate leaching across organic and conventional agricultural systems (Pimentel et al. 2005).

While some campesinos, like Jovita Tejada and her neighbors in Las Cebollas, Jalisco, cling to their environmentally sound traditional farming practices against the pressure of market forces and the promotion of "modernized" agriculture, most farmers in Mexico and farmworker interviewees in this study view their traditional practices as being *atrasados* (backward) and perceive U.S. agriculture as being *avanzada* (advanced) and modern. Agrochemical distributors throughout the countryside encourage this perception and use it as a selling point for "modern" agricultural products imported from the United States and elsewhere.

Both the hybrid or genetically altered corn seeds and the agrochemicals required to grow these crops are referred to by west-central Mexican farmers with innocuous terms that belie the enormous environmental, genetic, and health risks posed by their introduction and presence. As discussed earlier, the new introduced strains of corn seeds are referred to as *maíz mejorado* or *maíz superado* (improved seeds)—terms suggesting that the traditional *maíz criollo* strains are of comparatively inferior quality.

Granulated chemical urea fertilizer is referred to as *sal de la tierra* (salt of the earth) in San José de Guadalupe near Tlalpuhajua, Michoacán, rather than as chemical fertilizer. All liquid agrochemicals sold in liter containers, even those so toxic that they are classified as Dirty Dozen agrochemicals (see appendix A), are referred to as *líquidos* (liquids) rather than *venenos* (poisons). Powdered agrochemicals, regardless of their identity or toxicity, are all simply referred to collectively and innocuously as *polvos* (powders).

Brand names further mask the potentially venomous nature of agrochemical products. *Faena* translates to "task" or "job." Faena is Roundup (glyphosate). *Assadon,* an herbicide, and *Azadón* (pronounced in an identical manner) translate to "hoe" in English, the implication being that Assadon will take the place of *azadón* by killing off the weeds a farmer would use a hoe to dislodge in the field. *Matador,* a Bad Actor insecticide, translates to "killer" in English.

For Mexican farmers who are able to read them, the toxicity labels on agrochemical containers in Mexico often do not reflect their true, inherent danger. There are many discrepancies between container toxicity labeling in Mexico and the toxicity labeling of comparable compounds by the U.S. EPA and Pesticide Action Network. For example, in Mexico a container of Zeneca's (now Syngenta) Gramoxone is labeled as "moderately toxic," when in fact it is a member of the highly toxic Dirty Dozen, is listed as a Class I dangerous herbicide by the EPA, and is a Restricted Use Product. Another highly toxic Dirty Dozen herbicide—2,4,5-T—is labeled also "moderately toxic." Total 5g (diazinon) is labeled "mildly toxic," when in fact it is a Pesticide Action Network Bad Actor, is listed by the EPA as a Class 2 insecticide, and is a Restricted Use Product in the United States.

Transnational Corporations, Poisoning, and Death

Over half the world's one hundred largest economic entities are transnational corporations, not nations. The top ten agrochemical corporations account for 80 percent of global agrochemical sales (ETC Group 2003). These agrochemicals are responsible for an estimated 39 million global agricultural worker incidents of pesticide poisoning each year (Reeves et al. 2006), and every year three million cases of severe poisoning occur worldwide (Tinoco-Ojanguren and Halperin 1998). More than 200,000 people are reported killed by pesticide poisoning worldwide every year (WHO, as cited in Giuliano 2005).

Every minute, one person in the Third World is poisoned by pesticides (Luján 1995). Every day, 547 children, women, and men die from pesticide poisoning, and four million children die each year from the effects of contaminated water and other toxic hazards; that's nearly 11,000 per day (WHO, as cited in Giuliano 2005). Organophosphate pesticides ac-

Figure 17. Monsanto Faena herbicide advertisement on the road to San Agustín, Jalisco.

count for most of the deaths in Third World countries (Tinoco-Ojanguren 1998).

The United States exported 65 million pounds of pesticides that are banned or severely restricted for U.S. use between 1997 and 2000. More than half of these pesticide products were sent to developing countries (Beyond Pesticides 2002; LaDou 2001). Only one-fourth of the total world utilization of pesticides occurs in the Third World, yet the majority of the poisonings and 99 percent of the resulting deaths occur in developing countries (Tinoco-Ojanguren and Halperin 1998).

It is estimated that at least five thousand people die each year from acute pesticide poisoning in Mexico alone (PANNA 1990; Simon 1997). The Asociacion Mexicana de Estudios para la Defensa del Consumidor (AMEDC), a consumer group in Mexico, confirmed 750 severe poisonings among 4,400 adults studied in 1990 (PANNA 1990). A central finding in Tinoco-Ojanguren's work on pesticide poisoning in Chiapas is that individuals from the poorest communities were exposed to the most toxic insecticides, and poorer agricultural workers were most affected by toxic compounds. He further claims that the poorest workers may not be able to afford to purchase less toxic insecticides. Though there are no studies of the long-term health effects of insecticide exposure among the poorest Chiapan farmers, potential poisoning from the most toxic insecticides may aggravate the effects of the already impoverished living conditions (Tinoco-Ojanguren and Halperin 1998).

The Agrochemical Market in Mexico

From 1988 to 1992, imports of organophosphate insecticides into Mexico for agricultural use doubled from 3,000 to 6,000 tons (Tinoco-Ojanguren and Halperin 1998). More recently, commercial pesticide use and the use of cancer-causing chemicals and organophosphates appear to be dropping worldwide (Rogers 2001) due to a global farm crisis that includes the combination of overproduction and rock-bottom commodity prices (RAFI 2001). Still, the transnational pesticide market in Mexico continues to grow in recent years. In 1980, Mexico spent an estimated $199 million on pesticides. Accurate information regarding agrochemical exports to Mexico and agrochemical production by U.S. transnational subsidiaries in Mexico has become increasingly more difficult to obtain since NAFTA went into effect. But by 1990 Mexico had spent $565 million on pesticides (Tinoco-Ojanguren and Halperin 1998), in 1999 Mexico produced nearly 25,000 metric tons of pesticides for agricultural use, and pesticide sales continued to rise (INEGI 2000).

The pesticide business in Mexico includes sales by huge multinational corporations and a network of privately owned formulation plants (Wright 1990). Fertimex, once Mexico's government pesticide monopoly, was the largest manufacturer and wholesaler of pesticides in Mexico (Wright 1990). In 1990 the Fertimex monopoly was privatized. Today transnational chemical giants including Monsanto (annual sales $3.9 billion in 2000), Syngenta (largest agrochemical company in the world, annual sales over $7 billion in 2004), Dupont (annual sales over $2.5 billion in 2000), Dow (largest U.S. chemical company, 2005 first-quarter sales of nearly $12 billion), and Bayer (almost €30 billion sales in 2004) are represented on liter containers of the harshest, most toxic agrochemicals sold to subsistence farmers throughout west-central Mexico (see appendix A).

In 2005, the UN Food and Agriculture Organization estimated that there are 30,000–50,000 tons of obsolete toxic pesticides in Latin America. The obsolete pesticides were originally shipped to Latin America as a result of campaigns promoted by the chemical industry, often supported by U.S. agricultural interests. After the pesticides were banned or replaced, they remained in Latin America and were not disposed of or removed. For example, 86.7 tons of obsolete DDT is now sitting in Latin America; its use is highly restricted to malaria prevention and control (Beyond Pesticides 2005).

Storage facilities for agrochemicals in Mexico are sometimes not adequate or secure, leading to fires and explosions that compromise the health of employees and local residents. In 1991 fiery explosions engulfed the Veracruz National Agriculture Pesticide Warehouse and Mixing plant. An estimated 8,000 liters of methyl parathion (an extremely toxic Dirty Dozen pesticide), 8,000 liters of paraquat (an extremely toxic Dirty Dozen herbicide), 3,000 liters of 2,4-D, and 500 liters of pentachlorophenol-PCP (an extremely toxic Dirty Dozen fungicide) were burned or spilled from the site.

Five hundred people became ill from the toxic clouds, and army troops evacuated two thousand people from fifteen neighboring districts around the plant (RAPAM 1991). Three hundred local residents were hospitalized in serious condition. Of 540 local residents interviewed after the explosion, 485 complained of headaches, 379 reported pharyngeal mouth pain, 282 experienced skin irritation, 241 complained of dizziness, 229 reported nausea, 134 vomited, 132 experienced abdominal pain, 120 complained of weakness, 118 reported coughing, and 97 experienced insomnia. Five years after the accident, 87 people had died from conditions related to pesticide poisoning.

A member of the state ecology commission indicated that after the explosions the area was probably heavily contaminated by highly carcinogenic dioxins. The commission further charged that local authorities were unprepared to undertake an appropriate response to an agrochemical industrial fire in view of the fact that firefighters flushed the toxins into a nearby river, thereby contaminating the local water supply (RAPAM 1991).

Complaints of damage to health and property, lawsuits, and other efforts by the local population to acquire compensation for their losses were largely suppressed or ignored by government authorities and the agrochemical company (Blanco and Manila 2001). Whereas the larger, disastrous Bhopal, India, incident has received international press and pressure on Dupont to compensate the victims of its predecessor corporation, Union Carbide, the Veracruz incident has received comparatively little international publicity.

In another incident, in September 1993, more than five thousand residents in Los Mochis, Sinaloa, Mexico, were evacuated because of a fire at a pesticide warehouse. The fire, caused by a short circuit in the wiring, released a toxic cloud more than 50 meters in diameter and disrupted supplies of toxic chemicals including methyl parathion. At least fifty people suffered severe symptoms of pesticide poisoning.

In both incidents, citizens' complaints to government and industry officials regarding the safety of the plants prior to the explosions were ignored (RAPAM 1993).

Agrochemical Availability in West-Central Mexico

When asked about the origin of agrochemicals in west-central Mexico, campesinos and distributors alike agree that most come to Mexico from the United States or are manufactured by U.S. companies in Mexico. Billboards and impressive, newly painted signs placed on the sides of homes and small stores in the most remote villages advertise deadly agrochemicals to an often uninformed population (*IPCS News* 1993; PANNA 1990; Wright 1990). They also confirm the exhaustive penetration of transnational agrochemical corporations into the west-central Mexico countryside.

During the summer growing season, farmers and their hired workers don backpack agrochemical applicators, or *mochilas de bomba*. Manual spraying devices are viewed as an inexpensive and flexible means of applying agrochemicals (Wright 1990). The use of protective clothing while spraying with these applicators is almost nonexistent in west-central Mexico. Most campesinos wear traditional *huaraches* (open sandals) on their feet while spraying. Some farmers spray with exposed skin. When the corn is several feet tall, many enter cornfields to spray herbicides without protective masks. In the comparatively enclosed environment of a mature cornfield, the worker inhales spray the entire time that the agrochemicals are applied.

While studying the farms of west-central Mexico, my research assistants and I surveyed the stock of agrochemicals offered for sale by methodically taking agrochemical inventories throughout the region. We inventoried commercial establishments and farmer residences where agrochemicals acquired from local distributors were stored. Two of the inventories are provided in appendix A.

We later evaluated each inventory by the classification systems developed by the Pesticide Action Network, the Rachel Carson Council, and the U.S. EPA. Of the twenty-six agrochemicals on the shelves for sale at Veterinaria "Tepa" in Cuquio, Jalisco, in summer 1998, over half (four-

Figure 18. Worker with backpack applicator *(mochila)*.

teen, using 1999 classifications; eighteen, using updated 2005 classification revisions) were either Dirty Dozen or Bad Actor agrochemicals. Four are prohibited from use in the United States, and twelve are Restricted Use Pesticides available in the United States only to certificated pesticide applicators or to be used only under the direct supervision of a certified applicator.

In summer 2004, Fertilizante Gonzalez in Cuquio, Jalisco, offered thirty-nine products for sale. Three are Dirty Dozen pesticides, eighteen are Bad Actors, three are prohibited in the United States, one is prohibited in Mexico, and fifteen are Restricted Use Pesticides.

The owner of Veterinaria Tepa stopped stocking agrochemicals in 2000, claiming that he had seen too much harm from agrochemicals done to both livestock and farmers in the region. However, financial necessity required that he restock his shelves once again in January 2006. He justified his decision by claiming to stock only herbicides, not pesticides, and comparatively innocuous herbicides at that. But a later analysis of the chemicals he stocked tells another story. Of the fourteen chemicals I was able to record on his shelves in summer 2006, eight are Bad Actors and one, paraquat, is a Dirty Dozen herbicide (see appendix A).

Perhaps most disturbing is the regular purchase of deadly agrochemicals by uninformed farmers. Two farmers who enthusiastically support agrochemical use in their farming practices were chosen for personal inventories of their agrochemical supplies at their residences. Gabino Ayala of San Agustín, Jalisco, not only is committed to agrochemical use on his land, but he also informed me that he *mixes* the different agrochemicals together to discover "the best combinations." Of the ten agrochemicals stored in his adobe shed in July 1999, four were Dirty Dozen and four more were Bad Actor agrochemicals. Seven have been banned in the United States or Mexico or are Restricted Use Pesticides.

Agrochemical Symptomatology

According to Greenpeace Mexico, an estimated 124,000 tons of Dirty Dozen agrochemicals were applied in Mexico in the twenty-year period from 1975 to 1995 (Barry 1995). The Dirty Dozen herbicide paraquat, frequently sold under the trade name Gramoxone and produced by Syngenta, was found in almost every inventory taken in west-central Mexico from 1998 to 2006. It is the most toxic herbicide marketed over the past sixty years and the third most widely used in the world. Paraquat is so toxic that it is said to be the leading choice of people attempting suicide in the Third World. As little as one teaspoonful can be fatal (PANNA 2003). The poison is readily available in significant quantities without a prescription or any questions asked (Wright 1990). In the field, paraquat causes acute symptoms with skin rashes that can lead to serious illness and death within a matter of hours or days.

The deadly agrochemical is "effective" when inhaled, ingested, or absorbed through the skin. It is especially insidious because, with frequent low-dose exposure over a period of two to three years, paraquat can cause the proliferation of lung tissue, reducing the ability of the lungs to absorb oxygen. Compromised lung function can then lead to significant disability and death. In addition, paraquat is a probable carcinogen, disrupts reproductive functions, and causes birth defects (Wright 1990, 26–27).

Chlorinated hydrocarbons are also ubiquitous herbicides of choice in west-central Mexico. These compounds inhibit nerve membrane ion transport and block nerve signal transmission. They are fast acting and highly toxic, persist in nature for long periods of time, and are concentrated in the trophic levels of food chains where they are stored in the fatty tissues of organisms (Cunningham and Saigo 2001).

One of the most popular chlorinated hydrocarbons in use in west-

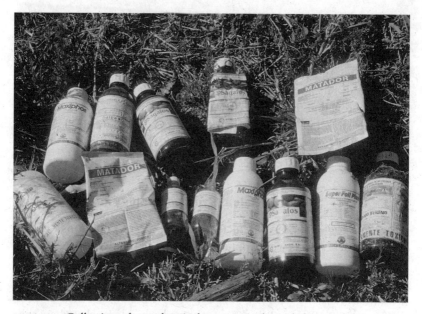

Figure 19. Collection of agrochemical containers discarded around the periphery of Joaquin Bejarano's strawberry field, Chaparaco, Michoacán.

central Mexico is the chloriphenoxy herbicide 2,4-D, which is often sold in combination with hazardous compounds such as 2,4,5-T. For example, 2,4-D is frequently sold as Esteron 2,4-D. The Esteron is 2,4,5-T, one of the Dirty Dozen that has been banned in the United States. A 50:50 mix of 2,4-D and 2,4,5-T is Monsanto's Agent Orange, a powerful herbicidal defoliant used in the Vietnam War. The utilization of Esteron 2,4-D and other hazardous 2,4-D combinations is commonplace throughout west-central Mexico.

Organophosphates are an outgrowth of nerve gas research during World War II. They are extremely toxic to mammals, birds, and fishes and are generally ten to one hundred times more poisonous than most chlorinated hydrocarbons. Organophosphates inhibit cholinesterase, which is essential for removing excess neurotransmitter from nerve synapses in the peripheral nervous system (Cunningham and Saigo 2001). Organophosphates break down quickly in the environment, usually within a few hours or days. However, they are extremely dangerous to work with and one of the most common sources of acute pesticide poisoning in Mexico (Wright 1990).

Organophosphate herbicides and insecticides are common and easily obtained in Mexico. Four of the most common organophosphate insecticides in west-central Mexico are methamidophos, a Bad Actor marketed under the trade names Monitor and Tamaron; chlorpyrifos, a Bad Actor marketed under the trade names Dursban, Lorsban, and Disparo; parathion, one of the Dirty Dozen marketed under the trade names Toxiton and Folidól; and malathion, a Bad Actor. In addition, as discussed earlier, organophosphate herbicides such as glyphosate, Monsanto's Roundup, and 2,4-D marketed in some locations under the trade names of Weed-B-Gon or Raid Weed Killer are also commonly in use.

The use of any of these compounds can result in serious health and environmental consequences. For example, the herbicide glyphosate is a suspected mammalian carcinogen and fetal endocrine disruptor (see chapter 8). The herbicide 2,4-D is a carcinogen, teratogen (may cause birth defects), immunotoxin, and may cause injury to the liver, kidneys, and central nervous system. Environmentally, chlorpyrifos is highly toxic to mollusks, fishes, crustaceans, bees, aquatic insects, and birds. In some mammals it acts as a delayed neurotoxin and may cause sterility.

The insecticide malathion is a suspected mammalian mutagen and teratogen. In addition, exposure results in immunosuppression (suppression of the immune system) and potential damage to eyesight. The compound is highly toxic to bees, amphibians, and aquatic insects.

The insecticide diazinon is a suspected mammalian mutagen, neurotoxin, and immunotoxin. Environmentally, the compound is highly toxic to birds, fishes, amphibians, crustaceans, bees, and aquatic insects. In birds diazinon acts as a teratogen. Although as an insecticide the compound is designed to target insects, in some cases it is toxic to plants (Cox 1992).

In 2000, the U.S. EPA announced that the production of Dow Chemical's Dursban and Lorsban would be halted in the United States by December 2000 (MSNBC News 2000). The primary component, chlorpyrifos, was cited as potentially damaging to children's nervous system and brain development. Yet sale of the common home-use and commercially applied pesticide was allowed to continue until December 31, 2001, "until stocks are depleted" (Owens 2000). Home treatment for termites was allowed through December 2002, and new home treatment was allowed until December 2005. Export of this product continues without restriction (Owens 2000), and chlorpyrifos products are commonly purchased by uninformed farmers in west-central Mexico.

Billboards sponsored by transnational corporations throughout west-central Mexico boldly advertise a wide variety of hybrid seeds and agrochemicals with information about their use and effectiveness. Though transnational corporate profits soar, the social costs of corporate penetration into the west-central Mexico countryside are truly unprecedented.

TWELVE

ENDANGERED MEXICAN FARMERS

Coke and beer are delivered in the morning to the pueblo before milk!

—Vicente Silva, former municipal president of Chilchota, Huancito, Michoacán

Yo pienso que con . . . tantas químicas y todo lo que le ponen a las tierras, ya a llegar un día que ya no va ver producción como que . . . cada ves va ocupar más y más de otras químicas más fuertes. Que se va cansar la tierra.

I think that with so many chemicals and everything else they put on the land, the day will come when there will no longer be [crop] production, since they're farming with more and more, ever stronger chemicals. The land will be [too] tired [to produce].

—Xóchitl Flores, Salinas farmworker from Tanaquillo, Michoacán

As the sun rises over the houses and verdant fields of the El Guaco *ejido,* near Uruapan, Michoacán, industrious resident farmers are already working in their fields. Most don backpack pesticide applicators, *bombas,* and are spraying their fields to rid them of the ever-competitive weeds, insects, and birds.

Luis Fernandez smiles broadly at his wife and children as they walk with him to the front door of their home. Before he leaves, he and his wife Ermelinda take a moment to enumerate the tasks of the day prior to the arrival of their relatives from a neighboring village. Ermelinda reminds Luis to return home early so he can join the family for their evening meal.

After a long hug and a good-bye, Luis heads out the door with his *bomba* and lunch, ready to begin the walk down the village's main road to the family's *parcela,* about 45 minutes away. As he walks down the road past his neighbors' planted *parcelas* Luis observes the many empty liter organophosphate pesticide containers of Lorsban and Disparo tossed to the side of his neighbors' fields. He is grateful that his *ejido* neighbors have joined him in signing a contract for a cooperative farming venture with a U.S. company. The company provides all seeds and agrochemicals for a melon and cucumber crop. The El Guaco farmers grow the crop, and company representatives return at a later date to purchase the harvest, for sale in the United States. Since he and his neighbors signed a contract with the company, their income has improved, and most have avoided the unwanted prospect of leaving their families alone in El Guaco to emigrate to Guadalajara or the United States in search of work.

Today, Luis is spraying Lorsban, a company-provided Bad Actor organophosphate insecticide, with chlorpyrifos as the active ingredient. By this afternoon, the pernicious bugs he discovered yesterday eating the leaves of his melon plants should be dead, and he won't have to worry about a reduced melon yield from *una plaga* (a pest infestation).

After spraying for half an hour, Luis begins to feel somewhat faint and fatigued. An unfamiliar nausea begins to creep into his awareness, diverting his attention away from the beauty of the dawning day over the fields. He puzzles for a moment about these unfamiliar bodily sensations and then walks over to the edge of his *parcela* to sit quietly on the rock boundary and rest for a few moments. However, his impatience to finish the task of spraying before the sun gets too high in the sky overrules the growing discomfort he senses in his body. After a short rest of 5–10 minutes, and with mustered resolve, Luis walks back to the center of his melon patch. He continues to spray as his symptoms become more intense. Without the recommended mask to breathe through, he continues to inhale the pesticide fumes.

Within moments of continued spraying, Luis is dizzy and vomits. His back feels wet. A jolt of terror runs through him like lightning as he suddenly realizes that his *bomba* has a leak in the plastic holding container pressed against his back. The toxic liquid has drenched his shirt and penetrated the skin. Luis yanks the *bomba* and his shirt off and tosses them both to the ground. He staggers to the edge of the field and, through blurred vision, attempts to locate the road leading back to the village. Finding the road at last, he attempts to navigate and stumbles along. He falls once, then manages to pick himself up. Once he is upright the dizziness overtakes him, and he vomits again. He shuffles along for what seems like an eternity.

Ermelinda is washing clothes in the yard when she sees her husband in the distance staggering toward their home with arms flailing. She quickly drops the clothes in the wash basin and runs up the road yelling, *"Qué te pasa! Qué te pasaste!"* ("What's going on! What happened to you!") Luis attempts to draw a strong enough breath to return a labored response, *"Es la química! . . . la química!"* And then he collapses unconscious in front of her.

By this time, people working in the nearby *parcelas* hear the shouts and become aware of the unfolding crisis. They toss their *bombas* to the ground and run toward Luis to offer assistance. Three men carry him to a villager's waiting vehicle. Luis and his wife are rushed to a hospital in nearby Nueva Italia. As Ermelinda quickly relates the morning's events to the doctor, a nurse hastily ushers Luis, now on a stretcher, into an emergency room while the doctor fits him with an IV drip of atropine. Treatment begins.

Luis remained in the hospital for a week. When his symptoms subsided and his recovery was certain, the doctor permitted him to return home to his family. However, the doctor cautioned him that he could never use agrochemicals again. The exposure he had sustained resulted in permanent nerve damage. Another exposure could cost him his life.

A LACK OF ENFORCEABLE REGULATIONS FOR AGROCHEMICALS

Government regulation of agrochemicals in the United States and Mexico differ in several ways. Both countries register pesticides and establish tolerance levels for pesticide residues. However, Mexico uses information from other countries in making its decisions; the United States does not. Tolerance levels differ geographically according to climatic and soil factors. Thus, the use of another country's data may not include a consideration of climatic and soil differences. Another difference between the two countries is that the U.S. government purportedly monitors produce imported from Mexico, whereas the Mexican government relies on inspection by the private sector (Luján 1995; Wright 1990).

The Mexican government largely ignores the health consequences of uncontrolled agrochemical application and does not enforce regulations to protect farmers and farmworkers from pesticide poisonings and deaths (Barry 1995; Luján 1995; Wright 1990). Indeed, government brochures recommend and promote the use of restricted pesticides, and the secretary of health acquires large quantities of dangerous pesticides, including Aldrin, a Dirty Dozen insecticide, for the control of malaria and dengue fever (Luján 1995).

Because the Mexican government does not monitor produce for pesticide residues, U.S. chemical manufacturers are able to produce and export deadly agrochemicals to Mexico that are not authorized for use in the United States because of their dangerous toxicity levels (Barry 1995). Without inspection, residues of these toxic substances are never detected in the country's food supply. The outcome appeared in a 1993 report by the National Human Rights Commission that confirmed that Mexicans have one of the world's highest levels of toxic substances in their bloodstreams (Comisión Nacional de Derechos Humanos, as cited in Barry 1995).

Trade liberalization may allow pesticide manufacturers even greater freedom and fewer restrictions in product promotion. The secretary of trade and industrial growth (SECOFI) has historically put pressure on CICOPLAFEST, the commission that regulates pesticide use in Mexico, to deregulate pesticide sales and trade completely. SECOFI advocates eliminating permits now required to import pesticides, arguing that deregulation will lead to "modernization." Regulations to protect health and the environment are viewed as obstacles to free trade. Deregulation, on the other hand, is perceived as necessary for encouraging more foreign investment in Mexican agriculture by making it easier for investors to avoid responsibility for harm caused by their practices (RAPAM 1991).

I asked campesinos throughout west-central Mexico about regulations on the use of agrochemicals. Javier Borrego of Tuxcueca, Jalisco, informed me that agrochemicals could not be sold to children under the age of 15. All other farmers questioned informed me that anyone at any age could purchase agrochemicals anywhere in Mexico. In 2002, Hector Figueroa, then municipal government president of Cuquio, Jalisco, informed me that he attempts to discourage parents from sending their children shopping for agrochemicals, alcoholic beverages, and cigarettes. Any 2-year old can purchase colorful liter containers of deadly agrochemicals in the west-central Mexico countryside.

Figure 20. Agrochemical establishment, Tecolotlán, Jalisco.

When I queried Joaquin Bejarano of Chaparaco, Michoacán, about government-sponsored legislation designed to protect farmers and farm laborers from agrochemical exposure, he informed me that the government "could care less. If a worker dies, another can be hired in his or her place." No information is given to farmers regarding agrochemical risks or toxicity at the time of purchase. He insisted that chemical inputs are purchased "as easily as groceries." He also indicated that some of the agrochemical containers do have labels that warn workers of potential hazards. However, many laborers can't read or don't pay attention to the message.

There is also widespread misinformation among subsistence farmers regarding agrochemical danger (*IPCS News* 1993; PANNA 1990; Wright 1990). Jovita Tejada of Las Cebollas, Jalisco, insists that agrochemicals are only poisonous if the farmer is smoking cigarettes or drinking while applying them. Sergio Camacho Machado of Pueblo Rincón de López, Colima, insists that the collapse of three men in a field from herbicide overexposure occurred as a result of the men's habit of smoking while applying herbicides. Jesus Acosta of Los Sauces de Pérez, Jalisco, and Eduardo Ramos of Catalina/Apatzingán, Jalisco, both claim that all chemical herbicides are safe and can be used without protective clothing; only insecticides are potentially harmful.

I asked. L. I. Gallardo, a veterinarian who practices medicine in a pueblo near Cuquio, Jalisco, how veterinarians who are licensed to treat animals can sell agrochemicals when they are not trained as agronomists. He informed me that a local company, Asgrow, with subsidiaries elsewhere in the country, provides a brief training in agrochemical use to any shop owner of any kind who wants to become a local distributor. According to Dr. Gallardo, "Anyone can sell chemicals. Once they have completed the brief training, they are free to sell the chemicals." His clarification offered an explanation for the prevalence of agrochemicals throughout west-central Mexico in a wide variety of different business enterprises.

Many campesinos reported that the information they receive about agrochemicals is given to them by store owners and distributors at the time of purchase. When a rural resident becomes ill in Mexico, it is customary to visit a local *farmacia* and relate the symptoms to a pharmacist. The pharmacist then chooses a medicinal product designed to alleviate the symptoms. This form of over-the-counter medical advice and treatment obviates the necessity for a potentially costly visit to a doctor. The practice of over-the-counter medical advice given by pharmacists in Mexico is common and remarkably effective. Rural residents often view their local pharmacist as a trusted ally who is in the business of safeguarding their health and the health of family members.

Agrochemical distributors are considered experts in crop health in much the same way that local pharmacists are viewed as medical experts. Farmers whose crops are besieged by an insect or weed infestation, or whose soils are depleted, resulting in diminished productivity, consult agrochemical distributors for solutions to their crops' or soils' maladies in much the same way they consult pharmacists regarding their own or a family member's illness (Luján 1995, 99). Agrochemical distributors then recommend a chemical solution.

Additionally, Jesus Acosta claims that agrochemicals and hybrid seeds are advertised on the radio. While working in their fields many campesinos listen to the radio and become informed about the best chemical means of increasing their land's productivity. Eduardo Ramos informed me that *ingenieros* (agronomist engineers) attend monthly *ejido* meetings in Catalina to discuss the dangers and necessary precautions for agrochemical use in the region.

AGROCHEMICAL EXPOSURE AND EXPOSURE PREVENTION

Dr. Hector Figueroa of Cuquio, Jalisco, has been strongly committed to improving the health of residents in his pueblo and in the contiguous 124 villages associated with Cuquio. He is widely respected as both a doctor and a two-term PRD municipal president. Not only has he been responsible for the establishment of seven clinics in Cuquio and nearby villages, he takes time from his busy schedule to enter local bars on the weekend. When he enters a bar, the music stops, people stop drinking for a moment, and Dr. Figueroa informs his captive audience about the dangers associated with unprotected sex, AIDS, and drug use.

He also takes time to organize an annual march against drug abuse and addiction in Cuquio. An assortment of interest groups, including students from local schools, senior citizens, and mothers, participate by carrying large homemade signs and posters through the streets of Cuquio while a school band plays lively music. Signs admonish readers to consider their future, a future that could be destroyed by drug addiction. Other signs suggest that the town's people talk to a friend when they are depressed instead of using drugs.

The parade proceeds through all the principal streets of Cuquio while people cluster together on street curbs, watching and clapping. Eventually the parade stops in the plaza. All the signs and posters are placed around the kiosk, and people are asked to vote for the poster they think is most effective. Shortly after the crowd organizes itself in front of the kiosk, Dr. Figueroa emerges, wearing his white laboratory coat. He gives an impassioned speech to the crowd about the perils of illegal drugs and concludes with a fervent plea for *un Cuquio sin drogas* (a Cuquio without drugs).

I asked Dr. Figueroa about his view of the health and environmental consequences of agrochemical use in the region. He informed me that the most common sources of agrochemical poisoning are the carbamates and organophosphates and that the incidence of agrochemical poisoning in the region is high, particularly between the months of June and October during the rainy season when agrochemicals are typically applied. He claims that two of every ten people who visit his clinic during these critical months are poisoned by agrochemicals. Most of those affected are men, but not all. Of those poisoned, three of every ten are women. Three or four people die each year from organophosphate poisoning.

When I spoke with Dr. Figueroa in March 2002, he informed me that there were eighty-six reported cases of agrochemical poisoning near Cuquio in 2001. He cautioned that the number reflects only the number of reported cases and assured me that the number would be much higher if every agrochemical poisoning in the area was reported.

He also told me that two of the most common cancers he sees in the region, which he attributes to agrochemical exposure, are skin cancers in both sexes and cervical cancers in women. His information corroborates a California state agency's study in the *American Journal of Industrial Medicine* indicating that Latino farmworkers in California have higher rates of brain, leukemia, skin, stomach, and uterine cancer than other Latinos in California (Baca 2002; *San Jose Mercury News* 2002a)

Eighty-eight percent of poisoned farmers arriving at Dr. Figueroa's clinics experience nausea. Seventy-eight percent experience vomiting. Fifty-nine percent experience abdominal pain, and 51 percent experience anxiety and agitation. He informed me that the symptoms of most cases of agrochemical poisoning he treats occur within less than 24 hours of exposure. However, poisoning symptoms may first appear as long as fifteen days after exposure (Figueroa 1995).

I asked him about data, records, or anything factual that could serve as a recorded history of agrochemical poisoning and death in the region. He informed me that good records are not kept at the clinic. Primarily interns use the clinics to complete their residencies in medicine at the University of Guadalajara. Even though he encourages them to maintain good notes and records, few follow his instruction.

In addition, Dr. Figueroa informed me that no investigative autopsies are done to verify the exact cause of death. The coroner might sign the death certificate as a case of heart failure when in fact the initiating factor was agrochemical exposure. Dr. Figueroa visits the families of the deceased to ask them personally about the circumstances surrounding deaths that he suspects are the result of agrochemical exposure. He agreed with my assessment that the lack of consistent records and accurate autopsies provides agrochemical industries with a free license to promote any chemicals they deem profitable without risking accountability.

Some farmers hire agrochemical advisors *(ingenieros agrónomos)* to visit their fields or orchards and recommend an agrochemical regimen that will maximize production. In Uruapan, Michoacán, Guillermo Acevedo signed a three-year rental contract with the owner of a neglected avocado orchard in the nearby remote mountain village of Milpillas. Guillermo paid for the three years in advance and assumed full responsibility for the 2-hectare orchard's maintenance and productivity.

While the rental contract was in effect, Guillermo was entitled to all profits generated from the avocado harvest, derived from the approximately
two hundred 20-year old trees.

Since his father was killed in El Guaco several years ago, Guillermo,
as the oldest son, worked in California agribusiness to support his
mother and siblings with remittances. To forestall future undocumented
immigration to California, he hoped that his rented avocado trees would
produce an ample harvest for export, to provide the financial support in
Mexico the family depends on.

Each month Guillermo paid an *ingeniero agrónomo* from a local enterprise called Agroquímicos Pancho's S.A. de C.V. 100 pesos to visit his
orchard and recommend inputs that maximize avocado production. I
was appalled at the misleading and inaccurate recommendations. The *ingeniero agrónomo* recommended an agrochemical solution for the elimination of earthworms, whose contributions to soil quality are only positive. Discarded agrochemical containers littered the orchard in several
areas and included containers of Tordon, 2,4-D, an extremely toxic herbicide and a Bad Actor (see chapter 11), and Captan, a powerful fungicide, proven carcinogen, and Bad Actor.

I asked Guillermo if he had attempted to hire an independent agronomist. He responded affirmatively but indicated that the independent
agronomist was not reliable. I reminded him that he was working alone
in the orchard with extremely toxic, damaging chemicals, miles away
from anyone who could help him at the remote site of his orchard. His
mother and siblings could lose him as the primary support person for
their family. I suggested that he explore less toxic alternatives to increase
his orchard's productivity.

There is widespread international recognition of the problems associated with the lack of controls, data, and official inquiries into problems
associated with pesticide poisoning and deaths in Mexico and other
Third World countries (Figueroa 1995; *IPCS News* 1993; Lujan 1995;
PANNA 1990; Wright 1990). Until 1988, no institution kept any sys-
tematic, reliable and verifiable records of pesticide poisoning, though the
incidents of poisoning were well known by almost anyone who lives in
Mexico's countryside (Figueroa 1995; Luján 1995, 266).

Obscuring the lethal legacy of agrochemicals further is the fact that
deaths from agrochemical exposure may be vastly underreported worldwide. They initially result in damage to the human immune system,
which then later leads to deadly illness. Many deaths that are attributed
to cancer, infectious diseases, and other illnesses, particularly in farming

areas and developing countries, may originate with exposure to agrochemicals that compromise the body's immune system, rendering the body incapable of warding off the illness (Repetto and Baliga 1996).

In our discussion, Dr. Figueroa addressed the consequences of indiscriminate disposal of empty agrochemical containers in the countryside. He cited several instances of uninformed children finding the often colorful containers, filling them with water, and drinking the contents. Fortunately, most children near Cuquio used old containers in which the contents had already evaporated. As of January 2000, there had not been any childhood casualties.

AGROCHEMICAL POISONING AND DEATH IN THE COUNTRYSIDE

Agrochemical deaths and poisonings are frequent topics of conversation among those who inhabit the villages and towns of west-central Mexico. I did not encounter a single person there who could not relate the story of at least one neighbor or family member who was poisoned or expired as a result of agrochemical exposure. Indeed, during the summer months I personally witnessed potentially dangerous and lethal agrochemical exposure occurring almost everywhere I traveled.

On my visit to El Loreto/La Barca, Jalisco, I noticed several small planes used as crop dusters parked adjacent to the village and surrounding cornfields. As I entered El Loreto, a crop duster began spraying an adjacent field. Drift from the sprayed agrochemical filled the air. A family member informed me that the entire village is regularly sprayed with agrochemicals despite the protests of local residents. By the time I finished meeting with and interviewing the family, both my research assistant and I experienced the familiar pesticide/herbicide exposure symptoms including headache, stomachache, and a feeling of nervous agitation.

Sixty percent of the national production of strawberries in Mexico occurs in the region of Zamora. Forty percent of the acreage in the area is planted in strawberries, potatoes, and tomatoes, primarily for export. These export crops require a massive use of agrochemical inputs (Luján 1995, 61). When I visited Joaquin Bejarano in nearby Chaparaco, Michoacán, he took me on a drive through two adjacent *pueblo-ejidos,* Jacona and Platanal. While on this outing, his wife Maribel informed me that her godfather died from toxic pesticide exposure. We eventually stopped alongside the road in Jacona to observe a state-of-the-art high-tech strawberry field on the *pequeña propriedad* of a religious order that maintains a well-manicured school on a hill overlooking the fields. Approximately 8 hectares were planted in strawberries on a slightly sloping hill. Rows of strawberry plants were equipped with drip irrigation and black plastic covering to encourage root growth and prevent weed development.

Approximately twenty-five day laborers were bent over in the field working with the plants. Two teenage boys wearing only jeans and cotton T-shirts were applying a powdered agrochemical. As the boys moved through the fields, bare skin on their backs and around their waists was exposed. They wore no protective masks or even handkerchiefs over their mouths and noses.

One boy carried a type of motorized machine as a backpack. Extending from the machine was a large woven duct pipe punctured with holes. A second boy held the end of the pipe, which stretched 20 feet across several rows of strawberries. Once the duct pipe was in place, the boy carrying the machine started a motor that pushed the powdered agrochemical, presumably a pesticide or fungicide, through the pipe and out the holes onto the crop. During this process, the boys were completely enclosed in a cloud of powdered agrochemical, with their skin, eyes, mouth, and noses exposed.

On one of my trips to visit the family of Tomasina López Santos in Confradia de Duendes, Jalisco, her grandson, Arturo López Navarro, led me and my research assistant to his grandfather's *parcela*, an approximately one-hour walk from his home in the village. Among the seven discarded agrochemical containers we found strewn alongside the cornfields were the following: Lorsban 400, a Bad Actor insecticide suspected of causing developmental brain and nervous system abnormalities in children and banned in the United States from most household uses; Gesaprim Combi, a Bad Actor herbicide containing atrazine; Primagram 500 FW containing atrazine, a Bad Actor herbicide; Hercules 5G (diazinon), a Bad Actor insecticide; and Tordon, an extremely toxic Bad Actor herbicide. Later, Arturo, a young adolescent at the time, showed me his collection of full bottles of these compounds, which he keeps on hand for use when needed.

On my first trip to Cuquio, while I was staying at Consuelo Morales's "hotel," the visiting family members of a local Cuquio resident informed me that on August 8, 1998, their relative, Adalberto Aguirre, was found slumped over dead from apparent herbicide poisoning in his cornfield while wearing his backpack chemical applicator. Mr. Aguirre was in his early 50s and had emphysema and diabetes. His family members specu-

Figure 21. Arturo López Navarro, an adolescent, with his bottles of agrochemicals, Confradia de Duendes, Jalisco.

lated that the herbicides he was spraying put too much stress on his already compromised health. When he sat down in his field to rest, he expired from overexposure to the herbicide.

On my third research trip to Cuquio, just prior to my departure, news spread through the pueblo of the death of Octavio Villa. He collapsed in his field while spraying an herbicide.

While visiting Cocula, Jalisco, en route to San Nicolás to meet with the family of Salvador Alfaro and his wife Candelaria Segunda Campos, Cocula residents were bustling with the news of the death of 72-year-old Mario Ramirez the night before my visit on July 14, 1999. Mario was spraying Tordon and became very ill. He returned to his home and then collapsed. Shortly before his death, the town doctor ruled his illness as a case of herbicide poisoning. Mario was known in the community as one of the first campesinos to migrate to the United States to work in agribusiness.

Eduardo Ramos of Catalina/Apatzingán, Michoacán, informed me that several years earlier he fumigated melon with malathion, a possible carcinogen, suspected endocrine disruptor, and Bad Actor organophosphate cholinesterase inhibitor. He claims that on one occasion he suddenly began vomiting and became very dizzy. He was rushed to a doctor in Apatzingán, where he was fortunate to be treated in time so that he has not suffered any lasting ill effects from the experience.

Eduardo also spoke of a young boy who worked with agrochemicals that were loaded onto planes when cotton was sprayed by crop dusters years ago. The boy collapsed and was near death when he was airlifted to a hospital in Apatzingán. Miraculously, he recovered.

Many agrochemical stores are poorly ventilated. I found that spending time in them while taking inventories, even among unopened containers, produced physical symptoms ranging from nausea to trembling. When my research assistant and I left Dow Agrosciences' Veterinaria Partido in Tecalitlán, Jalisco, we were both shaking, felt nauseous, and had bad headaches. The young woman tending the store informed us that her brother inadvertently dropped some 2,4-D on his hand and subsequently fainted. He was taken to a hospital and treated for agrochemical poisoning. The day after taking the agrochemical inventory at Veterinaria Partido, I became very ill and required medical treatment.

An anonymous informant, an *ingeniero agrónomo* who lives in Palo Alto, Jalisco, near Cuquio, informed me that a woman friend of his family worked for several years in a store that sold a variety of agrochemicals. When she married and attempted to become pregnant, each pregnancy ended in a miscarriage. He also claimed that a doctor friend of his reports at least forty-five agrochemical poisonings in the region each year.

Sergio Camacho Machado related that agrochemicals have been used in his state of Colima since the 1960s (see chapter 3). He has personally used agrochemicals in farming for the past thirty years. He currently uses Tordon and Gramoxone (paraquat), a Dirty Dozen herbicide, to rid his land of unwanted weeds. He also uses Folidol (parathion), a Dirty Dozen insecticide and one of the world's most acutely toxic pesticides, to rid his corn plants of corn worm. Agrochemicals are available literally a stone's throw away from his home at the store, two doors down the street.

When asked about agrochemicals, Sergio's wife Esmeralda spoke in a very agitated manner as she stressed how harmful the chemicals are for the body, noting the cancers and other diseases she has seen develop in her neighbors as a result of agrochemicals. Esmeralda then launched into a diatribe about four or five people in the immediate vicinity of her house who had died of cancer. She spoke of one who went to the United States for treatment as their only hope. The treatment was ineffective, so she watched helplessly as her neighbor wasted away and finally died.

Sergio recounted the experience of three men who collapsed in the field from herbicide overexposure while wearing their backpack applicators. I asked him which herbicide the men were spraying. He could not recall, but he told me that all three men were taken to the local hospital. Two of them died and the third survived and continues to live in the village. As discussed earlier, Sergio rationalized the men's collapse by claiming that they were all smoking while applying the herbicides. With their hands close to their mouths while smoking, they ingested the poison.

MINORS EXPOSED TO AGROCHEMICALS IN MEXICO

Hiring minors to apply dangerous chemicals is common throughout Mexico (Luján 1995; Wright 1990). In 1997, the United Nations Children's Fund reported that two million Mexican children were at risk because of living in extreme poverty, and a million minors under the age of 14 were working in agriculture (Cockcroft 1998, 183). Young people are more susceptible to the harmful consequences of agrochemical poisoning because of their relative inexperience as farm laborers, low body weight, and comparatively small overall body surface area (Luján 1995, 127).

Elizabeth Guillette, a University of Arizona medical anthropologist, studied the developmental damage that occurs in children who are regularly exposed to high levels of pesticides over the course of several growing seasons (Cunningham and Saigo 2001; Guillette et al. 1998; Luoma 1999). She chose two groups of 4- and 5-year old Yaqui children from northwestern Mexico as study participants. The children were similar in all respects except for their level of regular pesticide exposure. One group included children who lived in the foothills on ranches where pesticide use was almost nonexistent. The other group lived in the farming area of the Yaqui Valley, where pesticides have been used heavily for the past fifty years. Their mothers had been exposed to high levels of pesticides for several growing seasons, including Dirty Dozen compounds such as Lindane and Endrin, long banned from agricultural use in the United States.

Guillette adapted a series of motor and cognitive tests into simple games the preschool children could play, such as playing with a ball and drawing pictures. After testing the children, Guillete claimed, "I was shocked. I couldn't believe what was happening." The lowland children had much greater difficulty with hand-eye coordination tests and showed less physical stamina.

The most striking difference was discernible in the children's drawings of people. Most of the pictures drawn by foothill children looked like recognizable versions of a person, an expected result for their developmental stage. The pictures from most of the lowland children, however, were merely random lines and unintelligible scribbles, more characteristic of a toddler developmental stage (Guillette et al. 1998; Luoma 1999, 62). These findings are particularly disturbing in light of a recent study with experimental results indicating that the effects of pesticides on parents can be passed down through generations (Anway et al. 2005).

WHO PAYS THE SOCIAL COSTS OF MODERN AGRICULTURE?

The social costs of pervasive agrochemical poisoning in the west-central Mexico countryside include the disability and potential death of rural families' often key income-generating persons. Social costs extend binationally. J. Luis Seefoó Luján, a professor at the Center for Rural Studies at El Colegio de Michoacán in Zamora, Michoacán, claims that the external social costs of pervasive agrochemical poisoning in the region are not borne by modern agriculture, agrochemical companies, or federal and state agencies (Luján 1995). Rather, the external costs are borne by the afflicted person's immediate and extended family members. Ultimately, it is the poisoned person's immediate family members who may lose the income-generating capacity of a family member, and who are also required to reconcile the high medical bills for the potentially comprehensive treatment of an afflicted family member.

The social costs are not confined to Mexico. They extend across the international border to the United States, where extended family members may be required to send home hard-earned remittances to assist an afflicted family member's recovery. While agribusiness enjoys the elevated sales of U.S. products in Mexico, and its representative corporations showcase economic success on webpages and in glossy portfolio summaries designed to attract shareholders, its representatives in Mexico promote the very seeds of death, destruction, and further accelerated cultural disintegration.

THE CAMPESINO DIET

Prior to the introduction of Green Revolution technology and corporate penetration into the countryside, rural campesinos enjoyed a diet of comparatively simple, healthy foods grown on their own land, purchased at the local market, or collected from the surrounding countryside. Corn consumed with beans provided a diet of complementary proteins, even for the poorest campesinos. Those who owned animals could supplement their diets with additional sources of protein including meat, dairy products, poultry, eggs, and fish from a local river or pond.

Tortillas, hand-made daily from the traditional, nutritious *maíz criollo,* were a constant staple. *Huertas familiares* (family gardens) provided fruit, vegetables, herbs, spices, flowers, and a plethora of medicinal plants. In warm regions of Mexico some gardens even provided coffee. Studies of these campesino family gardens have confirmed that as many as three hundred different prolific plants in several strata may be growing near the home in these gardens on less than an acre of land.

As yet another example of the rural farm family's dependence on and integration into the natural environment, children were often sent into the countryside surrounding the villages to collect a variety of wild plants for consumption by the family. For example, every January in Los Sauces de Perez children head for the hills with buckets in hand to locate the famous *camote del cerro* (mountain sweet potato). Though much of the tropical scrub is dormant at this time, the children learn early to identify the dried leaves of the *camote* plant.

Once they find them, the children dig into the rocky hillside beneath the dried plant with a small trowel or shovel, until the branching tubers and white flesh are exposed. Village tradition exhorts children to leave some of the *camote* tuber in the ground so that the leaves will return during the summer rains and produce new tubers for the following year. After several hours of scavenging, the children return to their families in the village to roast the *camote* in the fire. Roasted *camote* has a very delicate, sweet starchy flavor and provides a filling addition to any meal.

Other dry winter foods provided by the natural environment include *guizache,* a sweet bean pod chewed as a natural source of sugar, and *guaje,* another legume with pods that have a variety of uses; they can be made into salsa, inserted into tacos, or mixed with beans. Edible fruit can be collected from wild guava trees growing by a river or stream.

Men take slingshots or rifles and hunt squirrels, which are later roasted and eaten; *venado,* wild deer that provide a source of meat; and *javelines,* wild pigs that are cooked in a variety of ways. Finally, children and adults catch fish in nearby streams, rivers, and ponds.

In the wet summer season, the countryside provides several foods for consumption including wild melons; mesquite, a leguminous shrub that produces sweet bean pods and seeds; and *guamuchil,* another leguminous shrub with a curled edible bean pod. The seeds are removed and the pod is eaten raw.

Along with guavas, *pitaya*, a red fruit harvested from the organ pipe cactus, and yellow *tunas*, fruits from beavertail (*Opuntia*) cacti, are available.

The replacement of traditional *maíz criollo* with hybrid corn has not only contributed to genetic erosion and potential intellectual deficits in the developing brains of children (see chapter 11) but also created indignation among many campesinos who claim that hybrid corn is so lacking in both nutrients and fat that their animals don't grow or gain weight on a diet of hybrid corn.

Additionally, in recent years small village stores sell an abundance of different types of junk food, mostly manufactured in Mexico and mimicking many forms of U.S. junk food. These small stores are full of varieties of soft drinks, potato chips, french fry–type products, candy bars, and a glut of other sugary products including gum, popsicles, and ice cream—all for sale to anyone with the money to purchase them.

Several village elders and municipal government officials throughout the west-central Mexico countryside decry the manufacture and influx of these health-compromising products resulting from corporate penetration into the countryside. Many claim that children used to eat the healthful food they grew with their family members on their land. Instead, in recent years children sell chicken eggs, *camote del cerro*, and other healthful foods grown on their land or collected near their villages to the village store or at a town market, then use the income to purchase health-compromising junk foods. Two of the worst junk food providers are the U.S.-originating transnational corporations Coca-Cola Company and PepsiCo.

Coca-Cola and PepsiCo are represented by ostentatious advertising everywhere in west-central Mexico. Their advertisements and products are as common as those of agribusiness. My research assistant, Andres Anaya, summed it up beautifully in January 2000 when he stated, "The pueblos and ranchos are literally wallpapered in Coca-Cola and Pepsi-Cola signs." Billboards, painted signs, hanging signs, and every other imaginable form of advertising are present in populated areas almost everywhere in the countryside.

Both Coca-Cola and Pepsi-Cola contain substances of questionable nutritional value including sugar, high fructose corn syrup, and phosphoric acid. The sugar content in soft drinks in general is so high that it

Figure 22. Jovita Tejada with her husband and two of their children, Las Cebollas, Jalisco. Note the contents of the baby's bottle.

has prompted the Centre for Science in the Public Interest to reference them collectively as "liquid candy" (Greg 2000). In addition, both Coca-Cola and Pepsi-Cola contain caffeine. Coca-Cola contains 23 mg of caffeine per 8-ounce serving, and Pepsi-Cola contains 25 mg (according to Coca-Cola and Pepsi-Cola websites). The medical community recognizes caffeine as an addictive substance that often results in withdrawal symptoms when abruptly eliminated from the diet (*American Family Physician* 1984; Glass 1994; Greenberg et al. 1999; Greg 2000; Uhlig and Pook 1999).

Coca-Cola Company

The soft drink giant Coca-Cola is the largest manufacturer, distributor, and marketer of nonalcoholic beverage concentrates and syrups in the world, with a business system that operates in nearly two hundred countries worldwide. Every day, 1.3 billion Coca-Cola beverage product servings are consumed worldwide. Gross profits for 1994 were $8.4 billion. Ten years later they had risen to $14.3 billion. Net income nearly doubled during the same period, from $2.55 billion in 1994 to $4.85 billion in 2004 (data here and below from Coca-Cola Company website).

Of Coca-Cola's five targeted worldwide regions, the Latin America Group accounts for 24 percent of unit case volume sales; 530 million Latin Americans consume nearly four servings of Coca-Cola products per week. Mexico accounted for almost half the unit case volume sold in Latin America in 2002 and bottles more than 200,000 bottles of product per minute. The Mexico "company per capita consumption" of all commercial beverages produced by Coca-Cola in 2000 was the highest in the world, at 459.

Of Coca-Cola's product list, the products I observe to be most frequently available, advertised, and consumed in west-central Mexico are Coca-Cola, Coca-Cola Lite, Fanta, Fresca, Ciel bottled water, and *pan Bimbo*. Coca-Cola aggressively promotes the consumption of both Coca-Cola and Fresca in west-central Mexico. On December 23, 1999, at about 7:00 in the evening, I was typing field notes in my room in a central Zamora, Michoacán, hotel. I was distracted from typing by whistles blowing and traffic noise from a street choked with cars outside of my hotel room.

When I stopped my work to investigate and arrived on the street, I found a steady stream of cars and pedestrians entering the plaza area near the hotel. A whistle-blowing policeman directed traffic. I walked to the plaza and found a stage with enormous speakers blaring Christmas songs in the corner of the plaza next to the church. The lyrics of the Christmas songs had been altered to include reference to Coca-Cola. Behind the stage stood a massive Christmas tree with a large, lighted five-pointed star on top. The tree was decorated with huge Christmas ornaments bearing the words "Coca-Cola." There were also huge semblances of silver bottle caps hanging on the tree with the words "Coca-Cola" inscribed on them. The Christmas tree display was completed with huge wrapped Christmas "gifts" under the tree.

The tree was cordoned off from the crowds, and a guard inside the cordoned area made certain that no one entered. A massive sign with a picture of a tree and toys was positioned next to the tree. The message on the sign translated to "Enjoy Coca-Cola; Coca-Cola increases the magic of Christmas in your city." In the lower right-hand corner was the DIF (Integrated Family Development) insignia, the organization thereby identified as a Coca-Cola supporter. To the right of the sign a Coca-Cola stand was set up with workers offering free cups of Coke and Fresca to

Figure 23. Coca-Cola Christmas celebration, Zamora, Michoacán.

the enthusiastic crowd. Three Disney-like bear characters, two brown ones and a white one, all wearing Coca-Cola signs, danced around the plaza while children eagerly ran up to the bears for a hug and handshake.

I later asked the director of DIF in Cuquio why an organization interested in family health would endorse Coca-Cola Company when it was peddling addictive, health-compromising substances. She responded that Coca-Cola is one of DIF's few and only financial supporters and sources of income.

On a trip to Cuquio in 1999, I observed similar marketing tactics to those in Zamora. On a warm Sunday afternoon, a Coca-Cola stand was set up in front of the marketplace facing the plaza. Young women wearing short green skirts offered free cups of Fresca to members of the crowd. On the following day, the stand was converted to a store where shoppers could purchase duffle bags, hats, T-shirts, and other items with the Coca-Cola insignia.

Coca-Cola signs throughout Mexico appear to be brand new. Refrigerators and their soft drink cache in the adobe huts of many impoverished residents of outlying pueblos and ranchos also are brand new. The brightness and newness of the signs, refrigerators, and other Coca-Cola advertising paraphernalia juxtaposed against the dusty poverty that characterizes the region belies the health-destructive properties of the product. One cup of Coca-Cola contains 27 grams of sugar and another 27 grams of other carbohydrates (*Consumer Reports* 2005). Soft drinks with high sugar content exacerbate diabetes, a recognized health problem among Hispanics (Villarejo et al. 2000). One in ten Mexicans has diabetes (Lizárraga 2006), and in west-central Mexico the lack of access to adequate health care for the majority of rural inhabitants precludes many from even knowing they are afflicted with this condition until it has become life threatening.

Coca-Cola's ethical stance in other countries is equally disturbing. The *Multinational Monitor,* a monthly magazine that examines the activities of multinational companies, holds a yearly contest to judge corporations according to their propensity to price-gouge, pollute, bust unions, support dictators, commit fraud, and destroy the environment. Coca-Cola was chosen as one of 2004's ten worst corporations (Mokhiber and Weissman 2005). Workers claim that the transnational giant has been involved in 179 human rights violations at its Colombian bottling plants, where workers have been regularly terrorized by paramilitary forces for years (Mokhiber and Weissman 2005). In 2004, the California Federation of Teachers asked members to join in a worldwide boycott of Coca-Cola products because of Coke's anti-union activities at its Colombian bottling plants (*California Teacher* 2004, 5). In London, Coca-Cola admitted that its Dasani bottled water is nothing but tap water (Datson 2004).

In the United States, Coca-Cola Company agreed to pay $540,000 to a former finance manager to settle a whistleblower lawsuit. The suit accused Coke of rigging a marketing test to inflate the popularity of Frozen Coke at Burger King Restaurants in Virginia (Weber 2003). In Dallas, Texas, workers claimed that in 2002 Coke took the nearly expired soda off the shelves in white neighborhood stores and sold it at predominantly minority neighborhood stores (Associated Press 2002). Coca-Cola has contracts with at least 6,000 of the more than 14,000 public school districts in the United States (Feller 2003).

Fortunately, as of the start of 2006, the general public is becoming more informed about Coca-Cola's unethical business practices. The multinational soft drink giant is facing the wrath of rights advocacy groups in the United States and abroad. Some U.S. universities have banned the sale of Coke products on their campuses, and mounting pressure from student bodies throughout Europe is pushing hundreds of schools to terminate their contracts with the company. New York University, the largest private school in the country, recently declared that it would ban all Coke products from campus (Rizvi 2005).

The company is also under fire in Asian and Latin American countries. Labor unions, peasant groups, and consumer associations are persistently campaigning to force Coca-Cola out of their countries. In India, thousands of demonstrators are demanding the closure of Coca-Cola plants, claiming that the corporation is responsible for severe water shortages due to ground water depletion and soil contamination (Rizvi 2005).

A website has been established with ongoing stories about the corporation's alleged involvement in murder. "We believe the evidence shows that Coca-Cola and the corporate network are rife with immorality, corruption, and complicity in murder" (Rogers 2006).

PepsiCo

Though less frequently advertised in west-central Mexico than its competitor, PepsiCo follows similar marketing strategies. The corporation displays enormous, like-new signs throughout the countryside. Often the two corporations showcase signs on the same wall in pueblos and ranchos.

PepsiCo exemplifies the modern trend toward corporate food consolidation. The corporation is the world's third-largest food and beverage company, after Kraft and Nestlé, and includes Frito-Lay North America, PepsiCo Beverages North America, PepsiCo International, and Quaker Foods North America. These corporate subdivisions further include Frito-Lay, Pepsi-Cola, Gatorade, Tropicana, and Quaker. The companies showcase a dizzying array of often unrelated food brands and products, including Quaker puffed wheat, Gatorade Thirst Quencher, and Doritos tortilla chips.

PepsiCo's 1998 revenues were over $22 billion. By 2004, net revenues grew to over $29 billion, with almost $7 billion operating profit. At 26 percent, PepsiCo has the leading share of the liquid refreshment beverage market in the United States, with noncarbonated soft drinks generating the largest revenues. PepsiCo beverages are available in about 175 countries and contain health-compromising ingredients similar to those in Coca-Cola. Their snack brands are distributed in 170 countries, making PepsiCo the largest salty snack company in the world (data here and below from PepsiCo website and 2004 annual report).

With 35,000 associates, Mexico has the largest concentration of PepsiCo associates outside the United States. Sabritas potato chips, sold in even the remotest rural Mexican villages, reach more than 700,000 Mexican retail outlets weekly. Other PepsiCo products sold in the Mexican countryside include Gamesa cookies, 7-Up, Quaker Mágica, and Magico chocolate powder. In 2004, Mexico generated almost $3 billion in PepsiCo profits, up from $2.6 billion in 2003. With such a high level of corporate profitability, it is interesting that a 2003 study in India concluded that nine out of twelve soft drink samples produced by Coca-Cola and PepsiCo operators failed to meet European Union safety standards for pesticide residues (George 2003). Researchers at the Center for Science and Environment conducted several studies that show that pesticide residues in Coca-Cola and Pepsi products in India were twenty-four times higher than European Union standards (Rizvi 2006).

PHILIP MORRIS AND MARLBORO CIGARETTES

The Marlboro Man and Marlboro cigarettes are alive and well in the west-central Mexico countryside. Indeed, one of the first visible billboards displays outside the Guadalajara airport is the familiar Marlboro Man advertising Marlboro cigarettes in his idealized country setting. With a symbol of U.S. masculinity juxtaposed against the romanticized "open range," the brand enjoys widespread appeal, especially among men, in west-central Mexico. Marlboro is the brand of choice among west-central Mexican farmers.

Philip Morris is another example of food product consolidation. In 2003, Altria Group became the parent company of Kraft Foods, Phillip Morris USA, Philip Morris International, and Philip Morris Capital Corporation. This giant corporate structure is responsible for the manufacture of a great variety of products including tobacco products, beverages, desserts, cereals, biscuits, snacks, confections, cheese and other dairy products, meals, enhancers, meats and pizza, coffee, powdered soft drinks, and beer. Kraft Foods alone manufactures many familiar supermarket brands including Maxwell House, Milka chocolate, Nabisco, Oreo, Oscar Mayer, Philadelphia, Post, and Tang.

Philip Morris International is the world's leading tobacco company outside the United States. The company employs more than 40,000 people worldwide, and its brands are made in seventy cigarette factories around the world. The vertically integrated company distributes cigarettes in more than 160 countries.

Philip Morris produces forty-five brands of cigarette. Familiar brands include Benson & Hedges, Chesterfield, L&M, Parliament, Virginia Slims, and, of course, Marlboro. In Mexico, Philip Morris International has achieved a 60.2 percent share of the market for tobacco products, largely because of Marlboro. Two new brands of Marlboro were introduced into Mexico in 2004: Marlboro Mild Flavor and Marlboro Medium (data here and below from Altria website).

Net revenues from the international sale of tobacco products in 2000 totaled $26 billion. By 2004, net revenues had jumped to $39.5 billion. Total 2000 operating revenues for both domestic and international tobacco sales in 2000 amounted to $49 billion. By 2004, this sum had jumped to $57 billion. Net corporate consolidated revenues for 2004 amounted to a whopping $89.6 billion.

While enjoying huge profits worldwide, largely from the sale of tobacco products, the transnational corporation supported a global treaty on tobacco control and "reiterated our commitment to finding solutions to tobacco-related issues" at the October 2000 World Health Organization hearings on a proposed Framework Convention on Tobacco Control (Philip Morris website). The corporation supports worldwide minimum-age laws and more than one hundred youth smoking prevention programs in nearly ninety countries (Altria website).

At the same time, Philip Morris has made a protracted effort over the past several years to increase sales by luring women into the smoking habit. Elaborate research proposed solutions that included the production of chocolate-flavored cigarettes that would curb appetite and cigarettes designed to give women the illusion that they could puff their way into a better life (Henningfield et al. 2005).

Although tobacco products, according to a former U.S. surgeon-general, are the leading preventable cause of death and disease in the United States, the addictive properties of nicotine (Briton 1998; Cinciripini et al. 1997) make withdrawal from cigarette smoking extremely difficult. Nicotene dependence provides the link through which smokers are repeatedly exposed to carcinogenic and genotoxic elements associated with tobacco consumption (Cinciripini et al. 1997). In addition, from 1998 to 2004 the amount of nicotine in most cigarettes increased an average of 10 percent, with the brands most popular with young people and minorities registering the greatest increases and highest nicotine content (Brown 2006).

Tobacco use worldwide is epidemic. The World Health Organization estimates that, unless the epidemic is curbed, one in ten people will die of a tobacco-related disease. In the United States about one-quarter of the adult population and one-fifth of high school seniors smoke. There are an estimated 434,000 deaths per year from tobacco use, or about 1,200 people per day and fifty per hour. The yearly death toll in the United States from tobacco use is greater than the yearly death toll from alcohol, cocaine, heroin, homicide, suicide, car accidents, fires, and AIDS combined (Cinciripini et al. 1997).

Just as accurate data on the incidence and extent of agrochemical poisoning are scarce in developing countries, reliable data on the extent of tobacco-related devastation in developing countries are difficult to obtain. The only real certainty is that the practice of tobacco smoking is most common among men (Cinciripini et al. 1997), which is immediately and empirically obvious to any visitor to west-central Mexico. I could not find any accurate medical records reporting the incidence of tobacco-related illnesses in west-central Mexico, but smoking is very common among campesino farmers, and Marlboro signs are ubiquitous.

A slowed tobacco industry in the United States and Britain resulting from the public's greater awareness of tobacco's health-damaging attributes led to the exportation of tobacco addiction to developing countries (Britton 1998). By 2025, worldwide smoking rates among women are expected to increase by 20 percent (Kunzelman 2005). Most of this growth will occur in developing countries like Mexico. Philip Morris represents yet another U.S.-originating transnational corporation operating with contradictory ethical policies. On one hand, the corporation promotes an addictive, health-compromising practice in Mexico; on the other, it offers solutions to tobacco addiction in the form of international smoking prevention programs for young people.

Whereas tobacco consumers in the United States are using litigation to force tobacco companies to pay for the health-damaging consequences of their wares (Daynard and Gottlieb 2001), no such recourse is available in west-central Mexico. Most people cannot afford to see a doctor for a definitive diagnosis of a tobacco-related illness. As with the health-damaging consequences of agrochemicals described previously, it is the impoverished family members of the afflicted who are most likely to bear the social costs of tobacco addiction, not the transnational corporate purveyors of disease and death. As campesino family members are driven further into poverty by escalating medical bills, transnational corporations continue to showcase robust annual profits for their shareholders.

THIRTEEN

INSTITUTIONAL OPPRESSION IN THE WEST-CENTRAL MEXICO COUNTRYSIDE

En los Estados Unidos, la mujer manda, pero en México, es el hombre que manda.

In the United States, women are in charge, but in Mexico, it is the men who are in charge.

—Jesus Acosta, Los Sauces de Pérez, Jalisco

From the time of one's birth into the west-central Mexico farming culture, the Catholic Church, male heads of the family, government leaders, and educators provide and encourage basic training in docility, compliance, and subservience. Uneducated rural inhabitants, who only very rarely have opportunities to develop critical thinking skills, easily and readily absorb and generally accept subjugation to those institutions and persons viewed as higher authorities. The internalized subjugation is later projected onto others, including corporate representatives and their products.

When corporations aggressively promote their destructive products with symbolism, including bright new signs juxtaposed upon the harsh realities of crumbling, dingy adobe walls, Marlboro masculinity, an association with DIF, and the like, the products are met with acceptance. They are often embraced rather than resisted or rejected, because they offer a "lift" and short-term relief from the pain of ever-visible poverty and hunger.

The authoritarian system, with its full range of institutions including the government, Catholic Church, and education, collaborate and reinforce each other. Corporations that align themselves with one or more of these authoritarian establishments in the countryside in the manner exemplified by Coca-Cola and its Christmas display in front of the Catholic Church in Zamora, Michoacán, encounter a readily exploitable consumer market for their products. Heedless of the potential risks and inappropriateness of their products for an impoverished, hungry, often ill population, U.S.-originating transnational corporations continue to market their goods with the full support of both the U.S. and Mexican governments, with impunity and without ethics. This damaging and deadly transnational corporate contribution constitutes the United States' shameful legacy in the west-central Mexico countryside.

Within the context of deserted pueblos and ranchos, abandoned and depressed women, transnational corporate penetration, and environmental destruction, the authoritarian institutions impact the lives of the west-central Mexican campesinos—controlling them, influencing them, contributing to the tragedy of rural disintegration, and ultimately rendering escape from their impoverished, ever-deteriorating circumstances a near impossibility. The most embedded and influential of these institutions are the Mexican government and army, the Roman Catholic Church, the educational system, commercial intermediaries, a tradition of caciques, and machismo.

THE MEXICAN GOVERNMENT AND
THE LEGACY OF THE PRI AND PAN

The Mexican government and the PRI (Partido Revolucionario Institucional) were almost universally cited among farmers and family members in my study as a formidable, combined source of oppression and neglect. The PRI appeared to be more interested in controlling and containing campesinos than in working democratically with them to improve their circumstances. As an example, Eladio Ramirez, former governor of Oaxaca, asked Vicente Silva, a former municipal president, to consider an appointment as director of the CNC (Confederación Nacional Campesina [National Peasant's Confederation]) in Michoacán. The CNC initially served as a vehicle to mobilize Mexican farmers but soon degenerated into an instrument for maintaining state control (Barry 1995, 139). The CNC is perceived by many campesinos as a branch of the PRI government, with an agenda of campesino control.

Vicente agreed to become the director with the understanding that the organization would be managed democratically with an advisory board of campesino members. Vicente was informed that he would not be allowed to manage the organization democratically and would have to follow the dictates of the PRI. Vicente subsequently refused the directorship.

The PRI made a mockery of free elections. I learned from Marisol Carranza that party representatives were sent to Uruapan during the 1994 presidential election. In spite of Uruapan's widespread allegiance to PRD candidates, the city voted in PRI candidates because PRI representatives offered voters 1,500 pesos at the polls as an incentive to vote for PRI candidates.

In Tototepec, Guerrero, the PRI bribed local campesinos with bags of free fertilizer for their agrochemical-dependent lands. Hundreds of bags of fertilizer arrived in Tototepec just prior to the election and were stacked neatly in the town hall. The following day, as the bags of fertilizer were handed out to the farmers, they were sternly warned that if they did not vote for the PRI there would be no more fertilizer (Simon 1997).

Campesinos throughout the countryside told stories about government and PRI neglect until election time. A campaign ploy always included the arrival of PRI trucks and buses full of hats, T-shirts, bags, and other campaign paraphernalia as gifts designed to garner votes from the countryside at election time.

> It was not the Mexican government's intention to destroy the rural environment, but since the destruction translated into greater dependence and greater political control, there was no incentive to halt it. And in many communities it is too late. When the peasants finally abandon their plots, they leave behind devastated landscapes of eroded soils, clearcut forests, and depleted wildlife. What has already been lost includes not only the land itself, but millennia of highly refined biological and natural knowledge— Mexico's natural heritage. (Simon 1997, 51)

The PRI's defeat by PAN's Vicente Fox in July 2000 was viewed optimistically by everyone in the countryside I spoke with as a potential source of government political improvement. Many farmers emphasized that conditions couldn't be worse; they could only improve. Yet, several years after Fox's election, and in spite of his rhetorical speeches promising poverty reduction, elimination of graft and corruption, and a commitment to human rights, little has changed for most poor subsistence campesinos in the countryside. The legacy of corruption continues to dominate the lives of Mexico's rural poor.

Indeed, on August 9, 2001, thousands of farmers from across Mexico descended on the Mexican capital as part of a nationwide rally to protest one of the country's worst agricultural crises in decades. Fox insisted that farmers should "modernize, adopt new crops, and rely less on the government." Fox's secretary of agriculture and president of a successful agribusiness enterprise, Javier Usabiaga, insisted that the solution to the farmers' problems in the countryside was the adoption of increasingly "advanced" technologies, improving efficiency, and upgrading physical infrastructure (Cevallos 2001; Mandel-Campbell 2001; Moreno 2001).

In October 2001, the Mexican Chamber of Deputies approved a revision of President Fox's original rural development law. The original law was designed to support large corporate farmers to the exclusion of small farmers. However, the revised law, referred to as La Ley de Desarrollo Rural Sustentable (Sustainable Rural Development Law) promises a rural development fund of $7.5–$8.5 million for rural development in the form of housing, health services, and education for subsistence farmers. The law's enactment began in April 2002, and its ameliorating effects on the lives of impoverished campesinos remain to be seen. However, my visits with farm families from 2004 to 2007 did not reveal any changes at all in their impoverished circumstances.

A comprehensive rural development program and agricultural policy that included subsistence and small producer corn farmers could have been developed, promoted, and enacted before NAFTA's initiation (Appendini 1997; Barry 1995). However, like their PRI predecessors, President Fox and his government associates continue to neglect the development of a program that might serve to forestall continued excessive rural emigration from west-central Mexico. Instead, in recent years they continue to support temporary programs that provide only stopgap measures to assist *ejidatarios* who attempt to participate in markets, such as Alianza Para el Campo and Procampo. They have done little to develop these programs into institutions that could provide both support for small farmers competing in the international marketplace and continuity for rural development planning (Appendini 1997).

In July 2006, Felipe Calderón of the conservative PAN ran for the presidency of Mexico against populist candidate Andrés Manuel López-Obrador. López-Obrador, former governor of Mexico City, promised to renegotiate NAFTA on behalf of the campesinos and provide other assistance to Mexico's disenfranchised, impoverished millions. Following the election, the Federal Electoral Judicial Tribunal, a government organization in charge of election oversight, announced Calderón as the winner. Huge protests in Mexico City and elsewhere erupted immediately after the announcement, and López-Obrador and his followers demanded a ballot recount.

Those I spoke with from the state of Jalisco during summer 2006 insisted that Calderón did, in fact, win the election, but nearly everyone I spoke with in Michoacán and Guerrero insisted that the election was fraudulent. Victor Toledo at the Morelia UNAM claimed that sixty mathematics professors in Mexico City conducted a mathematical analysis of the election and proved unequivocally that the election was rife with irregularities and fraud.

Newspapers in the region provided a step-by-step description of the manner in which the election was stolen by Calderón (Méndez 2006), and the huge plaza in Morelia, the state capital of Michoacán, was completely taken over by protestors giving impassioned speeches of protest, displaying artwork and posters, and handing out literature about electoral fraud. One huge artistic work was particularly noteworthy and overshadowed all others in the plaza: an enormous 15-foot-tall effigy of a dragon with "Foxzilla" written on the chest. The dragon was in the process of giving birth to the head of Calderón.

In conversations with farmers in Michoacán and Guerrero, I found it interesting that they and disgruntled family members spoke passionately of the election being "stolen," in much the same way that some in the United States have claimed that Bush "stole" elections. The difference in the two countries' public reaction to this possibility is notably different, however. In Mexico, people were visibly angry and even talked of a revolution and the creation of a new constitution. By comparison, reaction to a possible stolen election in the United States was quiet. One thing is certain. With Felipe Calderón as president of Mexico, unless his party's policies change dramatically, the status quo will be maintained, and little if anything will change for Mexico's subsistence farmers.

Subsistence farmers remain disenfranchised from government participation. The government hierarchy is vertical and undemocratic rather than horizontal and democratic. There are no checks and balances that could promote some level of government accountability. Rather, graft and corruption are commonplace at all levels in the bureaucratic hierarchy. Government funds earmarked for mitigation of the impoverished circumstances of campesinos are siphoned off at each level from the top down, leaving little or nothing for the people at the bottom for whom the funds were intended.

A MILITARY PRESENCE IN THE COUNTRYSIDE

Another effective mechanism for controlling campesinos besieged with the realities of NAFTA is the use of armed military personnel. Claiming to be interested in controlling drug traffic in the countryside, truckloads of military personnel regularly course through backcountry roads and set up checkpoints at crossroads. The Mexican military quietly and consistently supported the PRI for many years. The military's antidrug effort expanded from 5,000 soldiers in the 1970s to 25,000 soldiers in the late 1980s. As a result, the military has taken on the role as the primary, and sometimes the only, authority in several states in Mexico, including Jalisco and Guerrero (Pacific Council on International Policy 2000).

Some rural residents appreciate the military for the "protection" and social control it is able to provide. At the same time, many campesinos greatly fear the military's potential to accuse them of crimes that were never committed, kidnap, torture, kill, and even expropriate property. In 2001, after Fox's election, the National Human Rights Commission released a 2,846-page report that documents the appalling travesties wrought by the Mexican army and a secret police, which systematically kidnapped, brutalized, and "disappeared" hundreds of Mexicans in the 1970s as it attempted to crush an array of guerrilla movements. The report examined 532 cases and confirmed that at least 275 people were forcibly taken away by military agents from 1970 to 1985, never to be seen or heard from again (Smith and Fineman 2001).

Tuxcueca, Jalisco, on the edge of Lake Chapala, illustrates the many contrasting realities evident in the lives of residents in the region. The town appears to be peaceful and quiet, a sort of oasis on the road between the busy cities of Zamora and Guadalajara. The town is dominated by Ford pickups, mostly of 1970s vintage, and a few old Chevy pickups. However, off and on from summer 1998 through 2007, an entire military installation was set up next to the town at the crossroads of Mazamitla. Military personnel with AK-47s sat behind barricades made of urea fertilizer bags. Vehicles and anyone appearing suspicious were stopped for extensive questioning.

The contrast became even more striking after 9 P.M., when fully armed soldiers dressed in green army fatigues, some helmeted, frequented Mary's Restaurant at the edge of town. There they bought meals and flirted with the owner and her staff of young women. The innocence and

Figure 24. Soldier at Mary's Restaurant, Tuxcueca, Jalisco.

adoring glances of the women provided sharp contrast to the harshness of the military demeanor.

In Zinapecuaro, Michoacán, truckloads of armed military personnel traversed the town's roads. I asked Lorenzo Vasquez how he felt about having armed soldiers coursing through the streets of his pueblo. He informed me that he didn't like their presence, but that there really wasn't much anyone could do about it. If the townspeople organized to protest, they would be arrested and thrown in jail. Lorenzo viewed any interaction with the military as dangerous. If a soldier didn't like someone, he could arrest the person on trumped up charges and jail him or her indefinitely. Lorenzo said that he attempted to ignore and avoid the military in his town as much as possible.

On the way up the mountain to visit his home village of Pueblo Viejo, Lorenzo's van veered around a sharp curve, and Lorenzo pointed to a grassy fallow area of land with a few buildings and livestock next to the road. He informed me that the approximately 4-hectare *parcela* once belonged to his father and him. However, several years earlier government officials expropriated the land, claiming that they needed it for government housing. Lorenzo related that if they had really used the land for housing, he would not have been so distressed about the theft of his land.

However, housing was never constructed on the land, which was subsequently sold for government profit.

In winter 1999, two research assistants and I were returning by bus to Guadalajara after visiting Cuquio and Los Sauces de Pérez, Jalisco. Military personnel stopped the bus several miles outside Guadalajara. All passengers were required to exit the bus while soldiers conducted an extensive and protracted search. One of the research assistants was detained in a separate location at the roadside. All of his belongings were searched. I became somewhat alarmed because the assistant was not fluent in Spanish, so I presented myself to the soldiers and offered to assist with any translation. Fortunately, when they learned that the assistant was my student, and when I introduced the other assistant to them, the detained assistant was dismissed.

On another occasion I was stopped at a military checkpoint while traveling by taxi en route to Tecomán, Colima, from Maquilí, Michoacán. A ferocious military officer demanded that I unpack my backpack and computer. I was very concerned that both would be confiscated. However, when the officer saw that I was carrying only a computer, and no firearms or drugs, he gestured for the taxi driver to continue on his journey.

Most campesinos I spoke with view the Mexican federal military as the government's own personal military. They perceive the military presence in the countryside as a mechanism for both discouraging drug traffic and warding off any unrest or revolutionary organizing among the post-NAFTA impoverished throngs of disgruntled campesinos. The memories of the 1910 Mexican revolution are alive and well in the minds of those who hold the reins of power.

THE CATHOLIC CHURCH

With 90 percent of Mexicans claiming to be at least nominally Catholic, the Roman Catholic Church is one of the most influential, subtle, and repressive forces in west-central Mexico (Cockcroft 1998, 345). Historically, wealthy conservative landholders made generous financial contributions to the church. In return, the church has consistently opposed agrarian reform (Cockcroft 1998, 118) while promoting and protecting the status quo with the use of religious symbols and imagery such as the Virgin Mary, Jesus, and the saints. The symbols and imagery, in turn, are internalized and elicit emotional responses leading to recognized appropriate behavior that includes docility and supplication (Becker 1995).

The church-controlled subsistence farmers are humbled by and submissive to the church and its powerful images. With verbal and behavioral reinforcement from the clergy, the likelihood of unrest is greatly reduced.

Women in particular are trained into the symbolic system that calls for abnegation, conformity, and subjugation, though the clergy refers to these personality characteristics in women as attributes of purity (Becker 1995). Older Mexican women, for example, might focus on Our Lady of Guadalupe's maternal and self-sacrificing aspects as qualities to emulate. The religious symbol offers comfort and faith that all will be well, despite the torment, pain, alienation, loneliness, confusion, and suffering (Rodriguez 1994). Hope and redemption are associated with endurance, suffering, and the promise of a better afterlife in heaven.

In the past forty years both the Catholic Church and the Mexican government have jointly promoted campaigns to defend the virtues of motherhood and family life along with policies designed to repress "revolutionary" clerics who advocate and practice liberation theology. The only point of disagreement between the church and the government has centered on the government's birth-control program and provision of free school textbooks. Both the church and the Mexican government reject feminist proposals for the legalization of abortion (Cockcroft 1998).

Priests in Mexico who have promoted liberation theology and attempted to encourage and organize peasants to confront their repression have met with unrestrained resistance from both the Mexican government and the church. A papal nuncio issued in 1993 mounted a full-scale offensive against any member of the clergy who favored liberation theology. Bishop Ruíz of Chiapas is credited in part with fomenting the Chiapas uprising in 1994 and encouraging Indians to "recover dignity" (Cockcroft 1998). Subsequently, several clergymen who advocated liberation theology received death threats, and in 1997 Bishop Ruíz escaped an assassination attempt.

In more recent years, Archbishop Norberto Rivera Carrera, supported by conservative business adherents and politicians, has promoted an extreme version of "family values" by publicly censuring "feminists, homosexuals, third-worldists, pacifists, liberationists, and malcontents of whatever kind." Carrera's supporters are afforded access to television networks from which they publicly promote sexual abstinence, condemn condom use, criticize people with AIDS, and champion patriarchical values (Cockcroft 1998).

The Catholic Church plays a significant spiritual role in the lives of most of the poorest campesinos in west-central Mexico, while priests in the countryside follow the cardinal's proclamation and promote the conservative agenda. Even in the face of serious nutritional deficiencies and outright starvation among their constituents, the clergy encourage campesinos to have faith and endure the oppression as character components of a good Catholic. I found that the poorest subsistence farmers were those who were most heavily invested in the spiritual balm offered by Catholicism.

In Las Cebollas, Jalisco, Jovita Tejada claims that "God will help you, if you pray," in reference to the uncertainty of seasonal rainfall for her corn, bean, and squash intercrop. One of the poorest elderly couples in this study, Rogelio Durán and his wife, devoted an entire room of their concrete dwelling in Charo, Michoacán, to a large ornate altar of the Virgin Mary, with offering vessels for flowers and food. Other poor campesinos showcase religious crosses and other symbols and images liberally on the walls of their homes.

In contrast, Gerardo Fernandez, a former agrochemical distributor in Tuxcueca, Jalisco, who practiced commercialized agriculture in the early years of the millennium, would never consider leaving his crops to "faith in God." Instead, he had access to and utilized every modern agricultural intervention available to ensure a successful, productive harvest. The interior of his home reflects only a rudimentary reference to religion, with a few small, incidental religious items hung on the wall.

EDUCATION

West-central Mexican farmers and their families have access to only limited educational opportunities. Many never attended school because they were needed on the farm. Others completed only second or third grade of elementary school. While formal education is scarce, those children who are fortunate enough to attend school encounter authoritarian standards and school personnel. The excitement of social interaction and new knowledge is marred by the freedom of school personnel to practice corporal punishment, which is a norm, allowed and even expected, in Mexico's schools.

In Chiapas, only a quarter of Indian children ever attend school. For years prior to and since the Chiapas uprising, indigenous groups have consistently demanded reforms in the quality of education their children receive. Their demands include more schools, more teachers from the Indians' own linguistic communities, and an end to teachers beating children who cannot understand or speak Spanish fluently (Cockcroft 1998).

Adrienne Jerman, a Salinas, California, elementary school teacher, described the adjustment process of children who have received elementary education in Mexico and then enter her classes when they immigrate to California. She claims that initially they view her as someone to fear because she will slap or hit them. After they have attended her class for several weeks and received repeated reassurances that they will never be punished corporally, they relax and are attentive enough for her to work with them.

The expected corporal punishment in Mexico sometimes collides with California's educational and legal values. Juan Borrego of Salinas spoke angrily about the "permissive" California educational system. He asserted his right to discipline any of his three daughters in any way he felt appropriate. He ranted about the injustice inherent in the California educational system when teachers and other school personnel inform his daughters of their rights to freedom from abuse. He claimed that his daughters had threatened to call the police and report him on numerous occasions. He could not reconcile the concept of his potential arrest and a jail term with his right as a parent to discipline his children using corporal punishment.

COMMERCIAL INTERMEDIARIES

Many campesinos are oppressed because they do not have viable markets for their crops. Without direct connections to buyers in the big cities, they are forced to sell their crops to intermediaries who have developed economic liaisons with merchants or owners of packinghouses and distilleries. The generally despised *intermediarios* pay a pittance to the farmers and then turn around and sell the crop for twice as much or more than they paid for it. The farmers then remain impoverished while the *intermediarios*, who did not engage in the work and risks associated with farming, reap impressive profits.

For example, the sale of a dollar's worth of coffee from Mexico in the United States provides the original grower with only $0.08. About $0.19 is funneled off for federal taxes; $0.28 goes to traders, *intermediarios*, and shippers; $0.25 goes to processors and wholesalers; and $0.20 goes to retailers in the United States (Cunningham and Saigo 2001). The grower who invested all the time and labor and withstood the vagaries and risks associated with a potentially unstable market receives only a meager amount.

José Martínez Espino, a former dive master and current mango grower in Coacoyul, Guerrero, confirmed that prior to NAFTA the government attempted to regulate the exploitative practices of the *intermediarios*. Since NAFTA's initiation, though, all restrictions on brokers have been removed, and they have been given virtual free reign to exploit farmers in the countryside at any level they choose.

José is a member of an organic mango growing cooperative in Zihuatanejo. Because there is no market for his mangos, he has allowed his orchards to decline while he supports his family as the municipal government director of rural development. He claims that he actually loses money if he sells mangos to local *intermediarios*, who offer him only 5 centavos (less than 1 cent) for a full box of mangos.

On my first trip to San Agustín, Jalisco, in summer 1998, Gabino Ayala described in great detail his resentment of the local distillery's then-recent decision to use an intermediary for the purchase of agave stems from local growers. Until the tequila industry strengthened in summer 2000 (see chapter 10), he focused on the income-generating potential of cattle ranching. He informed me that he could raise cattle and sell them directly to any *carnicería* (meat market) locally or in Guadalajara. He concluded our conversation by forcefully stating that, if the meat industry begins to employ *intermediaries* as liaisons between ranchers and butcher shops, he will emigrate to the United States.

Vicente Silva, an organic blackberry grower, is desperately seeking an export market in the United States for his countercyclic blackberry crop. He claims that, without an export opportunity, he is forced to sell his blackberries to *intermediarios* in Zamora for only 40 centavos per kilogram, approximately 4 cents for about two pounds of organic blackberries. He was visibly astonished when I informed him that during the summer months in California the New Leaf Market in Felton sells 6-ounce plastic containers of organic blackberries for $2.45.

CACIQUISMO

The opportunity for campesinos to organize into unions and other alliances for the purpose of local empowerment is often undermined by the development of *caciquismo*—an institution developed early in the twentieth century as a federally supported system for the introduction and spread of capitalism into the countryside (Cockcroft 1998).

One individual or a small group of individuals amasses wealth, influence, and power over others within a rancho or pueblo, union, or branch of the local government. As a means of gaining political power, higher social status, and recognition, caciques often engage in indiscriminate, conspicuous spending while hosting impressive parties for prominent regional politicians. In addition, many attempt to play a part in community social projects such as health committees and public works committees by being the first to contribute economic support (Zendejas and De Vries 1995).

Operating paternalistically within the *ejido,* political bosses and corrupt *ejidal* officers are the bane of many individual *ejidos* in west-central Mexico (DeWalt et al. 1994). By instituting an ethic of favoritism and often fear, caciques are able to gain control of ranchos, pueblos, or various organizations and run them as the dominant "kingpins." The cacique and his/her allies then make all significant decisions over matters affecting the domain they control. They often accumulate property and profit personally from handling credit arrangements with banks and development projects.

When caciques take control of *ejidos,* they sometimes engender a state of corruption and lawlessness. Democracy within the organization is shattered and replaced by an arbitrary and authoritarian form of governance. *Ejidatarios* live with corruption and the constant threat of violence should they confront cacique authority (DeWalt 1994). Moreover, the capricious and coercive power caciques wield may allow privileged *intermediarios* to prevent the entry of potential broker competitors (Johnston 1987). Today caciques continue to function as agents who are loyal to the government while simultaneously penetrating and wielding control within local rural societies (Lomitz-Adler 1992).

On several *ejidos* long dominated by a cacique, campesinos surprisingly expressed support and gratitude for the overturning of Article 27 of the Mexican Constitution because it restored control of their land to them exclusively. Prior to constitutional reform, many complained that the local cacique would almost inevitably arrange for the expropriation of their land if they were unable or unwilling to farm it for a time because of short-term immigration to the United States.

Marisol Carranza and Adela Lozano recall their experiences with the caciques of the El Guaco pueblo in Michoacán. At election time, armed caciques visited each family to tell them how they should vote in upcoming elections.

When I arrived in San José de Guadalupe near Tlalpujahua, Michoacán, to visit José Moreno's family and farm, Javier Moreno greeted me as soon as I stepped out of the taxi. Everyone who lives in the valley is a "Moreno," by blood or marriage. Javier, the valley's elder cacique, guards the valley's entrance and greets everyone who journeys down the single road leading into the valley.

After I visited José Moreno's family in one of the numerous small houses scattered over the face of the mountain adjoining the valley, I returned to the narrow road that leads into the valley. Javier greeted me and sent a young boy across the valley to order his son-in-law to give me a ride back to the hotel in Tlalpujahua. While waiting for his son-in-law, he told me many stories exalting his political prowess and financial success. Several people walked past us and addressed him submissively as "Don Javier." It became obvious that he was in complete command of every life in the "Valle de los Morenos."

Vicente Silva was once the administrative manager of credit for the campesino-empowering Union de Jesus Montenegro, which was organized in 1973. The union included 114 *ejidos* and managed 35,000 tons of solid fertilizer per year so that campesinos could avoid the more costly purchase of chemical fertilizers from private enterprises. In addition, the union developed seventy pig farms, with four hundred pigs per farm, and produced its own sorghum as pig feed.

According to Vicente, the union grew and was eventually able to invest in education. Union members built schools, including the Eduardo Ruíz High School. The most successful high school students were sent to universities, including the national university, at union expense. The students, in turn, agreed to return to their villages upon completion of their studies and offer their newly acquired expertise to improve rural communities.

Other union activities that benefited the rural communities included the purchase of equipment designed for the construction of deep wells. Some union members produced alfalfa, wheat, corn, sorghum, and pork, while others produced strawberries and purchased their own strawberry cooler/storage facility. Several members developed an improved strain of sorghum called Purépecha and subsequently established a factory in which the sorghum was milled for animal feed. The union was so successful that members formed a union bank with shareholders, and union members continued to amass capital.

Women organized the Unidades Agricolas y Industrias para la Mujer Campesina (UAIM, Campesina Women's Agricultural and Industrial Units) within the Union de Jesus Montenegro. Women cared for 400,000 chickens and regularly sold eggs and chickens to the military in Mexico City and Jalisco. They also grew ornamental flowers for sale in the national market in Mexico City and produced headcheese, ham sausages, and chorizo from pigs.

During its most productive period in the 1980s, there were a total of 14,000 *ejidatario* members of the union. Eventually, as the union continued to grow, Vicente claims that the organization "lost direction." *Caciquismo* developed in the administrative council and the council of vigilance. The caciques weakened and eventually destroyed the union, which disbanded altogether in 1990. Today the Union de Jesus Montenegro exists only on paper, though, according to Vicente, some of the women continue their union activities.

MACHISMO

Ironically, even though women have a history of assuming the highest rank in Mexico's two most influential political parties and hold 17 percent of the seats in the Congress of Mexico, perhaps the most oppressed and exploited people of Mexico are women (Sandoval 2000). A legacy of oppression originating in European patriarchy (Cockcroft 1998,396), machismo ranks high in the traditional image of Mexican culture (Powell 1995). Since colonial times the Roman Catholic Church has reinforced patriarchy and machismo as the ideology and practice of male supremacy, with its emphasis on bravery, virility, women's intellectual inferiority, and women's assigned, subjugated role as caretaker of the family (Cockcroft 1998,12). The term *macho* has other more positive contemporary meanings as well, including reference to a man of courage, integrity, and strength (Zavella 1987). Men, however, often function as the ultimate authority in the family, while women are relegated to an inconsequential, subordinate position (Rodriguez 1994).

Despite the growing political influence of women in Mexico, the country continues to be dominated by the machismo ethic. In a 2000 survey, 92 percent of 128,000 Mexican men polled indicated that a woman's main role should be that of housekeeper and mother. About 4 percent of men disagreed with the statement that "women have a right to live free of violence" (Sandoval 2000).

In spite of the fact that the majority of voters are women in all but one Mexican state, the laws that reinforce women's oppression are still active. Penalties for spousal abuse are light. Issues of primary concern to women such as child care and women's rights in family law have largely been legislatively ignored. Women can be fired for being pregnant, and, as recently as 1974, Mexican men could legally object to their wives working outside the home (Sandoval 2000). Men's objections to women working outside the home were based on the assumption that such work challenged their manhood by calling into question their ability to support the family and control "their" women's movements (Mummert 1994).

Some scholars explain the existence of machismo as an adaptive characteristic of a conquered people. To compensate for their feelings of inadequacy elicited by the inability to protect their families from the conquerors' rape and plunder, males developed an exaggerated masculine and aggressive response to women. Thus, machismo is viewed as the response of the conquered to the dominant culture's oppression (Rodriguez 1994).

Regardless of its origin, the extreme form of rural patriarchy practiced in many remote ranchos and pueblos in west-central Mexico includes the brutal subjugation of women as standard practice. Women are expected to work to care for and maintain the family *and* work on the farm. If they work outside the family or farm, they are typically paid substandard wages. Many women of the countryside are literally beaten into submission (Cockcroft 1998, 149).

According to the DIF director in Cuquio, many campesinos refuse to use any form of birth control. Their stubborn refusal continues even after they have families with several underfed children who lack the barest necessities of life such as a bed and blanket. Continued forced births are promoted even when women's lives are at risk. Women's time is then consumed with the constant care and concern for too many children rather than in organizing to improve their economic circumstances. Continued, unremitting births give rise to yet another generation of impoverished campesinos.

Jorge Rosales's uncle near Apatzingán, Michoacán, has a wife in one village and a mistress in another. He has produced twenty-three offspring with the two women. José Moreno's grandfather in San José Guadalupe, Michoacán, also has a wife and a mistress. He has produced twenty-two offspring with the two women. Earlier I discussed the case of Jorge Becerra, who lives with his California wife in Salinas and is also married to a woman in El Loreto Occidental, Jalisco. He has produced seven children with the Mexican wife and two with the Californian wife.

Baby markets are also a reality in some pueblos. Wealthy Americans visit the pueblos and typically approach men with offers to purchase their children, without consulting the women. I met one farmer who was offered $30,000 for one of his children. A Cuquio father of twins I met in a local eatery arranged to sell one of his twins to an American who offered him a brand new truck and 15,000 pesos. The deal was called off when the man's wife learned of the arrangement and refused to sell her child.

In spite of the dismal, pervasive disempowered state of women common in the rural countryside, the introduction of limited opportunities to work outside the home is providing an opening for a redefinition of women's roles. Gail Mummert (1994) studied the spatial, institutional, and cultural changes resulting from agricultural commercialization and extensive male outmigration in a village near Zamora, Michoacán. The opening of strawberry packing plants in Zamora that hired mostly women, offering them an opportunity for salaried work, led to broad socioeconomic changes. Residents reported that the village progressed as a result of women's salaried labor. Further, the opportunity to earn a salary improved families' economic circumstances so that they were able to purchase food and clothing. Women felt freer to go out alone, leave the village on their own, and even marry men outside the village. Young wives were no longer willing to tolerate physical abuse and adultery.

These women exemplify the empowerment potential for women who are fortunate enough to participate in salaried labor opportunities, but such opportunities are still the very rare exception rather than the rule in the west-central Mexico countryside. The majority of women continue to endure oppressive, subordinate roles. Several women I met were virtually cloistered in their homes.

As pueblos and ranchos transform into veritable ghost towns, and NAFTA-supported efforts to exploit the environment continue virtually unabated, those left behind struggle with the absence of their family members who have emigrated to the United States. The authoritarian institutions that have long oppressed campesinos for centuries continue relentlessly unabated and add to the difficulties of living life in the face of cultural disintegration.

FOURTEEN

TOWARD AN ENLIGHTENED PERCEPTION OF CALIFORNIA'S MEXICAN AGRICULTURAL IMMIGRANTS

The Heart of a Nation Lies in its Villages.
—Anonymous

Sustainable development recognizes that poverty is the ultimate polluter and hunger has no environmental conscience.
—Frank Popoff, chairman, Dow Chemical Corporation

A riot is, at the bottom, the language of the unheard.
—Dr. Martin Luther King, Jr.

From the farms of west-central Mexico to California's corporate agribusiness there exists a dense, interlocking, co-reinforcing framework of social, political, and economic institutions and practices that extends binationally. The gridlocked framework unremittingly mars, disenfranchises, and oppresses small farmers and their families in Mexico and farmworkers in California all along the migrant circuit. Human rights violations are the norm at every juncture of the binational circuit (see appendix B).

This framework that enshrouds the lives of campesinos and California farmworkers is so pervasive and penetrating that escape is nearly impossible. Some farmworkers do, however, escape and then join the ranks of the farmers who lease or manage farms in California. They then find themselves in the untenable position of contributing to the disenfranchisement of those who follow them.

If the NAFTA originators had taken the time to consult with a representative sample of corn-producing subsistence farmers in the region, they would have been in a position to make informed decisions in the creation of a far more enlightened trade policy. However, campesinos were excluded from trade policy formulation, and the Mexican government largely ignores the post-NAFTA plight of impoverished, disenfranchised subsistence farmers while corporations and government elites enjoy the fruits of the NAFTA economy. Indeed, government elites and the NAFTA originators predicted that millions of rural inhabitants would be driven from their land as economic refugees, even before NAFTA went into effect.

The campesino forced flight from hunger would have been difficult enough. NAFTA, however, does not recognize a common labor market between the United States and Mexico, and NAFTA provisions for environmental protection have been largely ineffective. Many small subsistence farmers from Mexico perceive that their only survival choice is migration to the United States. However, when they arrive at the U.S. border they encounter life-threatening difficulties in the form of perilous border crossings led by costly *coyotes*. Ironically, if they survive the border crossing and secure employment in California, they live in constant fear of deportation while desperately missing their families, friends, towns, and villages in Mexico.

FORGOTTEN IN MEXICO

The plight of farmers in Mexico and the historic uneasy relationship between Mexico's government and campesinos can be traced to the Spanish conquest of Mexico, when indigenous people were driven off their communal lands and the Spanish introduced the concepts of private property and slave labor. Until the revolution of 1910, rural peasants were largely relegated to the status of a subordinate labor class on rural haciendas.

After the Cárdenas administration in the 1940s, presidential successors focused on opportunities for large-scale capital gains internationally and spent huge sums of money to fortify large-scale privately owned agriculture. The introduction of Green Revolution technologies at this time furthered the movement toward large-scale commercial agriculture, and it continues to penetrate the rural countryside, encouraging subsistence farmers to abandon their sustainable polyculture farming practices and adopt more "modern" methods. The small subsistence farming sector, however, has been historically neglected and largely excluded from any coherent, abiding government-sponsored agricultural policy. Further, the government of Mexico has neglected the formulation and enforcement of effective environmental legislation designed to protect Mexico's varied natural resource base and biodiversity from exploitation.

The Mexican government's neglect of the campesino sector has been historically punctuated with attention breaks when campesinos mobilize and threaten the existing order, or when the government is motivated to garner rural political support to maintain its power. The most dramatic historic example of peasant mobilization was the Mexican revolution of 1910, which forced government elites to finally pay attention to peasant oppression and enact agrarian reform legislation with the creation of Article 27 of the Mexican Constitution. The aim of the land reform, however, was to placate landless peasants who brought about the revolution without threatening the future development of capitalist agriculture— not to include them as players in a government-sponsored agricultural policy.

In the 1970s, campesino mobilization throughout Mexico forced President Echeverría to institute a series of government programs designed to assist rural small-scale farmers, including CONASUPO. In 1988, President Salinas de Gortari instituted PRONASOL, another government-sponsored program, as a means of garnering popular rural state support. Finally, the government-sponsored Procampo, Alianza Para el Campo, and Progresa programs were instituted during the NAFTA transition purportedly as a means of assisting rural small-scale farmers in their adjustment to the NAFTA economy. According to both scholars and my study participants, both Procampo and Alianza Para el Campo were palliative at best and did not contribute to the development of a new farm policy that includes small producers. The Progresa program, renamed Oportunidades in 2004, continues today and is also fraught with many difficulties.

In August 2001, thousands of small-scale and subsistence farmers traveled to Mexico City for an extended protest of their government's abandonment of small producer farmers since NAFTA's initiation. Once again the government's response to the protest was to appropriate millions of dollars, in this case to institute La Ley de Desarollo Rural Sustentable, to take effect in April 2002, and not to engage in the democratic development of government agricultural policies that include small subsistence farmers.

Democracy is even thwarted by government-sponsored organizations purportedly designed to support campesinos, such as the Confederación Nacional Campesina (CNC, National Peasants' Confederation). Vicente Silva declined the opportunity to become the director of the CNC when his request to include an advisory committee of campesinos was denied. The social institutions and those who represent them (see chapter 13) further support campesino acquiescence to a government agenda that excludes them by promoting fear, compliance, and submission.

MARGINALIZED IN CALIFORNIA

Post-NAFTA economic refugee campesinos from Mexico who manage to survive an undocumented border crossing to secure employment in California's corporate agribusiness become part of an institutional and legislative framework that has afforded agribusiness growers mastery and supremacy over capitalist crop production and concomitant agribusiness labor force repression. In California, the Farm Bureau, governor, and state government (heavily financed at election time by agribusiness), the Agricultural Labor Relations Board, the Pesticide Regulatory Commission, and local and state authorities all conspire and function to reinforce agribusiness supremacy and the continued oppression of the farmworker underclass.

From its statehood in 1848, California has enacted legislation against ethnic farmworker employees designed to maintain their invisibility in mainstream society and their disenfranchisement from full participation in any agricultural endeavor other than as farm laborers. In addition, farmworkers risk subjection to violence and even murder if they organize to confront their oppressive employment conditions. Historically, whenever an ethnic group associated with farm labor becomes too militant for growers to control, growers threaten to employ tactics including violence and murder to suppress potential strikers. Local, state, and federal law enforcement agencies acquiesce and support them in reinstating and maintaining the repressive status quo.

California farmworkers are subject to employment laws that are unique to the farming system and different from those affecting workers in manufacturing. "Agricultural exceptionalism" excludes agriculture and agricultural workers from most protective labor legislation, since agriculture has consistently been presented as a special case that should be governed by separate laws in order to protect the nation's food supply.

Farmworkers on small farms are excluded from the protective legislation of the New Deal Fair Labor Standards Act, designed to curtail poverty among workers by establishing a minimum wage. They are not entitled to overtime pay for work performed beyond the federally mandated forty-hour workweek. Lack of protective legislation further permits the employment of children age 12 and older in agriculture.

Only a small minority of farmworkers receive health insurance benefits from employers. They are the population in the state most exposed to agrochemicals, and the longer they work in California the sicker they become. For their hard labor, compromised health, and overtime work, their meager salaries provide them only the barest essentials and force them into a life of poverty in crowded, untenable housing situations because of the statewide scarcity of adequate low-income housing. Even the hopes of their children receiving an education with which to escape farmwork altogether are often shattered when farmworker parents and children encounter a state-wide educational system and curriculum that are frequently unresponsive to their culture and needs.

The post-NAFTA California immigrant backlash that extends across the country engenders further hardship as immigrants confront the many forms of nativism and racism expressed by an uninformed mainstream public. Lack of compassion or perspective on how this country created the conditions that force immigrants into the United States in the first place leads to votes in favor of punitive legislation such as California's Propositions 187 and 209, which further exacerbate the immigrants' plight.

Should an undocumented immigrant be unlucky enough to be apprehended by the *migra,* he or she encounters U.S. immigration law and court proceedings that operate with a separate, unique interpretation of due process that is unlike proceedings in U.S. civil and criminal trial proceedings.

Historically, the institutional and legislative framework that impacts subsistence farmers in Mexico could be penetrated, with a favorable outcome, when campesinos mobilized to confront the established authority. Likewise, effective strikes and union activity in California have served to provide some temporary relief and justice for farmworkers. However, the gains garnered by enormous mobilization efforts and strikes, as exemplified by the UFW activity in the 1960s, are comparatively short-lived and in no way permanently alter the rigidified system. Indeed, the creation of the Agricultural Labor Relations Board during Governor Brown's term in the 1960s was intended to arbitrate farmworker grievances. But the ALRB was later co-opted by subsequent

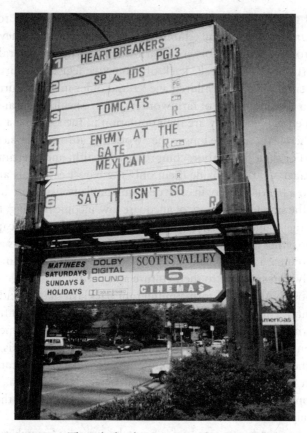

Figure 25. Though the theater received repeated complaints about the inappropriate concurrence of *Enemy at the Gate* and *Mexican*, theater personnel continued the offensive juxtaposition for several weeks in spring 2001.

agribusiness-friendly governors who appointed agribusiness-supportive board members and has become an auxiliary of the repressive institutions and regulations.

HUMAN RIGHTS VIOLATIONS

The legislative and institutional framework that oppresses small producer farmers in Mexico and farmworkers in California is the primary contributor to multiple human rights violations from the farms of west-central Mexico to California's corporate agribusiness, as a look at the UN Universal Declaration of Human Rights makes clear.

> Article 7: All are equal before the law and are entitled without any discrimination to equal protection of the law. All are entitled to equal protection against any discrimination in violation of this Declaration and against any incitement to such discrimination.

> Article 9: No one shall be subjected to arbitrary arrest, detention or exile.

> Article 10: Everyone is entitled in full equality to a fair and public hearing by an independent and impartial tribunal, in the determination of his rights and obligations and of any criminal charge against him.

In Mexico, subsistence farmers and family members may be subject to arbitrary arrest and even "disappearance" by military personnel.

In California, farmworkers are often subjected to arbitrary arrest and detention. Furthermore, they are governed by unique immigration and labor legislation with court proceedings that are separate and not equal to civil and criminal court proceedings, often in a language they do not understand.

> Article 16: (3) The family is the natural and fundamental group unit of society and is entitled to protection by society and the State.

Clearly under NAFTA the family as the natural and fundamental group unit of campesino society is not receiving protection from the state. Indeed, NAFTA promotes family separation and immigration, as predicted by the NAFTA originators. In the United States, stringent immigration laws often preclude family reunification for years, resulting in grief, loneliness, isolation, abandonment, and unhealthy coping strategies in both Mexico and the United States.

> Article 17: (2) No one shall be arbitrarily deprived of his property.

Property is commonly expropriated without payment in the west-central Mexico countryside. I encountered government water theft from the farmland of a small producer farmer living in San José Ixtapa, near Zihuatanejo. The water was redirected from his land to the hotel chain on the beach in Ixtapa, resulting in a precipitous decline in his coconut yields. Farther up the coast, fishermen were run off their beachfront land by the military in the 1970s in order to make way for a Club Med. Some of Lorenzo Vasquez and his father's farmland near Zinapécuaro, Michoacán, was expropriated without payment by the military, purport-

Figures 26. Faces of poverty in the west-central Mexico countryside, Ojo de Agua, Jalisco.

edly for the construction of military housing. The housing was never built, and the land was never returned.

> Article 21: (1) Everyone has the right to take part in the government of his country, directly or through freely chosen representatives. (3) The will of the people shall be the basis of the authority of government; this shall be expressed in periodic and genuine elections which shall be by universal and equal suffrage and shall be held by secret vote or by equivalent free voting procedures.

Campesinos in the west-central Mexico countryside experience separation from and abandonment by the Mexican government as well as undemocratic exclusion from participation in the development of government policies that impact their lives. Past government policies that have negatively impacted the countryside have created widespread fear, anger, and distrust.

The PRI recognized the importance of the campesino vote for ultimate election gains. The party engaged in manipulative election tactics and practices that effectively nullified free voting procedures, including the purchase of votes in a predominantly PRD area, bribery, and even threats made by cacique party representatives to residents living in *ejidos*. The 2000 and 2004 U.S. presidential elections have also received considerable criticism for improper election protocol, particularly in minority districts. The 2006 presidential election in Mexico resulted in massive protests against alleged voting irregularities.

> Article 23: (1) Everyone has the right to work, to free choice of employment, to just and favorable conditions of work and to protection against unemployment. (3) Everyone who works has the right to just and favorable remuneration ensuring for himself and his family an existence worthy of human dignity and *supplemented, if necessary, by other means of social protection* [my emphasis].

Article 23 is violated binationally by NAFTA and labor legislation in both Mexico and California. Beginning with the World Bank's sectoral adjustment loan to Mexico, which required the removal of all price supports and subsidies in preparation for NAFTA, small producer farmers in Mexico have been denied the right to free choice of employment on their own land. When they are forced to migrate from Mexico to California in order to work in corporate agribusiness, they are paid wages so low that they live beneath the poverty level, often in conditions lacking human dignity.

> Article 24: Everyone has the right to rest and leisure, including reasonable limitation of working hours and periodic holidays with pay.

In California, the number of hours worked by farmworkers is established by the grower, not by state or federally mandated legislation. From June through August during the height of the harvest season, some farmworkers work thirteen-hour days, six or seven days per week, without overtime pay. Years of overwork in combination with a poor diet and agrochemical exposure methodically lead to a compromised health status and shortened lifespan.

> Article 25: (1) Everyone has the right to a standard of living adequate for the health and well-being of himself and of his family, including food, clothing, housing and medical care and necessary social services, and the right to security in the event of unemployment, sickness, disability, widowhood, old age or other lack of livelihood circumstances beyond his control. (2) Motherhood and childhood are entitled to special care and assistance. All children, whether born in or out of wedlock, shall enjoy the same social protection.

The binational legislative and institutional framework along with transnational corporations preclude these basic human rights from being realized on either side of the border. Campesinos are often born hungry from the impoverished bodies of their mothers. They grow up and live in a constant paradigm of hunger, illness, and scarcity. They experience the worst of the Third World. When they immigrate to California as economic refugees, their health deteriorates further as they experience the worst of the First World as farm laborers. Most farm laborers do not enjoy sufficient food, clothing, or adequate housing and medical care because of the inadequate salaries they earn in California's corporate agribusiness.

Motherhood and childhood are afforded no special care and assistance on either side of the border. On the contrary, children are often painfully separated from their parents and left in Mexico, often for years, while their parents work in the United States in the hopes of providing them an improved life. Whole families of women and children are abandoned in Mexico with no support when an emigrating husband or partner disappears from their lives.

The agrochemicals, agricultural products, soft drinks, and nicotine products that are aggressively promoted by U.S.-originating transnational corporations in Mexico poison children and adults alike. Some children raised on Green Revolution hybrid corn may sustain intellectual deficiencies resulting from the corn's inability to absorb micronutrients essential for proper intellectual development. Their intellectual impairment is exacerbated by agrochemical exposure that can impede motor and cognitive development from birth.

> Article 26: (1) Everyone has the right to education. Education shall be free, at least in the elementary and fundamental stages. Elementary education shall be compulsory. (2) Education shall be directed to the full development of the human personality and to the strengthening of respect for human rights and fundamental freedoms. It shall promote understanding, tolerance and friendship among all nations, racial or religious groups, and shall further the activities of the United Nations for the maintenance of peace.

The binational legislative and institutional framework does not support farmer or farmworker education on either side of the border. Campesinos throughout Mexico bemoan the fact that either they were unable to pursue an education, even at the elementary level, because they were needed on the farm, or they were unable to continue their education past the third grade. Many of the poorest campesinos do not have the money required to send their children to elementary school, where they could acquire basic math and literacy skills. Education in Mexico requires the purchase of uniforms and school supplies at a nominal cost. However, many of the poorest campesinos don't have sufficient funds to avert malnutrition and starvation. Under these circumstances, education is considered an unattainable luxury.

When they immigrate to California, campesinos come with the desire to pursue their own education, and they are passionate about their children's pursuit of an education. However, overwork and seasonal underemployment force migration throughout the state and make educational pursuit for farmworker parents next to impossible. Their children often enter schools and classrooms with school personnel and a curriculum that are indifferent to their needs, culture, and families. Academic success under these circumstances is greatly compromised and ultimately contributes to the deplorably high Latino dropout rate.

> Article 28: Everyone is entitled to a social and international order in which the rights and freedoms set forth in this Declaration can be fully realized.

It is impossible to guarantee human rights for the subsistence farmers of Mexico and the farmworkers of California under the current NAFTA social and international order. The NAFTA accords create conditions for millions of binational subsistence farmers and farmworkers that are anathema to the full realization of the human rights cited above.

DOING SOMETHING ABOUT IT

The most obvious viable solution to these pervasive, institutionally and legislatively mandated violations is the development of binationally enforceable legislation with the full participation of both Mexican and U.S. governments. This legislation must recognize and honor the agonizing predicament the functionally binational NAFTA-driven Mexican farmer/U.S. farmworker population of immigrants finds itself in.

This binational legislation must be given a priority that goes beyond large NAFTA-garnered government profits and embraces the recognition that California's multibillion dollar agricultural industry would not exist without the hard labor of the migrant farmworker population. Provisions must be made at each stage of the migrant circuit from Mexico to California for improving the well-being of all individuals in this population and for maintaining family unity as a priority.

I propose that a portion of the billions of U.S. tax dollars spent unproductively enforcing country-specific border legislation and fighting drug wars could be better utilized in a legislated program designed to correct the innate human rights violations in the current migrant circuit. Such a program would improve the lives of both the small producer farmers of Mexico and the farmworkers of California. The following proactive recommendations provide the first steps toward program implementation:

1. The United States and Mexico must develop effective border legislation that fully recognizes that the border is the responsibility of *both* Mexico and the United States, and that therefore border legislation must be binationally generated with the recognition of a common binational labor market.

2. The United States must contribute U.S.-sponsored financial and sustainable agricultural development institutions to the Mexican countryside that operate on a small scale and are designed to offer small loans and assistance to subsistence and small producer farmers. With a small loan, instruction, and commentary on the most efficient ways they can make their

lands productive again and restore sustainability to their farming practices, farmers will be able to choose to remain in Mexico with their families and thus avoid the unwelcome prospect of emigration.

3. Rather than continually escalating punitive militarization, a portion of U.S. tax dollars should be directed specifically toward rural development projects for the key immigrant-sending states of Jalisco, Michoacán, and Oaxaca. Many international organizations provide successful models of rural development worldwide, including Mohammed Yunus's Grameen Bank in India, the International Heifer Project, and the Jane Goodall Foundation in Africa. These organizations have the potential to establish sustainable farming communities with local rural economies. Again, successful rural economies provide the means by which Mexican campesinos can farm and earn a living while remaining in Mexico to support their families.

4. The United States must earnestly put pressure on the government of Mexico and join in partnership with its leaders by lending expertise to the process of developing a comprehensive, coherent farm policy in Mexico that includes the millions of subsistence and small producer farmers.

5. The U.S. and Mexican governments must pursue international policies that serve to reclaim some measure of control over and restrict the activities of profit-seeking transnational corporations and the spread of their deadly and health-compromising products throughout the west-central Mexico countryside. U.S.-originating corporate activity is out of control in west-central Mexico. Corporate activity must be restricted so that the promotion of products that result in poisoning, death, addiction, and other health-compromising conditions is curtailed.

6. The State of California must promote the creation of a domestic, state-controlled contracted agricultural labor force that is funded with joint revenues contributed by agribusiness growers and tax dollars garnered from California's residents who enjoy the inexpensive fruits of farm labor.

7. The State of California must promote and allot funds for the construction of sufficient low-income affordable housing to provide for the housing needs of its agricultural labor force.

In addition, farmworkers must be afforded health insurance provided by a statewide health insurance program. Clinics that are staffed with physicians who have expertise in the health concerns of farmworkers must be set up near agribusiness fields.

8. The State of California must aggressively recruit, train, and provide attractive salaries for enthusiastic teachers at all levels of the educational system who can provide an effective curriculum of culturally relevant bilingual education for farmworkers and their children. The education of farmworker children must provide for the ongoing inclusion of the parents in their educational pursuits so as to mitigate the deplorable Latino dropout rate in the state.

Every September 11th since 2001, the president of this country memorializes people who died on that date. He speaks of the American commitment to human life and family values. He laments the loss of family members who will be forever separated by death. But he continues to promote trade policies internationally and support corporations that force family separation and often destroy the lives of farm family members in Mexico. There is no commitment to the lives of Mexican farmworkers or to subsistence farmers in Mexico, or to the binational integrity of their families. The painful binational separation of members of these families is a subject never mentioned in his speeches.

The inherent misery of this huge binational population in its inescapable oppression within the framework of contemporary legislation and the institutions described here, as well as the multitude of human rights violations occurring at each juncture of the migrant circuit, must be afforded top binational remediation priority. It is the responsibility of citizens in both countries who are not caught up in the impossible life circumstances of the subsistence farmers of Mexico and the farmworkers of California to call for the recognition by their legislators and policymakers that the persistence of poverty in this population without hope for improved circumstances is intolerable, violates any standards of human decency, and compromises the humanity and dignity of all citizens in both countries.

Californians must recognize that the state's cheap food supply is borne on the shoulders of farmworkers who are consistently exploited and impoverished by their employment circumstances. California citizens must demand that the food that nourishes their bodies reflect human rights and social justice values. Without reform and with continued apathy and complacency, the dignity and humanity of all of California's citizens succumb to the role of perpetrators by omission of the binational legislative and institutional framework of oppression.

EPILOGUE

"Our lives begin to end the day we become silent about
things that matter."
—Dr. Martin Luther King, Jr.

In spite of the dismal circumstances the binational farmworker community finds itself in, there is an emerging awareness about its plight internationally, in Mexico and in the United States. In spring 2006, the extent of the migrant population became visible to mainstream America
for the first time when more than three million people took to the streets
of major cities all over the country to protest peacefully against punitive legislation and to push for legalized status. The emergence and organization of Mexican civil society in the United States continues. In
Mexico, some of the farmers themselves are becoming informed about
imported industrialized agriculture's risks and hazards, and indeed the
world in general is waking up to the potential health and environmental perils inherent in planting genetically modified crops and using toxic
agricultural and industrial chemicals. There is also an international
movement among sustainable agriculture advocates, largely outside the
United States, to include social justice and human rights in organic certification standards.

Whenever I have given presentations about the information in this
book, people in the audience are often taken aback and scandalized by the
extent of the oppression faced by the binational farmworker population.
Many are motivated to take immediate action and always ask how they can
assist in reversing the human rights tragedy occurring in their "backyard."
At the end of this epilogue, you will find some suggestions for action.

AN INTERNATIONAL TREATY ON PERSISTENT
ORGANIC POLLUTANTS

On May 17, 2004, the International Treaty on Persistent Organic Pollutants (POPs) officially became legal, ninety days after France became the fiftieth country to ratify the treaty. The POPs treaty, also known as the Stockholm Convention, targets twelve persistent organic pollutants for elimination. Nine of these chemicals identified by the Convention are pesticides; the other three are chemicals used frequently in industry. POPs chemicals are toxic, persist in the environment, accumulate in body fat, concentrate in food chains, and are transported around the world. Chemicals scheduled for elimination are DDT, aldrin, dieldrin, endrin, chlordane, heptachlor, hexachlorobenzene, mirex, toxaphene, polychlorinated biphenyls, dioxins, and furans.

Ironically, the United States, one of the first countries to propose an international treaty to restrict the manufacture and use of some of the most toxic chemicals, has yet to ratify the treaty. Many other POPs chemicals are still in widespread use in the United States. Pentachlorophenol (PCP), lindane, and endosulfan are highly toxic and still in use. Because of their levels of toxicity, there is an international movement to add these chemicals to the Stockholm Convention for eventual elimination from use and manufacture.

GROWING AWARENESS AMONG FARMERS IN MEXICO

In July 1999, when I interviewed agrochemical distributor and farmer Gerardo Fernandez, who lives with his family in a farming community along the shore of Lake Chapala, he was completely committed to the importation of U.S. industrial agricultural technology, including seeds, agrochemical fertilizers, pesticides, and machinery. With excitement in his voice, he spoke of the higher yields garnered through the more "advanced" U.S. agricultural technology. He invited me to his land nearby so that I could observe him planting corn seed with a rented, computerized seed-sowing tractor. In addition, Gerardo spoke of the "backward" rural villages nearby that refused to give up their traditional intercrops for more "advanced" monoculture corn production with agrochemicals.

When I interviewed him again five years later in July 2004, he had arrived at completely different conclusions. He acknowledged that, though his *parcela* planted in *maíz mejorado* yielded 10 tons of corn the first year after seed purchase, seeds from this harvest planted the next year yielded only 3 tons of corn of greatly reduced quality. He further conceded that farmers continue to use agrochemicals in the farming process, but that there is increasing interest among them in the use of organic farming input alternatives. "Farmers are beginning to recognize how damaging chemicals can be to their own health, to the health of their children and livestock, and to the environment."

The day after that interview, representatives from Agromar, a bio-organic distributor based in Ensenada, Baja California, visited the region and presented several organic fertilizer alternatives to the chemical urea in common use in Mexican farming. Most are manufactured from fish emulsion. They also introduced several organic pesticide and herbicide alternatives. Ten local farmers attended the meeting.

I presented information about the classification of agrochemicals (see appendix A). This was subsequently translated into Spanish, and each farmer received a Spanish summary of the agrochemical classification and a list of the most commonly used agrochemicals in the west-central Mexico countryside, along with their potential health and environmental impacts.

When the farmers were given an opportunity to respond to the presentations with questions and comments, most expressed astonishment at the hazards implicated in agrochemical use. They acknowledged that there were many cases of agrochemical poisoning and death in the area, and some farmers recognized their own agrochemical exposure symptoms of headaches, anxiety, watering eyes, nausea, rashes, and so forth. However, most farmers concurred that they had never heard about the dangers associated with agrochemical use, only the benefits.

In summer 2006, the farmers themselves organized to establish the entire region as an organic farming region. Some even talked about introducing mandatory municipal laws requiring the use of only organic farming practices within the boundaries of their *municipio*. To support their efforts, they have sponsored a candidate of the Mexico Green Party to run for municipal president in the next election. One farmer has applied for admission to the 2008 apprenticeship program at the Center for Agroecology and Sustainable Food Systems at the University of California, Santa Cruz, in order to learn effective sustainable, economically viable, organic farming practices so that she can then return to the region and teach others.

AN INTERNATIONAL MOVEMENT TO INCLUDE SOCIAL JUSTICE
AND HUMAN RIGHTS IN ORGANIC CERTIFICATION

Many U.S. consumers of organic produce assume that social justice and human rights standards are included in the sustainable agriculture/ organic production process. In fact, fair treatment of workers is *not* a prerequisite for organic certification. Though workers are probably better off working in organic agriculture because they are not exposed to harmful pesticides, there are no regulations to ensure that they are treated with dignity or provided with a contract and living wage as a condition of employment. Furthermore, there is no social justice enforcement policy or agency, because social justice and human rights standards have yet to be defined specifically in agriculture.

There is, however, a movement among sustainable agriculture/organic producer and labor organizations worldwide to include fair treatment of workers in the organic certification process. IFOAM, the International Federation of Organic Agriculture Movement, the largest international body of organic agricultural producers, accredits organic certifiers around the world. At least on paper, this organization favors the inclusion of social justice standards in the certification process (per Chapter 8 of the IFOAM Basic Standards).

RAFI, The Rural Advancement Foundation International, and CATA, the Comité de Apoyo a los Trabajadores Agricolas (Farm Worker Support Committee) both have put the issue of social justice for farm employees on the table in the past couple of years as part of their Agricultural Justice Project. Along with collaborating and supporting organizations that include members of the sustainable agriculture community as well as workers' organizations such as UITA (Unión Internacional de Trabajadores de la Alimentación), they have developed model standards that encourage a "high bar" for inclusion of social justice and human rights standards in organic labeling—rights that comply with conventions of the International Labour Organization (ILO) and include freedom of association (unionizing), collective bargaining rights, grower transparency, bargaining and negotiation rights, freedom from abuse, a contract, and a living wage.

The issue of resolving the disparity between current farmworker living and working conditions in California and elsewhere and the ideals presented in Article 23 of the Universal Declaration of Human Rights (see appendix B and chapter 14) is now at the forefront of the sustainable agriculture movement. The ultimate goal, fueled by public pressure, is for this trend to lead to policy change internationally.

ACTION PLAN FOR INFORMED CONSUMERS

Congratulations! Now that you have read this book, you are one of a growing number of informed consumers who are in a position to make intelligent choices regarding product purchases and your diet. California farmworker injustice continues because there is a lack of political will to develop policy designed to guarantee farmworkers the same rights that others in mainstream American society take for granted. Informed citizens can make the difference by insisting upon a socially just context of employment for farm workers. You can begin by calling or writing your local organic certifier and requesting that the social justice and human rights standards that embrace the provisions listed in the previous paragraphs be included in the organic certification process. Your closest organic certifying agent can be located on the USDA National Organic Program website at www.ams.usda.gov/nop/indexNet.htm.

There are other actions that informed consumers must take. Contact your congressional and state representatives and express your interest in immigration reform (chapters 4 and 5), renegotiating NAFTA to include the replacement of "free trade" with fair trade standards (chapter 3), developing an enforcement mechanism to hold U.S.-originating transnational corporations accountable for health and environmental damage (chapters 11 and 12), and curtailing U.S. farm subsidies that put Mexican subsistence and small producer farmers out of business (chapters 1 and 11). In the meantime, purchase fair trade products, such as fair trade Mexican coffee. By doing so, you are indirectly providing funds that give campesinos the option of staying home in Mexico on their land with their families, where the overwhelming majority of campesinos want to be.

In addition, there are many, nearly inexhaustible ways you can participate to improve the lives of the binational farmworker community (see the Preface for a review of some projects). I and a group of associates are starting a nonprofit foundation designed to provide assistance of many kinds to farmworkers in California and to Mexican subsistence farmers and their families in Mexico. If you would like to participate in or donate to the Farm Worker Family Foundation, please go to our websites: www.farmworkerfamily.org or www.familiascampesinas.org. We will regularly update you about our work and the many ways you can participate.

One might argue that it is the responsibility of the U.S. and Mexican governments to address the issues described in this book. However, the governments in fact are not addressing these issues proactively. Having studied this issue for many years, I firmly believe that it is up to concerned citizens at the grassroots level in both countries to take a stand and demand that the inordinate pain and suffering experienced by this binational population be rectified as an international priority, immediately. To that end, please join us in our efforts to clean up this often invisible, yet quite extensive social blight of our times.

You the reader and compassionate human being will make the difference. It's up to you.

AGROCHEMICAL INVENTORIES AND CLASSIFICATIONS

APPENDIX A AGROCHEMICAL INVENTORIES AND CLASSIFICATIONS

Veterinaria "Tepa," Cuquio, Jalisco, 1998 (agrochemical classifications updated May 2005)

Product	Active Ingredient(s)	PAN Rating[1]	EPA Warning[2]	Producer	Container Notes
Manzate 200 DF (66 pesós/kg)[3]	Mancozeb (most banned in U.S.)	Bad Actor	3 caution	DuPont	Fungicide; for use on tomatoes, chilis, and potatoes
Karate (65 pesos/200 mL)	Lambda-cyhalothrin (RUP[4])	Bad Actor	1 danger	Ciba Agro	Insecticide; kills corn "worm"
Gesaprim Combi 500 FW (94 pesos/L) Furadan (156 pesos/L)	Atrazine (RUP[4]) Carbofuran (RUP[4])	Bad Actor Bad Actor	3 caution 1 danger	Ciba Agro FMC Agrochemical	Herbicide Carbofuran insecticide; general insecticide; nematocide; kills corn and tomato "worm"
Sanson 4SC (360 pesos/L)	Nicosulfuron	—	3 caution	Cisk	Nicosulfuron; corn herbicide
INEX-A	—	—	—	Cosmocel	Applied prior to herbicide and/or pesticide application
Rogor 400 (73 pesos/L)	Dimethoate	Bad Actor	2 warning	Anajalsa	Insecticide
Vydate Loxamil (140 pesos/L)	Oxamyl (RUP[4])	Bad Actor	1 danger	DuPont	Insecticide/Acaracide (Altamente Toxico)
Metamidofos 600 (85 pesos/L)	Methamidophos (RUP[4])	Bad Actor	1 danger	DuPont	Insecticide; moderately toxic

Product (price)	Active ingredient	Dirty Dozen / Bad Actor	Toxicity	Company	Description
Gramoxone (65 pesos/L)	Paraquat dichloride (RUP[4])	Dirty Dozen	1 danger	Zeneca	Herbicide; applied before planting crop; moderately toxic
Disparo (126 pesos/L)	Chlorpyrifos; Permethrin (both RUP[4])	Bad Actor	2 warning	DowElanco	Fertilizer; moderately toxic
Arrivo-200CD (66 pesos/240 mL)	Cypermethrin (RUP[4])	—	—	FMC Agrochemical	Insecticide; moderately toxic
Lorsban-480EM (98 pesos/L)	Chlorpyrifos (RUP[4])	Bad Actor	2 warning	DowElanco	Insecticide; eliminates corn and sorghum "worm"; sorghum "mosca miche"
Agroc-N-20	—	—	—	Agrofriends	Insecticide
Counter FC-156	Terbufos (RUP[4])	Bad Actor	1 danger	Cyanamid	Mixed with fertilizer; applied as pesticide for soil pests
Asufre-Paration Metalico	Parathion (banned in U.S.)	Dirty Dozen	1 danger	—	Insecticide; for use on strawberries
Previcur N	Propamocarb hydrochloride	—	3 caution	AgroEvo-US	Fungicide; root diseases
SuperCoral ADH-30% 22 pesos/L	—	—	—	INCO	Fertilizer
Bayfolan (90 pesos/L)	(Vitamin)	—	—	Bayer de Mexico	Foliar fertilizer
Marvel (95 pesos/L)	Dicamba; Atrazine (both RUP[4])	Bad Actors	3 caution	Sandoz Agricola	Herbicide; destroys spiny weeds
Tamaron 600 (90 pesos/L)	Methamidophos (RUP[4])	Bad Actor	1 danger	Bayer	Mining insects; highly toxic
Navajo 2,4-D Amina (55 pesos/L)	2,4-D Amine (not registered for use in U.S.)	—	3 caution	DuPont	Herbicide
Basagran-408 (185 pesos/L)	Bentazon, sodium salt	Bad Actor	1 danger	BASF Corporation	Herbicide

Product	Active Ingredient(s)	PAN Rating[1]	EPA Warning[2]	Producer	Container Notes
Toxiton 50%; Paration Metalico	Parathion (banned in U.S.)	Dirty Dozen	1 danger	IDOSA	Insecticide; extremely toxic
Folidol M-50-Paration Metalico	Parathion (banned in U.S.)	Dirty Dozen	1 danger	Bayer	Insecticide; for use on bean pests
Nuvanol 50LS	Fenitrothion	Bad Actor	2 warning	—	Insecticide; extremely toxic

Veterinaria "Tepa," Cuquio, Jalisco, Summer 2006

Product	Active Ingredient(s)	PAN Rating[1]	EPA Warning[2]	Producer	Container Notes
Desmonte-A	2,4-D amine	Bad Actor	—	—	Herbicide; moderately toxic
Hierbamina	2,4-D	—	—	Syngenta	Herbicide; moderately toxic
Chapoleo-A	2,4-D amine	Bad Actor	—	Cheminova Agro de Mexico	Moderately toxic
Secazone	Paraquat dichloride (RUP[3])	Dirty Dozen	—	Cheminova Agro de Mexico	Moderately toxic
Aatrex Combi	Atrazine-terbutrin (RUP[3])	Bad Actor	—	Ducor: Sociedad de Dupont	Slightly toxic
Nufarmester 2,4-D	2,4-D butyl ester	—	—	Ducor: Sociedad de Dupont	Moderately toxic

Product	Active Ingredient(s)	PAN Rating	EPA Warning	Manufacturer	Toxicity
Estéron, 47M 2,4-D	2,4-D, butyl ester	—	—	Dow Agrosciences	Moderately toxic
Tordon 101	Picloram; 2,4-D triisopropanolamine salt (RUP[3])	Bad Actor	1 danger	Dow Agrosciences	Moderately toxic
Arrasina 90 DF	Atrazine (RUP[3])	Bad Actor	—	Cheminova Agro de Mexico	—
Harmony	Trifensulfuron-methyl; Tribenuron methyl	—	3 caution	DuPont	Slightly toxic
Foley-50	2,4-D, 2-ethylhexyl ester	Bad Actor	—	—	—
Gesaprim	Atrazine (RUP[3])	Bad Actor	—	—	—
Atranex	Atrazine (RUP[3])	Bad Actor	—	—	—
Ultraquat	Poly(oxyethylene) (dimethylimino); ethylene (dimethylimino); ethylene dechloride	—	3 caution	—	—

SOURCE: The product information on this inventory was derived and cross-referenced from information obtained from the following organizations: Pesticide Action Network (www.pesticideinfo.org), the Environmental Protection Agency (www.epa.gov), and the Rachel Carson Council (http://members.aol.com/rccouncil/ourpage/samples.htm). Product formulations and pesticide classifications are subject to continuing review and potential reclassification into different categories.

[1]PAN Rating: Rating by the Pesticide Action Network. Bad Actors are chemicals that are one or more of the following: acutely toxic, cholinesterase inhibitor, known/probable carcinogen, known groundwater pollutant, or known reproductive or developmental toxicant. PAN's "Dirty Dozen" includes the world's most hazardous pesticides, which have been banned or restricted in many countries.

[2]EPA Warning: Information from the U.S. Environmental Protection Agency's acute toxicity rating by the EPA, which is reflected in the warning label on the pesticide container. The EPA gives a warning label of category 1 to the most acutely toxic pesticide products and category 4 to the least acutely toxic pesticide products. Formulated pesticide products (which usually include inert ingredients) are required to carry an acute toxicity rating by the EPA.

[3]In 1998, 8.9 pesos = US$1; the minimum wage in Zinapecuaro was 30 pesos/day.

[4]RUP: Categorization based on the restricted use products (RUP) report database as maintained by the Office of Pesticide Programs of the EPA. This compilation, last updated in 2003, includes products classified by the EPA as "restricted use." Under the rules of this classification, a product may be appled only by a certified pesticide applicator or under the direct supervision of a certified applicator.

THE UNIVERSAL DECLARATION OF HUMAN RIGHTS

On December 10, 1948 the General Assembly of the United Nations adopted and proclaimed the Universal Declaration of Human Rights the full text of which appears in the following pages. Following this historic act the Assembly called upon all Member countries to publicize the text of the Declaration and "to cause it to be disseminated, displayed, read and expounded principally in schools and other educational institutions, without distinction based on the political status of countries or territories."

Preamble

Whereas recognition of the inherent dignity and of the equal and inalienable rights of all members of the human family is the foundation of freedom, justice and peace in the world,

Whereas disregard and contempt for human rights have resulted in barbarous acts which have outraged the conscience of mankind, and the advent of a world in which human beings shall enjoy freedom of speech and belief and freedom from fear and want has been proclaimed as the highest aspiration of the common people,

Whereas it is essential, if man is not to be compelled to have recourse, as a last resort, to rebellion against tyranny and oppression, that human rights should be protected by the rule of law,

Whereas it is essential to promote the development of friendly relations between nations,

Whereas the peoples of the United Nations have in the Charter reaffirmed their faith in fundamental human rights, in the dignity and worth of the human person and in the equal rights of men and women and have determined to promote social progress and better standards of life in larger freedom,

Whereas Member States have pledged themselves to achieve, in co-operation with the United Nations, the promotion of universal respect for and observance of human rights and fundamental freedoms,

Whereas a common understanding of these rights and freedoms is of the greatest importance for the full realization of this pledge,

Now, Therefore THE GENERAL ASSEMBLY proclaims THIS UNIVERSAL DECLARATION OF HUMAN RIGHTS as a common standard of achievement for all peoples and all nations, to the end that every individual and every organ of society, keeping this Declaration constantly in mind, shall strive by teaching and education to promote respect for these rights and freedoms and by progressive measures, national and international, to secure their universal and effective recognition and observance, both among the peoples of Member States themselves and among the peoples of territories under their jurisdiction.

Article 1

All human beings are born free and equal in dignity and rights. They are endowed with reason and conscience and should act towards one another in a spirit of brotherhood.

Article 2

Everyone is entitled to all the rights and freedoms set forth in this Declaration, without distinction of any kind, such as race, colour, sex, language, religion, political or other opinion, national or social origin, property, birth or other status. Furthermore, no distinction shall be made on the basis of the political, jurisdictional or international status of the country or territory to which a person belongs, whether it be independent, trust, non-self-governing or under any other limitation of sovereignty.

Article 3

Everyone has the right to life, liberty and security of person.

Article 4

No one shall be held in slavery or servitude; slavery and the slave trade shall be prohibited in all their forms.

Article 5

No one shall be subjected to torture or to cruel, inhuman or degrading treatment or punishment.

Article 6

Everyone has the right to recognition everywhere as a person before the law.

Article 7

All are equal before the law and are entitled without any discrimination to equal protection of the law. All are entitled to equal protection against any discrimination in violation of this Declaration and against any incitement to such discrimination.

Article 8

Everyone has the right to an effective remedy by the competent national tribunals for acts violating the fundamental rights granted him by the constitution or by law.

Article 9

No one shall be subjected to arbitrary arrest, detention or exile.

Article 10

Everyone is entitled in full equality to a fair and public hearing by an independent and impartial tribunal, in the determination of his rights and obligations and of any criminal charge against him.

Article 11

(1) Everyone charged with a penal offence has the right to be presumed innocent until proved guilty according to law in a public trial at which he has had all the guarantees necessary for his defence.

(2) No one shall be held guilty of any penal offence on account of any act or omission which did not constitute a penal offence, under national or international law, at the time when it was committed. Nor shall a heavier penalty be imposed than the one that was applicable at the time the penal offence was committed.

Article 12

No one shall be subjected to arbitrary interference with his privacy, family, home or correspondence, nor to attacks upon his honour and reputation. Everyone has the right to the protection of the law against such interference or attacks.

Article 13

(1) Everyone has the right to freedom of movement and residence within the borders of each state.

(2) Everyone has the right to leave any country, including his own, and to return to his country.

Article 14

(1) Everyone has the right to seek and to enjoy in other countries asylum from persecution.

(2) This right may not be invoked in the case of prosecutions genuinely arising from non-political crimes or from acts contrary to the purposes and principles of the United Nations.

Article 15

(1) Everyone has the right to a nationality.

(2) No one shall be arbitrarily deprived of his nationality nor denied the right to change his nationality.

Article 16

(1) Men and women of full age, without any limitation due to race, nationality or religion, have the right to marry and to found a family. They are entitled to equal rights as to marriage, during marriage and at its dissolution.

(2) Marriage shall be entered into only with the free and full consent of the intending spouses.

(3) The family is the natural and fundamental group unit of society and is entitled to protection by society and the State.

Article 17

(1) Everyone has the right to own property alone as well as in association with others.

(2) No one shall be arbitrarily deprived of his property.

Article 18

Everyone has the right to freedom of thought, conscience and religion; this right includes freedom to change his religion or belief, and freedom, either alone or in community with others and in public or private, to manifest his religion or belief in teaching, practice, worship and observance.

Article 19

Everyone has the right to freedom of opinion and expression; this right includes freedom to hold opinions without interference and to seek, receive and impart information and ideas through any media and regardless of frontiers.

Article 20

(1) Everyone has the right to freedom of peaceful assembly and association.

(2) No one may be compelled to belong to an association.

Article 21

(1) Everyone has the right to take part in the government of his country, directly or through freely chosen representatives.

(2) Everyone has the right of equal access to public service in his country.

(3) The will of the people shall be the basis of the authority of government; this will shall be expressed in periodic and genuine elections which shall be by universal and equal suffrage and shall be held by secret vote or by equivalent free voting procedures.

Article 22

Everyone, as a member of society, has the right to social security and is entitled to realization, through national effort and international co-operation and in accordance with the organization and resources of each State, of the economic, social and cultural rights indispensable for his dignity and the free development of his personality.

Article 23

(1) Everyone has the right to work, to free choice of employment, to just and favourable conditions of work and to protection against unemployment.

(2) Everyone, without any discrimination, has the right to equal pay for equal work.

(3) Everyone who works has the right to just and favourable remuneration ensuring for himself and his family an existence worthy of human dignity, and supplemented, if necessary, by other means of social protection.

(4) Everyone has the right to form and to join trade unions for the protection of his interests.

Article 24

Everyone has the right to rest and leisure, including reasonable limitation of working hours and periodic holidays with pay.

Article 25

(1) Everyone has the right to a standard of living adequate for the health and well-being of himself and of his family, including food, clothing, housing and medical care and necessary social services, and the right to security in the event of unemployment, sickness, disability, widowhood, old age or other lack of livelihood in circumstances beyond his control.

(2) Motherhood and childhood are entitled to special care and assistance. All children, whether born in or out of wedlock, shall enjoy the same social protection.

Article 26

(1) Everyone has the right to education. Education shall be free, at least in the elementary and fundamental stages. Elementary education shall be compulsory. Technical and professional education shall be made generally available and higher education shall be equally accessible to all on the basis of merit.

(2) Education shall be directed to the full development of the human personality and to the strengthening of respect for human rights and fundamental freedoms. It shall promote understanding, tolerance and friendship among all nations, racial or religious groups, and shall further the activities of the United Nations for the maintenance of peace.

(3) Parents have a prior right to choose the kind of education that shall be given to their children.

Article 27

(1) Everyone has the right freely to participate in the cultural life of the community, to enjoy the arts and to share in scientific advancement and its benefits.

(2) Everyone has the right to the protection of the moral and material interests resulting from any scientific, literary or artistic production of which he is the author.

Article 28

Everyone is entitled to a social and international order in which the rights and freedoms set forth in this Declaration can be fully realized.

Article 29

(1) Everyone has duties to the community in which alone the free and full development of his personality is possible.

(2) In the exercise of his rights and freedoms, everyone shall be subject only to such limitations as are determined by law solely for the purpose of securing due recognition and respect for the rights and freedoms of others and of meeting the just requirements of morality, public order and the general welfare in a democratic society.

(3) These rights and freedoms may in no case be exercised contrary to the purposes and principles of the United Nations.

Article 30

Nothing in this Declaration may be interpreted as implying for any State, group or person any right to engage in any activity or to perform any act aimed at the destruction of any of the rights and freedoms set forth herein.

REFERENCES

Associated Press and Agence France Presse news reports are archived by Lexis-Nexis and can be accessed by searching author or keyword at www.lexis-nexis.com. Inter Press Service reports are archived at www .ipsnews.net.

Acevedo, D., and T. J. Espenshade. 1992. Implications of the North American Free Trade Agreement for Mexican Migration into the United States. *Population and Development Review* 18(4): 729–744.

Agence France Presse. 2001. Freed Mexican Ecologists Call for Democracy, End of Torture. November 9.

Agricultural Worker Charitable Trust. 2005. *Fact Sheet: Who Is the American Agricultural Worker?* www.awct.org/FactSheet1.

Aguirre International. 2000. No Longer Children: Case Studies of the Living and Working Conditions of the Youth Who Harvest America's Crops Executive Summary, submitted to the Office of the Assistant Secretary for Policy, U.S. Department of Labor, Washington, DC.

———. 2005. *The California Farm Labor Force: Overview and Trends from the National Agricultural Workers Survey.* www.epa.gov/region09/ag/docs/final -naws-s092805.pdf.

Ahn, C., M. Moore, and N. Parker. 2004. Migrant Farmworkers: America's New Plantation Workers. *Backgrounder* (Food First: Institute for Food and Development Policy) 10(2): 4.

Alarcón, R., and R. Mines. 2001. Options for U.S. Labor Intensive Agriculture: Perpetuation of the Status Quo or Transition to a New Labor Market? In A. López (ed.), *Forum for Transnational Employment: A Dialogue on Alternatives to the Status Quo in Immigrant-Labor Dominated Industries.* California Institute for Rural Studies, Davis.

Allen, J. L., Jr. 1998. Activists See Threat to Food Supply in Form of New "Terminator Technology." *National Catholic Reporter* 34(28): 6.

Almaguer, T. 1994. *Racial Fault Lines: The Historical Origins of White Supremacy in California.* University of California Press, Berkeley.

Alonso, A. M. 1992. Work and Gusto: Gender and Re-creation in a North Mexican Pueblo. In J. Calagione et al. (eds.), *Workers' Expressions: Beyond Accomodation and Resistance.* State University of New York Press, Albany.

Alonso-Zaldivar. 2005. High-Tech Border Fence along Mexico Is Proposed. *San Jose Mercury News,* October 4.

Alvarez-Icaza, P., G. Cervera, C. Garibay, P. Gutiérrez, and F. Rosete. 1993. *Los Umbrales del Deterioro: La Dimensió Ambiental de un Desarrollo Desigual en la Región Purépecha.* Programa de Aprovechamiento Integral de Recursos Naturales y Desarrollo Social en Areas de Subsistencia. PAIR-UNAM Michoacán.

American Family Physician. 1984. Caffeine Addiction. *American Family Physician* 30(1): 272.

Amnesty International. 2001. Montiel and Cabrera Released. Environmental Defenders Still Experiencing Harassment: Urgent Action Needed, November 8. www.amnestyusa.org/justearth/countries/mexico2.html.

Anderson, S. 1999. *Five Years under NAFTA.* Institute for Policy Studies, Washington, DC.

Andow, D. H. Daniell, P. Gepts, K. Lamkey, E. Nafziger, and D. Strayer. 2004. Technical Report. In D. Andow (ed.), *A Growing Concern: Protecting the Food Supply in an Era of Pharmaceutical and Industrial Crops.* Union of Concerned Scientists, UCS Publications, Cambridge, MA.

Annerino, J. 1999. *Dead in Their Tracks: Crossing America's Desert Borderlands.* Four Walls Eight Windows, New York.

A.N.S.W.E.R. 2006. The Largest Demonstration in the History of California: Over 1 Million Protest in Los Angeles for Immigrant Rights! www.answer coalition.org.

Anway, M. D., A. S. Cupp, M. Uzumcu, and M. K. Skinner. 2005. Epigenetic Transgenerational Actions of Endocrine Disruptors and Male Fertility. *Science* 308:1466–1469.

Appendini, K. 1997. Changing Agrarian Institutions: Interpreting the Contradictions. In W. A. Cornelius and D. Myhre (eds.), *The Transformation of Rural Mexico: Reforming the Ejido Sector.* Center for U.S.-Mexican Studies, University of California, San Diego.

Appleby, A. 2004. Conservationists Strive to Bring Peace and Pride to Communities Plagued by Conflict. Rare newsroom, December 15. www.rare conservation.org.

Arax, M. 2000. Farmers Using More Chemicals. *Los Angeles Times,* March 29.

Arlacchi, P. 2000. (Director General, UN Office for Crime Control and Drug Prevention) quoted in *Migration World* 28(4): 4.

Armas, G. C. 2002. Population of Illegal Immigrants in U.S. Doubled in 1990's, Census Bureau Says. Associated Press, January 23.

———. 2003. "Hispanics Comprise Most of U.S. Growth." Associated Press, June 18.

————. 2004. Hispanic, Asian Populations Still Growing. Associated Press, June 14.

Arnold, A. 2002. Stressed by Housing Costs, Californians Can't Afford to Feed Their Children. *Weaving the Food Web: Community Food Security in California.* Community Food Security Coalition, Venice, CA.

Associated Press. 2001. Commission Will Make It Easier for Mexicans Living in the U.S. to Send Money Home. Associated Press, November 13.

———— 2002. Coke Accused of Selling Old Soda to Minorities. Associated Press, May 21.

———— 2003 People in 96 Percent of Mexican Cities and Towns Migrate to the U.S. Associated Press, June 26.

AWQA. 2005. Crop Statistics. Agriculture Water Quality Alliance. www.mb nms.nos.noaa.gov/awqa/ag/statistics.

AxKC. 2006. www.AxKC.net.

Baca, K. 2002. Farm Workers More Likely to Get Cancer, Report Says. *Santa Cruz Sentinel,* March 18.

Bach, R. L. 1978. Mexican Immigration and the American State. *International Migration Review* 12(4): 536–558.

Bacon, D. 2005a. *Talking Points on Guest Workers.* www.truthout.org/cgi-bin/artman/exec/view.cgi/36/12611.

————. 2005b. The Border Is a Common Ground between Us. Truthout/Perspective. www.truthout.org/docs__2005/121905G.shtml.

Bada, X., J. Fox, and A. Selee. 2006. Al Fin Visibles: La Presencia Cívica de los Migrantes Mexicanos en los Estados Unidos. Woodrow Wilson International Center for Scholars. www.wilsoncenter.org/news/docs/Invisible%20No%20More.pdf.

Badger, T. A. 2003. Putting Names to Bodies on Border. *USA Today,* October 1.

Baird, P., and E. McCaughan. 1979. *Beyond the Border: Mexico & the U.S. Today.* North American Congress on Latin America, New York.

Baldassare, M. 2004. *Special Survey on Californians and Their Housing.* Public Policy Institute of California, San Francisco.

Barbassa J. 2006. Organic Growers Suffer from a Labor Shortage. *Albuquerque Journal,* August 20.

Barkema, A. 1992. The North American Free Trade Agreement: What Is at Stake for U.S. Agriculture? *Economic Review* 77: 5–20.

Barnett, A. 2000. "Junkie" GM Gene Threat to Third World Farmers. *Observer,* April 2.

Barnett, P. G. 1989. Survey of Research on the Impacts of Pesticides on Agricultural Workers and the Rural Environment. California Institute for Rural Studies, Working Paper 2, Davis.

Barry, T. 1992. *Mexico: A Country Guide.* Inter-Hemispheric Education Resource Center, Albuquerque, NM.

————. 1995. *Zapata's Revenge: Free Trade and the Farm Crisis in Mexico.* South End Press, Boston.

————. 2003. *Death on the Border.* Americas Program, Interhemispheric Resource Center, Silver City, NM. www.americaspolicy.org/columns/am prog/2003/0303death.html.

Bazeley, M., and C. Kang. 2001. Region's Wealth Leads U.S. *San Jose Mercury News,* November 20.

BBC News 2006. DDT "Link" to Slow Child Progress. http://newsvote.bbc .co.uk/2/hi/health/5145450.stm.

Beamish, R. 2005. Despite Ban, Farmers Still Use Pesticide. Associated Press, November 27.

Becker, M. 1995. *Setting the Virgin on Fire: Lázaro Cárdenas, Michoacán Peasants, and the Redemption of the Mexican Revolution.* University of California Press, Berkeley.

Bejarano, F. G. 1993. NAFTA Threatens Mexico's Rural Sector, Neglects Crucial Issues. *Global Pesticide Campaigner.* Pesticide Action Network North America. February. www.panna.org/resources/pestis/PESTIS.burst.368.html.

Benbrook, C. M. 2003. *Impacts of Genetically Engineered Crops on Pesticide Use in the United States: The First Eight Years.* Biotech InfoNet. Technical Paper Number 6. Benbrook Consulting Services. Northwest Science and Environmental Policy Center, Sandpoint, ID. www.biotech-info.net/Technical_Paper_6.pdf.

Berkowitz, B. 2005a. The Minutemen and the Media: Mainstream News Overlooks Vigilante Group's Ties to White Supremacists. Working for Change. www.workingforchange.com/article.cfm?itemid = 19008.

———. 2005b. Minutemen to Spread Wings: Anti-Immigrant Group Pledges to Bring 15,000 Volunteers to Both the Mexican and Canadian Borders for Month-Long Vigils Starting October 1. Working for Change. www.work ingforchange.com/article.cfm?itemid=19501.

Bethel, J. W., and M. B. Schenker. 2005. Acculturation and Smoking Patterns among Hispanics: A Review. *American Journal of Preventive Medicine* 29(2).

Beyond Pesticides. 2001a. Glyphosate. ChemicalWATCH Factsheet 21, no. 1. www.beyondpesticides.org.

———. 2001b. Scientists Find Strong Evidence That Pesticides Play a Role in Parkinson's. Daily News Archives, April 2. www.beyondpesticides.org.

———. 2002. Increase in U.S. Pesticide Exports. Daily News Archives, January 14. www.beyondpesticides.org.

———. 2005. Genetically Modified Corn Causes Blood, Kidney Abnormalities in Rats. Daily News, June 6. www.beyondpesticides.org.

——— 2006. Research Reveals Link between Pesticides and Motor Neuron Disease. February 3. www.beyondpesticides.org/news/daily_news_archive/2006/02_03_06.htm.

Billeaud, J. 2006a. Ariz. Governor Orders Troops to Border. Associated Press, March 8.

———. 2006b. Business Raids Breathe Life into Plans for Boycott, Work Stoppage. Associated Press, April 24.

Blanco, J. L., and R. R. Manila. 2001. Consecuencias de la Explosión de Una Planta Mezcladora de Plaguicidas. *La Jornada,* April 26.

Bletzer, K. V. 2004. Open Towns and Manipulated Indebtedness among Agricultural Workers in the New South. *Ethnologist* 31(4): 530–551.

Boerner, H. 2001. Housing Crunch Caps County Report. *Santa Cruz Sentinel,* October 14.

Bogado, A. 2006. California Students Defy Lockdown, Walk out for Immigrant Rights. *NewStandard,* March 30.

Booth, W. 2000. Immigrants/Ranchers in Border Battle. *San Jose Mercury News,* March 22.

Border Action Network. 2004. *Globalization and Migration.* December 1. www.borderaction.org/resources2.php?articleID=4.

Bower, B. 2004. Immigration Blues: Born in the U.S.: Mental Health Deficit. *Science News,* December 18.

Brand, C. 2003. EU OKs Tough New Rules on Biotech Foods. Associated Press, July 2.

Brasher, P. 2002. Farmers Increase Compliance with Biotech Corn Rules, Survey Says. Associated Press, February 5.

Brezosky, L. 2005. Border Volunteers Not So Welcomed in Texas. Associated Press, June 4.

Britton, J. 1998. Exporting Tobacco Addiction from the USA. *Lancet* 352(9122): 152.

Brown, D. 2006. Study: Smokes Pack Bigger Punch. *San Jose Mercury News,* August 31.

Bruno, K. 1992. *The Greenpeace Book on Greenwash.* Greenpeace International, Washington, DC.

Burton, M. L., and D. R. White. 1987. Sexual Division of Labor in Agriculture. In M. D. Maclachlan (ed.), *Household Economics and Their Transformations.* Monographs in Economic Anthropology. University Press of America. Lanham, MD.

Burton, T. 1997. Can Mexico's Largest Lake Be Saved? *Ecodecision: An Environmental and Policy Magazine* 23 (Winter).

———. 2000. Can Mexico's Largest Lake Be Saved? A Year 2000 Update: The State of the Lake. www.mexconnect.com/mex_/travel/tonysarticles/tblagunasaved2.html.

———. 2001. Can Mexico's Largest Lake Be Saved? A Year 2001 Update, Part 3: The Future of Lake Chapala, Suggestions for Discussion. www.mexconnect.com/mex_/travel/tonysarticles/tblagunasaved2.html.

Bustamante, J. A. 1989. Measuring the Flow of Undocumented Immigrants. In W. A. Cornelius and J. A. Bustamante (eds.), *Mexican Migration to the United States: Origins, Consequences, and Policy Options.* Dimensions of U.S.-Mexican Relations, Vol. 3, Center for U.S.-Mexican Studies, University of California, San Diego.

Bybee, R., and C. Winter. 2006. Immigration Flood Unleashed by NAFTA's Disastrous Impact on Mexican Economy. April. www.CommonDreams.org.

Cain, B. 2002. Oregon Measure Aims at Modified Foods. Associated Press, August 12.

Calavita, K. 1989. Recent Works on Immigration Policymaking: A Review Essay and Agenda for the Future. *Law and Society Review* 23(5): 779.

California Agricultural Statistics Service. 1997. *1997 County Agricultural Commissioner's Data.* U.S. Department of Agriculture and State of California Department of Food and Agriculture, Agricultural Statistics Branch. Sacramento.

————. 2003. *2003 County Agricultural Commissioners' Data*. U.S. Department of Agriculture. Agricultural Statistics Branch, State of California Department of Food and Agriculture, Sacramento.

California Statistical Abstract. 2003. California Department of Finance, Sacramento.

California Strawberry Commission. 2001. 2001 Acreage Survey Results. Strawberry Review. January 2001. www.calstrawberry.com.

————. 2004. California Strawberry Export Report 2004. www.calstrawberry.com.

————. 2005. Strawberry Review: 2005 Acreage Survey Results. www.calstrawberry.com.

California Teacher. 2004. Union Joins International Boycott of Coca-Cola Products. *California Teacher* 58(2): 5.

Call, W., J. Ross, and Mexico Solidarity Network. 2002. New Corporate Development from Southeastern Mexico to Panama: Plan Puebla Panama. Acción para La Comunidad y La Ecología en Las Regiones de Centroamericana. www.asej.org/ACERCA/plan_pueblo_panama.

Camarota, S. A. 2004. *Economy Slowed, But Immigration Didn't: The Foreign-Born Population, 2000–2004*. Center for Immigration Studies, Washington, DC.

Campos, P. V., and S. Kotkin-Jaszi. 1987. *California Farmworkers Enumeration Report*. California Department of Health and Human Services, Sacramento.

Carlsen, L. 2003. *Analysis on the Tenth Anniversary of NAFTA*. Institute for Public Accuracy. www.americaspolicy.org/columns/amprog/2003/0305nafta_body.

Carpentier, C., and H. Herrmann. 2004. *Maize and Biodiversity: The Effects of Transgenic Maize in Mexico*. Issues Summary. Secretariat of the Commission for Environmental Cooperation of North America, Montreal, Quebec.

Carral, M. 2003. *Migration and Security Policy Post-9/11: Mexico and the United States*. Second North American Meeting of the Trilateral Commission, Mexican National Migration Institute. October 14–16. www.trilateral.org/NAGp/regmtgs/nycpdf_folder/migration_security.pdf.

Carrol, S. 2003. Arizona Border Grows Deadlier. *Arizona Republic,* July 17.

Carter, C. A. 1997. International Trade and Pacific Rim Issues. In J. Siebert (ed.), *California Agriculture: Issues and Challenges*. University of California, Department of Agriculture and Natural Resources, Oakland.

Castañeda, X., and P. Zavella. 2003. Changing Constructions of Sexuality and Risk: Migrant Mexican Women Farmworkers in California. *Journal of Latin American Anthropology* 8(2): 126–150.

Castro, G. L. 1986. *La Casa Dividida: Un Estudio de Caso sobre la Migración a Estados Unidos en Un Pueblo Michoacano*. El Colegio de Michoacán, Zamora.

CBS News. 2005. More Migrants Dying to Get In. *60 Minutes,* December 10.

CEC. 1999. *Assessing Environmental Effects of the North American Free Trade Agreement (NAFTA): An Analytic Framework (Phase II)and Issues Studies*. Environment and Trade Series. Commission for Environmental Cooperation, Montreal.

Cevallos, D. 2001. México: Farmers Protest Fox's Policy. Inter Press Service, September 10.

Chavez, L. R. 1992. *Shadowed Lives: Undocumented Immigrants in American Society*. Harcourt Brace Jovanovich, New York.

———. 1997. Immigration Reform and Nativism: The Nationalist Response to the Transnationalist Challenge. In J. Perea (ed.), *Immigrants Out! The New Nativism and the Anti-Immigrant Impulse in the United States*. New York University Press, New York.

Ching, L. L. 2006. Moratorium on Terminator Technology Reaffirmed, but with Qualifications. Organic Consumers Association. January 29. www.organic consumers.org/ge/terminator013106.cfm.

Cinciripini, P. M., S. S. Hecht, J. D. Henningfield, M. W. Manley, and B. S. Kramer. 1997. Tobacco Addiction: Implications for Treatment and Cancer Prevention. *Journal of the National Cancer Institute* 89:1852–1867.

Clancy, M. 2006. Arizona Guard Heads to Mexico Border. *Arizona Republic*, June 14. www.news.azcentral.com.

Clapp, R. W., G. K. Howe, and M. M. Jacobs 2005. *Environmental and Occupational Causes of Cancer: A Review of Recent Scientific Literature*. Lowell Center for Sustainable Production, University of Massachusetts, Lowell.

Cleeland, N. 1999. When the Foreman Is Dad. *Los Angeles Times*, September 23.

Cockcroft, J. D. 1998. *Mexico's Hope: An Encounter with Politics and History*. Monthly Review Press, New York.

Coghlan, A. 2005. Exposure to Pesticides Can Cause Parkinson's. NewScientist.com, June 7. www.newscientist.com.

Cohn, D. 2001. Experts Ponder Apparent Spike in Number of Illegal Immigrants. *San Jose Mercury News*, March 18.

Consejo Nacional de Población. 2004. *Migración Mexicana Hacia los Estados Unidos*. www.conapo.gob.mx/prensa/migracion.htm.

Consumer Reports. 1999. Seeds of Change. *Consumer Reports*, September.

———. 2005. Lower-Sugar Foods: Some Are Diet Traps. *Consumer Reports*, February.

Contreras, C. C. 1987. The Agricultural Sector's Contributions to the Import Substituting Industrialization Process in Mexico. In B. F. Johnston, C. Luiselli, C. C. Contreras, and R. D. Norton (eds.), *U.S.-Mexico Relations: Agriculture and Rural Development*. Stanford University Press, Stanford, CA.

Cooper, M. 2006. Pro-Immigrant Marches Surging Nation. *Nation*, April 10.

Cordoba, A. 1974. *La Política de Masas del Cardenismo*. ERA, Mexico City.

Cornelius, W. A. 1989a. Impacts of the 1986 U.S. Immigration Law on Emigration from Rural Mexico. *Population and Development Review* 15(4): 695.

———. 1989b. The U.S. Demand for Mexican Labor. In W. A. Cornelius and J. A. Bustamante (eds.), *Mexican Migration to the United States: Origins, Consequences, and Policy Options*. Center for U.S.-Mexican Studies, University of California, San Diego.

Cornelius, W. A., and P. L. Martin. 1993. *Uncertain Connection*. Center for U.S.-Mexican Studies, University of California, San Diego.

Cox, C. 1992. Diazinon Fact Sheet. *Journal of Pesticide Reform* 12(3). Northwest Coalition for Alternatives to Pesticides. Eugene, OR. www.panna.org/resources/pestis/PESTIS.burst.708.html.

————. 1995. Glyphosate, Part 2: Human Exposure and Ecological Effects. *Journal of Pesticide Reform* (Northwest Coalition for Alternatives to Pesticides, Eugene, OR) 15(4).

Cumberland, C. 1968. *Mexico: The Struggle for Modernity*. Oxford University Press, New York.

Cunningham, W. P., and B. W. Saigo. 1999. *Environmental Science: A Global Concern*. 5th ed. WCB McGraw-Hill, Burr Ridge, IL.

————. 2001. *Environmental Science: A Global Concern*. 6th ed. WCB McGraw-Hill, Burr Ridge, IL.

Dalton, J. 2003. Immigrating to Doubts on Globalization. *Arizona Republic*, June 19.

Dane, A. J., C. R. Havey, and K. J. Voorhees. 2006. The Detection of Nitro Pesticides in Mainstream and Sidestream Cigarette Smoke Using Electron Monochromator-Mass Spectrometry. *Analytical Chemistry* 78(10): 3227–3233.

Daniell, H., and P. Gepts. 2004. Alternative Pharma Crops. In D. Andow (ed.), *A Growing Concern: Protecting the Food Supply in an Era of Pharmaceutical and Industrial Crops*. Union of Concerned Scientists, Cambridge, MA.

Das, R., A. Steege, S. Baron, J. Beckman, and R. Harrison. 2005. *Pesticide-Related Illness among Migrant Farm Workers in the United States*. California Department of Health Services. Occupational Health Branch, Oakland.

Datson, T. 2004. Coca-Cola Admits That Dasani Is Nothing but Tap Water. Reuters, March 4. www.commondreams.org/headlines04/0304-04.htm.

Davis, S. 2000. OSHA Issues Proposed Ergonomics Standard Excluding Farmworkers. *Farmworker Justice News* 12(1): 1–2.

Daynard, R. A., and M. Gottlieb. 2001. Tobacco Class Actions Fire Up: Courts Are Certifying More Class Actions Brought against the Tobacco Industry by Injured Consumers Seeking Damages or Help with Their Addiction and by Other Parties Harmed by Cigarette Makers. *Trial* (Association of Trial Lawyers of America) 37(12): 18–24.

de Anda, J., H. Shear, U. Maniak, and P. F. Z. del Valle. 2004. Solids Distribution in Lake Chapala, Mexico. *Journal of the American Water Resources Association* 40(1): 97–109.

de Janvry, A., D. Runsten, and E. Sadoulet. 1988. Toward a Rural Development Program for the United States: A Proposal. In *Agriculture and Beyond: Rural Economic Development*. College of Agriculture and Life Sciences, University of Wisconsin, Madison.

de la Torre, A. 2002. *Children of Immigration* (book review). *Journal of Latinos and Education* 1(2): 145–146.

del Castillo, G., and R. A. Garcia. 1995. *Cesar Chavez: A Triumph of Spirit*. University of Oklahoma Press, Norman.

Delgado, J. J. 1996. *Los Migrantes en Tijuana*. Análisis de la Realidad Mexicana No. 21. Universidad Iberoamericana, Mexico City.

Delgado-Gaitan, C. 1990. *Literacy for Empowerment: The Role of Parents in Children's Education*. Falmer, Philadelphia.

del Pinal, J., and J. M. Garcia. 1993. Hispanic Americans Today. In *Current Population Reports*. U.S. Census Bureau, Population Division, Washington, DC.

del Pinal, J., and A. Singer. 1997. *Generations of Diversity: Latinos in the United States*. Population Bulletin, Population Reference Bureau, Washington, DC.

del Toro, A. L., and L. Vives. 2006. Major Church Groups Back Undocumented Workers. Inter Press Service, March 28.

De Sá, K. 2001. Culture Central in Case against Gynecologist. *San Jose Mercury News*, July 23.

Devraj. R. 2005. Calls to Ban GM Crops Intensify after Rats Suffer. Inter Press Service, June 6.

DeWalt, B. R., M. W. Rees, and A. D. Murphy. 1994. *The End of Agrarian Reform in Mexico: Past Lessons, Future Prospects*. Center for U.S.-Mexican Studies, University of California, San Diego.

Diringer, J. D., and A. Gilman. 2006. Paradox in Paradise: Hidden Health Inequities on California's Central Coast. Diringer and Associates, San Luis Obispo, CA.

Dominican Hospital. 2003. Santa Cruz County Community Assessment Project: Summary Report. *Focus on Health* 8(6): 6–7.

———. 2004. Santa Cruz County Community Assessment Project: Summary Report, Economy. *Focus on Health* 8(7): 8–9.

Drewnowski, A., and S. E. Specter. 2004. Poverty and Obesity: The Role of Energy Density and Energy Costs. *American Journal of Clinical Nutrition* 79:6–16.

Durand, J. 2000. Tres Premisas para Entender y Explicar la Migración México-Estados Unidos. *Relaciones: Estudios de Historia y Sociedad* (El Colegio de Michoacán, Zamora) 21(83): 19–35.

Dyer-Leal, G., and A. Yúnez-Naude. 2003. *NAFTA and Conservation of Maize Diversity in Mexico*. Commission for Environmental Cooperation, Montreal.

Elias, P. 2002. Corn Study Spurs Debate over Corporate Meddling in Academia. *Santa Cruz Sentinel*, April 22.

Ellington, K. 2001. INS Begins Tougher Checks at Mexican Border. *Los Angeles Times*, October 18.

Elser, A. 2005. US Republicans Introduce Tough Immigration Bill. Reuters, July 19. www.amren.com/mtnews/archives/2005/07/US_republicans.php.

Employment Development Department. 2000. *Occupational Employment and Wage Data 1998: Occupational Employment Statistics (OES) Survey Results*. U.S. Department of Labor, Bureau of Labor Statistics, Washington, DC.

Engdahl, W. 2005. Seeds of Destruction: The Geopolitics of Frankenfoods. Organic Consumers Association. February 14. www.currentconcerns.ch/archive/2004/05/20040505.php.

Enriquez, S. 2006. Maps Show Illegal Migrants Best Routes. *Los Angeles Times*, January 25.

Environmental Protection Agency. 2001. U.S. Methyl Bromide Phase Out: Historical Notes on the U.S. Phase Out Schedule. www.epa.gov.

Environmental Working Group. 2006a. Across Generations: Mothers and Daughters. The Industrial Chemical Pollution Mothers and Daughters Share and Inherit. www.ewg.org/reports/generations.php.

————. 2006b. Stolen Inventory: Bush Proposal Would Allow Industry to Pollute California Communities without Notifying the Public. www.ewg.org/reports/ca_tri2006/php.

Environment News Service. 2001. Tortured Appeal of Mexican Ecologists Denied. Lycos Network. http://ens.lycos.com/ens/jul2001/2001L-07-18-02.html.

ETC Group. 2003. Rural Advancement Foundation International (RAFI) Oligopoly, Inc.: Concentration in Corporate Power: 2003. Communiqué, No. 82. www.etcgroup.org.

————. 2006. UN Upholds Moratorium on Terminator Seed Technology. March 31. www.etcgroup.org/article.asp?newsid=556.

Evans, D. 2002. EU: Global GM Crop Plantings Top 50 Million Hectares. www.farmsource.com/News_Trends/newsarticles.asp?ID = 31734.

Fanjul, G, and A. Fraser. 2003. *Dumping without Borders: How US Agricultural Policies Are Destroying the Livelihoods of Mexican Corn Farmers.* Oxfam Briefing Paper. Oxfam International, Washington, DC.

Farm Worker Pesticide Project, Farmworker Justice Fund, and United Farm Workers. 2005. *Messages from Monitoring: Farm Workers, Pesticides and the Need for Reform.* February 8. www.fwjustice.org.

Faux, J. 2003. "How NAFTA Failed Mexico: Immigration Is Not a Development Policy. *American Prospect* 14(7).

————. 2006. What Bush's Speech on Immigration Will Miss. *Counterpunch,* May 15.

Feagin, J. R. 1997. Old Poison in New Bottles: The Deep Roots of Modern Nativism. In J. F. Perea (ed.), *Immigrants Out! The New Nativism and the Anti-Immigrant Impulse in the United States.* New York University Press, New York.

Feder, B. 2001. Study Cites Barriers to Treatment of Mental Ills. *San Jose Mercury News,* August 27.

Federal Interagency Forum on Child and Family Statistics. 2005. *America's Children: Key National Indicators of Well-Being 2005.* http://childstats.gov.pubs.asp.

Feller, B. 2003. Coca-Cola, Education Groups Agree on Guidelines for Drink Sales. Associated Press, November 14.

Fernandes, F. 2005. Hunger for Jobs Forces Laborers to Put Their Health on the Line. *UC Mexus News* 42:6–15.

Fernández, A. T. 1987. Research and Technology for Mexico's Small Farmers. In B. F. Johnston, C. Luiselli, C. C.Contreras, and R. D. Norton (eds.), *U.S.-Mexico Relations: Agriculture and Rural Development.* Stanford University Press, Stanford, CA.

Figueroa, H. 1995. Uso de Insecticidas y Pesticidas en el Campo Agrícola del Edo. De Efectos Adversos en la Salud Humana y del Medio Ambiente. *CICOPLAFEST Journal de Medicine* 4:chap. 2.

Financial Times Information. 2001. México-US Remittances of Mexicans in U.S. Increase 40 Percent This Year. *Financial Times Information* (London), November 2.

FitzSimmons, M. 1986. The New Industrial Agriculture: The Regional Integration of Specialty Crop Production. *Economic Geography* 62(4): 334–353.

Flores, M. L. 2000. Atraviesa la Industria Tequilera una Crisis Histórica. *Ocho Columnas,* July 2.

Forest Stewardship Council. 2004. Greenpeace Mexico Hand over a Presidencial Chair to President Vicente Fox. *Environment News Service* 2(5): 3.

Fox, B. 2001. Aid Bundles Left for Immigrants. *San Jose Mercury News,* December 30.

———. 2002. Southwest Border Still Being Crossed. Associated Press, July 16.

Fox, J. 1992. *The Politics of Food in Mexico: State Power and Social Mobilization.* Cornell University Press, Ithaca, NY.

Friedland, W. H., and A. Barton 1975. *Destalking the Wily Tomato: A Case Study in Social Consequences in California Agricultural Research.* Research Monograph No. 15, Department of Applied Behavioral Sciences, College of Agricultural and Environmental Sciences, University of California, Davis.

Friedland, W. H., A. Barton, and R. J. Thomas. 1978. *Manufacturing Green Gold: The Conditions and Social Consequences of Lettuce Harvest Mechanization.* Department of Applied Behavioral Sciences, California Agricultural Policy Seminar, College of Agriculture and Environmental Studies, University of California, Davis.

Friends of the Earth International 2006a. Biotech Foods: International Safety Laws Agreed. March 18. www.globalresearch.ca/index.php?context=view Article&code=FRI20060318&articleId=2123.

———. 2006b. Who Benefits from GM Crops? January. www.foei.org/publica tions/pdfs/gmcrops2006full.pdf.

Furillo, A. 2001. Toiling under Abuse: Farm Workers' Struggle Goes On. *Sacramento Bee,* May 20; Farm Labor Abuses Alleged, May 26; Farm Labor Dangers Detailed, May 27.

Furlong, C. E., N. Holland, R. J. Richter, A. Bradman, A. Ho, and B. Eskenazi. 2006. PON1 Status of Farmworker Mothers and Children as a Predictor of Organophosphate Sensitivity. *Pharmacogenetics and Genomics* 16:183–190.

Gailbraith, J. K. 2006. Morning in America Again. *Guardian/UK,* April 13.

Gamsky, T. E., S. A. McCurdy, P. Wiggins, S. J. Samuels, B. Berman, and M. B. Shenker. 1992. *Epidemiology of Dermatitis among California Farm Workers.* Division of Occupational and Environmental Medicine, Department of Internal Medicine, University of California, Davis.

Gaouette, N. 2006. What Was behind the Big Raid. *Los Angeles Times,* April 22.

Garcia, E. 2001. Merciless Epidemic Has Spread Worldwide. *San Jose Mercury News,* June 3.

Garcia, S. 2004. *The ABCs of Immigration Reform.* Ameritas Program, Interhemispheric Resource Center, Silver City, NM.

García y Griego, M. 1989. The Mexican Labor Supply, 1990–2010. In W. A. Cornelius and J. A. Bustamante (eds.), *Mexican Migration to the United States: Origins, Consequences, and Policy Options.* Dimensions of U.S.-Mexican Relations, Vol. 3, Center for U.S.-Mexican Studies, University of California, San Diego.

Gardner, J. L. (ed.). 1986. *Mysteries of the Ancient Americas*. Reader's Digest Association, Pleasantville, NY.

Gay, L. 2006. Fruits, Vegetables Not as Nutritious as 50 Years Ago. Scripps Howard News Service. www.ucsaction.org/ct/p7_lfnd1Ym5K/.

Gazzar, B. 2005. Border Patrol Supporters Train for Patrols. *Inland Valley Daily Bulletin*, September 13.

Gedda, G. 2001. Immigration Reform on Hold, U.S. Says: Terrorism Concerns Delay U.S.-Mexico Pact. *San Jose Mercury News*, November 21.

Geitner, P. 2004. EU to Approve Genetically Modified Corn. Associated Press, May 14.

George, N. 2003. India Says Coke, Pepsi Fail EU Standards. Associated Press, August 21.

Gershon, D. 1992. Programme Aids Developing World. *Nature* 356(6372): 735.

Girón, V. M. C. 1995. *Sólo Dios y el Norte: Migración a Estados Unidos y Desarrollo en una Región de Jalisco*. Universidad de Guadalajara.

Giuliano, J. A. 2005. Biological and Chemical Warfare Are Here Now. Emerging Worlds. www.emergingworlds.com.

Giuriato, M., C. Johnson-Lyons, and E. Wood. 2001. *Farmworker Housing and Health Needs Assessment Study of the Salinas and Pajaro Valleys*. Applied Survey Research, Watsonville and San Jose, CA.

Glass, R. M. 1994. Caffeine Dependence: What Are the Implications? *JAMA* 272(13): 106–107.

Gledhill, J. 1995. *Neoliberalism, Transnationalization and Rural Poverty: A Case Study of Michoacán, Mexico*. Westview Press, Boulder, CO.

Gliessman, S. R. 1982a. Nitrogen Distribution in Several Traditional Agroecosystems in the Humid Tropical Lowlands of South-Eastern Mexico. *Plant and Soil* 67: 105–117.

———. 1982b. Polyculture Cropping Has Advantages. *California Agriculture* 36(7): 14–16.

———. 1992. Agroecology in the Tropics: Achieving a Balance between Land Use and Preservation. *Environmental Management* 16(6): 681–689.

———. 1998. *Agroecology: Ecological Processes in Sustainable Agriculture*. Ann Arbor Press, Chelsea, MI.

Glipo, A., L. Carlsen, A. T. Sayeed, R. S. D. Rindermann, and J. Cainglet. 2003. *Agreement on Agriculture and Food Sovereignty Perspectives from Mesoamerica and Asia*. Interhemispheric Resource Center, Americas Program, Silver City, NM.

Global Pesticide Campaigner. 2005. Terminator Technology Rises Again. *Global Pesticide Campaigner* 15(1): 20.

Golash-Boza, T. M., and D. A. Parker. 2006. Dehumanizing the Undocumented May 15. www.counterpunch.org/golasho5152006.html.

Gonzalez, J. 2006. Reigniting a Call to Action. *New York Daily News*, March 30.

González, R. J. 2006. Youthful Demonstrators Carry on Great American Tradition. *San Jose Mercury News*, March 31.

Grebler L. 1965. *Mexican Immigration to the United States: The Record and Its Implications*. Advance Report 2, Mexican-American Study Project Division of Research, Graduate School of Business Administration, University of California, Los Angeles.

Greenberg, J. L., S. E. Lewis, and D. K. Dodd. 1999. Overlapping Addictions and Self-Esteem among College Men and Women. *Addictive Behaviors* 24(4): 565–571.

Greenhouse, S. 2001. Latino Immigrants Die at Work More Often. *New York Times,* July 16.

Greenpeace. 2004a. Corrobora PNUMA: Desastrosa la Política Ambiental Mexicana. July 26. www.greenpeace.org/mexico/news/corrobora-pnuma-desas trosa-la.

———. 2004b. El Gobierno Es Culpable de la Desaparición de Bosques y Selvas en México. Boletín 0403, February 3. www.greenpeace.org/mexico/press/releases/el-govierno-se-cupable-de-la.

———. 2004c. El Presupuesto 2005 Acelerará la Destrucción de los Bosques. November 23. www.greenpeace.org/mexico/news/el-presupuesto-2005-acel erara.

———. 2004d. Exigen Ambientalistas Libertad para el Campesino Ecologista Felipe Arreaga. Boletín 0559, May 12. www.greenpeace.org/mexico/press/releases/exigen-ambientalistas-libertad.

———. 2004e. Medio Ambiente, el Gran Ausente en el Cuarto Informe de Gobierno. 9/2/2004. www.greenpeace.org/mexico/news/lo-ambiental-ausente -en-el-in.

———. 2005a. Emboscan a Líder Campesino Ecologista y Asesinan a Dos de Sus Hijos en la Sierra de Petatlán, Guerrero. Boletín 0562, May 20. www.green peace.org/mexico/press/releases/emboscan-a-l-der-campesino-eco.

———. 2005b. La Invasión de los Transgénicos. www.greenpeace.org/mex ico/news/la-invasi-n-de-los-transgenico.

———. 2006a. El Medio Ambiente: El Verdadero Perdedor en el Debate. Boletín 0633, April 26. www.greenpeace.org/mexico/press/releases/el-medio-ambi ente-el-verdader.

———. 2006b. Vende Estados Unidos Arroz Transgénico no Aprobado para Consumo Humano . . . Méxicoes el Principal Importador de ese Grano. Boletín 0664, August 23. www.greenpeace.org/mexico/press/releases/vende -estados-unidos-arroz-tra.

Greg, C. 2000. Soft-Drink Sugar Content Is High. *Gazette* (Montreal), January 31.

Griffith, D., and E. Kissam. 1995. *Working Poor: Farmworkers in the United States.* Temple University Press, Philadelphia.

Grillo, I. 2005. Mexico Criticizes U.S. Immigration Bill for Security Fence: Measure Would OK Partial Fence on Border, Impact Worker Permits. Associated Press, December 17.

Grindle, M. S. 1986. *State and Countryside: Development Policy and Agrarian Politics in Latin America.* John Hopkins University Press, Baltimore.

Guerin-Gonzales, C. 1985. *Labor Control in California Industrial Agriculture.* Dissertation. UMI Dissertation Services, Ann Arbor, MI.

Guillette, E. A., M. M. Mesa, M. G. Aguilar, A. D. Soto, and I. E. Garcia. 1998. An Anthropological Approach to the Evaluation of Preschool Children Exposed to Pesticides in Mexico. *Environmental Health Perspective* 106(6): 347–353.

Gumbel A., and A. Buncombe. 2006. Two Million Join Protests as Immigrant Debate Grips US. *Independent.* www.commondreams.org/headline s06/0411–03.htm.

Hall, K. G. 2006. Desperation Fuels Border Attempts: More Kids Apprehended as Families Try to Reunite. *San Jose Mercury News,* June 4.

Hall, M., and P. O'Driscoll. 2005. Border Patrols Growing in Arizona. *USA Today,* March 29.

Hamilton, L. M. 2004. Strawberries: Worldwide Red Delight. *CCOF Magazine* 21(1): 24–26.

Hanson, G. H., and A. Splimbergo. 1999. *Political Economy, Sectoral Shocks, and Border Enforcement.* Working Paper Series No. 7315, National Bureau of Economic Research, Cambridge, MA.

Havice, E. 2005. Remittance-Based Development? *Berkeley Review of Latin American Studies* (Center for Latin American Studies, University of California, Berkeley),Winter, 18–21.

Hayes, T., K. Haston, M. Tsui, A. Hoang, C. Haeffele, and A. Vonk. 2003. Atrazine-Induced Hermaphroditism at 0.1 ppb in American Leopard Frogs (*Rana pipiens*): Laboratory and Field Evidence. *Environmental Health Perspectives* 111(4): 568–575.

Healey, J. F. 1997. *Race, Ethnicity, and Gender in the United States: Inequality, Group Conflict, and Power.* Pine Forge Press, Thousand Oaks, CA.

Heifer Project International 1996. *HPI in Mexico.* Heifer Project International, Little Rock, AR.

Henderson, A. T. 1987. *The Evidence Continues to Grow: Parent Involvement Improves Student Achievement.* National Coalition of Citizens in Education, Columbia, MD.

Henningfield, J. E., P. B. Santora, and F. A. Stillman. 2005. Exploitation by Design: Could Tobacco Industry Documents Guide More Effective Smoking Prevention and Cessation in Women? *Addiction* 100(6): 735.

Heppel, M. L. 1995. Immigration and Agriculture: Policy Issues. In P. L. Martin, W. Huffman, R. Emerson, J. E. Taylor, and R. I. Rochin (eds.), *Immigration Reform and U.S. Agriculture.* Publication 3358, Division of Agriculture and Natural Resources, University of California, Oakland.

Heppel, M., and D. Papademetriou. 2001. Government Intervention and the Farm Labor Market: How Past Policies Shape Future Options. In A. López (ed.), *Forum for Transnational Employment: A Dialogue on Alternatives to the Status Quo in Immigrant-Labor Dominated Industries.* California Institute for Rural Studies, Davis.

Hernandez, J. 2005. *The Elephant in the Room: Latinos and Mental Health.* Eastern Group Publications, Los Angeles.

Herrera, L. 1998. *The Impact of the Immigration Policy of the United States on the US-Mexico Relationship.* Working Paper, University of California Institute on Global Conflict and Cooperation, University of California, San Diego.

Hill, L. E. 2004. *The Socioeconomic Well-Being of California's Immigrant Youth.* Public Policy Institute of California, San Francisco.

Himelstein, D., and I. G. Lascuraín. 1993. The California-Mexico Connection in Tables and Figures. In A. F. Lowenthal and K. Burgess (eds.), *The California-Mexico Connection.* Stanford University Press, Stanford, CA.

Hobbs, R. 2001. Immigration Is Not a Matter of Choice but of Survival. *San Jose Mercury News,* August 12.

Hondagneu-Sotelo, P. 1994. *Gendered Transitions: Mexican Experiences of Immigration.* University of California Press, Berkeley.

Hondagneu-Sotelo, P., and E. Avila. 1997. I'm Here, But I'm There: The Meanings of Latina Transnational Motherhood. *Gender and Society* 11(5): 548–571.

Howie, M. 2001. EPA Says Bt Corn Poses Little Risk to Butterflies. *Feedstuffs* (Miller Publishing) 73(33): 15.

Huffman, W. E. 1995. Immigration and Agriculture in the 1990s. In P. Martin et al. (eds.), *Immigration Reform and U.S. Agriculture.* Publication 3358, Division of Agriculture and Natural Resources, University of California, Oakland.

Human Rights Watch. 2000. *Fingers to the Bone: United States Failure to Protect Child Farmworkers.* www.hrw.org/reports/2000/frmwrkr.

Hutcheson, R. 2005. Tough Talk: Business Likes Cheap Labor, but Voters Want Secure Borders. *San Jose Mercury News,* November 29.

INEGI. 2000. *Encuesta Industriál Mensual.* Instituto Nacional de Estadística Geografía e Informática, Mexico City.

International Herald Tribune. 2005. Discovering Transgenic Corn, Mexicans Suspicious of U.S. *International Herald Tribune,* March 28.

International Labour Conference. 2004. *Towards a Fair Deal for Migrant Workers in the Global Economy.* 92d Session, Report 6.

International Labour Office. 2003. *Facts on Agriculture.* Department of Communication Fact Sheet, International Labour Office.

IPCS News. 1993. Poisoning by Pesticides. *IPCS News: The Newsletter of the International Programme on Chemical Safety,* April.

Ivins, M. 2006. *More Immigrant Bashing on the Way.* July 5. www.truthdig .com/report/item/20060705_molly_ivins_immigrant_bashing.

Jacobi, P., and M. Lee. 1999. Who Can Afford to Live Here? The Number of Jobs and Optimism Are up, but So Is the Cost of Living in Santa Cruz County. *Focus on Health* (Dominican Hospital, Santa Cruz) 5(3): 6–7.

Jacobs, P. 2004. Altered Seeds Found with Regular Variety. *San Jose Mercury News,* February 24.

James, W. D. 2001. Amnesty Would Reward Those Who Broke the Law. *San Jose Mercury News,* August 12.

Johnson, G. E. 2001. Bad Investment: Take It from a Businessman: The War on Drugs Is Just Money down the Drain. *Mother Jones,* July 10.

Johnston, B. F. 1987. The Implications of Rural Development for Employment and Welfare: Experience in the United States, Mexico, Japan, and Taiwan. In B. F. Johnston, C. Luiselli, C. C. Contreras, and R. D. Norton (eds.), *U.S.-Mexico Relations: Agriculture and Rural Development.* Stanford University Press, Stanford, CA.

Johnston, P. 2001. Rethinking Cross-Border Employment in Overlapping Socicties: A Citizenship Movement Agenda. In A. López (ed.), *Forum for Transnational Employment: A Dialogue on Alternatives to the Status Quo in Immigrant-Labor Dominated Industries*. California Institute for Rural Studies, Davis.

Johnston, W. 1997. Cross Sections of a Diverse Agriculture: Profiles of California's Production Regions and Principal Commodities. In J. Siebert (ed.), *California Agriculture: Issues and Challenges*. University of California, Department of Agriculture and Natural Resources, Oakland.

Jourdane, M. 2004. *The Struggle for the Health and Legal Protection of Farm Workers: El Cortito*. Arte Público Press, Houston, TX.

Kaiser, J. 2000. Biotechnology: USDA to Commercialize "Terminator" Technology. *Science* 289(5480): 709–710.

Kaplan, T. 2000. Housing Sets off Struggle in Salinas. *San Jose Mercury News,* August 20.

Karliner, J. 1997. *The Corporate Planet: Ecology and Politics in the Age of Globalization*. Sierra Club Books, San Francisco.

Kasirye, O. C., J. A. Walsh, P. S. Romano, L. A. Beckett, J. A. Garcia, B. Elvine-Kreis, J. W. Bethel, and M. B. Schenker. 2005. Acculturation and Its Association with Health-Risk Behaviors in a Rural Latina Population. *Ethnicity and Disease* 15: 733–739.

Katel, P., and M. Lloyd. 2001. The Towns They Left Behind: As Poor Mexicans Head North, Their Villages Slowly Disappear. *Time,* June 11.

Kaufman, M. 2000. Search, Buyback in Progress of Grain Meant for Animal Use. *San Jose Mercury News,* October 19.

Kegley, S., A. Katten, and M. Moses. 2003. *Secondhand Pesticides: Airborne Pesticide Drift in California*. Californians for Pesticide Reform, Pesticide Action Network Northern California, San Francisco.

King, P. H. 2001. That's It. Vamanos. Gone. *Los Angeles Times,* February 28.

Kingsolver, A. 1996. *Plurinationality and Multilocality: Some Explanations of Identity and Community before and after NAFTA in Mexico and the U.S.* Working Paper No. 11, Chicano-Latino Research Center, University of California, Santa Cruz.

Klug, F. 2002. 14 Illegal Immigrants Found Dead in Arizona Desert in Past Few Days. Associated Press, December 6.

Kluger, J. 1999. The Suicide Seeds: Terminator Genes Could Mean Big Biotech Bucks—But Big Trouble Too, as a Grass-Roots Protest Breaks out on the Net. *Time,* February 1.

Koons-Garcia, D. 2000. *The Future of Food* (video). Lily Films, Mill Valley, CA.

Krauze, E. 1999. *México Siglo XX: El Sexenio de Lázaro Cárdenas*. Editorial Clío, Mexico City.

Kunzelman, M. 2005. Cigarette Industry Targeted Women. *San Jose Mercury News,* June 1.

Kushner, S. 1975. *Long Road to Delano*. International Publishers, New York.

LaDou, J. 2001. Obsolete Pesticide Stocks Poison Latin America. *International Journal of Occupational and Environmental Health* 7(4).

Lauritzen, E. 2000. *Monterey County Crop Report 2000*. Monterey County Agricultural Commissioner, Salinas, CA.

————. 2003. *Monterey County Agriculture, California*. Monterey County Agricultural Commissioner, Salinas, CA.

Lean, G. 2000. Hi-tech Crops Are Bad for the Brain. *Independent,* April 23.

————. 2006. Rice Contaminated by GM Has Been on Sale for Months. *Independent,* August 27.

Letourneau, D. K. 1986. Associational Resistance in Squash Monoculture and Polycultures in Tropical Mexico. *Environmental Entomology* 15: 285–292.

Levey, N. 2002. Pesticide near Schools Raises Concern: State Officials Say Regulations Are Adequate. *San Jose Mercury News,* October 14.

Liebman, J. 1997. *Rising Toxic Tide: Pesticide Use in California, 1991–1995.* Pesticide Action Network, San Francisco.

Lizárraga, P. 2006. Tiene Diabetes Uno de Cada 10 Mexicanos. *Ocho Columnas,* August 24.

Llamas, R. 2000. *Heat Sabotages Border Crossings.* Associated Press, July 12.

Lloyd, J., P. L. Martin, and J. Mamer. 1988. *The Ventura Citrus Labor Market.* Giannini Foundation Information Series, No. 88–1. University of California, Berkeley.

Lohse, D., and K. McPherson. 2006. Senate Panel OKs Immigration Bill. *San Jose Mercury News,* March 28.

Lomitz-Adler, C. 1992. *Exits from the Labyrinth: Culture and Ideology in the Mexican National Space.* University of California Press, Berkeley.

López, M. E. 1999. *When Discourses Collide: An Ethnography of Migrant Children at Home and in School.* Peter Lang, New York.

Los Angeles Times. 2006 UFW: A Broken Contract (4 part series). *Los Angeles Times,* January 8–11.

Lowell, B. L., and R. Suro. 2002. How Many Undocumented: The Numbers behind the U.S.-Mexico Migration Talks. *Pew Hispanic Center Report,* March 21.

Luján, J. L. S. 1995. *Quién Paga los Platos Rotos? Costos Sociales de la Agricultura Moderna: El Caso de las Intoxicaciones por Plaguicidas en Zamora, Michoacán, 1980–1989.* Master's thesis, Centro de Estudios Rurales, El Colegio de Michoacán, A.C. Zamora.

Luoma, J. R. 1999. System Failure. *Mother Jones* 24(4): 62–66.

Lyons, J. S., and M. Bazeley. 2002. Health Care Bias Harms Minorities, Study Finds. *San Jose Mercury News,* March 21.

Maestas-Flores, M. 1997. 25,000: March for Strawberry Workers and the UFW. *Raza Teca.* San Jose, CA.

Magis-Rodríguez, C., C. Gayet, M. Negroni, R. Leyva, E. Bravo-Garcia, P. Uribe, and M. Bronfman. 2004. Migration and AIDS in Mexico: An Overview Based on Recent Evidence. *Journal of Acquired Immune Deficiency Syndromes* 37(4): S215–226.

Majka, L., and T. Majka. 1982. *Farm Workers, Agribusiness and the State.* Temple University Press, Philadelphia.

Malone, J. 2002. Study Documents America's Reliance on Labor of Illegal Immigrants. *Santa Cruz Sentinel,* March 22.

Mandel-Campbell, A. 2001. Mexican Farmers in Big Protest Rally. *Financial Times,* August 9.

Mangaliman, J. 2001. Univision Deal Sparks Worry. *San Jose Mercury News,* December 2.

———. 2006. Amnesty Foes: We Represent Mainstream. *San Jose Mercury News,* March 3.

Markusen, J. R., and S. Zahniser. 1997. *Liberalization and Incentives for Labor Migration: Theory with Applications to NAFTA.* Working Paper 6232, National Bureau of Economic Research, Cambridge, MA.

Martin, P. 1989. *The California Farm Labor Market.* Working Group on Farm Labor and Rural Poverty, Working Paper No. 4, California Institute for Rural Studies, Davis.

———. 2001. *Farm Labor in California: Then and Now.* Working Paper No. 37, Center for Comparative Immigration Studies, University of California, San Diego.

Martin, P., and B. Mason. 2003. Hired Workers on California Farms. In J. Siebert (ed.), *California Agriculture: Dimensions and Issues.* UC Giannini Foundation of Agricultural Economics, Berkeley, CA.

Martin, P., and J. E. Taylor. 1995a. *Good Intentions Gone Awry: Immigration Reform and Agriculture.* Program for Research on Immigration Policy, Urban Institute, Washington, DC.

———. 1995b. Introduction; and IRCA's Effects in California Agriculture. In P. L. Martin, W. Huffman, R. Emerson, J. E. Taylor, and R. I. Rochin (eds.), *Immigration Reform and U.S. Agriculture.* Division of Agriculture and Natural Resources, Publication 3358, University of California, Oakland.

———. 1995c. *Merchants of Labor: Farm Labor Contractors and Immigration Reform.* Program for Research on Immigration Policy, Urban Institute, Washington, DC.

Martin, P., and J. Widgren. 1996. *International Migration: A Global Challenge.* Population Bulletin, Population Reference Bureau, Washington, DC.

Massey, D. S. 1998. March of Folly: U.S. Immigration Policy after NAFTA. *American Prospect* 37:22–33.

Massey, D., R. Alarcón, J. Durand, and H. González. 1987. *Return to Aztlan: The Social Process of International Migration from Western Mexico.* University of California Press, Berkeley.

May, P., M. A. Ostrom, and R. Foo. 2006. A Call for Rights: 100,000 March through Downtown San Jose. *San Jose Mercury News,* May 2.

McCurdy, S. 1997. *Occupational Injury among California Migrant Hispanic Farm Workers: Fighting the Invisible Epidemic.* Department of Epidemiology and Preventive Medicine, University of California, Davis.

McLaughlin, K. 2004. Immigrant Youths' Health Deteriorates in U.S., Study Finds. *San Jose Mercury News,* October 5.

McWilliams, C. 1939. *Factories in the Field: The Story of Migratory Farm Labor in California.* Little Brown, Boston.

Mekay, E. 2003. NAFTA: North American Deal Dismal after a Decade. Inter Press Service, December 27.

Mellon, M., and J. Rissler. 2004. *Gone to Seed: Transgenic Contaminants in the Traditional Seed Supply.* Union of Concerned Scientists, Cambridge, MA.

Mena, J. 2000. AIDS Now a Migrant to Mexico. *Los Angeles Times,* September 15.

Méndez, E. 2006. No Hay Crimen Perfecto: Autopsia al Fraude Electoral. Jornadas Políticas. *La Jornada Michoacán,* August 10.

Mendoza, M. 2006. Cost to Remove 12M Illegal Immigrants Huge. Associated Press, April 7.

Meredith Corporation. 2001. Study Shows Monarch Danger Is Exaggerated. *Successful Farming* 99(2).

Mexico Solidarity Network. 2003. *Weekly News and Analysis from Mexico,* October 4.

Miga, A. 2006. Feds Warn Companies Using Illegal Workers. Associated Press, April 20.

Milanese, M. 2001. Migrant Dreams and Realities. *San Jose Mercury News,* October 26.

Milius, S. 2003. When Genes Escape: Does It Matter to Crops and Weeds? *Science News* 164(15): 232–233.

Mines, R., and R. Anzaldua. 1982. *New Migrants vs. Old Migrants: Alternative Labor Market Structures in the California Citrus Industry.* Monograph Series, No. 9, Center for U.S.-Mexican Studies, University of California, San Diego.

Mines, R., N. Mullenax, and L. Saca. 2001. *The Binational Farmworker Health Survey.* California Institute for Rural Studies, Davis.

Mintz, H. 2006. A Sympathetic Public. *San Jose Mercury News,* April 3.

Modesto Bee. 2003. Census Reveals Huge Rise in Non-English Speakers. *Modesto Bee,* October 9.

Moeller, D. W. 1999. *Parasol Brand Apples: A Report on Apples and Other Crops for 1999.* County of Santa Cruz, Office of the Agricultural Commissioner, Watsonville, CA.

———. 2003. *Santa Cruz County Agricultural Crop and Livestock Report.* County of Santa Cruz, Office of the Agricultural Commissioner. Watsonville, CA.

Mokhiber, R., and R. Weissman. 2005. The 10 Worst Corporations of 2005. Posted by Organic Consumers Association, Little Marais, MN. www.organic consumers.org/10worst012505.cfm.

Moll, L. C., C. Amanti, D. Neff, and N. Gonzalez. 1992. Funds of Knowledge for Teaching: Using a Qualitative Approach to Connect Homes and Classrooms. *Theory into Practice* 31(2): 132–141.

Molloy, T. 2006. Immigration Rallies Draw Thousands Nationwide. Associated Press, March 24.

Morales, M. P. 1994. Michoacán: Crisis Agrícola y Deterioro de Vida en el Medio Rural. In E. H. T. Barragán, G. V. Uribe, and A. S. Daza (eds.), *México en Los Noventa: Globalización y Reestructuración Productiva.* Universidad Autónoma Metropolitana-Azcapotzalco, Departamento de Economía, Area de Teoría y Análisis Económico, Universidad Michoacana de San Nicolás de Hidalgo Escuela de Economía.

Moreno, J. 2001. Mexican Farmers Protest Fox Policies; Demands Include More Government Aid. *Houston Chronicle,* August 9.

———. 2003. Mexico Farmers Say U.S. Subsidizes Corn. *Houston Chronicle,* August 27.

Morris, D. 2006. *Blame NAFTA.* www.alternet.org/story/34768.

Moses, M. 1993. Farmworkers and Pesticides. In *Confronting Environmental Racism: Voices from the Grassroots.* South End Press, Boston.

Mountjoy, D. C. 1996. Ethnic Diversity and the Patterned Adoption of Soil Conservation in the Strawberry Hills of Monterey, California. *Society and Natural Resources* 9:339–357.

Moyers, B. 1990. *The Global Dumping Ground.* Frontline. KQED: A Special Report. Corporation for Public Broadcasting, Washington, DC.

MSNBC News. 2000. Popular Pesticide to Be Phased Out: Dursban/Lorsban Seen as Risk to Children's Nervous Systems and Brains. MSNBC News, June 8.

Muller, T. 1997. Nativism in the Mid-1990s: Why Now? In J. F. Perea (ed.), *Immigrants Out! The New Nativism and Anti-Immigrant Impulse in the United States.* New York University Press, New York.

Mummert, G. 1994. From *Metate* to *Despate:* Rural Mexican Women's Salaried Labor and the Redefinition of Gendered Spaces and Roles. In H. Fowler-Salamini and M. K. Vaughan (eds.), *Creating Spaces/Shaping Transitions: Women of the Mexican Countryside, 1850–1990.* University of Arizona Press, Tucson.

———. 2003. Dilemas Familiars en un Michoacán de Migrantes. In G. L. Castro (ed.), *Diáspora Michoacana.* El Colegio de Michoacán, Zamora.

Nadal, A. 1999. *Environmental Effects of NAFTA on Corn Production in Mexico.* Environmental Studies Seminar, University of California, Santa Cruz.

———. 2000. *The Environmental and Social Impacts of Economic Liberalization on Corn Production in Mexico.* Oxfam GB, Oxford, and WWF International, Gland, Switzerland.

Najar, J. 1999. *Beyond Ellis Island: Latino Immigration to the United States.* Document M24, National Council of La Raza, Washington, DC.

National Agricultural Workers Survey. 2002. *Agricultural Workers.* www .doleta.gov/agworker/report9/toc.cfm.

National Center for Farmworker Health. 2004. HIV/AIDS Farmworker Fact Sheet. National Center for Farmworker Health, Buda, TX.

National Safety Council. 2002. Help Celebrate National Farm Safety and Health Week. NSC News Center, August 27. www.nsc.org/news/nr082702.htm.

———. 2003. Focus on Farm Security. NSC News Center, August 22. www.nsc.org/news/nr082203.htm.

Natoli, J., et al. 2001. A Path to Citizenship: Immigration: Who Is Welcome Here? *San Jose Mercury News,* September 2.

Nauman, T. 2002. Balance Sheet: Tallying up Fox's Environmental Record. Americas Program, Policy Brief. www.americaspolicy.org/briefs/2002/body_0203foxenv.html.

Navarrete, L., and C. Muñoz. 2001. *Statement of NCLR on the Current Immigration Policy Debate.* National Council of La Raza, Washington, DC.

Navarrete, L., and S. Perez. 2001. *Census Results Point to an "American Agenda" to Help Ensure Positive Future for Hispanics and the Nation.* National Council of La Raza.

Nesmith, J. 2004. Feds Petition to Postpone Phaseout of Much-Used Ozone-Eating Pesticide. *San Francisco Chronicle*, March 24.

Netting, R. McC. 1993. *Smallholders, Householders: Farm Families and the Ecology of Intensive, Sustainable Agriculture*. Stanford University Press, Stanford, CA.

Nevins, J. 2000. How High Must Operation Gatekeeper's Death Count Go? *Los Angeles Times*, November 19.

New York Times. 2006. Editorial: Young Latinas and a Cry for Help. *New York Times*, July 21.

Nieto, S. 1996. *Affirming Diversity: The Sociopolitical Context of Multicultural Education*. 2d ed. Longman, White Plains, NY.

Ohlemacher, S. 2006. Estimate: Illegal Immigrant Population in Country Hits 12 Million. Associated Press, March 7.

Ohmart, J. 2003. SAREP Sponsors First Organic Strawberry Production Short Course. *Sustainable Agriculture* (University of California Sustainable Agriculture Research and Education Program) 15(1): 20.

Olivo, A. 2001. Ghosts of a 1931 Raid: A Random INS Roundup Set the Tone for Decades of Ethnic Tension. *Los Angeles Times*, February 25.

Olvera, J. E. 2001. Season in the Sun: Introduction. *Fresno Bee*, May 14.

OnEarth. 2002. OnEarth update. (Environmental Activist Rodolfo Montiel Flores). *OnEarth* (Natural Resources Defense Council) 23(4): 5.

Oppenheimer, A. 1996. *Bordering on Chaos: Guerrillas, Stockbrokers, Politicians, and Mexico's Road to Prosperity*. Little, Brown, Boston.

Organic Consumers Association. 2006a. Biosafety Protocol Negotiations Maintain Weakened GMO Labeling Requirements. March 18. www.organicconsumers.org/ge/biosafety032106.cfm.

———— 2006b. World Leaders Vote against the Terminator and Frankentrees. March 29. www.organicconsumers.org/ge/trees060324.cfm.

————. 2006c. EPA's Scientists Condemn EPA. May 25. www.organicconsumers.org/2006/article_540.cfm.

————. 2006d. New Study Links Monsanto's Roundup to Cancer. June 22. www.organicconsumers.org/Monsanto/glyphocancer.cfm.

Organista, K. C., H. Carrillo, and G. Ayala. 2004. HIV Prevention with Mexican Migrants: Review, Critique, and Recommendations. *Journal of Acquired Immune Deficiency Syndromes* 37(4): S227–239.

Organista, K. C., and A. Kubo. 2005. Pilot Survey of HIV Risk and Contextual Problems and Issues in Mexican/Latino Migrant Day Laborers. *Journal of Immigrant Health* 7(4): 269–281.

Orme, W. A. 1993. The NAFTA Debate: Myths versus Facts; The Whole Truth about the Half-Truths. *Foreign Affairs* 72:2–12.

Orozco, E. S. 2000. Inquieta Posible Desaparición del Lago de Chapala. *Ocho Columnas*, July 2.

Osava, M. 2006a. Biodiversity: Environmentalists, Indigenous People Disappointed by COP8. Inter Press Service, March 31.

————. 2006b. Biodiversity: Terminator Seeds Suffer Defeat at Global Conference. Inter Press Service News Agency. April 11.

Ostrom, M. A. 2006. S.J. Marchers Back Immigrant Rights. *San Jose Mercury News,* March 26.

Osuna, J. A. P. 1998. México-Estados Unidos: El Impacto de Las Remesas. *Nexos* 21(252): 51–59.

Owens, K. 2000. Environmentalists Urge Homeowners, Applicators and Farmers to Stop Use and Retailers to Stop Sale of Common Pesticide Subject to Partial Ban. Press Release, June 8. Beyond Pesticides/National Coalition against the Misuse of Pesticides, Washington, DC.

Oxfam. 2004. *Like Machines in the Fields: Workers without Rights in American Agriculture.* Oxfam America, Boston.

Pacific Council on International Policy. 2000. *Mexico Transforming.* Pacific Council on International Policy, Los Angeles, CA.

Palerm, J. V. 1991. Farm Labor Needs and Farm Workers in California, 1970–1989. Unpublished report for the California Employment Development Department, Sacramento.

———. 1993. A Binational System of Agricultural Production: The Case of the Mexican Bajio and California. In D. Aldrich and L. Meyer (eds.), *Mexico and the United States: Neighbors in Crisis.* Proceedings from Neighbors in Crisis: A Call for Joint Solutions, February 1989. UC Mexus, Borgo Press, University of California.

———. 1994. *Immigrant and Migrant Farm Workers in the Santa Maria Valley, California.* Center for Chicano Studies and Department of Anthropology, University of California, Santa Barbara.

———. 2000. The Expansion of California Agriculture and the Rise of Peasant-Worker Communities. In N. Klahn, P. Castillo, A. Álvarez, and F. Manchón (eds.), *Las Nuevas Fronteras del Siglo XXI.* Desarrollode Medios, S.A. de C.V.

PANNA. 1990. 5000 Pesticide Deaths in Mexico. *Dirty Dozen Campaigner,* January. Pesticide Action Network North America. www.panna.org/resources/pestis/PESTIS.burst.175.html.

———. 1995. *Alternatives to Methyl Bromide: Excerpts from the U.N. Methyl Bromide Technical Options Committee 1995 Assessment.* Pesticide Action Network North America Regional Center, San Francisco.

———. 2000. News Note: Ethyl Parathion Uses Cancelled in U.S. *Global Pesticide Campaigner* 10(3). www.panna.org/resources/gpc/gpc_200012.10.3.21.dv.html.

———. 2001a. Methyl Bromide Use in California. www.panna.org/resources/documents/mbUseInCA.dv.html.

———. 2001b. PANUPS: Dupont Withdraws Benlate from the Market. World Bank Accountability Project, May 7. www.panna.org/resources/panups/panup_20010507.dv.html.

———. 2001c. PANUPS: Top Seven Agrochemical Companies in 2000. World Accountability Project, May 23. www.panna.org/resources/panups/panup_20010521.dv.html.

———. 2003. Position Paper of Pesticide Action Network (PAN) International on Paraquat. November. www.panna.org/resources/panups/PANParaquatP Paper.pdf.

———. 2005a. PAN Sues for Healthy Air. *Partners Update,* Spring. www
.panna.org/about/pu/pu_200504.06.dv.html.

———. 2005b. PANNA Corporate Profile: Bayer AG. May 2005. www.panna
.org/campaigns/caia/corpProfilesBayer.dv.html.

———. 2005c. Pesticide Action Network Spearheads Public Comments on
EPAHs Fumigant Assessments. *Partners Update,* Fall 2005. www.panna.org/
about/pu/pu_200511.07.dv.html.

Parsons, L. 2001. Agriculture Survey: Study Paints a Harsh Picture: Farm Workers Deal with Low Pay, Costly Housing. *Californian,* June 5.

Passel, J. S. 2005a. *Estimates of the Size and Characteristics of the Undocumented Population.* Pew Hispanic Center Report, Washington, DC.

———. 2005b. *Unauthorized Migrants: Numbers and Characteristics.* Pew Hispanic Center Report, Washington, DC.

Perea, J. F. 1997. Introduction. In *Immigrants Out! The New Nativism and
Anti-Immigrant Impulse in the United States.* New York University Press.
New York.

Perian, N. 1999. Fields of Greed: "Terminator Technology" Could Make Monsanto Rich . . . and Devastate the Environment. *Greenpeace* 4(1): 11.

Perrin, S., J. Ruiz, and D. Williams. 1998. Building Solutions for Farm Worker
Housing. *Rural California Report* (California Institute for Rural Studies,
Davis) 9(4): 1, 6–7.

Perrin, S., and D. Williams.1999. Undocumented Farm Workers Pay Estimated
$337–$410 million in Taxes. *Rural California Report* (California Institute for
Rural Studies, Davis) 10(3): 1.

Pimentel, D., P. Hepperly, J, Hanson, D. Douds, and R. Seidel. 2005. Environmental, Energetic, and Economic Comparisons of Organic and Conventional
Farming Systems. *BioScience* 55(7): 573–582.

Poovey, B. 2005. Hispanics New Target of Hate Groups. Associated Press, July
29.

Porter, E. 2005. Illegal Immigrants Are Bolstering Social Security with Billions.
New York Times, April 5.

Powell, D. R. 1995. Including Latino Fathers in Parent Education and Support
Programs: Development of a Program Model. In R. E. Zambrana (ed.), *Understanding Latino Families: Scholarship, Policy, and Practice.* Sage, Thousand Oaks, CA.

Prengaman, P. 2006. Thousands March in L.A. over Immigration. Associated
Press, March 26.

Prentice, S., and J. Broome. 2004. Methyl Bromide Alternative Results for Strawberries. *Sustainable Agriculture* 15(3): 1, 14–17.

President's Advisory Commission on Educational Excellence for Hispanic Americans. 1996. Our Nation on the Fault Line: Hispanic American Education.
Washington, D.C. www.ed.gov/offices/OIIA/Hispanic.

Pritchard, J. 2004. The Jobs That Lure Mexican Workers to the United States Are
Killing. Associated Press, March 14.

Public Citizen's Global Trade Watch. 1996. NAFTA's Broken Promises: Evidence
of NAFTA's Failure. In K. Danaher (ed.), *Corporations Are 'Gonna Get Your*

Mama': Globalization and the Downsizing of the American Dream. Common Courage Press, Monroe, ME.

———. 2001. Down on the Farm: NAFTA's Seven-Years War on Farmers and Ranchers in the U.S., Canada and Mexico. *Public Citizen,* June.

Quist, D., and I. H. Chapela. 2001. Transgenic DNA Introgressed into Traditional Maize Landraces in Oaxaca, Mexico. *Nature* 414:541–543.

RAFI (Rural Advancement Foundation International). 2001. Globalization Inc.—Concentration in Corporate Power: The Unmentioned Agenda, July/August. www.rafi.org.

Ramírez, H. R. 2003. Migración Internacional y Remesas en Michoacán. In G. L. Castro (ed.), *Diáspora Michoacana.* D.R. El Colegio de Michoacán.

RAPAM (Red de Acción sobre Plaguicidas y Alternativas en México). 1991. Fire at Mexican Pesticide Plant. *Global Pesticide Campaigner* 1(3).

———. 1994. Pesticide Fire Forces Evacuation in Mexico. *Global Pesticide Campaigner* 4(2).

Reeves, M., A. Katten, and M. Guzmán. 2002. *Fields of Poison 2002: California Farmworkers and Pesticides.* Pesticide Action Network North America, San Francisco.

Reeves, M., and K. Schafer. 2003. Greater Risks, Fewer Rights: U.S. Farmworkers and Pesticides. *International Journal of Occupational and Environmental Health* 9:30–39.

Reeves, M., K. Schafer, K. Hallward, and A. Katten. 1999. *Fields of Poison: California Farmworkers and Pesticides.* Pesticide Action Network North America, San Francisco.

Reeves, M., K. Schwind, and R. Silberblatt. 2006. The Invisible Epidemic: Global Acute Pesticide Poisoning. Pesticide Action Network. www.panna .org/magazine/summer2006/inDepthGlobalPoisoning.html.

Reiche, R., U. Horn, S. Wölfl, W. Dorn., and H. H. Kaatz. 1998. The Bee as a Vector of Gene Transfer from Transgenic Plants into the Environment. *Apidologie* 219:401–403.

Reinhardt, S. 2000. Court: Hispanic Appearance Cannot Be Considered in Border Stops. Associated Press, April 12.

Repetto, R., and S. S. Baliga. 1996. *Pesticides and the Immune System: The Public Health Risks.* World Resources Institute, Washington D.C. http://sustag .wri.org/pubs_toc.cfm?PubID = 2704.

Reuters. 2001. U.S., Mexico Step up Patrols for Desert Migrants. *San Jose Mercury News,* June 16.

———. 2002. Migrant Deaths Soar in Intense Border Heat. www.cnn.com/ 2002/WORLD/americas/06/24/mexico.migrants.reut/index.html.

———. 2005a. Immigrants Do Not Overwhelm Healthcare—Study. Reuters, July 25. www.azteca.net/aztec/immigrat/overwhelm.html.

———. 2005b. U.S. Hazardous to Health of Mexican Entrants, Study Says. Reuters, October 14. www.azstarnet.com/dailystar/news/97727.php.

Revolutionary Worker. 2001. Fox Plan for Mexico: More Exploitation, No. 1094, March 11. http://rwor.org.

Richard, S., S. Moslemi, H. Sipahutar, N. Benachour, and G. E. Seralini. 2005.

Differential Effects of Glyphosate and Roundup on Human Placental Cells and Aromatase. *Environmental Health Perspectives* 113(6): 716–720.

Ríos, V. M. 1999. El Mercado Mexicano de Plaguicidas en 1997. *Industria de Agroquimicos: Plaguicidas e Insumos de Nutrición Vegetal* 3(7): 15–17.

Risch, S. 1980. The Population Dynamics of Several Herbivorous Beetles in a Tropical Agroecosystem: The Effect of Intercropping Corn, Beans and Squash in Costa Rica. *Journal of Applied Ecology* 17:593–612.

Rivera, M. 2001. Mexican Energy Policy, Subordinate to the U.S. *La Jornada,* May 14.

Rizvi, H. 2005. Coca-Cola Faces Mounting Pressure over Abusive Practices at Plants Worldwide, December 15. www.OneWorld.net.

———. 2006. Bush-Coke-Pepsi Triumvirate under Fire. August 21. www .OneWorld.net.

Rochín, R. I., and M. D. Castillo. 1995. *Immigration and* Colonia *Formation in Rural California.* Chicano/Latino Policy Project Working Paper, Berkeley, CA.

Rodebaugh, D. 2000. Farm Worker Health Probe. *San Jose Mercury News,* March 28.

Rodriguez, J. 1994. *Our Lady of Guadalupe: Faith and Empowerment among Mexican-American Women.* University of Texas Press, Austin.

Rodriguez, R. 2006. Immigration and the Scapegoating of Children. Column of the Americas. xcolumn@qmail.com. July 14.

Rogers, P. 2001. Commercial Pesticide Use Dropped Sharply in 2000. *San Jose Mercury News,* October 24.

Rogers, R. 2006. Campaign to Stop Killer Coke. www.KillerCoke.org.

Rosenblum, M. R. 2000. *U.S. Immigration Policy: Unilateral And Cooperative Responses to Undocumented Immigration.* Institute on Global Conflict and Cooperation, Policy Paper No. 55, University of California, San Diego.

Rosenzweig, M. R., and Kenneth Wolpin. 1985. Specific Experience, Household Structure and Intergenerational Transfers: Farm Family Arrangements in Developing Countries. *Quarterly Journal of Economics* 100:961–987.

Rosés, J. H. 2003. Conservation Perspectives. *MonarchWatch Email Updates,* September 23. www.monarchwatch.org/update/2003/jordi092203.html.

Ross, J. 1995. *Rebellion from the Roots: Indian Uprising in Chiapas.* Common Courage Press, Monroe, ME.

———. 2005. What the Indocumentados Leave Behind: Lost and Found in the Arizona Desert. *CounterPunch* (El Paso, TX), April 7.

Rouse, R. 1991. Mexican Migration and the Social Space of Postmodernism. *Diaspora* 1(1): 8–23.

Rubenstein, S. 2001. Hanging Hat in Bay Area Costs Bundle: $70,000 a Year Needed to Rent S.F. Apartment. *San Francisco Chronicle,* October 3.

Rubin, J., and C. H. Cho. 2006. High School Students Extend Immigration Protests into Third Day. *Los Angeles Times,* March 27.

Rubio, L., and G. Trejo. 1993. Reform, Globalization, and Structural Interdependence: New Economic Ties between Mexico and California. In A. F.

Lowenthal and K. Burgess (eds.), *The California-Mexico Connection*. Stanford University Press, Stanford, CA.

Ruiz, O. 2006. Immigrant Surge Is Tied to the Failure of NAFTA. *Star Tribune* (Minneapolis, MN), April 22.

Ruiz, V. L. 1987. *Cannery Women, Cannery Lives: Mexican Women, Unionization, and the California Food Processing Industry, 1930–1950*. University of New Mexico Press, Albuquerque.

Runsten, D. 1981. *Mechanization and Mexican Labor in California Agriculture*. Center for U.S.-Mexican Studies, University of California, San Diego.

———. 1987. Competition in Strawberries. In *Competitiveness at Home and Abroad*. Report of a 1986–87 Study Group on Marketing California Specialty Crops: Worldwide Competition and Constraints. University of California Agricultural Issues Center, Davis.

———. 1998. *Building the North American Development Bank's Community Adjustment and Investment Program: The Watsonville Experience*. Environmental Studies Department Seminar, February 17, University of California, Santa Cruz.

Runsten, D., and K. Moulton 1987a. Competition in Frozen Vegetables. In *Competitiveness at Home and Abroad*. Report of a 1986–87 Study Group on Marketing California Specialty Crops: Worldwide Competition and Constraints, University of California Agricultural Issues Center, Davis.

———. 1987b. Competition in Processing Tomatoes. In *Competitiveness at Home and Abroad*. Report of a 1986–87 Study Group on Marketing California Specialty Crops: Worldwide Competition and Constraints, University of California Agricultural Issues Center, Davis.

Runsten, D., and C. Zabin 1995. A Regional Perspective on Mexican Migration to Rural California. In J. E. Taylor, P. L. Martin, and M. Fix (eds.), *Poverty amid Prosperity: Immigration and the Changing Face of Rural California*. Urban Institute Press, Washington, DC.

Rural California Report. 1998. Did You Know? *Rural California Report* 9(4): 1.

Russel, D. 2002. Mexico's Marine Life Threatened by Development Plans. *Ecologist*, March 22.

Sagara, E. 2006. Schools Powerless vs. Protest Momentum. *Tucson Citizen*, March 31.

Salgado de Snyder, V. N. 1993. Family Life across the Border: Mexican Wives Left Behind. *Hispanic Journal of Behavioral Sciences* 15(3): 391–401.

———. 1996. *Dios y el Norte*: The Perceptions of Wives of Documented and Undocumented Mexican Immigrants to the United States. *Hispanic Journal of Behavioral Sciences* 18(3): 283–296.

Salgado de Snyder, V. N., A. Acevedo, M. D. J. Díaz-Pérez, and A. Saldivar-Garduño. 2000. Understanding the Sexuality of Mexican-Born Women and Their Risk for HIV/AIDS. *Psychology of Women Quarterly* 24:100–109.

Salgado de Snyder, V. N., R. C. Cervantes, and A. M. Padilla. 1990. Gender and Ethnic Differences in Psychosocial Stress and Generalized Distress among Hispanics. *Sex Roles* 22(7/8): 441–452.

Sanchez, M. A., and G. F. Lemp. 2003. *The Epidemiology of HIV, STDs, and TB among Mexican Migrants and Recent Immigrants in California*. California

Program on Access to Care (CPAC) and Universitywide AIDS Research Program (UARP) Policy Briefing, April 24, Sacramento.

Sanderson, S. 1981. *Agrarian Populism and the Mexican State*. University of California Press, Berkeley.

Sandoval, R. 2000. Female Voters Slowly Helping Mexico to Change Political Habits. *San Jose Mercury News*, April 7.

San Jose Mercury News. 2001a. Immigrants More Likely to Be Injured on the Job Than U.S.-born Workers. *San Jose Mercury News*, October 22.

———. 2001b. Teresa Martinez, Fieldworker, Recently Gave Birth to Twins. *San Jose Mercury News*, October 19.

———. 2001c. U.S. Leaders Looking to Immigration Reform. *San Jose Mercury News*, November 18.

———. 2002a. Hispanic Farm Workers Experience Higher Rates of Leukemia, Brain, Skin Cancers. *San Jose Mercury News*, March 18.

———. 2002b. Population Jump Prompts SF's Mexican Consulate to Find Bigger Digs. *San Jose Mercury News*, September 15.

———. 2003a. Mexican Farmers Stage Mass Protest against U.S. Imports. *San Jose Mercury News*, January 31.

———. 2003b. Spotlight on Latino Health: Lack of Insurance Is a Big Problem, Especially in California. *San Jose Mercury News*, April 2.

———. 2005a. Bush Tries to Straddle Divide over Illegal Immigration to U.S. *San Jose Mercury News*, November 29.

———. 2005b. Tough Talk Isn't Enough to Stem Illegal Immigration. *San Jose Mercury News*, November 30.

Santa Cruz Sentinel. 2002. Farm Neighbors Charge Pesticide Makes Them Ill. *Santa Cruz Sentinel*, March 21.

Santos, J. 2006a. *Immigration Endgame*. April. www.dissidentvoice.org/Apr06/Santos28.htm.

———. 2006b. *Immigration: A Nation of Colonists and Race Laws*. April. www.dissidentvoice.org/Apr06/Santos07.htm.

Sassen, S. 1990. U.S. Immigration Policy toward Mexico in a Global Economy. *Journal of International Affairs* 43(2): 369–383.

Schmitt, E. 2001. Bush Amnesty Plan Ignites Opposition. *New York Times*, July 16.

Scripps-McClatchy Western Service. 2001. Agriculture Exports Strong. *San Jose Mercury News*, October 21.

Seewer, J. 2001. Toledo Hispanics Wary of Free Trade. Associated Press, September 9.

Segura, D. A. 1994. Working at Motherhood: Chicana and Mexican Immigrant Mothers and Employment. In E. N. Glenn, G. Chang, and L. R. Forcey (eds.), *Mothering: Ideology, Experience, and Agency*. Routledge, New York.

Shatz, H. J., and L. F. López-Calva. 2004. *The Emerging Integration of the California-Mexico Economies*. Public Policy Institute of California, San Francisco.

Sherman, J. 1998. Shortage or Surplus? The Guest Worker Debate. *Rural California Report* (California Institute for Rural Studies, Davis) 9(2): 1, 3.

Shields. J. D. 2005. *Quaker Group Plans to Document Human Rights Abuses on Arizona-Mexico Border*. American Friends Service Committee, Philadelphia, PA.

Shields, M. K., and R. E. Behrmann. 2004. Children of Immigrant Families: Analysis and Recommendations. *Future of Children* (Packard Foundation)14(2).

Shorey, A. 2001. Unions Push Immigrant Labor Rights. Associated Press, August 27.

Silverman, M., and J. Nagiecki. 2001. The Momentum of 245(i): Central Valley Partners Mobilize to Meet Immigration Deadline. *Rural California Report* (California Institute for Rural Studies, Davis) 12(2): 1–10.

Simon, J. 1997. *Endangered Mexico*. Sierra Club Books, San Francisco.

Smaller, C. 2005. *Planting the Rights Seed: A Human Rights Perspective on Agriculture Trade and the WTO*. Institute for Agriculture and Trade Policy, Backgrounder No. 1 in the Thread Series. http://creativecommons.org.

Smith, J. F. 2001. Mexico's Grupo Beta Tries to Make Life Safer for Migrants. *Los Angeles Times*, June 17.

Smith, J. F., and K. Ellingwood. 2001. When the Trek North Becomes a Slow March toward Death. *Los Angeles Times*, June 10.

Smith, J. F., and M. Fineman. 2001. Mexicans Shine Light on State's Dark Secrets. *Los Angeles Times*, December 9.

Sociedad Amigos del Lago de Chapala. 2005a. Problems/Solutions: Politics. www.amigosdelago.org/politics-e.html.

———. 2005b. Problems/Solutions: Pollution. www.amigosdelago.org/pollution-e.html.

Solorzano, D., and A. Ornelas 2007 (forthcoming). Reaffirming Affirmative Action: An Equal Opportunity Analysis of Advance Placement Courses and University Admissions. In P. Zavella, D. Trevino, D. Segura, J. V. Palerm, and R. Gutiérrez (eds.), *Mexicans in California: Transformations and Challenges*. University of Illinois Press, Urbana.

Southern Poverty Law Center. 2005a. Blood on the Border. Intelligence Report, October 15. www.splcenter.org/intel/intelreport/article.jsp?aid=230.

———. 2005b. The Immigrants: Myths and Reality. Intelligence Report, October 15. www.splcenter.org/intel/intelreport/article.jsp?sid=173.

Spagat, E. 2005. Judge Clears Way for Border Fence. Associated Press, December 12.

Spitzer, S. 2003. Industrial Agriculture and Corporate Power. *Global Pesticide Campaigner* 13(2). August. www.panna.org/resources/gpc/gpc_200308.13.2.pdf

Stebbins, C. 2006. U.S. Agriculture and Immigration Tied in a Knot. Reuters, April 26. www.freerepublic.com/focus/f-news/1621730/posts.

Stefancic, J. 1997. Funding the Nativist Agenda. In J. F. Perea (ed.), *Immigrants Out! The New Nativism and the Anti-Immigrant Impulse in the United States*. New York University Press, New York.

Stevenson, M. 2006a. Mexico to Give Desert Maps. *Albuquerque Journal*, January 25.

———. 2006b. Mexico Harsh to Undocumented Immigrants. Associated Press, April 18.

———. 2006c. Mexicans March to Support Migrants in U.S. Associated Press, May 1.

Sterngold, J. 2001. Ditched by Smugglers in Desert, 14 Mexican Border Crossers Die. *San Jose Mercury News*, May 25.

Stuart, G. S. 1985. *The Mighty Aztecs*. National Geographic Society, Washington, DC.

Stuart, G. E., and G. S. Stuart. 1985. *The Mysterious Maya*. National Geographic Society, Washington, DC.

Suppan, S., and K. Lehman. 1997. *Food Security and Agricultural Trade under NAFTA*. Institute for Agricultural and Trade Policy, Minneapolis.

Sutton, B. J. 2001. Amnesty Would Reward Those Who Broke the Law. *San Jose Mercury News*, August 12.

Tactaquin, C. 2001. Immigration and Globalization: The UN Conference against Racism Takes on Migrant Issues. CorpWatch: Holding Corporations Accountable, Issue Library 101. www.corpwatch.org/issues/golb101/featured /2001/ctactaquin. html.

Tanner, L. 2002. Illness More Common in Hispanic Kids. Associated Press, July 2.

Taylor, J. E., P. L. Martin, and M. Fix. 1997. *Poverty amid Prosperity: Immigration and the Changing Face of Rural California*. Urban Institute Press, Washington, DC.

Tedford, D. 2003. Migrant Deaths Rise on U.S.-Mexico Border. Reuters, October 1. http://sf.indymedia.org/mail.php?id=1650091.

Thomas, R. J., and W. H. Friedland. 1982. *The United Farm Workers Union: From Mobilization to Mechanization?* Working Paper No. 269, Center for Research and Social Organization, University of Michigan, Ann Arbor.

Thompson, A. 2006. Mexican Consumers Plan "Great American Boycott." *Financial Times*, April 20.

Thompson, G. 2001. Chasing Mexico's Dream into Squalor. *New York Times*, February 11.

Tinoco-Ojanguren, R., and D. C. Halperin. 1998. Poverty, Production, and Health: Inhibition of Erythrocyte Cholinesterase via Occupational Exposure to Organophosphate Insecticides in Chiapas, Mexico. *Archives of Environmental Health* 53(1): 29–36.

Tobar, H., S. H. Verhovek, and S. Moore. 2003. A Scourge Rooted in Subsidies: From Uruguay to Kenya, Farmers Face Ruin, Unable to Profit as Rich Nations Prop up Their Growers. *Los Angeles Times*, September 22.

Tokar, B. 1999. Biotech Corn and the Deaths of Butterflies. *Food and Water Journal*, Summer, 20–23.

Toledo, V.M. 1995. *Peasantry, Agroindustriality, Sustainability: The Ecological and Historical Basis of Rural Development*. Working Paper 3, Interamerican Council for Sustainable Agriculture. Michoacán, Mexico.

UC Mexus. 2004. Maize Experts Tussle with Transgenes. UC Mexus, Publication No. 41, Spring 2004. www.ucmexus.ucr.edu.

Uhlig, R., A. Irwin, and S. Pook. 1999. The British Association: Fillip from Morning Coffee "Is Just a Fix." *Daily Telegraph*, September 15.

Union of Concerned Scientists. 2006. UCS Pharma Crop Database. http://go.uc susa.org/food_and_environment/pharm/index.

United Farm Workers of America, AFL-CIO. 2000. Newsletter, August 2000. Keene, CA.

United Nations. 2002. *International Migration Report 2002*. Department of Economic and Social Affairs, Population Division, New York. www.un.org/esa/population/publications/ittmig2002/press-release-eng.html

———. 2005. *World Migration 2005: Costs and Benefits of International Migration*. International Organization for Migration, Geneva. www.iom.int/en/news/pr882_en.shtml.

Uranga, R. 2005. A Woman's Work: Female Immigrants Supporting Families Far from Home. *Los Angeles Daily News*, March 27.

USDA. 1997. *Census of Agriculture*. National Agricultural Statistics Service, U.S. Department of Agriculture, Washington, DC.

———. 2001. *Agricultural Statistics*. National Agricultural Statistics Service, U.S. Department of Agriculture, Washington, DC.

———. 2003. *Agriculture Fact Book 2001–2002*. Office of Communications, U.S. Department of Agriculture, Washington, DC.

———. 2004. *Agricultural Statistics*. National Agricultural Statistics Service, U.S. Department of Agriculture, Washington, DC.

USDL. 2000. National Agricultural Workers Survey 1997–1998. *A Demographic and Employment Profile of United States Farmworkers*. Research Report No. 8, U.S. Department of Labor, Washington, DC.

———. 2002. *National Agricultural Workers Survey 2001–2002*. www.doleta.gov/agworker/report9/toc.cfm.

Vallejo, M. 2005. En el Estado, de Acuerdo con la SEDESCO, Padece Pobreza Alimentaria 45% de la Población. *Cambi de Michoacán* (Morelia), January 24.

Vasquez, O. A., L. Pease-Alvarez, and S. M. Shannon. 1994. *Pushing Boundaries: Language and Culture in a Mexicano Community*. Cambridge University Press, New York.

Vause, J. 2001. Migrants Take Increasing Risks to Reach U.S. CNN News, September 5.

Vega, W. A., B. Kolody, and J. R. Valle. 1987. Migration and Mental Health: An Empirical Test of Depression Risk Factors among Immigrant Mexican Women. *International Migration Review* 21(3): 512–529.

Vélez-Ibañez, C. G., and J. B. Greenberg. 1992. Formation and Transformation of Funds of Knowledge among U.S.-Mexican Households. *Anthropology and Education Quarterly* 23(4): 313–334.

Villagran, G. 2006. The Great Immigrant March of San Jose Not a Demand but a Plea for Just Treatment. *El Observador*, May 5–11. www.el-observador.com.

Villarejo, D. 2001. Foreward. In A. López (ed.), *Forum for Transnational Employment: A Dialogue on Alternatives to the Status Quo in Immigrant-Labor Dominated Industries*. California Institute for Rural Studies, Davis.

Villarejo, D., D. Lighthall, D. Williams III, A. Souter, and R. Mines. 2000. *Suffering in Silence: A Report on the Health of California's Agricultural Workers*. California Endowment and California Institute for Rural Studies, Davis.

Villarejo, D., and S. Perrin. 1999. Trends in California Farmland Use: California Agriculture Is Growing, Despite Urbanization. *Rural California Report* (California Institute for Rural Studies Davis) 10(2): 1, 5.

Villarejo, D., and D. Runsten. 1993. *California's Agricultural Dilemma: Higher Production and Lower Wages*. California Institute for Rural Studies, Davis.

Villarejo, D., and M. Schenker. 2005. *Policies to Improve the Health and Well-Being of California's Hired Farm Laborers*. Research Report commissioned by California Program on Access to Care, California Policy Research Center, University of California.

Wade, N. 1974. Green Revolution (I): A Just Technology, Often Unjust in Use. *Science* 728.

Wagner D., and P. Flannery. 2000. Questions Trump Answers in War on Drugs: Lots of Cash, Little to Show for All of It. *Arizona Republic,* January 16.

Warwick, H. 2000. Terminator Too. *Ecologist* 30(1): 50.

Watson, J. 2000. Deforestation, Overfarming, and Overgrazing Threaten Mexico's Land. Associated Press, June 17.

Watte, C. 1992. *NAFTA Report*. California Farm Bureau Federation, Sacramento.

Webby, S. 2003. Doctor's License Revoked: Medical Board Finds Gynecologist Gave Inappropriate Examinations. *San Jose Mercury News,* April 22.

Weber, H. R. 2003. Coke to Pay $540,000 in Whistleblower Case. Associated Press, October 7.

Weiner, M. (ed.). 1993. *International Migration and Security*. Westview Press, Boulder, CO.

Weiner, T. 2002. In Corn's Cradle, U.S. Imports Bury Family Farms. *New York Times,* February 26.

Weissert, W. 2004. GM Corn Threatens Mexico's Crops. Associated Press, March 11.

Wells, M. J. 1996. *Strawberry Fields: Politics, Class, and Work in California Agriculture*. Cornell University Press, Ithaca, NY.

Wheelwright, J. 2001. Don't Eat Again until You Read This. *Discover* 22(3): 35–43.

White, M. C. Salas, and S. Gammage. 2003. *Trade Impact Review: Mexico Case Study. NAFTA and the FTAA: A Gender Analysis of Employment and Poverty Impacts in Agriculture*. Women's Edge Coalition, Washington, DC.

Wides, L. 2005. Celebs Backing Immigrant Driver's Licenses. Associated Press, January 24.

Wides-Muñoz, L. 2006. Raid Rumors Spark Fear among Immigrants. Associated Press, April 28.

Wilken, G. C. 1987. *Good Farmers: Traditional Agricultural Resource Management in Mexico and Central America*. University of California Press, Berkeley.

Williams, D. 1998. Work at Your Own Risk: Summer Accidents Magnify Dangers of the Agricultural Workplace. *Rural California Report* (California Institute for Rural Studies, Davis) 9(4): 8–9, 11.

Wolkomir, R. 1995. Bringing Ancient Ways to Our Farmers' Fields. *Smithsonian* 26(8): 99–107.

Worldwide Forest/Biodiversity Campaign News. 2000. Action Alert: Protest Conviction of Mexican Environmental Activists & Unchallenged, Illegal Logging, September 4. http://forests.org/web/.

Wright, A. 1990. *The Death of Ramón González: The Modern Agricultural Dilemma.* University of Texas Press, Austin.

Yang, S. 2006. Susceptibility to Pesticides Highly Variable among Latina Women and Children. www.berkeley.edu/news/media/releases/2006/03/02_pesticides .shtml.

Zabin, C., M. Kearney, A. Garcia, D. Runsten, and C. Nagengast. 1993. *A New Cycle of Poverty: Mixtec Migrants in California Agriculture.* California Institute for Rural Studies, Davis.

Zahm, S. H., and A. Blair. 2005. *Cancer among Migrant and Seasonal Farmworkers: An Epidemiologic Review and Research Agenda.* National Cancer Institute, Occupational Studies Section, Rockville, MD.

Zangerl, A. R., D. McKenna, C. L. Wraight, M. Carroll, P. Ficarello, R. Warner, and M. R. Berenbaum. 2001. Effects of Exposure to Event 176 *Bacillus thuringiensis* Corn Pollen on Monarch and Black Swallowtail Caterpillars under Field Condition. *Proceedings of the National Academy of Sciences of the United States* 98(21): 11908.

Zavella, P. 1987. *Women's Work and Chicano Families: Cannery Workers of the Santa Clara Valley.* Cornell University Press, Ithaca, NY.

———. 1996. Living on the Edge: Everyday Lives of Poor Chicano/Mexicano Families. In A. F. Gordon and C. Newfield (eds.), *Mapping Multiculturalism.* University of Minnesota Press, Minneapolis.

———. 1997. The Tables Are Turned: Immigration, Poverty, and Social Conflict in California Communities. In J. F. Perea (ed.), *Immigrants Out! The New Nativism and the Anti-Immigrant Impulse in the United States.* New York University Press, New York.

———. 2000. Engendering Transnationalism in Food Processing: Peripheral Vision on Both Sides of the U.S.-México Border. In N. Klahn, P. Castillo, A. Álvarez, and F. Manchón, *Las Nuevas Fronteras del Siglo XXI: Dimensiones Culturales, Políticas y Socioeconómicas de las Relaciones México-Estados Unidos* [New Frontiers of the 21st Century: Cultural, Political and Socioeconomic Dimensions of U.S.-Mexico Relations]. Centro de Investigaciones Colección: la democracia en México, La Jornada Ediciones, Mexico City.

———. 2005. Sexuality and Risks: Gendered Discourses about Virginity and Disease among Young Women of Mexican Origin. *Latino Studies* 3:226–245.

Zendejas, S., and P. De Vries. 1995. *Rural Transformations Seen from Below: Regional and Local Perspectives from Western Mexico.* Transformation of Rural Mexico Series, No. 8. Ejido Reform Project, Center for U.S.-Mexican Studies, University of California, San Diego.

Zlolniski, C. 1996. *Working but Poor: Mexican Immigrant Workers in a Low-Income Enclave in San Jose.* CLPP Working Paper, Chicano/Latino Policy Project, Berkeley, CA.

INDEX

Page numbers in italics *indicate illustrations.*

Text: 10/13 Sabon
Display: Sabon
Cartographer: Bill Nelson
Indexer: Thérèse Shere
Compositor: Binghamton Valley Composition, LLC
Printer and binder: Maple-Vail Manufacturing Group